Preaching through

Isaiah

Exegetical Sermons in the book of Isaiah

By Pastor Paul Wallace

Contents

God's Lament - Isaiah 1:1-9

Isaiah, his name is his message. Isaiah means "God is salvation." Thank you for your prayers as to which book was to be our next study. The Lord did make it clear and as usual it is fitting in ways I didn't see before I began studying for the first sermon in Isaiah. For one thing, Isaiah refers to God as the Holy One of Israel 25 times in his book. There are only six other times in the Old Testament when the name is used. Since we finished the series on the attributes of God with the holiness of God, we can see the connection.

The setting is also clearly something we can relate to in our day. The people to whom Isaiah prophesied sensed the insecurity of their wealth and could see that things were about to change. The kingdom was in a time of transition. It was being tested to see if it would rely on things of this world to assist them against the foreign threats or if they would rely upon God. I think we can all see that this is the challenge that we face.

Isaiah's father was Amoz. Jewish tradition tells us that Amoz was the brother of Amaziah, king of Judah. This would make Isaiah of royal lineage and give him access to the kings. We know he lived in Jerusalem and was married and had children (7:3; 8:3, 18). He wrote one other book, a historical account of the reign of Uzziah, which has never been found (2 Chronicles 26:22). He prophesied between the years 740 to at least 681 B.C., sixty or more years of ministry.

Textual critics have decided that the book of Isaiah was written by three different prophets in three distinct time periods. They note that the middle portion appears to be written to the exiles and that there seem to be three writing styles. This is in part due to their denial of anything super-natural. Isaiah couldn't write to the exiles because he was before the exiles. That is unless he was a seer, which is exactly what he claimed to be.

As for different styles, he was addressing different subjects and writing over decades. I challenge anyone to find a writer whose style remains the same over 60 years writing on different topics. My writing has changed dramatically in 20 years. There is also the fact that there is a theme that runs through the book. The theme is that God is purifying his people for the coming of the Messiah. The people of Judah were a mess, but through captivity and testing they would become the ones ready for the days of the Messiah. That is why the three sections focus on their current sinful condition which would result in exile, encouragement during exile, and finally the days of the Messiah.

Josephus, the Jewish historian, and one of the intertestamental books[1] tell us Isaiah was the sole author. The Qumran caves held an entire scroll of Isaiah which showed no sign of segmentation and dated to around 200 B.C. But perhaps most convincing of all to us who believe in the inspiration of Scripture is that fact that all three sections of Isaiah are quoted in the New Testament and ascribed to Isaiah.

To whet your appetite for what is to come, listen to what Jesus said about Isaiah. *⁴¹ Isaiah said these things because he saw his glory and spoke of him.* John 12:41 Isaiah saw the glory of Jesus and spoke of Him! Isaiah is mentioned by name 20 times in the New Testament. Quotations from Isaiah run throughout because his message is the message of the New Testament. The Messiah is coming to save the world!

The ESV study Bible introduction to Isaiah tells us, *Isaiah's message makes an impact on every reader in one of two ways. Either this book will harden the reader's pride against God (6:9-10; 28:13; 29:11-12) or it will become to the contrite reader a feast of refreshment in God (55:1-3; 57:15; 66:2).* I can say that I have seen that to be the case. Isaiah challenges us to see things not as the world sees, but as God sees them. This will not be an easy study. Isaiah is a seer and a poet. His lines are filled with metaphor and simile. The book does not flow like a narrative. It is a collection of different prophecies. It jumps from judgment to hope and comfort and then back again to judgment. Nevertheless, many have found Isaiah to be the richest of the Old Testament books.

Ray Ortlund Jr. began his commentary on Isaiah with a quotation from William Henry Green that I'd like you to consider. *Who can tell us whether this awful and mysterious silence, in which the Infinite One has wrapped himself, portends mercy or wrath? Who can say to the troubled conscience whether He, whose laws in nature are inflexible and remorseless, will pardon sin? Who can answer the anxious inquiry whether the dying live on or whether they cease to be? Is there a future state? And if so, what is the nature of that untried condition of being? If there be immortal happiness, how can I attain it? If there be an everlasting woe, how can it be escaped? Let the reader close his Bible and ask himself seriously what he knows upon these momentous questions apart from its teachings. What solid foundation has he to rest upon in regard to matters which so absolutely transcend all earthly experience and are so entirely out of the reach of our unassisted faculties? A man of facile faith may perhaps delude himself into the belief of what he wishes to believe. He may thus take upon trust God's unlimited mercy, his ready forgiveness of transgressors, and eternal happiness after death. But this is all a dream. He knows nothing, he can know nothing about it, except by direct revelation from heaven.* (Raymond Ortland Jr. *Preaching the Word Commentary, Isaiah,* p 17)

What do we know? How can we know anything about the spiritual realm unless God reveals it? And God has revealed it to His prophets and sovereignly seen that it was written down for us to know spiritual truth in the midst of this fallen world.

Without any more introduction, let us begin. *¹ The vision of Isaiah the son of Amoz, which he saw concerning Judah and Jerusalem in the days of Uzziah, Jotham, Ahaz, and Hezekiah, kings of Judah.* Isaiah 1:1 Isaiah prophesied during the reign of four kings. Early in his ministry the threat was from Syria in league with the northern tribes of Israel. Later it was Assyria that was conquering the known world. Isaiah had visions that he often expressed in poetic form. He was seeing the Word of the Lord (2:1). The world sees and interprets with its limited abilities and is usually nowhere near understanding what is really taking place. The prophet is not influenced by worldly perception. He sees what God reveals of reality. This is why we so need our minds renewed by the Word of God today (Romans 12:2). How often we simply take a pundits limited perceptions as factual. We need to move beyond the limited resources of man and walk in the light of the Lord (2:5).

Are you dumfounded as to why the world can't see things that are black and white to you? Without spiritual eyes they are unable to see (1 Corinthians 2:14). They take their opinion from someone else that is as blind as they (Luke 6:39). The Christian is often astonished at the lack of discernment expressed by the world. We can't understand why bad behavior is rewarded and destructive things are encouraged. We should know that those who walk in darkness cannot see. But when Isaiah's words confront *us*, we should also be aware that areas of our understanding may still be in darkness. Let us revere the Lord enough to be open to what He is trying to show us and willing to have a change in our thinking.

² Hear, O heavens, and give ear, O earth; for the LORD has spoken: "Children have I reared and brought up, but they have rebelled against me. Isaiah 1:2 Isaiah makes it clear that this is the Word of the Lord. The heavens and the earth as inanimate objects without feeling are to bear witness to the rebellious condition of God's children. It was the language Moses used when he warned them of the cost of disobedience (Deuteronomy 30:19). God called Abraham and chose his descendants to be His children, to represent Him to the world (Deuteronomy 7:6). He reared them and brought them up for that purpose.

God delivered them from captivity and gave them a revelation on Sinai of how to live. He led them to the Promised Land. He gave them Judges to help guide them and delivered them from their enemies. When they cried out for a king, he gave them their request, knowing it was their rejection of God as their king (1 Samuel 8:7).

When they failed to represent God to the world, but became in every way as vile as the world and more so (2 Kings 21:9), He declared, "They have rebelled against me." There is pain in that decree. Some of you parents have felt that pain and are feeling it even now. Children have a choice. We tell them what is right for their own good, but the allurements of this world deceive them into thinking there is a better way. God knows that pain, as He watched Judah return to idolatry. Appearances deceived them. The apparent prosperity of their neighbors was not due to their false gods. Salvation does not come from leaning upon the powerful. The Lord is salvation. If they could only see. God help us see.

Do you really think electing a different set of leaders will save the nation? That is idolatry. Our answer is not politics! It is turning to the Lord with all our heart (Deuteronomy 10:12). If our nation won't, you still can. But don't take up their idols. God sets up leaders, but He often gives us leaders we deserve. It's not enough to know that God reigns. We need to know that God is reigning.

Vote for the person that has the godliest stand, but don't put your hope in them. They can't save us. Only God can save! The way we speak reflects our hearts (Matthew 12:34). Are you looking to the Lord as the only hope for this nation? Or do you talk as if man has the answer? God has reared and brought us up as well. Hasn't He? God help us to stop rebelling against Him in our words and actions.

³ The ox knows its owner, and the donkey its master's crib, but Israel does not know, my people do not understand." Isaiah 1:3 The Lord is telling them they are stupider than a cow or donkey. And so is everyone that doesn't know where to turn in times of need. It shows a lack of basic understanding that our hope is *only* found in the Lord (Psalm 62:2). Nothing in this world is dependable. Things aren't going to go like you hope. But God is there through it all and will strengthen you if you will let Him. He may rescue you or give you the perseverance to endure, but He won't fail you. This world will certainly fail you!

Believing the lie of self-dependence shows we have a lack of understanding an essential truth. God is the only One that is reliable, not reliable to do what you want, but to do what is right (Psalm 73:26). In the end, that is all that matters. Isaiah is declaring a convicting message. We lean on our own understanding and no different than the world (Proverbs 3:5).

In our modern world, "conviction" is a bad word. Nothing is wrong with anything. But in reality, lack of conviction is psychopathic. Let me share one more Ortland quote. *Conviction of sin is the lance of the divine Surgeon piercing the infected soul, releasing the pressure, letting the infection pour out. Conviction of sin is a health-giving injury. Conviction of sin is the Holy Spirit being kind to us by confronting us with the light we don't want to see and the truth we're afraid to admit and the guilt we prefer to ignore. Conviction of sin is the severe love of God overruling our compulsive dishonesty, our willful blindness, our favorite excuses. Conviction of sin is the violent sweetness of God opposing the sins lying comfortably undisturbed in our lives. Conviction of sin is the merciful God declaring war on the false peace we settle for. Conviction of sin is our escape from malaise to joy, from attending church to worship, from faking it to authenticity. Conviction of sin, with the forgiveness of Jesus pouring over our wounds, is life.* (Ibid p 26)

Do we understand where to turn in times of difficulty? Or are we rebellious children that are dumber than a donkey? That is pretty tough poetry. Is that too harsh? Is God being too tough on us? That very thought proves our rebellious nature. We don't want to hear the truth about ourselves. We'd rather not be disturbed in our mediocrity (Revelation 3:15-16).

These last two verses are really an expression of God's broken heart toward His children. Next God points out our broken strength. *⁴ Ah, sinful nation, a people laden with iniquity, offspring of evildoers, children who deal corruptly! They have forsaken the LORD, they have despised the Holy One of Israel, they are utterly estranged.* Isaiah 1:4 The "Ah" tells us this is God's lament for our condition. Has any idol ever told you, "My yoke is easy!" It probably has, but then you find out it's a lie (Matthew 11:30). The idol's burden is crushing, constantly demanding more. It results in estrangement from God. That is a burden that is more than we can bear (Psalm 32:3). Our strength is cut off. Our comfort and hope are gone.

This is God's lament for what had become of those for whom He had such a glorious intent (Deuteronomy 28:1). How did they go from such promise to such bondage? They forsook the Lord and despised the Holy One of Israel. Is this what we are observing in our nation, or in our lives? Or is the Lord all our hope and strength, the One upon Whom we are depending?

Do we recognize our true condition? The Lord goes on to describe Judah as a man who is horribly wounded and sick but doesn't even realize it. *5 Why will you still be struck down? Why will you continue to rebel? The whole head is sick, and the whole heart faint. 6 From the sole of the foot even to the head, there is no soundness in it, but bruises and sores and raw wounds; they are not pressed out or bound up or softened with oil.* Isaiah 1:5,6 Do we realize how desperately needy we are? Don't we want to begin to return to real health? Will we lie to ourselves and pretend we are not at death's door? (See Luke 10:25f where Jesus portrays Himself as the Good Samaritan who could care for this condition.)

God's next illustration of Judah's need for God was a picture of an overpowered nation. *7 Your country lies desolate; your cities are burned with fire; in your very presence foreigners devour your land; it is desolate, as overthrown by foreigners. 8 And the daughter of Zion is left like a booth in a vineyard, like a lodge in a cucumber field, like a besieged city.* Isaiah 1:7-8 Some people think that this is literal, but it didn't come to that at this point in Judah's history. Spiritually they were like a shack left in field that had been picked over by their enemies. Little was left standing and nothing of substance remained. The enemy of their soul had plundered their spiritual wealth. God had such plans for them, but they had fallen to such a pathetic condition. Is the church today a tottering shack, our land overthrown by the enemy or are we charging the gates of hell (Matthew 16:18)?

Our last verse tells us of God's unfailing grace. *9 If the LORD of hosts had not left us a few survivors, we should have been like Sodom, and become like Gomorrah.* Isaiah 1:9 Left to ourselves we would become as vile as Sodom and Gomorrah and come under the wrath of God. But God is gracious. He would not let Judah be utterly destroyed for the promised Messiah was to come from the house of David (Isaiah 9:7). He keeps a remnant then and now that His witness might remain in the earth. It is the grace of God that reaches out and saves us, keeps us, strengthens us, leads us on to sanctification, and finally to glory in His presence. A few were still following the Lord then and now, only because God is faithful.

Isaiah's prophecies challenge us to examine our spiritual condition from God's perspective. Are we being honest with Him and with ourselves? Do we turn to Him first in our time of need? Are we burdened with our sin? Have we rebelled and become estranged? His grace reaches out with healing in His hand and invites us to return. Will you take His hand?

Questions

1 What is the meaning of "Isaiah?"
2 How are Isaiah's and our times similar?
3 Why should we believe Isaiah wrote the whole book?
4 How can we know about any spiritual reality for certain?
5 How did God describe the people in vs 2-3?
6 What is modern day idolatry?
7 Why is conviction good?
8 What is God's heart in these verses?
9 How did God describe their condition?
10 Where do we see God's grace in these verses?

Perfect Religion - Isaiah 1:10-20

Last week we were challenged by Isaiah's prophecy to examine where we turn in time of difficulty. Does our speech show that we trust in man or in God? We tried to see ourselves as God sees us and discern whether or not we are fooling ourselves. The people of Judah were like a man who was sick and beaten within an inch of his life, and they thought they were just fine. We saw the importance of receiving conviction, and that it is *the violent sweetness of God opposing the sins lying comfortably undisturbed in our lives.*

That passage ended by saying that the grace of God in leaving them a remnant was the only reason they hadn't been destroyed like Sodom and Gomorrah (Isaiah 1:9). The next section begins by calling them rulers of Sodom and people of Gomorrah. *[10] Hear the word of the LORD, you rulers of Sodom! Give ear to the teaching of our God, you people of Gomorrah!* Isaiah 1:10 The entire nation was to hear what God was about to say to them. We know it's not going to be pretty because God is calling them Sodomites (Ezekiel 16:48-49). While God had not treated them as he did those wicked cities, it wasn't because they didn't deserve it.

Now if we heard God begin to speak to us like that, what would our reaction be? We would probably start listing all the good things that we do, which is probably where their minds went. But that is what God is about to address, the very things we think should earn us favor in God's sight. The first thing we might think of is our faithful fulfilment of religious duties, our perfect doctrinal stances, and the way we are consistent to attend church and Bible study. That is why what followed was shocking to the hearers.

12

[11] "What to me is the multitude of your sacrifices? says the LORD; I have had enough of burnt offerings of rams and the fat of well-fed beasts; I do not delight in the blood of bulls, or of lambs, or of goats. Isaiah 1:11 God is describing sacrifices that He requested in Leviticus. Not only had the people been offering exactly what God requested, they had done so in abundance. They had perfected religious ritual. They fed those animals until they were good and fat. They gave God the best. How could God say He had enough of what He requested? The people may have been a bit dumbfounded at first (Proverbs 15:8).

Today it would be like God saying, "What to me is your faithful and consistent church attendance? I've had enough of you being at church every Sunday and at your weekly Bible study. I do not delight in your tithing a full 10% without fail. What would you say? I might say, "Huh? Is that you God?"

He continues to help us get the point. *[12] "When you come to appear before me, who has required of you this trampling of my courts?* Isaiah 1:12 To appear before Him, was to come into the Temple, into the courts of the LORD before the Holy Place that housed the throne of God, the ark of the covenant. When we come into God's presence, who required us to be seen all over the church?

Once again, we might ask, "Where else would you want us to be?" God seems to have forgotten that He was the One that insisted that all males come to at least three of the annual feasts to appear before Him (Exodus 23:17). "Who required us to come trample the courts? You did (Exodus 34:23)!"

The next verse begins to clarify just what God was addressing. It was not their perfect religious activity, but the heart and actions behind it. *[13] Bring no more vain offerings; incense is an abomination to me. New moon and Sabbath and the calling of convocations— I cannot endure iniquity and solemn assembly.* Isaiah 1:13 Offerings are only vain when there is a wrong motivation in the heart of the giver. Samuel spoke for God when he declared, "To obey is better than sacrifice, and to harken than the fat of rams" (1 Samuel 15:22). If there is no intention to hear and obey God, the offering is meaningless. Worse than that, it is an affront to God.

In the east, there is a tradition of giving and expecting something back. If you wanted something from someone, you just keep giving them gifts until they finally give you what you want. It is somewhat manipulative. It is the way people treat their idols and false gods. They think if they keep giving gifts to pacify the god that they will win its favor. That is thinking of God in human terms. I give Him what He wants and He will give me what I want. That is treating God like an idol. God doesn't need anything. He doesn't need the meat on the altar or your $20 in the offering plate. He doesn't really smell the incense. That is all for us to have a physical picture to understand deeper truths (Colossians 2:17).

Without a heart to hear and obey, offerings are in vain. Do we really think we can manipulate God? That is misguided and insulting to God. God makes the problem clear when He says He can't endure iniquity and solemn assembly. Solemn assembly was a time for the people to come and examine their heart and repent (Leviticus 23:36). But they would come together in fasting, bow their heads, and shed some tears while thinking about how they can do some wicked action. God says He can't endure that! He just can't put up with it.

¹⁴ Your new moons and your appointed feasts my soul hates; they have become a burden to me; I am weary of bearing them. Isaiah 1:14 God has listed about every biblical worship gathering that Israel was instructed to have. The people would come, but God hated the events. Those perfectly performed religious ceremonies mock Him. Worship without a heart to hear and obey is a declaration that the worshiper sees God on par with an idol that is pleased with mere performance or physical gifts. The various worship services had become a burden to God.

Does God get tired? That's not possible, but so that we could understand, He calls these meaningless worship services something He is weary of bearing. He'd rather they quit coming to the Temple and going through the motions than to take the God prescribed forms of worship and see them treated like pagans treat their idols.

God isn't a great genie in the sky who gives us what we want when we give Him what He wants. Prayer isn't a means to make life easy and avoid problems. God Almighty has every detail of every day in the palm of His hand. Nothing, absolutely nothing happens without His consent. And regardless of Him allowing evil to do its worst, He will through it all be glorified and held in awe by all who see what He has done. It's a blessing to serve Him and do His will and give an offering. This way of seeing worship is a huge contrast with those who go through the worship motions thinking they are making God happy with them so they can get something they desire. That thinking is missing the reality of who God is and who we are.

¹⁵ When you spread out your hands, I will hide my eyes from you; even though you make many prayers, I will not listen; your hands are full of blood. Isaiah 1:15 Prayer is the opportunity to join in what God is doing, not for Him to join in what you are doing. He doesn't exist to help you do what you want; you exist for His glory. If you are willing to respond to His gracious invitation, you get to serve Him by praying His will into the earth. Your desires are transformed to match His (1 John 5:14). Then you experience real prayer as you pray His heart.

What God was seeing in Judah wasn't just selfish prayers, it was requests for blessings from those who would not bless others. Whether or not God is saying they are literally guilty of shedding the blood of others or not I do not know. Some of the people of Judah may have been covering all their bases with child sacrifices to Molech (Leviticus 18:21). They thought, "If YHWH wasn't pleased enough with their sacrifices to bless them, maybe Molech would be."

It may be that God is referring to murder in the way that Jesus would 700 years later (Matthew 5:22). To hate another is to murder them in your heart. God may be referring to un-forgiveness and hatred. Jesus said that if we would not forgive others, our heavenly Father would not forgive us (Matthew 6:15). If they were praying for forgiveness or blessing with hatred in their hearts, God would see their hands symbolically covered in blood.

Whatever the case, they were guilty and God wasn't going to listen to their requests until they dealt with their guilt. We can't come before a holy God unless we are in Christ (1Timothy 2:5). If their sacrifices were in vain, they were missing the whole symbolism in sacrifice. They thought God was pleased with the meat when it was intended for them to see the cost of sin and how one-day God would provide the ultimate and effectual sacrifice for sin.

In the New Testament, Peter tells men that if we don't want our prayers to be hindered, we better treat our wives right (1 Peter 3:7). Our spiritual state has a lot to do with how we pray and if our prayers are effective (James 5:16).

So what were they to do? God couldn't tolerate their ritual worship regardless of how perfectly it was performed. He wouldn't listen to their prayers because of their guilt. Those were the two things they were relying on to be right with God. What now?

16 Wash yourselves; make yourselves clean; remove the evil of your deeds from before my eyes; cease to do evil, Isaiah 1:16 But how do they wash themselves? When the people of Israel were preparing to meet with God on Sinai, they washed themselves (Exodus 19:10). Cleaning up the outward body is symbolic of cleaning up our heart and our actions. Stop doing evil. But how could they do that?

God wanted from them what He wants from us, to look to Him and see our true condition. If we would come before Him we must recognize our need for Him to cleanse us. It begins with repentance, but then it must be followed with our total dependence on God to change us. We can choose to intentionally stop doing what is wrong, but we can't keep from doing what is wrong without God's help (John 15:5). We do all that we are able to make things right, like Zacchaeus who gave away half his wealth and restored fourfold anything he had taken fraudulently (Luke 19:8). True repentance takes immediate action to change what is wrong.

17 learn to do good; seek justice, correct oppression; bring justice to the fatherless, plead the widow's cause. Isaiah 1:17 They had fallen so far they needed someone to teach them what a good action was. God began pointing out a few things. Seek justice. Don't try to get away with unjust gain. God is just so we should be just in all we do, regardless of how much it costs us.

Correct oppression. If there were slaves that were being treated more like property than like people, then attitudes and actions needed to change. If you see people oppressing others, warn them. Do what you are able to help the oppressed.

Seek justice for the orphan and widow. God often brings up their need because they were vulnerable and taken advantage of (James 1:27). Someone needed to stand up for them. God was telling Judah that everyone needs to stand up for them. We can stand up for justice, against oppression, and for the vulnerable in our society. Who is being taken advantage of, and what can you do to help them?

18 "Come now, let us reason together, says the LORD: though your sins are like scarlet, they shall be as white as snow; though they are red like crimson, they shall become like wool. Isaiah 1:18 While God's indictment is severe, His invitation is gracious. In spite of their hypocritical worship that God detested, and their failure to turn to God in their desperation, God still invited them to come and reason with Him.

God had called them on their bloody hands, but now He is telling them that they can be white as snow. Though they are red like crimson, they shall become like wool. How? What could change a sinner's bloody hands to pure white? Only Another who could take our sin and whose blood could be spilled in our place. Only when we accept that we can never wash our own hands clean. We don't have the solvent strong enough, but God does (Colossians 1:20). He provides it in Christ for those who will come and reason with Him.

Here is His promise: *19 If you are willing and obedient, you shall eat the good of the land;* Isaiah 1:19 When you come to the Almighty, when you appear before Him, it isn't to offer Him something that will appease Him. He is the One who has provided the One who has made us acceptable to God. It is to reason with us. It is to have us accept the reality that He is God and we are created for His glory (Isaiah 43:7).

If we are willing to see things as God sees them, and willing to be obedient to His good will by receiving His Son, He will cleanse our blood stained hands. The land will be healed when we are healed. Instead of the empty field picked over by foreigners, we will eat the good of the land. The spiritual condition we saw last week of bareness will be transformed into fruitfulness.

In the nation of Israel, God promised physical blessing for obedience to the Laws of God (Leviticus 26:3-4). This promise for them was both physical and spiritual. While some claim the same is true today, in Christ we prize spiritual prosperity above all. To have the fruits of the Spirit expressed in our life and be transformed into the image of Christ is our desire (Romans 8:29). To enjoy the good of the land is to enjoy the presence of the Holy Spirit and His fruits. It's to enjoy the fellowship of believers and grow together with them. That's eating the good of this new kingdom we've become a part of.

The Spirit of God is the same with all of us. He invites us to come and reason with Him. He sets before us the promise of goodness if we are willing and obedient. Notice it takes both. Some say they are willing, but never get around to being obedient. We have to take the step of obedience, making Jesus the Lord of our life, and following where He leads.

16

The promise is followed by a warning. *²⁰ but if you refuse and rebel, you shall be eaten by the sword; for the mouth of the LORD has spoken."* Isaiah 1:20 In verse 2 the Lord has already declared Judah was in rebellion. They now have an invitation to make a change. The invitation comes with the promise of God. It's another chance, one after so many that had been given previously. But if they refuse and rebel against this gracious invitation, they will face the sword. The last verse of Isaiah is the fulfillment of this verse. It tells us of the destruction of the rebellious (Isaiah 66:24).

This is the declaration that comes from the mouth of YHWH. Repent and be cleansed and enjoy God's promises or refuse and continue to rebel and die by the sword. If we will not be cleansed, we will be judged. Promise or punishment, it's up to us. It's up to you. Will you come and reason with God? Are you willing and obedient or will you stubbornly refuse the good grace of God offered to you?

Questions
1 How did God describe Judah's worship?
2 How did God feel about it?
3 What does "appear before me" mean?
4 What does "trample my courts" mean?
5 What burdens God?
6 Why does God refuse to hear prayer?
7 What is God's solution?
8 What is the invitation?
9 What is the promise?
10 What is the warning?

Refiners Fire - Isaiah 1:21-31

God's first charge against Judah was rebellion (1:2). The second indictment was hypocritical worship (1:13). And in our passage today He brings the third charge with a warning and a prophecy. This time the charge is that His people have become His enemies.

²¹ How the faithful city has become a whore, she who was full of justice! Righteousness lodged in her, but now murderers. Isaiah 1:21 This is God's lament over the backslidden condition of Jerusalem. It begins with the indictment of whoredom. The prophets often used this analogy (Jeremiah 2:20). Since God was to be loved with all their heart, to turn to other gods was described as playing the whore. The city was once faithful to worship God and truly love Him, but now they only sought after other gods. He specifically points to her former faithfulness to execute justice. The implication is that now injustice is the norm (Ezekiel 9:9).

Justice often has to do with financial obligations. Injustice is due to bribes or favors to those with wealth and power. The other lover that lured the people from the love of God was wealth. By perverting justice people were enriching themselves at the expense of those who were unjustly treated. Because God is just, this injustice was giving a false message to the people of the nation and to the foreigners who passed through the land.

When I was building my home I tried to hire Christian contractors. The one who had the cement contract claimed to be a prophet. Whenever someone has to tell you they are a prophet, it often has something to do with personal profit – for themselves.

When our slab was ready to pour we noticed there were footings that weren't dug. My wife and I rushed to make up for his mistakes. After the next advance he never returned to finish his work. We heard a few more stories of disastrous work he had done for his next clients, and eventually found out he never had a license and left the state. How many people heard about him representing Christ but then saw his actions were all about greed? I've heard people say, "Don't hire anyone with a fish on their name card." Misrepresenting Christ can turn one into an enemy of Christ. *How the faithful city has become a whore!*

Righteousness lived in Jerusalem, but now murderers. There was a day under kings Josiah and Hezekiah that the nations could observe the blessings of living under the Law of God. Foreigners inquired about the God of Israel. People encouraged one another to walk in the ways of God and treat one another with dignity and respect. Now they stab you in the back and rob you.

God's complaint in the previous section was that when they lift their hands in prayer, that they are covered in blood (1:15). Again, I don't know if this is literal or poetically saying they have hearts filled with un-forgiveness. Either way, they have gone from righteousness that honors life, to being unrighteous, disregarding the gift of life. 57 million babies have been aborted in this nation since Roe vs. Wade. Worldwide the number is more than a staggering 1.3 billion! The most innocent among us have been snuffed out, the majority because of inconvenience or financial burden.

The cry of God here is the contrast of what once was to how far they have fallen. We expect the world to be sinful. They don't really know any other way. But we expect those who have the truth to be different. God expected them to be different as well! You see, sin is all the more hideous when the sinner knows that what he or she is doing is absolutely wrong and forbidden by their Creator (Romans 7:13).

22 Your silver has become dross, your best wine mixed with water. Isaiah 1:22 I believe Isaiah is poetically saying that the very best among them have a watered down version of being a child of God. For silver to become dross is to say they went from being valuable to being garbage. The best wine mixed with water is not quite so bad a statement, but carries the same loss of real quality. This reminds us of the letter to the church of Laodicea, the lukewarm. God was about to spew them out of his mouth (Revelation 3:16).

As civilizations decline, their coinage becomes more and more dilute. The Romans had a coin that was 40% silver, the Antoninianus. Over

18

time it had less and less silver until it simply had a silver wash. The Denarius, a day's wage, started out as silver with 5% alloy and eventually ended up with 50% alloy. This dilution often goes hand in hand with morals and integrity of a country. It's the way of man.

²³ Your princes are rebels and companions of thieves. Everyone loves a bribe and runs after gifts. They do not bring justice to the fatherless, and the widow's cause does not come to them. Isaiah 1:23 The leaders of the country are rebels against God. The thieves they hang out with are lobbyists who offer bribes to push projects that will be lucrative to them. They lose a friendly wager on the golf course, intentionally. It's all about lining your pockets. And that quarter million dollar speaking engagement, that's all legal. That prince didn't push that project just because of that. Am I being too cynical or does this sound a bit too much like articles from the New York Times?

When the leaders should be bringing justice to the needy, they spend all their time with the fat cats wheeling and dealing. The poor and needy they could truly help by the leader's position and influence go without. That is the real crime. It's not just what is done but also what is left undone (Isaiah 58:6-7).

²⁴ Therefore the Lord declares, the LORD of hosts, the Mighty One of Israel: "Ah, I will get relief from my enemies and avenge myself on my foes. Isaiah 1:24 Because of this backslidden condition that misrepresents God, because the needs of the poor and oppressed are not met, the God of angel armies, the all-powerful God who plagued Egypt has something to say.

Ah! Or Alas! Or Woe! God will get relief from His enemies. Judah had gone from being His children and His bride to becoming His enemies. They are like a wayward wife who has gone to seek other lovers. The people of Judah had become God's foes upon whom He would avenge Himself (Hosea 1:2).

Considering the history of Israel and the times they had seen God miraculously devastate their foes, this was a wakeup call. If God could annihilate the Egyptian army in the Red Sea, you don't want to be opposed to Him. You don't want to be on the list of His foes (Job 41:10). But their backsliding had placed them on that list. Is America on that list or is there still hope? Are you on that list?

God said He would get relief from them. Their hypocritical worship was weighing on Him (1:14). Their bad example was angering Him. I was told about a man who had gone with my mother to visit scenic site in Arizona. He used a Christian vocabulary and put off a sense of being mister religion. They stopped at a restaurant for lunch. My mother said she was embarrassed by how he treated the waitress, demanding and verbally abusive. But to make matters worse, he left a tract instead of a tip. Is that a friend of God or His foe? Is that kind of person drawing people to God or away? God help us always be aware of how we represent Him lest we go from being the friend of God to His enemy.

Next follows a promise and then a warning. *²⁵ I will turn my hand against you and will smelt away your dross as with lye and remove all your alloy.* Isaiah 1:25 While the hand of God had been against their enemies, it was now turned against Judah. But this was not to destroy them, but rather to purify them. The hand of the Lord was not going to a gentle tap on the shoulder as in the previous invitation, "Come and let us reason together (1:18)." It will be like a catalyst that sets the dross in a smelting pot ablaze. It is the hand of God's discipline. All the impurity was going to be removed. The compromising alloy that degraded the quality would be removed.

What a wonderful promise! What trying means. The harder we become, the heavier God's hand of discipline upon us to turn us back. The greater our grief for having rebelled against or loving Creator. As we go through Isaiah we will see God is referring to the destruction of the Temple and the 70 years of captivity. God would have a people ready for the coming of the Messiah no matter what it took. And He will have a bride adorned for her husband Jesus no matter what it takes. The dross of backsliding and the alloy of compromise must be removed and He knows exactly how to do it. How much better to listen to the invitation to come and reason with Him and let Him wash us white as snow.

Christian, are you silver or dross? How does God see you? And if you are silver how much alloy is there in that silver? He loves you enough to purify you. Make it easy on yourself and sit down and be honest with Him. Turn and let Him strengthen and transform you.

²⁶ And I will restore your judges as at the first, and your counselors as at the beginning. Afterward you shall be called the city of righteousness, the faithful city." Isaiah 1:26 God was not going to let them remain in their present compromising condition. He would restore them to their former state of integrity. The testimony of righteousness in Jerusalem would be restored. It would once again be called "the city of righteousness, the faithful city." This was fulfilled to some degree before the coming of the Messiah. We see the struggle in the books of Ezra and Nehemiah. The people decided to follow the Lord and quit compromising. Their leaders were godly. The nation was preparing for the coming of the Messiah.

Once again the ultimate fulfillment is in God preparing the bride of Christ for the Second Coming of the Messiah. The true believers around the world should be "the city of righteousness, the faithful city." But God has to do a lot of purging before we are seen that way in the eyes of the world.

The faithful judges are the elders of godly congregations that only want to see God's will be done. They are like the counselors Israel had in the beginning.

²⁷ Zion shall be redeemed by justice, and those in her who repent, by righteousness. Isaiah 1:27 Zion is a hill in Jerusalem but was often used as another name for Jerusalem. It would be redeemed by justice. In other words, when the city is known again for justice, its name will be redeemed. It is justice or the lack thereof that makes a city what it is.

The inhabitants who repent are redeemed by righteousness. Their lives are witness to the validity of their repentance. That will one day be validated by the death and resurrection of Jesus who makes our repentance legally acceptable to God. After the heavy hand of God is upon the people, justice will again prevail and the people will repent of their sins. It often takes tragedy and hardship to wake us up. Man seems to need something to slap him out of his stupor so that he considers what is really of importance. Sometimes that is the death of a loved one, or the loss one's fortune, or an illness. War can certainly turn many to God. And while God may not desire it, He allows man to do as he will and uses the situations to turn the lost to Him.

Considering the depressing view of their current condition, this was quite a promise for their future. It was something they could look forward to in hope. Just as the Lord encourages us with the promise of the future. Now for the warning. *28 But rebels and sinners shall be broken together, and those who forsake the LORD shall be consumed.* Isaiah 1:28 That is a stern and specific warning like the one in verse 20. They are rebels now, as we saw in verse 2. God is telling them that they must change or face the sword. If they don't change, they will remain the enemies of God and the last verse of Isaiah speaks of their fate (Isaiah 66:24).

Judgment will not hold off forever. The day will come when those who insist on remaining in rebellion will face the God they have been resisting. To rebel and to forsake God, you had to know of Him first. We can't rebel against someone we are unaware of. We can't forsake something that was never offered to us. Those who will be broken and consumed are those who have fought the love of God and remain stubbornly opposed to it in their selfishness. It's all about them. They refuse to accept the love, care about others, and especially yield to another, even if He is their Creator.

29 For they shall be ashamed of the oaks that you desired; and you shall blush for the gardens that you have chosen. Isaiah 1:29 This is a reference to places where pagan gods were worshiped. You can see the same thing today in Hindu and Buddhist areas. Old large trees become focal points of worship. Prayer centers to the gods are often made into gardens. God is telling the people of Judah that once God gets done dealing with them, they will be embarrassed that they ever worshiped these false gods. It will be a shameful part of their past.

They chose these gods who can neither hear nor see over their Creator who had done such great things for them. It is just like today when we choose money, or pleasure, or a drug, or anything other than the Lord. When we come to the Lord we are ashamed of how we once looked to those things as having any lasting value. We ask ourselves if we were so depraved as to put our hope in those things; and we have to confess that we were.

30 For you shall be like an oak whose leaf withers, and like a garden without water. 31 And the strong shall become tinder, and his work a spark, and both of them shall burn together, with none to quench them. Isaiah 1:30-31 We tend to become like what we worship. God said they would become

21

like those oaks they worshiped, but no longer strong and secure but rather dried up and dead. Once they are dried they become tinder, fuel with which to start a fire. The work of those who were once so strong in worldly ways is their own spark (1 Corinthians 1:27).

Both the strong and their works, represented by tinder and the spark, will burn together. In other word they will come to nothing. There will be nothing that remains of their work. No one will remember them. All that they did was for the present.

Are we investing in things that last? Are we strong in this world but without spiritual strength? There was an oak in eastern Maryland that was estimated to be 400 years old. The trunk was 32 feet in circumference. The crown spread over 158 feet and was 105 feet tall. A few years ago a storm blew it over. While parts of the tree might be worked into furniture, much of it probably dried and became firewood. We can make a big show in this world and look larger than life, but death comes to all. What will remain? Will it be fuel for the fire, or something that remains (1 Corinthians 3:15)?

So ends this third prophecy. The purging wind of God's discipline was coming. The individual's reaction to God would determine his or her fate. They could be refined and restored to former greatness, prepared for the Messiah, or broken and consumed. It looks like the choice was clear for them, and the choice is the same for us.

Questions
1 What were the past and present charges against Jerusalem?
2 What was so bad about their actions?
3 How does dross apply today?
4 What are the princes up to?
5 What is the promise?
6 What will it take?
7 What is the warning?
8 What is the ultimate fulfillment?
9 Why are difficulties necessary?
10 What is the oak analogy?

Thy Kingdom Come - Isaiah 2:1-5

The first chapter of Isaiah was a preview of the entire message of Isaiah. God challenged the people to see their true spiritual condition. He warned of the consequences of going on without hearing God and changing their rebellious ways. He graciously invited them to come and reason with Him as He was willing to change their bloody hands from crimson to pure white (1:18).

The beginning of chapter two is another invitation to experience now what will one day be a worldwide experience. There are two ways of interpreting the passage. This is true with many prophecies in Scripture. We often see an immediate or intermediate message and also an ultimate fulfillment of a future promise. For example, the first great promise of the coming Messiah in Genesis 3:15 tells us the Messiah will bruise the head of the Serpent while the Serpent will bruise His heel. Jesus defeated Satan on the cross. We could say it was fulfilled then, but there will be an ultimate fulfillment when Satan is cast into the lake of fire (Revelation 20:10). Or we could consider the reign of Christ on earth. A prediction later in Isaiah tells us that Jesus will reign on David's throne forever (9:7). Jesus is reigning now in the hearts of believers, but He will reign over the nations during the Millennium.

We also have to consider the poetic nature of Isaiah's prophecy that often uses allegory and the language of eschatology (end time prophecy). When prophets are speaking of the End of Days, they express things with extreme wording. It's not that they are exaggerating, but rather to give us a sense of the enormity of the situation, they have to use the most extreme language possible.

¹ The word that Isaiah the son of Amoz saw concerning Judah and Jerusalem. Isaiah 2:1 Isaiah saw God's word. It's an interesting expression. He is a seer of visions. He could see this happening, but what he is seeing is the Word of the Lord. The "word" in Hebrew is "dabar." It is what God is speaking or revealing. Instead of using "word" we could say it was the "communication" or "council" of the LORD that Isaiah saw.

This was a message to and concerning Judah and Jerusalem. While it was for them in that day, we'll see that it speaks to us today as well. It is almost the exact wording of Micah 4:1-3. Since Micah wrote around the same time as Isaiah, some believe that Isaiah was copying the Micah prophecy. Man always looks for a natural explanation. Could it be that Isaiah was seeing this vision and the words of Micah were quickened to his spirit and so perfectly fit what he was seeing that he wrote them down almost unchanged? It could also be that these two prophets heard the exact same thing from the Lord. Isaiah wrote that he saw this word, and that settles it for me.

² It shall come to pass in the latter days that the mountain of the house of the LORD shall be established as the highest of the mountains, and shall be lifted up above the hills; and all the nations shall flow to it, Isaiah 2:2 The latter days began at Pentecost. Under the inspiration of the Holy Spirit, Peter explained to those who heard the noise of the rushing wind and gathered to see what was happening, that the prophecy of Joel was being fulfilled before their eyes. In the last days God would pour out His Spirit on all flesh (Acts 2:17).

By the way, this Joel prophecy is another of those with multiple fulfillments. The rest of the prophecy says that the sun will be darkened and the moon turned into blood before the great and awesome day of the LORD (Joel 2:31). That did not happen in Peter's day, and yet the prophecy of the Spirit being poured out then did. In the end of the last days I believe we will see a greater pouring out of the Spirit and these signs in the heavens as the ultimate fulfillment comes to pass (Matthew 24:29).

The mountain of the house of the LORD is where the Temple was in Jerusalem. Mountain is also a symbol of a kingdom. Daniel tells us that that man's governments end when a rock from a mountain strikes the image of man and becomes a mountain that fills the whole earth (Daniel 2:35). God's kingdom will fill the earth. Isaiah's prophecy is saying that it will be exalted above all the other nations and the other nations will flow to it.

Here is where we begin to see the two possible interpretations. I'll follow this pattern through the prophecy, showing first its fulfillment in the spread of the gospel, and then the future of the millennial kingdom.

Since the preaching at Pentecost and the pouring out of the Spirit, the gospel has spread to the entire world (Matthew 24:14). There is not a nation on earth that has not had the witness of the gospel. It all began in Jerusalem. The Apostles went out from Jerusalem. That was their headquarters for the first four decades of the church. It is just as Jesus said, "Beginning in Jerusalem… (Luke 24:47).

The kingdom they were founding was not like those of this world. It does not have a capital, and our King reigns in our hearts rather than from a political center. Those who enter the kingdom through saving faith in Jesus have become a part of the New Jerusalem, Zion (Revelation 21:2; Ephesians 2:19-22; Hebrews 12:22-23).

As missionaries and evangelists travel the globe proclaiming the gospel in the languages of the world, the nations are flowing into the New Jerusalem. Over 25 million a year are converted to faith in Jesus. Like creeks flowing into rivers that run to the ocean of New Jerusalem, we see the prophecy fulfilled.

If you've ever been to Tel Aviv airport, you can see the New Jerusalem flowing to literal Jerusalem to see where their Lord walked and taught. The languages are numerous. You meet believers from everywhere in the world. You can see by the joy on their faces they love the same LORD. We speak different languages, but we sing the same songs with the same message. While they are flowing to literal Jerusalem, the greater flow around the world is to New Jerusalem. The testimonies are amazing. The dreams and visions Joel predicted are coming to pass with great frequency in the Middle East.

Is it any wonder that evil is surging as well? The vile practices of radical Muslims are a forewarning of what will happen when the anti-Christ reigns (Revelation 20:4). In the midst of the uncertainty people are forced to consider what really matters and to think about their eternal destiny. They are flowing into New Jerusalem, which is the kingdom that is exalted above all the kingdoms of man.

In the future sense of fulfillment, the government of Jesus' earthly kingdom during the Millennium will be centered in Jerusalem. The nations that refuse to come up to the Feast of Booths will be punished with drought (Zechariah 14:16-18; 8:22). The flow into Jerusalem in those coming days will make today's flow look like a trickle.

³ and many peoples shall come, and say: "Come, let us go up to the mountain of the LORD, to the house of the God of Jacob, that he may teach us his ways and that we may walk in his paths." For out of Zion shall go the law, and the word of the LORD from Jerusalem. Isaiah 2:3 Many people indeed! Christianity surpasses all other religions in conversions. About 31.5% of the world's population claim to be Christians. Only God knows how many of them have truly placed their faith in Jesus, but regardless, it is as the prophecy says "many people." Who would have reasoned in their natural mind that the builder from the little town of Nazareth would one day reign in the hearts of billions of people?

They come so that they may be taught the ways of the LORD. The ways of the LORD are the equivalent of His attributes that we studied recently. The current fulfillment is coming into the kingdom to learn to walk in the fruits of the Spirit (Galatians 5:22-23). The future fulfillment will be similar, but the trip will be to physical Jerusalem where the LORD Himself will be teaching.

Enoch and David both asked to be shown the ways of the LORD so that they could walk with Him (Exodus 33:13; Psalm 25:4). If we want to walk with Him, we need to walk in step with His Spirit (Galatians 5:25). He will not walk with the rebellious or prideful. There are two people in Scripture whom God declared to have walked with Him. Enoch was the first. His testimony is short but profound. He walked with God and God took Him without seeing death (Genesis 5:22). The other person is Noah, a preacher of righteousness whose obedience saved the human race (Genesis 6:9; 2 Peter 2:5). If we want to walk with God, we have to know His ways, His attributes. When we walk in His ways we know we are acting in accord with His character. We need the infilling of the Holy Spirit and a knowledge of the Word to check us when we are stepping out of the Lord's ways.

They go to New Jerusalem because the saints have learned the ways of God and can disciple them. They can learn from our mistakes and successes, but most of all from our understanding of God's Word (Matthew 28:20).

They will go to Jerusalem in the millennial kingdom because the law will go forth from there. That word for "law" in Hebrew is "torah." It means instruction, teaching, precepts, or the laws God applied to Israel. In this case it seems "teaching" would be the most applicable translation. The world will come to hear Jesus instruct them. Imagine that! Those in the Millennium will be able to go and hear Jesus teaching. With Jesus overseeing it all, there will be no false teaching going out of Jerusalem in those days.

The word of the LORD will go out from Jerusalem. That was what Isaiah was doing. He was in Jerusalem declaring the Word of the Lord. It was happening then as we are reading this prophecy. It is happening now with New Jerusalem, and it will happen in the future (Isaiah 52:10).

⁴ He shall judge between the nations, and shall decide disputes for many peoples; and they shall beat their swords into plowshares, and their spears into pruning hooks; nation shall not lift up sword against nation, neither shall they learn war anymore. Isaiah 2:4 This portion of the prophecy sounds like it only applies to the future earthly kingdom but let me try to make a current application.

Before Christianity took hold, clan was fighting clan, nation was conquering nation, and war was a normal part of life. That made every day full of uncertainty. While wars continue in our day, the influence of Christianity has brought peace to many parts of the world. The death toll from war has increased because of man's destructive capacity and population increase, but the chance of you being removed from your home because of a conquering nation has decreased dramatically. Now, when a nation invades another nation, the whole world protests the action.

The biggest warfare has always been man against God. That is the source of earthly wars. God tells us not to covet, but nations covet what belongs to others and go to war to take it (Exodus 20:17). The souls of man are in a war against God as they seek out ways of destroying their own lives and that of others through lust and selfishness. I believe we could apply this passage to the peace we have with God when we come to Jesus and repent of our sins and accept Him as Lord (Colossians 1:20). He judges our sins. He teaches us to forgive and let go of anger and disputes. He commands us to love one another and enables us to do so (John 15:12).

Swords and spears can be the words of our mouth used to attack others and have our way (Psalm 55:21). Certainly words can be weapons, but the Christian tames the tongue by the power of the Holy Spirit. We learn to speak the language of the Spirit which is love and truth in humility. We see the power of a soft word to turn away wrath (Proverbs 15:1). We express the fruits of gentleness and kindness resulting in animosity being disarmed.

While our words were used as swords, we see them transformed into plowshares. They break up the hard ground in others' hearts so that we can plant the seeds of the gospel. How much more fruitful to use our words to prepare a heart to hear the message than to drive them from us or hack them in pieces (Proverbs 25:15).

Our words that were spears are reshaped into pruning hooks. Jesus told the disciples that they were pruned through the word that He spoke to them (John 15:3). That is to use our words to disciple those that began to grow from the seeds we planted. And when we see this fruit from what we once used as weapons, we have no desire to learn war anymore. We are done with fighting men. It is much more meaningful to win them to the Prince of Peace (9:6).

The verse is certainly as fitting to the millennial kingdom, perhaps more so than to the present age. As the nations in the Millennium learn that Jesus settles all disputes and has all power to punish those nations which act out of selfish greed, they will find there is no need for weaponry. They will instead focus on productive use of their resources. The abundance of provision from a world where resources are not consumed by war but instead invested in agriculture will be amazing. Military academies will close. The art of war and tactics will be forgotten until Satan is released at the close of the Millennium (Revelation 20:3).

Isaiah closes the prophecy with a call to Judah to not wait until some future day, but to enter the kingdom under the reign of the LORD now. *⁵ O house of Jacob, come, let us walk in the light of the LORD.* Isaiah 2:5 The benefits of learning the ways of the LORD and walking with Him far outweigh anything the world has to offer. One way is light and the other is darkness. (Ephesians 5:8-9) One way is life and the other is destruction. One way is peace with God or to be at war against the Almighty.

Because the Messiah was coming, both in the days of Jesus with salvation and in the coming millennial kingdom to reign on earth, why would they wait? Why not experience it now by yielding our life to the light of the world, learning His ways, and walking with Him (John 8:12)?

History tells us the sad story that Judah refused the invitation. How it might have been different had they received it! They had to experience captivity to realize their wealth had no power to save. Comfort was not security. Other gods were a lie. They learned the hard way. Man seems to prefer that route, and seems unable to learn from the experience of others. I have had to take that hard route in areas of my life, and you have probably had to as well. Will we hear the invitation? Can we learn from Judah? O congregation of Wayside Bible Chapel, let us walk in the light of the LORD by the grace of God. Let us accept His reign over our lives each day. Let us be the New Jerusalem teaching truth and breaking up the hard hearts with the love of God and genuine concern for their souls.

Questions
1 How can prophecies have two meanings?
2 What are the two ways of seeing this prophecy?
3 When did the Latter Days begin?
4 What does a mountain symbolize?
5 How is the mountain being exalted now?
6 How are the nations flowing in?
7 Why will many peoples go to Jerusalem?
8 Why do we need to know the ways of God?
9 What are the weapons and how are they changed now and in the future?
10 What is the invitation?

Humiliated! - Isaiah 2:6 – 22

In the previous sermon we were encouraged by Isaiah's prediction of the kingdom of God. We saw the current fulfillment in the advancement of the gospel. The conversion rate of Christianity outpaces all other 12 religions combined.[1] We also considered the ultimate fulfillment in the Millennium when Christ Jesus will reign on the earth. But before that ultimate fulfillment, the Day of the Lord will come. As in many prophecies, this passage also has an intermediate fulfillment for the people of Judah and an ultimate fulfillment during the end of the Tribulation period.

Isaiah presented the glorious coming kingdom and invited us to walk in the light of the Lord right now. He was telling the people of Judah not to wait but be changed now. He first gives the positive reasons to do so, but now continues with the consequences of remaining in rebellion. *⁶ For you have rejected your people, the house of Jacob, because they are full of things from the east and of fortune-tellers like the Philistines, and they strike hands with the children of foreigners.* Isaiah 2:6 The house of Jacob was another way of saying the house of Israel. Isaiah uses the name of Israel's old nature, Jacob. They could have walked in the conversion of the man who became one who prevails with God, Israel, but they chose to walk in his old nature, the conniving and scheming youth who looked at everything through the eyes of selfish gain (Genesis 27:36).

God rejected Judah because they were full of things from the east. This is a contrast with the preceding prophecy of Jerusalem filled with the knowledge of the Lord (2:3). Presently they are filled with the pagan influence the caravans have brought from Syria, Assyria, and Ammon. The gods of those areas and their superstitions had infiltrated the thought life and private practice of the people. The high places and groves or gardens we saw two weeks ago are among those imports, even the detestable practice of sacrificing children to Moloch.

From the southwest they had let the fortune-tellers of the Philistines influence them (1 Samuel 6:2). King Uzziah had conquered several Philistine towns which brought with it a greater influence of the customs of those they conquered (2 Chronicles 26:6).

In our land of the United States of America, we have seen a repeat of the influence of the east and the fortune-tellers. Walk through our city. Everywhere you look you will see idolatry, eastern influence, and fortune-telling. You can get an aura photo, your chakra aligned, a class on skipping your 6th kamacitic life cycle, or some other eastern influence. Just as in Israel, it snuck in quietly at first. People looked into these practices privately. As the influence grew and the universities and elites increasingly welcomed the influence, we began to see it on book shelves, movies, and television shows. Then the temples were built and the shops began to

---

[1] http://fastestgrowingreligion.com/fgr.html

flourish. Now, as in the later stages of the nation of Judah, paganism is ingrained itself into our daily lives. It is "in." The parallel to Judah is a wakeup call (1 Corinthians 10:6).

Striking hands with the children of foreigners may be familiarity and acceptance of the evil ways of pagans. We call it acceptance of "diversity" and "tolerance" in our day. Christianity in American history for the most part has been tolerant of other faiths. It has not been accepting of them however. There is a world of difference. It is one thing to allow Muslims to practice their religion and build mosques. It is another altogether to be accepting of other faiths as equal to and as valuable as our own. Christians are prejudiced by the Word of God (8:20; Proverbs 30:5)!

We play such silly word games today and rely on the ignorance of our fellow man. Of course, we are prejudice. Only liberal Christians who don't believe the Bible is the Word of God think Christianity is just one of many valid religions. When I came to Wayside, there was a prominent attendee who told me Buddhism was just as valid as Christianity. How can it be when they contradict each the other? The Bible is truth, or it isn't, and if you are of the opinion that you can decide what parts of it are true and which are not, then you are playing God and making up your own personal religion. You have a right to do that, but I don't have to accept your belief system has the same validity as Christianity (John 14:6). We are so desperate to not offend that we are afraid to speak the truth. That is not love. If the Bible is true, we must speak the truth in love (Psalm 40:10). We must study to give an answer to the hope that we have (1 Peter 3:15). We need to understand where others are coming from so we know how to answer them.

I could stop with this one verse. Look at how it applies to the Western world. Listen to this quote of what is happening in Europe. *Today's Europe is spiritually beset by a morally relativistic post-modern worldview that encourages indifference to religion, especially of the Judeo-Christian variety. Religious apathy, induced by secular humanism, has emerged as the defining characteristic of contemporary European society; has created a huge spiritual vacuum that Islam is eager, willing and determined to fill.*

At the same time, Europe's near-wholesale rejection of the Judeo-Christian worldview is fueling a demographic time bomb, planted by Europeans who see no meaning to human life beyond the present, and who do not believe in the future enough to want to pass it on to the next generation. This is reflected by the fact that birth rates among native Europeans are far below replacement levels in most European countries. By contrast, Muslim immigrants in Europe are procreating at a breakneck pace, with birth rates that in many cases are double or triple those of native European populations.[2]

We exported secularism and imported eastern religions to fill the vacuum, and we will pay the price. We are already paying the price! Has the

---

[2] http://www.gatestoneinstitute.org/1536/islam-religion-of-europe

tragic declaration already been made over us, "You have rejected Your people?"

7 Their land is filled with silver and gold, and there is no end to their treasures; their land is filled with horses, and there is no end to their chariots. Isaiah 2:7 Have you seen any ads for silver or gold? The demand for precious metals is so high that whole industries have been created buying jewelry to refine and resell the metal. People actually think silver or gold will save them from the judgments of God (Ezekiel 7:19). The only thing that will save us is turning in repentance and having a personal relationship with Jesus (Psalm 3:8).

There is no end to their treasures. Judah was fantastically wealthy for as small a nation as it was (Isaiah 39:2). This made them a target. We are the wealthiest nation in the history of the world, which makes us a target as well. But it isn't so much the military threat, but rather the spiritual threat of relying on our wealth rather than God to be our security (Psalm 17:14). Our national debt makes our horded resources barely worth anything at all. We just haven't yet come to grips with that reality.

Only under Solomon were horses and chariots ever a large part of Israel's military. But for the wealthy in Isaiah's day, these were a show of status. This thought is along the lines of the abundance of silver and gold. Trusting in being the upper class of society was not going to save from the coming Day of the Lord. You may be riding in the latest handmade Rolls Royce. It won't deliver you. Only Jesus can deliver us on that day.

8 Their land is filled with idols; they bow down to the work of their hands, to what their own fingers have made. Isaiah 2:8 It sounds as if the people were still making household gods called *teraphim*. They were quite small, sometimes made of stone or clay and covered in gold or silver, and others made completely of precious metals. They represented gods of a foreign culture. Judah witnessed the prosperity or power of that culture and some thought it must be due to the worship of their gods; so they took up the practice.

How strange, today, that we take up the gods of cultures vastly inferior to our own. We are welcoming the gods of cultures that have enormous poverty, corruption on a grand scale, and a fraction of our life expectancy. As we adopt their gods we adopt the fruit of worshiping those entities. We can see the decline and yet we continue on in our stubborn walk into darkness (Psalm 115:4-8). What will it take to wake up America?

9 So man is humbled, and each one is brought low— do not forgive them! Isaiah 2:9 Trusting in idols, wealth, and prominence results in humiliation. God rejects us when we reject Him (2 Kings 23:27). If we insist on turning away from Him after all His goodness to us, and choose to exalt ourselves rather than God, we will be humbled, brought low! It is a principle in Scripture. Whoever exalts himself will be humbled, but whoever humbles himself will be exalted (Matthew 23:12). Why is that? Self-exaltation is self -enthronement. It is the rejection of the truth of our real condition. We don't like to hear that we are sinners with an evil nature. That is why some reject the idea and label rebellion against God and his Word as enlightenment. Imagine standing before the holy Creator of all things and telling him you are a god.

Humility is fitting because humility is the only appropriate behavior of fallen creatures that are redeemed by grace alone. When we realize what we are by nature and what we deserve, and then see it is only the loving grace of God that redeems us in spite of ourselves, how can you not be humble?

Isaiah is saying that even when they are humbled, even when they see the destructive end of their choices, don't forgive them. That doesn't seem in-line with New Testament teaching, but perhaps Isaiah is declaring that they are physically humbled but their heart is not changed. To restore them would only result in a repeat of the pattern (Proverbs 26:11). Only captivity will be momentous enough to truly change the direction of the nation.

Now the prophet seems to shift to the ultimate Day of the Lord. While it was coming to Judah upon their defeat by Babylon, the language points us forward to the day of God's wrath upon the earth. *10 Enter into the rock and hide in the dust from before the terror of the LORD, and from the splendor of his majesty.* Isaiah 2:10 Judah has numerous limestone caves in which the people would try to hide themselves when a conquering nation would invade the land. Isaiah is telling the people that it is coming. Get right with God now before it arrives. Conquering nations were said to be the instrument of God to execute judgment upon nations (Ezekiel 39:23). It is the same today. The book of Revelation echoes this thought on the day of God's wrath (Revelation 6:15-16). People will look for caves and bunkers to hide themselves from what is coming on the earth.

11 The haughty looks of man shall be brought low, and the lofty pride of men shall be humbled, and the LORD alone will be exalted in that day. Isaiah 2:11 Every arrogant leader in the secular and religious realms will know they are nothing. Every prideful person will know the vanity of their ways. The LORD alone will be exalted in that day! That is a glorious phrase to those who know Him, for we know He alone is worthy to be exalted (Psalm 96:4). We also know the exaltation of man is the source of this world's problems. It started in the Garden of Eden when Satan whispered the most powerful deception to enter the ears of man, "You shall be as gods (Genesis 3:5)!" No! God alone is God and worthy to be exalted.

12 For the LORD of hosts has a day against all that is proud and lofty, against all that is lifted up—and it shall be brought low; 13 against all the cedars of Lebanon, lofty and lifted up; and against all the oaks of Bashan; 14 against all the lofty mountains, and against all the uplifted hills; 15 against every high tower, and against every fortified wall; 16 against all the ships of Tarshish, and against all the beautiful craft. Isaiah 2:12-16 There are different interpretations of this passage. Are these literal trees and mountains or are they symbolic of people and kingdoms? It is my understanding that Isaiah is addressing people and kingdoms. At the same time, the earth will be purged through the Tribulation while the ultimate cleansing will take place at the end of the Millennium.

High towers and fortified walls were historically present and worked on in the days of the kings to whom Isaiah prophesied. They were building high towers and reinforcing walls. Ships of Tarshish were great ships that could trade with the distant city of Tarshish and withstand storms. This was addressing the things that men trusted in for security. The high towers and fortified walls were to protect against a siege while the ships kept trade flowing to increase their wealth. Judah would try and buy the protection of Assyria only to later have Assyria attack them (2 Kings 16:8).

[17] And the haughtiness of man shall be humbled, and the lofty pride of men shall be brought low, and the LORD alone will be exalted in that day. [18] And the idols shall utterly pass away. Isaiah 2:17-18 This is nearly a repeat of the previous paragraph. It declares the certainty of it coming to pass. The prophet's life was on the line if it did not (Deuteronomy 18:20). Isaiah is declaring he has no doubt that day is coming. It seemed impossible to those who received the prophecy as it seems impossible to us. Could their great wealth, their fortifications, their trading ability all come to an end? Could all these prideful people of power be brought to nothing? Can God humble a nation to such an extent? Isaiah had no doubt.

[19] And people shall enter the caves of the rocks and the holes of the ground, from before the terror of the LORD, and from the splendor of his majesty, when he rises to terrify the earth. [20] In that day mankind will cast away their idols of silver and their idols of gold, which they made for themselves to worship, to the moles and to the bats, [21] to enter the caverns of the rocks and the clefts of the cliffs, from before the terror of the LORD, and from the splendor of his majesty, when he rises to terrify the earth. Isaiah 2:19-21 They will hide from the splendor of the majesty of the LORD of the whole earth because they have rejected His right to reign over their life. They know He is bringing justice, and they know what they deserve. Isaiah mentions the splendor of the majesty of the LORD three times (2:10, 19, 21). Jesus is not coming again as the Lamb but as the Lion of the tribe of Judah and we will see the awesome splendor of His majesty (Revelation 5:5). To those who love Him it will be a welcome vision. To those who hate His authority that day will mean the end of all things for which they have wasted their lives.

[22] Stop regarding man in whose nostrils is breath, for of what account is he? Isaiah 2:22 Stop our breath for a few minutes and we are but dust. Why do we put so much faith in man and our personal abilities? When difficulties come is your first thought, "What can I do?" You can look to God for direction. Stop regarding man. Start looking to God, the maker of heaven and earth. Man will be humbled and the Lord alone exalted when He reveals the splendor of His majesty.

Questions
1 Why did Isaiah call Israel the house of Jacob?

2 How does verse 6 relate to the USA?
3 What is the difference between tolerant and accepting?
4 Review the quote regarding Europe.
5 How does it apply to the USA?
6 Has the tragic declaration already been made over us, "You have rejected Your people?"
7 In what ways does God's description of Judah match the USA?
8 Why would we choose to worship gods of an inferior culture?
9 Why should we be humble?
10 Why should we stop putting our hope in man?

Consequences - Isaiah 3:1-4:1

There are consequences for rebellion against God. We all experience the law of sowing and reaping (Galatians 6:7). We refuse to keep our marital commitments and we wonder why we have grown distant. We leave our Bible on the shelf and wonder why we are spiritually struggling. We slack off at work and are angry because we didn't get a raise. We quit exercising and can't figure out why we have gained so much weight. It must be a thyroid issue. We have a habit of looking outside ourselves for something or someone to blame when the problem is in our own heart (Genesis 3:12-13).

We had a vivid picture in chapter one of the future of Jerusalem if they chose not to repent and change their ways. Spiritually they were already a shack in the midst of a cucumber field picked over by foreigners (Isaiah 1:8). That spiritual condition would become their physical reality if they did not repent. Chapter two was filled with accusations and warnings and final plea to turn from putting faith in material goods and man (Isaiah 2:22).

God has warned them of the justice He would enact. He invited them to come to Him and promised He would wash them clean (Isaiah 1:18-19). He even gave them a view of the coming kingdom of God to motivate them. They would not be moved. This chapter now moves to a prophetic view of what will actually happen. Justice is on the way. It will refine them like a fire refines silver.

¹ For behold, the Lord GOD of hosts is taking away from Jerusalem and from Judah support and supply, all support of bread, and all support of water; ² the mighty man and the soldier, the judge and the prophet, the diviner and the elder, ³ the captain of fifty and the man of rank, the counselor and the skillful magician and the expert in charms. Isaiah 3:1-3

First, note who it is that declares this. It is the Lord of hosts! He is the Lord of angel armies. What He declares is what will be. This is certain. If the invitation didn't get their attention, a vivid description of the coming wrath might wake some up.

This is a list of everything they put their faith in. Food and water are the basic essentials. What would we do without them? How do people behave without it? More frightening than starvation is what humans will do when they are desperate. Imagine the water supply of any metropolitan city being cut off. Imagine grocery stores closed because there was no food to stock.

If that weren't bad enough, there will be no army to protect against invaders, and no power to enforce civility, for the mighty man, judge, and soldier will be removed. We've recently seen a bit of the chaos that erupts in a city that feels injustice is done. Overnight it turns from calm to terror. The unbelievers' trust in military and judicial defense will be dashed (Hosea 3:4).

Where do we turn when our supplies have run out, the police force has fled, and the courts are abandoned. Finally, we turn to God. But the prophet, diviner, and elder are also gone. Therefore, form a militia! But the captain of 50, the man of rank, and the counselor are gone too. There is nothing left but the corner fortune-teller and a lucky rabbit's foot. Now we realize how really powerless they are. That is why we turn to them last in the time of crisis.

So, who is in charge now? [4] And I will make boys their princes, and infants shall rule over them. [5] And the people will oppress one another, everyone his fellow and everyone his neighbor; the youth will be insolent to the elder, and the despised to the honorable. Isaiah 3:4-5 This could mean the leaders have such a lack of experience that they are like youth (1 Kings 3:7). It may be literal. The young, insolent gangs of youth take over because there is no one to stop them. This would happen because the people that were productive and influential were all taken into captivity. Only the poor were left in the land (2 Kings 25:12). When there is no teaching or example of righteousness, it's everyone for themselves. The elders who could give good advice are treated with insolence. Disrespect for the aged is a sign of barbarism. Good government is one of God's best gifts to a sinful race. (Edward Young, The Book of Isaiah Vol 1, p 145)

We have a youth fixated culture. We are absorbed with looking good and being physically healthy. As America's morality declines, we see this more and more. Youth take advantage of the elderly and treat them with contempt, ignoring their voice of experience (1Kings 12:8). I've done too many funerals in which the main thought of the survivors was not the godly testimony of that loved one but about who will get the most money.

[6] *For a man will take hold of his brother in the house of his father, saying: "You have a cloak; you shall be our leader, and this heap of ruins shall be under your rule"; [7] in that day he will speak out, saying: "I will not be a healer; in my house there is neither bread nor cloak; you shall not make me leader of the people."* Isaiah 3:6-7 There will be such a lack of leadership that a man with a basic cloak will be nominated to lead. That's not because they have leadership skills, but because of the desperation for a leader. No one would want to lead the rabble and rubble that is left. That is

the desperate state of what would remain in the land. It became the condition after the Assyrian invasion. Our next verse tells us why this happened.

⁸ For Jerusalem has stumbled, and Judah has fallen, because their speech and their deeds are against the LORD, defying his glorious presence. Isaiah 3:8 The literal meaning of "defying his glorious presence" is "before His glorious eyes". Our words and actions show we either delight in or defy His glorious presence. When a person goes back into sin they had once forsaken, we used to say, "They fell." I don't hear that expression much anymore. The implication was that they were walking with the Lord, and they fell back into sin, like falling into a pit. Their speech and their deeds were in defiance of the holy God before Whom we live. Speech and deeds are the whole expression of our hearts. Some might fall in speech but not in deeds or vice-versa. Jerusalem stumbled in both before the glorious eyes of God. And when the capital stumbles the nation falls.

The previous chapters spelled it out. They practiced injustice and worshiped false gods all the while going through the religious rituals God required (Isaiah 1:13). And it isn't as if they were convicted and felt bad about it. They were brazen in their sin. *⁹ For the look on their faces bears witness against them; they proclaim their sin like Sodom; they do not hide it. Woe to them! For they have brought evil on themselves.* Isaiah 3:9 You don't have to look far to see this evident today. It's everywhere. We call sin a lifestyle choice. If you dare to insist on calling it sin, you are intolerant. Never mind that your motive is for the person's good and the behavior is destructive. You are expected to welcome it as the new normal. They proclaim their sin as Sodom; they do not hide it. I see it on a daily basis, and it grieves my soul (2 Peter 2:7).

The consequences of those choices are well known. It's not as if the information isn't available. But it brings a momentary pleasure or is the preferred route for the flesh to take, so they run headlong to their own destruction. They bring evil on themselves. God doesn't have to judge them. The consequences of their actions do. I've seen it over and over, pleaded with people to see where they were headed. They want God to rescue them from a crisis resulting from their actions, but they are unwilling to change their ways.

In stark contrast God declared, *¹⁰ Tell the righteous that it shall be well with them, for they shall eat the fruit of their deeds. ¹¹ Woe to the wicked! It shall be ill with him, for what his hands have dealt out shall be done to him.* Isaiah 3:10-11 Most of the righteous went into captivity and prospered. There was a refining time of transition, but many did so well in the foreign land that they did not want to return. They sowed righteous actions and they reaped the fruit of their deeds. Both the godly and the wicked sowed speech and actions and each reaped the fruit of what they sowed. It is an eternal truth. What are you sowing? If you answer that question then you know what you will reap, as long as you aren't fooling yourself.

12 My people—infants are their oppressors, and women rule over them. O my people, your guides mislead you and they have swallowed up the course of your paths. Isaiah 3:12 How can infants oppress? When the inexperienced gain power without humility, pride becomes a vicious task-master. Women rule over them. This is not a condemnation of women leaders. It is a statement about the lack of male leadership. God had no problem with Deborah being a judge over Israel (Judges 4:4-5). The problem was that men who remained weren't sacrificial enough to lead.

Their guides had misled them. They had led them down a path of pseudo-religion that had a form of godliness without the power to change the life (2 Timothy 3:5). In fact, they excused the evil choices the people made. We have the exact same problem today. Our universities and denominations are overrun with post-modern nonsense. It is logically incoherent and fosters abandonment to one's desires. It is a message of living for the moment with abandon (1 Timothy 5:6). Sheri showed the admin board a graph of the S.A.T. average scores since the date prayer was taken out of schools. It was a slow steady upward trend until that year and has gone down steadily since. It's no wonder, because ideologies have trumped historical fact. Political correctness has triumphed over free speech. They have swallowed up the way we should go and replaced it with a path to destruction.

13 The LORD has taken his place to contend; he stands to judge peoples. 14 The LORD will enter into judgment with the elders and princes of his people: "It is you who have devoured the vineyard, the spoil of the poor is in your houses. 15 What do you mean by crushing my people, by grinding the face of the poor?" declares the Lord GOD of hosts. Isaiah 3:13-15 The Scriptures often declare the consequences of abusing the poor. You may wonder how leaders abuse the poor today. They foster a culture of dependency. The more children you have, the more welfare you receive. Why work when the government will pay you to stay at home. Of course there are those who truly need help in difficult times in their life. But extended support only encourages a dependent lifestyle keeping them in poverty but receiving their vote come next election (1 Timothy 5:8). *Rather than living to enrich others, false leaders ride on the backs of others. One way God judges His people is by depriving them of worthy leaders.* (Raymond Ortland - *Preaching the Word – Isaiah: God Saves Sinners*. Comment on 3:14)

There has been a lot of talk recently about the real problem being households where the father has abandoned the children. There are so many single moms. The selfishness of men and their failure to live up to their responsibilities is one reason, but I think the main reason is individual selfishness and a lack of Christ likeness from both men and women.

16 The LORD said: Because the daughters of Zion are haughty and walk with outstretched necks, glancing wantonly with their eyes, mincing along as they go, tinkling with their feet, Isaiah 3:16 Female stars today seem to think their way to fame is to act in an ever increasingly shocking way. Children are paying attention and imitating the depravity. There is nothing wrong with women modestly dressing tastefully and using makeup to enhance their looks. It crosses the line when it becomes sexually provocative. Ask yourself if it is lovely or sexy (1 Timothy 2:9-10). What a double standard we have in our culture! While complaining that women are objectified, they glorify women who display themselves as objects of pleasure.

The dress, jewelry, and make-up express the haughtiness in their hearts. "Outstretched necks" was a description of pride. And it all goes back to a self-centered attitude that it is all about me. "Where's the man that will treat me like the queen I am?" Until we realize that lasting happiness can't be found in things of this world, we will keep trying to fill our lives with things that inevitably fail us.

The justice of God is so harsh that it is hard to read, but remember it is meant to refine them. *17 therefore the Lord will strike with a scab the heads of the daughters of Zion, and the LORD will lay bare their secret parts. 18 In that day the Lord will take away the finery of the anklets, the headbands, and the crescents; 19 the pendants, the bracelets, and the scarves; 20 the headdresses, the armlets, the sashes, the perfume boxes, and the amulets; 21 the signet rings and nose rings; 22 the festal robes, the mantles, the cloaks, and the handbags; 23 the mirrors, the linen garments, the turbans, and the veils.*
24 Instead of perfume there will be rottenness; and instead of a belt, a rope; and instead of well-set hair, baldness; and instead of a rich robe, a skirt of sackcloth; and branding instead of beauty. Isaiah 3:17-24 If removal of all these worldly things women rely on to make them attractive and feel valued, even prideful, would turn them toward the true beauty of the heart (1 Peter 3:4), then it must be done. Our eternal good far outweighs our pleasure in what is passing.

Take a guess at how much the make-up and women's clothing industries take in each year? 100 billion dollars in the USA alone! And that isn't counting perfume, hair salons, nail salons, and jewelry. We spend our money on what we think is really important. Again, there is absolutely nothing wrong with looking lovely, but an excessive focus on one's pride being placed in their appearance shows they have missed what is truly of value. Beauty, wealth, possessions are all gifts from God. There is nothing wrong with any thing God gives us. It is how our heart relates to that gift. Do we see it as a gift to be used for His glory or does it feed our pride and rebellion against God?

25 Your men shall fall by the sword and your mighty men in battle. Isaiah 3:25 The men these women were chasing were going to die in battle. Their dreams of happily ever after would be shattered. That is what it took.

26 And her gates shall lament and mourn; empty, she shall sit on the ground. Isaiah 3:26 The gates were the place of news, of court cases, and the place of welcoming the in and out flow of goods (Psalm 100:4). No longer would it be a place of joy and excitement, but rather of grieving. Today it would be an airport where people happily greet loved ones that have been away, but now filled with mourners because of the destruction.

¹ And seven women shall take hold of one man in that day, saying, "We will eat our own bread and wear our own clothes, only let us be called by your name; take away our reproach." Isaiah 4:1 Like the men in verse six desperate for a leader, the women will be desperate for man to take away their personal shame.

This is so far the harshest of prophecies. There isn't an invitation as in previous prophecies. The only hope offered is that the righteous will reap the fruit of their deeds. But we must remember, this is what happened. Isaiah was God's instrument to warn them to turn. They wouldn't accept God's invitations, and so He told them the consequences that they were bringing on themselves.

Was it mean spirited of Isaiah to preach the harsh truth of this message? Or was it gracious of God to tell the rebellious people of Judah just what they were bringing upon themselves? How should the people have responded? How should we respond? *God knows how to enrich us through loss. Sometimes he takes away more than we would wish he would, but only to give us more of himself forever.* (Raymond Ortland, *Preaching the Word, Isaiah,* Introduction to chapter 3)

How much of this applies to our nation? They declare their sin as Sodom and do not hide it. Your guides mislead you. Is the Lord standing to judge those who devour the poor for their own advantage? Are women rising up to be senators and running for president because we don't have men that are godly leaders ready to serve the nation? Are our women focused on outer rather than inner beauty? Is our faith placed in our wealth and military might?

If it does apply to us as a nation, what should our response be to these warnings of what we as a nation will bring upon ourselves? Has our culture invaded our own homes and lives, our very way of thinking, or are we in agreement with God?

There is one line of hope in this passage, just one way to turn. As for the righteous, they will reap the fruit of their deeds. Are our speech and deeds sowing righteousness or evil? Will we reap good fruit or bring destruction upon ourselves? Each person must make the choice of what they will sow. Each person will reap what he or she has sown (Galatians 6:8).

Questions
1 What was God removing from Jerusalem?
2 What would that be like in the USA?
3 What would be the new condition?
4 Why must God do this?
5 Where is His glorious presence then and now?
6 Do verses 8 – 9 apply to Sedona?
7 What is the promise to the righteous?
8 Why is the Lord contending with the elders and princes?

9 What did the Lord oppose in the women?

10 What should have been their response?

The Beautiful Branch - Isaiah 4:2-6

Chapter one gave us an introduction to the deplorable spiritual condition of Judah. Chapter two set before them the glorious future when the Messiah would reign. The rest of chapter two and three predict that the people of Judah will have to go into captivity in order to purge out their idolatry and rebellion against God. Then like a book end opposite the beginning of chapter two, we have another glimpse of the glorious future. That future is in stark contrasting images from the preceding passage. The women had placed their pride in physical beauty. God is about to describe true beauty. Judah was going to reap the fruit of their sinful deeds. God is going to declare a different fruit of the land, His fruit. They were filthy and stained with blood, but they are to be washed clean. God's protective hand was being lifted, but it will return in an even more glorious way.

Like the prophecy in chapter two, chapter four has multiple fulfillments. We can see that in how the terms are used later in Isaiah. *2 In that day the branch of the LORD shall be beautiful and glorious, and the fruit of the land shall be the pride and honor of the survivors of Israel.* Isaiah 4:2 That day refers back to the Day of the LORD (2:12; 3:18). It is a day of judgment, a day of reckoning. However, for the righteous, it will be a glorious day! If Jesus has borne the judgment on your sins, then it will be a welcome day, a day to look for each and every day. If you will pay for your own sins, it will be a day in which you look for a hole in the ground to try to hide from the eyes of the glorious One.

The word "branch" is used in two different ways. Remember, this is end time poetry and the prophet is using metaphors. The branch he is referring to can be the Branch of Jesse, who is identified as the Messiah (Isaiah 11:1), or it can be the remnant that turn to the Lord (Isaiah 60:21). Since the Branch is the pride of the survivors, it must be a reference to the Messiah. Jeremiah and Zechariah have several passages in which they refer to the Messiah as a Branch raised up for David (Jeremiah 23:5; 33:15; Zechariah 3:8).

We can read the passage as saying that on the Day of the LORD, the Messiah, Jesus, shall be beautiful and glorious. He will come the second time in the splendor of His unveiled glory. For the redeemed it will be the beautiful sight we have longed to see (Zechariah 9:17). For those in rebellion it will be terror and dread (Matthew 24:30).

To some extent this was fulfilled in the first coming. Jesus manifested the glory of the Father in His teaching of truth, miraculous healing, deliverance from evil spirits, and especially in His atoning death for us (John 1:14: 2:11). He judged the religious leaders and cleaned the Temple courts. Within a generation the old system was demolished by the Romans. It was not in a 24-hour day, but it was a time in which God was manifest in Israel, and people had to decide if they were for or against Him.

The second half of the verse is: *the fruit of the land shall be the pride and honor of the survivors of Israel.* I agree with commentator Edward Young and others that this is not to be read literally but continues with the same metaphor, calling the Messiah the fruit of the land. The land and the people are the inheritance God gave to Abraham. This is emphasizing the human side of Jesus' lineage. Jesse, a descendent of Abraham, is the stump from whom came the branch. Jesse's son David is the king who received the promise that God would give him a descendant who would reign forever. Both the Branch and the Fruit are called glorious. Both should be capitalized. We could hardly compare our Savior with bananas and grapefruit. It is Jesus who will be the pride and honor of the survivors of Israel. The descendants of the ones who survived the Assyrian and Babylonian invasions would see the glorious One, Jesus, and many of them would witness His mighty acts. Those who accepted Him as Messiah saw Him as their pride and honor.

We who are redeemed certainly see Him as our pride and honor. Our value is found in the love of God that redeemed us and is preparing us for eternity with Him. What could we possibly boast in that would be greater than that? What greater honor could any human have? Is He your pride and honor? Does it show? Do others know He is your delight?

The ultimate fulfillment may be when the 144,000 see Jesus coming at the end of the tribulation. Their long-awaited King will have come to reign on David's throne for a thousand years. Those Jews who survive the tribulation will look on Him Whom they have pierced and mourn as one mourns for their only child (Zechariah 12:10). It will be a heartfelt repentance. He will be their pride and honor. This interpretation flows into the next verse.

[3] And he who is left in Zion and remains in Jerusalem will be called holy, everyone who has been recorded for life in Jerusalem, Isaiah 4:3 This could not have been the case after the Babylonian invasion, for those left in the land rebelled against the word of the Lord from Jeremiah (Jeremiah 42:18-19). In some sense it could be applied to those who returned. Ultimately it must be applicable to those Jews who have turned to the LORD at the end the tribulation and accepted Jesus as their Messiah, Lord and Savior. This is surely what the Apostle Paul was referring to in Romans 11 when he declared that all Israel would be saved (Romans 11:26), though his actual proof text was Isaiah 59. *[20] "And a Redeemer will come to Zion, to those in Jacob who turn from transgression," declares the LORD. [21a] "And as for me, this is my covenant with them," says the LORD* Isaiah 59:20-21a Paul adds, "when I take away their sins" from Isaiah 27:9.

The only way they can be redeemed, saved, and sanctified is by the atoning death of Jesus, their Messiah. The veil over their eyes will be lifted in a time of tragedy, called "Jacob's trouble," and they will accept Jesus as their Savior (Zechariah 13:1). That is the only way that everyone who remains could be holy and recorded in the Book of Life. Everyone who has accepted Jesus as their Savior is considered holy and written in that book. If you know Him as your Lord, your name is there too.

Isaiah is predicting the fulfillment of His own prophecy in chapter one verse 27. *27 Zion shall be redeemed by justice, and those in her who repent, by righteousness.* It is the righteousness of Jesus that redeems them, not their own. Justice had to be served and it was ultimately meted out on the cross. It would be the sacrifice of Jesus that would make their repentance acceptable to God. Through repentance and trust in God to provide for their sins, they would receive the righteousness of Jesus. All our own righteousness is as filthy rags (Isaiah 64:6). Our righteousness is of Him (1 Corinthians 1:30)

Isaiah 1:27 contains the basics requirements of salvation. There has to be justice. There has to be repentance. Those who repent are redeemed. They have the righteousness of Christ. The only factor missing is the means of that justice being meted out, which as the apostle Paul says, was still a mystery in Isaiah's day (Ephesians 3:4-6). Though it was clearly predicted by the prophets, they could not understand how it would come about through the cross.

The next verse tells us how this will happen. *4 when the Lord shall have washed away the filth of the daughters of Zion and cleansed the bloodstains of Jerusalem from its midst by a spirit of judgment and by a spirit of burning.* Isaiah 4:4 The immediate partial fulfillment would be the repentance the people would express when Jerusalem went into captivity. Then they would be forced to face the fact that it was their sins that had brought about the very thing that God had said would happen through the mouth of Moses (Deuteronomy 28:15). God had spoken in the previous chapters accusing them of shedding blood. The psalmist wrote that they sacrificed their innocent children to gods of the Canaanites (Psalm 106:38). That guilt would be taken away.

The spirit of judgment upon Jerusalem would be the wakeup call to repent and turn back to God. It did not happen all at once. God gave them numerous chances to turn. First it was the nation of Syria. Then it was Assyria. The final blow came from Babylon. We can see the grace of God with warning after warning. After all, Judah would see the northern tribes fall because of idolatry. They had an example right before their eyes, but they would not turn. God rescued them from Syria and Assyria by miraculous means, but they would not give Him the glory due His name.

God seems to follow similar patterns throughout history. That is because His love and mercy are unchanging. He warns and then warns again. He pleads through those who deliver His Word. But when people pass a point of no return, when repentance would only last until the threat was lifted, judgment must eventually come. Are we approaching this point in our nation?

Judgment and the removal of all they trusted in was the only way to bring true repentance of those who would turn. If we keep turning back to the things of the world when the danger passes, God will do what must be done for our sake. He will take away our filth by a spirit of judgment and burning. Let us not harden ourselves to that extent. Let us be repentant and continue to place our trust and hope in Jesus and not on the temporal things of this passing world. We thank God for His blessings and provision but we must never let things become our security or come between us and God. That is to turn them into idols.

In Isaiah we are seeing God speak to a nation that was His chosen people. That does not mean they were redeemed. Paul tells us only a remnant is saved and that is consistent with the words of the prophets (Romans 9:27). The majority were in rebellion toward God.

God deals with nations in a similar way that He deals with individuals. While the message is addressed to the nation of Judah, it applies to individual lives. As the redeemed of the Lord, we should be checking to see if there is any area in our own life where we are compromising in similar ways.

John the Baptist said the one who would come after him would baptize with the Spirit and with fire (Matthew 3:11). The Spirit convicts of sin and the fire of the Lord is His purging of our hearts' sinful ways. He purifies our inner thoughts and outward actions as we grow in Christ. The spirit of burning is the cleansing of fire. In the Old Testament, spoils of war were to be sanctified by fire (Numbers 31:23). Israel did not know it, but it was a way of not bringing disease back to their homes. The fire of the Holy Spirit purges our lives of the disease of sin.

Judah was about to be purged by the burning of everything they took pride in and trusted. That is what the Spirit of God does in the mind and actions of those who come to Jesus and let the Holy Spirit have His way in them. The Spirit of judgment and burning works in us too, if we will allow it. If we want to walk with the Lord, we need to let Him cleanse our life with that fire.

5 Then the LORD will create over the whole site of Mount Zion and over her assemblies a cloud by day, and smoke and the shining of a flaming fire by night; for over all the glory there will be a canopy. Isaiah 4:5 This is reminiscent of how the Lord led the children of Israel out of Egypt and through the wilderness (Exodus 13:21). There is no record of this happening upon the return from captivity in a literal way, so again we see Isaiah speaking in a figurative form explained in the next verse (Isaiah 25:4). The pillar of cloud and fire represented the LORD'S presence in their midst leading, protecting, and watching over them throughout their miraculous journey.

Upon the captives return, we can read in Ezra and Nehemiah how God miraculously gave them favor of the king, supplied their building materials, protected them from their enemies, and even guiding them to repentance as they restored the city walls and the Temple.

42

In New Jerusalem it must be figurative of His presence as well, for there is no night there (Revelation 21:24). More important than any literal fulfillment is what the pillar of cloud represents (Revelation 7:15). The canopy over us is a wedding canopy. It is ultimately fulfilled in us becoming the bride of Christ (Revelation 21:9). It is the loving presence of Jesus with us throughout eternity. It is joy unceasing and full of glory (1 Peter 1:8).

6 There will be a booth for shade by day from the heat, and for a refuge and a shelter from the storm and rain. Isaiah 4:6 The presence of the LORD in their midst would the shelter and refuge they needed from the storms of life. We see the partial initial fulfillment upon the return to Jerusalem. Then we see the fulfillment in Jesus during His three years of ministry. Jesus demonstrated this in a physical way by calming the storm on Galilee (Mark 4:39) and in guarding His disciples spiritually (John 17:12). In the Exodus, the LORD was said to be in the pillar of cloud (Exodus 14:24). Jesus was the pillar of cloud in the Old Testament and took on human form in the New. In the Millennial Kingdom and forever He will again be physically present with us, our shelter and refuge.

Chapter two and four and the closing chapters of Isaiah give us this wonderful picture of the coming kingdom. It is surrounded by chapters of God's declaration of our sinful nature and the justice we deserve. Isaiah's prophecies predict the coming of the Suffering Servant who will come and provide the justice that takes us from being children of wrath (Ephesians 2:3), to becoming children of God with the righteousness of God in Christ Jesus (2 Corinthians 5:21). It is no wonder then that after the captivity Isaiah became one of the favorite books of the Jews and quoted so often.

Isaiah is setting before the people of Judah the devastating result of their choices, but also the glorious plan of God to redeem them through it all. The Spirit sets the same before us. Is He your pride and honor? Is your life focused on Him, or on the things of this world? Let us not be as foolish as the people of Judah, neglecting God's warnings and going our own way. Let us choose the Lordship of Jesus and live for Him today. Amen?

Living with the beautiful Branch as your king is not a burden. He does the work through us. In fact, He is the one place we find our souls can rest. He is the canopy over us. When He is our King, we are in His Kingdom, and it is there we experience righteousness, peace, and joy in the Holy Spirit (Romans 14:17).

Questions
1 Who is the Branch? The Fruit?
2 Is Jesus the pride and honor of your life? How is that seen?
3 What is the future fulfillment of vs 2-3?
4 How could the people be holy?
5 How is 1:27 the Gospel?
6 What was required to cleanse them?
7 How can it be applied to us?
8 When is judgment inevitable?

9 What does the cloud represent?
10 What are the three fulfillments of verse six?

The Vineyard Song - Isaiah 5:1-7; Psalm 80:8-19

This study of Isaiah has begun with some very severe prophecies about the coming captivity of Judah, intermingled with words of hope about the coming Messiah and His kingdom. The purpose of the coming captivity is to purify the nation and prepare it for the coming Messiah.

This week's passage is a prophetic song that has repetitive sounds in its original language of Hebrew. If Psalm 80 was written by Asaph from the time of King David, then the inspiration originally came from his psalm (1 Chronicles 16:7). Jesus will take it up and use it to address His culture, which again shows us the multiple fulfillments of prophecy.

¹ Let me sing for my beloved my love song concerning his vineyard: My beloved had a vineyard on a very fertile hill. Isaiah 5:1 Isaiah begins by announcing in prose that he will sing this song for his beloved. I believe he is using the language of the Song of Songs (1:16) and sees the LORD as the One he loves. He sings the song of the LORD for the LORD concerning the LORD'S vineyard.

Isaiah calls is it a love song. It sounds like the prototype of country western songs. Everything that was good goes bad. We can see it as a love song if we see it as Isaiah singing of his grieving love for the LORD'S broken heart. Isaiah is one of those people that make up the vine. It is personal to him. It's about the Lord he loves and His people. It was the earliest of the songs that would later be sung in captivity when the people of Judah sat by the rivers of Babylon and wept for their homeland (Psalm 137:1).

Psalm 80 verse 8 tells us that the LORD brought this vine out of Egypt. It is a transplant of a choice vine carefully chosen by God and planted in a fertile place. You'll recall that when the spies came back from exploring the land they brought a giant bunch of grapes carried on a pole between two of them (Numbers 13:23). The physical condition of the land was a picture of the spiritual preparation for the success of the nation.

²ᵃ He dug it and cleared it of stones, and planted it with choice vines; he built a watchtower in the midst of it, and hewed out a wine vat in it; Isaiah 5:2a Israel is a land full of stones. There is an Arab saying that an angel had two bags of stones to distribute over the earth, but as he was flying off, one of them broke over Israel. Even today in the plowed fields of Israel you'll see white stones everywhere you look. It was a lot of work to clear the stones. This represents the work God did in the wilderness to clear the hearts of the people from all the stoniness they had taken with them out of Egypt, the murmuring and lack of faith in God (Joshua 5:6).

44

He does the same work in our lives as we journey through our own wildernesses. The trials and judgments teach us to quit murmuring and begin trusting and praising (1 Corinthians 10:10-11). Some of us are slower to learn than others. But God is faithful to break up our hard hearts and remove the stones.

He planted it with a choice vine. There is another more recent saying about God's choice of the Jewish people. "It's odd of God to choose the Jews; He chose which shows God knew His Jew." It has a similar assonance (repetition of sounds) as the poem we are studying. God chose the Jews because they are just like us. God chose them because of Abraham (Genesis 22:16-18), but He knew they would emphasize the plight of the human race, such potential, and such a disappointment, such high points of faith and low points of faithlessness.

God built a watchtower and hewed out a wine vat. This was a lot of work. Stones that are pulled from the field are used to make a small tower and shelter. From the tower you can oversee the whole vineyard and be shaded from the heat of the sun. The small room at the base was a shelter for the farmer and a place to store tools.

The wine vat was harder to make. There is a nice example in the Nazareth Village. A Christian group bought some land in Nazareth to recreate a first century village for pilgrims to see what the town was like at the time of Christ. As they cleared the land they uncovered an ancient wine vat and crushing pit. The pit is hewn into the limestone in the shape of a bowl with a trough on one side that runs into a vat, a hole in the limestone to hold the juice.

Everything was done that could be done to make this a fruitful vineyard. The rest of the verse tells the sad results. *2b and he looked for it to yield grapes, but it yielded wild grapes.* Isaiah 5:2b In the saddest of tones, Isaiah sings of the results. God, the vineyard owner, looked for the nation to bring forth fruit, but wild bitter grapes were all it bore. He looked for righteousness, justice, and worship from devoted hearts, but instead injustice and hypocrisy abounded.

We have wild grapes near my home. They are small and very bitter. Selfishness was the response to the generosity of God. How bitter it was to God to see His work result in bad fruit.

And what shall we say of our own nation? Has God not planted us in a fertile field? Did He not pick our ancestors fleeing from persecution to worship God in freedom? Did God not provide everything we needed to be just, righteous, and faithful worshipers of God in our heritage and constitution? The founders wanted the Bible to be available for every student, and our universities were founded to raise up ministers who could faithfully expound upon the Word of God. Now we hear reports of Bibles banned from classrooms.

In Psalm 80 we read of the early success of the vine, Israel, how it spread over the land and covered the high cedars. But now where is the fruit? Where is the justice, righteousness, and faithfulness to God and His Word? God looks out and sees a harvest of sour grapes.

But let us take this as individuals as well. What has God done for you? How has He cared for you? What does He have the right to expect from your life and mine, and is He reaping it? We can weep with Isaiah for our nation, but we must then be sure that we have not followed the selfish pattern that it took. Are we serious about our relationship with God and bearing the fruit that should be the result of all the goodness with which He has blessed us (Romans 7:4)?

³ And now, O inhabitants of Jerusalem and men of Judah, judge between me and my vineyard. Isaiah 5:3 Stand back and look what God has done for our nation, for each of us individually, and look at the fruit. Now consider if God is getting what He deserves from all His input.

We have a Fuji apple tree in our garden. It's about 12 years old. Every year we say, "One more year, and if it doesn't produce a better crop, it comes down." We brought in good soil in which to plant it. We water and feed it. We spray for bugs. We do everything we can, and it gives us a handful of mediocre apples. Isaiah was asking what the people thought should be done. This fall the apple tree comes down.

Listen to another prophet declare the aching heart of God for His people. *⁷ Therefore thus says the LORD of hosts: "Behold, I will refine them and test them, for what else can I do, because of my people?* Jeremiah 9:7 What else can God do? If we won't respond to His goodness, we may respond to His discipline (Hebrews 12:6). That is why we usually learn more in the trials and painful experiences of life than we do when times are easy and carefree. Refinement comes from heat. If we won't let the cool winds of God's goodness blow away the chaff, God will use the refining fires of difficulty to burn it up. Stubbornness in our hearts must be plowed through (Jeremiah 4:3).

⁴ What more was there to do for my vineyard, that I have not done in it? When I looked for it to yield grapes, why did it yield wild grapes? Isaiah 5:4 Think of all God did for Israel. He gave them homes and fields already in place (Deuteronomy 6:11-12). It was a fruitful land. He put the fear of them in the surrounding people so they were not invaded for a long while. He gave them godly leaders to help turn them back when they strayed. Numerous times He gave them victory over a far larger army. He blessed them with rules that helped them physically to not have the illnesses of people around them. His laws for the nation were far superior to any in the world, laws we adopt in the modern age because we see how beneficial they are. So what should have been the response?

If we were to list all of God's kindness to us, we might ask what more could He do for us? We, who are here today, live in one of the most prosperous nations in the history of the world. We are freer than most of the world from violence. We have the Word of God and more commentary and study material than anywhere else on earth. There are churches on every corner. We have the best medical care. What else could God do to cause us to yield the fruit we should?

⁵ And now I will tell you what I will do to my vineyard. I will remove its hedge, and it shall be devoured; I will break down its wall, and it shall be trampled down. Isaiah 5:5 God had a hedge of protection around Israel. He allowed enemies to harass them to turn them back to Him (Judges 2:18), but now it had to be more than that. The hedge had to be removed altogether. The vineyard had to be devoured and trampled down. The song is taking on a woeful sound. What follows the song is a description of the bad fruit.

That hedge is still about the nation of America, but it is thinning out. I can't say if God is allowing harassment so that we will turn back or if He is done and ready to remove the hedge altogether. But I do know we better wake up before it is too late. Either way, the believer can still walk in the protection of the Lord with the pillar of cloud over them by day and fire by night (Isaiah 4:5). Though we may suffer loss, the things that really matter to us cannot be taken from us. The hedge around Judah was utterly removed. God was true to His Word. His warning came to pass. But the song is not over.

⁶ I will make it a waste; it shall not be pruned or hoed, and briers and thorns shall grow up; I will also command the clouds that they rain no rain upon it. Isaiah 5:6 Thorns represent the curse of God on the earth from Genesis three (3:17-18). The lack of rain is also seen as God's judgment for disobedience and idolatry (Deuteronomy 11:16-17). The beautiful land would become a wasteland. And so it was during the captivity. But it was also more recently. There are some fascinating drawings of the land of Israel in the 1800s. It was barren inland and swampy along the coast. The last couple of generations have turned Israel once again into a fruitful land. That too was predicted by Isaiah in a song of the redemption of the vineyard (27:6). In fact, today Israel is one of the world's leading citrus fruit producers and exporters.

⁷ For the vineyard of the LORD of hosts is the house of Israel, and the men of Judah are his pleasant planting; and he looked for justice, but behold, bloodshed; for righteousness, but behold, an outcry! Isaiah 5:7 The prophet closes the song with the explanation of the analogy. The house of Israel is the vineyard. The fruit God looked for was justice. The bitter wild grapes were bloodshed. The other fruit that was sought was righteousness. Instead God saw those who were crying out like Abel's blood cried from the ground for justice (Genesis 4:10).

Jesus used the parable of the vineyard with a twist. In His retelling of the song, the vineyard was lent out to tenants, who were the spiritual leaders of the nation. That is in keeping with Isaiah's prophecy that the Lord is contending with the leaders (Isaiah 3:14). In that prophecy God was contending with the leaders because they were the ones that spoiled the vineyard.

In Jesus' parable, when the owner sent his servants to collect his share of the fruit, the tenants beat one, stoned another, and killed another. He sent more, and they treated them in the same way. Finally, he sent his son. Here is where the song and Jesus' use of it takes quite a different turn. They took the son out of the vineyard and killed him in hope that the vineyard would become theirs.

Then Jesus wrapped it up with a question and answer similar to the way the song ends. The song asked if God could have done anything more. Jesus asked what should be done to the tenants. The Luke account is more in line with Isaiah 5:5. Jesus answers His own question, telling the people the owner will kill the tenants and give the vineyard to others (Luke 20:15-16). The crowd knew the Isaiah vineyard song and so they answered, "Surely not!" The land of Israel's inheritance included Jerusalem. Would God remove the Jews and let it be occupied by Gentiles? That is exactly what happened during the captivity and again 40 years after Jesus' death.

The parallel between the song and Jesus' parable was that in Jesus' parable the rejection of the Son was the same as Judah's rejection of God. Isaiah was one of the servants in Jesus' parable that came looking for the fruit but was shamefully sent away empty handed. All Isaiah could see was bitter wild grapes.

In Jesus' parable the final straw was the killing of the Son which was about to take place a few days after the parable was spoken. Jesus pointed to Scripture to show them exactly what they were doing. They were rejecting the cornerstone as predicted in the Psalms (Psalm 118:22). Those who fall upon the stone would be broken. We come to Jesus and realize the sinners that we are and are broken, only to be remade as in the promise of the previous chapter of Isaiah (4:4-5). But those on whom the stone falls in judgment will be ground to powder. It happened in the Babylonian invasion and again in the Roman conquest of Jerusalem in 70 A.D.

Where is the vine today? Isaiah prophesied its redemption in another later vineyard song. The vine is now the Redeemer. When Jesus said, "I am the vine, you are the branches (John 15:5)," He was declaring a total change in how God was working in the world. No longer would it be the Jewish nation and their failure to keep the laws of God and constant turning back to idolatry, but now it would be in Jesus who lived the Law for us. Now those who trust in Jesus would become a branch on the vine. He would prune them and cause them to bear much fruit (John 15:8). His Holy Spirit would be the life-giving sap within that would empower them to live a life that is pleasing to God. It is His life in us that causes us to bear fruit.

There are still promises to the Jewish people that are yet to be fulfilled, but the greatest is that they would be grafted back into the vine by knowing that Jesus is their Redeemer (Romans 11:23). That is the same way any of us becomes a part of the vine. Once we are a part of the vine, He must prune us of the unproductive shoots in our life. It can be painful, but it means greater production of fruit. It means more love, joy, peace and all the fruits of the Spirit (Galatians 5:22). No longer were the leaders of Israel expected to produce fruit. God has taken over caring for the vineyard. He is the pruner. It is His very life in us, the branches, that assures we will bear the fruit He desires.

Are you in the vine? Are you bearing fruit? In the song, the reason the hedge was taken away was because the fruit was bitter wild grapes. In Jesus' analogy, the branches that didn't bear fruit, that didn't remain in Him, were cut off, gathered up and burned (John 15:2, 6). The nation of Judah did not remain faithful to the Word of God. Our nation has drifted away from the Word of God. I pray that you haven't. Remain in Him and He will remain in you. Then you will bear the fruit that God is seeking. It's Jesus' promise (John 15:4).

Questions
1 Who is the beloved? Is He yours?
2 What is the vineyard?
3 What did God do for the vineyard?
4 Where did He get the vine?
5 How did He prepare the vine?
6 Why should it have born good fruit?
7 What did God do when it didn't? Why?
8 What is different from Jesus retelling of the song?
9 Why were the hearers shocked?
10 How can anyone be a part of the vine?
11 How do we bear fruit?

Exalted in Justice - Isaiah 5:8-30

Isaiah was God's instrument to warn the nation of Judah of the consequences of their spiritual depravity. Twice so far, interspersed in those warnings, were predictions of the coming kingdom of God. His message is that they have fallen so far that captivity is the only thing that will prepare them for the coming Messiah and His kingdom. They need to lose all that they have and depend on so that they will repent and be washed clean.

Two weeks ago, we considered the beauty of the Branch, the coming Messiah, and how we should be praising Him for His goodness right now (Isaiah 4:2-4), which is what Judah refused to do. In our passage today, Isaiah describes the bitter grapes in the vineyard song. The passage consists of seven woes and their consequences. In the middle of these, there is a declaration of the central truth of the passage. The Lord of hosts is exalted in judgment!

8 Woe to those who join house to house, who add field to field, until there is no more room, and you are made to dwell alone in the midst of the land. 9 The LORD of hosts has sworn in my hearing: "Surely many houses shall be desolate, large and beautiful houses, without inhabitant. Isaiah 5:8-9 Woe! It is an interjection used 50 times in Scripture. It is usually used as a cry of warning of impending judgment. Six times it is used in mourning the dead (1Kings 13:30).

The idea in these verses is of the affluence of Jerusalem and the unconcern for the poor. We can see that in the use of the same word in both verses. The person that has nowhere to dwell is the same word in verse nine as the inhabitant that no longer lives in his or her beautiful home. The poor had no place to build because the wealthy bought up all the available land in cities for wall to wall housing. They bought up the country land and turned it all into cultivated fields. But when God's judgments would fall, the inhabitant that had no concern for the poor not having a place to dwell would be forced to leave their own beautiful home. As we saw in chapter three, support and supply would be taken from them along with bread and water. (Isaiah 3:1) It is not that investments and agriculture are somehow sinful. They were ignoring the Jubilee Laws that returned land to its original owner (Luke 12:48; also see Leviticus 25) and were unconcerned about the poor.

It is difficult in our culture to relate to this because we are so blessed. Those who have their hand out are often those who refuse to work or who have addictions. But we are beginning to see more and more genuine poverty that comes with the decline of a nation. Where we see genuine hardship, we should show the love of God by providing assistance (1 John 3:17).

Mariko had a person who was obviously a meth addict ask her for money last week. Mariko offered her a meal. The person turned and walked away. We see the cycle of professional beggars hit the heavy traffic hours at the freeway off ramps in Flagstaff. But we also know some single parent moms who are struggling to feed their kids and doing all they can to make ends meet. Be generous, but be discerning.

[10] For ten acres of vineyard shall yield but one bath, and a homer of seed shall yield but an ephah." Isaiah 5:10 The Spirit of God has come upon Isaiah and he is hearing the voice of God swear these things will happen. The abundance of blessing upon Judah is over! This verse literally means that what ten yoke of oxen can plow in a day won't produce enough in a year to feed those oxen for that day. The people will reap a tenth of what they sow. It is over! The time of prosperity should have resulted in their helping the poor and giving praise to God. The goodness of God should have drawn them to repentance (Romans 2:4). Instead, the people hardened their hearts and lived for their greed and selfish pleasures.

[11] Woe to those who rise early in the morning, that they may run after strong drink, who tarry late into the evening as wine inflames them! [12] They have lyre and harp, tambourine and flute and wine at their feasts, but they do not regard the deeds of the LORD, or see the work of his hands. Isaiah 5:11-12 Lots of entertainment, but no regard for God. Amusement means away from thinking. If the god of this world can just keep us absorbed with mind numbing games, depraved TV shows, and violent movies that have no value, we don't have to think about eternity and

whether or not we are living out the purpose for which we were created. They lived to party.

Preoccupation with manmade pleasures keeps us from seeing the work of the LORD, praising Him for our gorgeous sunsets, seeing Him work in our neighbor's life, watching how He directs our steps, and so much more. Enjoy a glass of wine if you are in control of it. Flee from it if it dominates or consumes you (1 Corinthians 6:12). Enjoy music, especially praise music, but don't let the message of worldly music indoctrinate your mind. When the rhythm of a song with an ungodly message comes into my mind, I enjoy changing the words to the opposite message. Try it. It's a good exercise. Instead of drowning out the voice of conscience, let music exercise our conscience to express spiritual truth.

I find that the more spiritually mature people are, the more they recognize and give thanks for the deeds of the LORD in the world around them and in their own lives. That is a factor in how joyful they are. They are always thanking God. Like the seraphim in the next chapter (Isaiah 6:3), they see the whole earth filled with the glory of God.

Now we come to the consequences that sprout from the spiritual condition God has described. *13 Therefore my people go into exile for lack of knowledge; their honored men go hungry, and their multitude is parched with thirst. 14 Therefore Sheol has enlarged its appetite and opened its mouth beyond measure, and the nobility of Jerusalem and her multitude will go down, her revelers and he who exults in her.* Isaiah 5:13-14 The knowledge they lack is the knowledge of the LORD and His Word (Hosea 4:6; Isaiah 1:3). They don't honor those who are truly honorable. In fact, they reject them. The people are dying of spiritual thirst (Amos 8:11), and that will become their physical condition as well.

That is why exile and the death of so many must take place to change the nation. Sheol is the grave. The nobility, the common man, the partiers that thought tomorrow would be like today, were about to answer to their Maker (Isaiah 56:12). The One who had given them so much, who invited them to be His priests to the world (Exodus 19:6), who warned them with miraculous deliverances from enemies and by the vivid example of northern Israel, would ask them why they refused His grace.

15 Man is humbled, and each one is brought low, and the eyes of the haughty are brought low. 16 But the LORD of hosts is exalted in justice, and the Holy God shows himself holy in righteousness. 17 Then shall the lambs graze as in their pasture, and nomads shall eat among the ruins of the rich. Isaiah 5:15-17 Isaiah described the haughty men in chapter two and the haughty women in chapter three (Isaiah 2:11; 3:16). Pride is the ugliest of all attitudes in the eyes of God (Proverbs 8:13). Pride declares its independence from the very One that gave him or her life, breath, strength, health, and all things. Everything we have is a gift from God (1 Corinthians 4:7), but we not only declare our independence, we pretend we are a product of chance and time. The arrogance of man looks at the marvel of creation and declares it to be a cosmic accident. That is haughtiness in the extreme.

If we think we can rob God of His glory, we are sadly mistaken. He will be exalted in justice! His justice upon our pride will show just how righteous He is. Righteousness demands that justice be met. His holiness is seen in His righteous justice. If He were not a holy God, He might let us continue in arrogant pride. But He is holy! There is a day when justice must be met on the cross or in hell. To some extent, there are times when we can see it in this life. Those beautiful homes that left no space for the poor would be pasture land and a place for nomads to dine.

Now for the second set of actions and consequences. You'll see some of the themes overlap but with a different emphasis. *18 Woe to those who draw iniquity with cords of falsehood, who draw sin as with cart ropes, 19 who say: "Let him be quick, let him speed his work that we may see it; let the counsel of the Holy One of Israel draw near, and let it come, that we may know it!"* Isaiah 5:18-19 This time the woes are to the ones that draw the heavy load of sin to themselves with their lies. Instead of fleeing from sin, they laboriously draw it to themselves. The lies are the deception that sin will somehow satisfy the emptiness within and that there won't be consequences (Proverbs 5:22). The lie is that God won't judge us for ignoring His just commands (Psalm 10:11).

The most repulsive act of all those condemned is the one in verse 19. They mockingly say, *19 who say: "Let him be quick, let him speed his work that we may see it; let the counsel of the Holy One of Israel draw near, and let it come, that we may know it!"* Isaiah 5:19 Allow me to paraphrase. "Let God hurry up and judge us. We want to see God act. If God wants to speak, bring it on. We are all ears." These are the mocking taunts that Isaiah had to put up with. We hear them today. Rarely are they this bold, but it is quickly approaching that state. We would hear it more if the church was bold enough to proclaim that we as a nation will be judged if we do not turn to God in repentance (Psalm 9:17).

20 Woe to those who call evil good and good evil, who put darkness for light and light for darkness, who put bitter for sweet and sweet for bitter! Isaiah 5:20 The reversal of God's standards is a sign of a nation's decline. When we justify sin and call it a good thing, we have put light for darkness. When false religions are lauded, idolatry encouraged, promiscuity called a necessity, divorce labeled as inevitable, and selfishness is called healthy, we have lost our way. When the Bible is called bigotry and Christianity is referred to as the cause of much of the wrong in the world, we have forgotten our roots and what made our nation great.

Individually it means that each person who practices and promotes those things reaps the fruit of them. Most people don't even take the time to consider the outcome of the lives they admire. We can be blinded by our own passions and desire to be accepted so that we can't see the consequences right before us. In declaring that it is up to us as individuals to decide what is right or wrong for us, we have declared ourselves to be our own god.

21 Woe to those who are wise in their own eyes, and shrewd in their own sight! Isaiah 5:21 Pride at its worst. "I know better than the prophet of God. I know better than the Word of God." Or it may be, "I know how to do as I please and still be acceptable to God." Basically, it is saying, "I can escape the justice of God (Proverbs 3:7)." That is not possible. Each of us will give an account of himself to God (Romans 14:12)! This kind of pride can hear nothing but their own opinion.

22 Woe to those who are heroes at drinking wine, and valiant men in mixing strong drink, 23 who acquit the guilty for a bribe, and deprive the innocent of his right! Isaiah 5:22-23 Once again we see the glory in excessive alcohol consumption. There is condemnation of the people's praise for the overindulgent and against the injustice in the judicial system. While bribery may be rarer here than in third world countries, it is still a factor. A more common problem is the wealth to hire an attorney that can spin the facts so the jury is dazzled into a wrong decision.

The innocent being deprived of their rights is increasingly common. As our nation adopts corrupted standards, judges are making decisions based on the current temperature of the nation's popular opinion (Deuteronomy 16:20). Back in the 70s my family had our own experience of coming before a judge to try to force a corrupt developer to honor the building codes. We didn't even get a chance to present our case. Grades were steeper than allowed, sewer and water lines were put in the same trench, our well was surrounded with changes in elevation that caused it to flood. Many of you have your own story. Injustice is evil because God is just (Deuteronomy 32:4).

Now for the consequences of drawing evil to themselves, mocking God, perverting what is good, distorting right and wrong, being prideful, indulgent, honoring the abuse of chemicals, and being unjust. *24 Therefore, as the tongue of fire devours the stubble, and as dry grass sinks down in the flame, so their root will be as rottenness, and their blossom go up like dust; for they have rejected the law of the LORD of hosts, and have despised the word of the Holy One of Israel.* Isaiah 5:24 Their root is their source of support and supply that God already declared would be taken away. When the root is dead, the tree is dead. Their blossom is all the outward manifestations of success. Like dust in the wind, it is gone (James 4:14).

The root of the Christian should be their faith in Jesus. What is the root of our nation? We may have once said it was our faith in God, but now it is more likely to be faith in ourselves, our military, our technology, our education, etc. And what is our blossom? Is it our wealth and status in the world? It should be, and to some extent still is, our assistance to those who face tyranny and injustice, but we are beginning to need it at home as much as it is needed abroad (Matthew 3:10). When people are unfairly targeted for their political affiliation, or for voting for moral principles, injustice abounds.

The reason justice must fall on them is stated in the previous verses, but now it summed up in another way. ... *they have rejected the law of the*

LORD of hosts, and have despised the word of the Holy One of Israel. That is the source of the injustice, pride and distorting right and wrong. Our nation at large is rejecting the Word of God and despising the Holy One of Israel. My daughter told me she was experiencing something I had warned her about. She bought our car that has "bible-sermons.org" on the back. Many drivers treat you quite differently when they see it, even giving you gestures. I've even had my tire punctured. There is an increased despising of the things of God in our nation. Ravi has said, "Immorality is always preceded by impiety." First we lose our respect and reverence of God and His Word, and the result is increasing immorality (Nehemiah 9:29).

²⁵ Therefore the anger of the LORD was kindled against his people, and he stretched out his hand against them and struck them, and the mountains quaked; and their corpses were as refuse in the midst of the streets. For all this his anger has not turned away, and his hand is stretched out still. Isaiah 5:25 After all God had done and the glorious future He intended for them, they despised Him. Now it was time for justice. Assyria defeated all but Jerusalem, which God miraculously spared. But God was not done. If they had then turned, their future may have been different, but even in the face of such a miraculous rescue, they would not fully turn back to God.

(See 2 Kings 19) The Assyrians laid siege to Jerusalem. The people were sure they would be defeated or die of starvation. The king asked the LORD to save them. Isaiah predicted the leader of the Assyrians would hear a rumor, return to his own land, and be killed. Soon after, an angel of God slew 185,000 Assyrians. Isaiah's prophecy came to pass, but the people still did not turn to the Lord with all their heart. The very next king was one of the wickedest in Israel's history (2 Kings 21:9).

²⁶ He will raise a signal for nations far away, and whistle for them from the ends of the earth; and behold, quickly, speedily they come! ²⁷ None is weary, none stumbles, none slumbers or sleeps, not a waistband is loose, not a sandal strap broken; ²⁸ their arrows are sharp, all their bows bent, their horses' hoofs seem like flint, and their wheels like the whirlwind. ²⁹ Their roaring is like a lion, like young lions they roar; they growl and seize their prey; they carry it off, and none can rescue. ³⁰ They will growl over it on that day, like the growling of the sea. And if one looks to the land, behold, darkness and distress; and the light is darkened by its clouds. Isaiah 5:26-30 The next invasion would be anointed by God to utterly defeat Judah. They would go into captivity. The survivors would once again honor God by repenting and seeking to follow the laws He had given them. What does it take to turn a nation whose hearts despise God? If hardship does not turn them, defeat may.

God is loving enough to do whatever it takes. He is exalted in justice. He even went to the extent of sending His own Son to take the just penalty for our sins. The cross is the greatest meeting place of love and justice. In it, God is highly exalted in justice. Only in Christ, the true vine, can we bear the fruit that God is seeking. Without Him we end up just like the people of Judah. If we are in Him, we will bear much fruit, but without Him, like the nation of Judah, we can do nothing (John 15:5). Only in Jesus do we produce the fruit God is seeking.

Questions
1 What is God's message so far in Isaiah?
2 What are verses 8 and 9 about?
3 What occupied the people's time?
4 How is God exalted in judgment? How does it show Him to be holy?
5 Why is pride so abhorrent to God?
6 Do we hear things like verse 19 today?
7 What are some common distortions of truth today? Have we fallen for any?
8 What is the root of all their sins?
9 Why does God hate injustice?
10 What must God do to Judah? Why?

God Calling - Isaiah 6

We looked at Isaiah chapter six when we studied the attribute of God's holiness. Today we will focus on the call of God to Isaiah and to us. This is such an important chapter because it gives us one of the first insights into the throne room of heaven (Job 1:6), but also because it shows us how God calls an individual into the privilege of serving Him.

It begins by telling us the time in which it took place. It was the year that King Uzziah had died (740 B.C.). I believe his 52-year reign was the longest in Judah's history. He started his reign at the age of 16 (2 Chronicles 26:3). He was a godly king and very successful. He strengthened the army and equipped it, added to the defense systems of Jerusalem, and subjugated the Amorites.

The temptation that those who are godly and successful often face is pride. It happens with nations and with individuals. When we do the right thing, the natural results are often prosperity. It isn't always the case. I'm not talking about the prosperity gospel. If we do our work as unto the Lord and are fair and honest, the usual result is often financial increase (Ephesians 6:7). People want to employ us because they can trust us. They don't want to lose us and so they give raises and promotions.

In the Old Testament, when Israel represented God to the world, God would prosper them when they were obedient. That drew the world to consider the God of Israel. Uzziah was an obedient king and so God prospered him. But then Uzziah began to think that he should be able to do the things the priests do. He thought he should be able to go into the Holy Place and offer incense. The law of God said that was only the privilege of the descendants of Aaron (Numbers 16:40). Uzziah thought God was so pleased with him that the Word of God did not apply to him.

It is the same cycle that many fallen spiritual leaders have followed. They became successful and influential. They allow demands on their time to keep them from time in prayer and the Word. They began to think it was something in them that brought their success. A temptation came along, whether financial or sexual, and they thought they were so favored that they were above the Word. That ends their ministry. The grace of God can forgive them when they repent, but rarely is the privilege of ministry restored.

Uzziah went into the Holy Place and offered incense at the altar of incense. The priests came to resist him, and God smote Uzziah with leprosy. That was a very humbling disease in Judah. It meant isolation from everyone (Leviticus 13:45). The fame he so relished could no longer be enjoyed. The grace of God humbled him and brought him back into a right relationship with his Maker. That same grace referred to him as a king who did what was right before the eyes of the Lord (2 Chronicles 27:2).

It must have been a shock to the nation when he died. Most people had only known his kingship and the prosperity of his reign. Perhaps it was this loss that sent Isaiah to the earthly Temple to pray when he suddenly saw the reality in heaven (Hebrews 8:5). *[1] In the year that King Uzziah died I saw the Lord sitting upon a throne, high and lifted up; and the train of his robe filled the temple.* Isaiah 6:1

When someone sees the Lord, they are seeing Jesus, the manifestation of the invisible God (Colossians 1:15). But this is Jesus in His glory. Perhaps that what John was referring to in John 12:41, *[41] Isaiah said these things because he saw his glory and spoke of him.* That glory filled the heavenly temple. The throne that He sits on is the heavenly Ark of the Covenant. He was sitting on the mercy seat upon which He would one day sprinkle His own blood (Hebrews 9:12). That blood would come between the Shekinah (the light of God) and the Law that condemns us within the Ark of the Covenant. Just as grace had intervened in the life of King Uzziah, so grace would intervene for all mankind in a future day. Isn't it wonderful that this is where Jesus was seated? It's as if He was waiting till that perfect time in history when He could pour out His blood and sprinkle it on that very place for all who would come to Him in repentance (Galatians 4:4).

[2] Above him stood the seraphim. Each had six wings: with two he covered his face, and with two he covered his feet, and with two he flew. [3] And one called to another and said: "Holy, holy, holy is the LORD of hosts; the whole earth is full of his glory!" Isaiah 6:2-3 Seraphim, the burning ones, are glorious beings. Their voices were created to praise God. Their eyes were made to see His glory, but they must cover them in His presence, for there is so much glory emanating from Him that they are unable to take it all in. Instead, they look into the earth and see the glorious deeds of the Lord in the lives of everyone He has created (Acts 17:26).

Everywhere they look they see God's gracious acts. They see God orchestrating every life to draw each one to Himself. They see the wonder that God would let man choose to reject Him. They marvel that sinful man could be given the grace to repent and receive forgiveness. Detail after detail in every life on the planet they see orchestrated by an all-knowing, all-powerful God. The attribute that fills their thoughts and praise is holiness.

"Holy" when applied to God means to be utterly different from fallen humanity. It is to be of another type altogether. It is the difference between the unlimited Creator and fallen, limited creation. We can't even imagine the extent of the holiness of God. We wouldn't just need to cover our eyes with our hands, we would be seeking for a hole in which to hide. And that is exactly how anyone would feel in the presence of the glorified Jesus as the foundations of the threshold tremble.

⁴ And the foundations of the thresholds shook at the voice of him who called, and the house was filled with smoke. Isaiah 6:4 The reference to smoke is another sign of grace. The High Priest would fill the Holy of Holies with smoke before he would enter on the Day of Atonement (Leviticus 16:13). The idea was that he needed something so that God could not see him clearly, for in spite of his preparations he was bound to be impure. Thus, smoke represented the grace that will overlook present sin and not bring judgment, for the payment for sin will one day be paid.

⁵ And I said: "Woe is me! For I am lost; for I am a man of unclean lips, and I dwell in the midst of a people of unclean lips; for my eyes have seen the King, the LORD of hosts!" Isaiah 6:5 The anointed prophet of God felt just as filthy as you or I would feel in the presence of the glorified Christ. He now realizes that the messages he has been proclaiming to the nation of Judah are for him as well. His lips are as unclean as theirs. He feels the weight of his sin and the justice his sins deserve (Romans 6:23). His filthiness is before the holy God of eternity, and he feels utterly lost.

The grace of God helps us see our sin. God was doing for Isaiah what He had done for Uzziah. He was bringing humility into Isaiah's life to keep him from the pride that separates us from God. Isaiah would not be the instrument God planned for him to be until he recognized the messages he would proclaim are for him as well. As long as he distanced himself from the people, his message would not have the passion and connecting power that it could have. Pride mutes our message. Humility conveys it.

This is the beginning of a call to true service. We can't really serve as we should until we see our sinfulness. We can't really be saved unless we are convicted of sin and recognize our need for a Savior (John 16:8). In many cases, recognition that we are as sinful as anyone else is essential to receiving the call of God to serve. If we are not humbled and repentant, our service is usually for our ego. But when we see the depths of our sin, the call of God to serve is realized as the extravagant grace of the God who loves us in spite of ourselves. We can then serve humbly out of a heart of gratitude and love (Psalm 2:11).

Isaiah was calling the nation to repentance while not realizing he was just as in need as his audience. Now he sees it and has confessed it. That is when sin can be atoned. *⁶ Then one of the seraphim flew to me, having in his hand a burning coal that he had taken with tongs from the altar. ⁷ And he touched my mouth and said: "Behold, this has touched your lips; your guilt is taken away, and your sin atoned for."* Isaiah 6:6-7 One of the burning ones took a coal from the altar with tongs and carried it in his hand.

Is this the altar of incense or the altar of sacrifice? I believe this is referring to the altar of sacrifice which foreshadowed the cross of Jesus, God's perfect sacrifice. Symbolically, this is pointing to the sacrifice of Jesus cleansing us from our sin and purging iniquity from our lives. This is the life transforming power of Christ in us, the hope of glory enabling us to serve Him now and forever in eternity. The Lord baptizes us with the Spirit and with fire (Matthew 3:11). He cleanses us in His sight, but then works it out in our everyday experiences throughout our lifetime.

Isaiah's sense of guilt was gone. He would have a prophecy of how that was possible in his 53ʳᵈ chapter (Isaiah 53:10). His sin was atoned for. Atoned means reconciled. The books balance. There is no more debt. And this is the second part of the call. First, we are convicted of our sin and repent. Next, we receive the gift of forgiveness made possible through the cross.

⁸ And I heard the voice of the Lord saying, "Whom shall I send, and who will go for us?" Then I said, "Here I am! Send me." Isaiah 6:8 Now Isaiah has his recall notice. He had already been serving, but now he would serve with a humble spirit and a clean heart. Now he can hear the voice of God calling personally to him. It wasn't that he couldn't hear it before, but now his heart is sensitized to hear it applied to him. The Lord is calling out to us all. "Whom shall I send, and who will go for us?"

Pray that the Lord of the harvest will send laborers into His harvest (Matthew 9:38). Do you hear the call go out from the throne room of God? Isaiah did. Now he could stand up as a new creation and say, "Here I am! I'm willing. I'm a recipient of grace. God is so great He can even use me (Ephesians 3:8). I'm a sinner saved by grace and I owe my very life to my Savior. Lord, would You give me the privilege of allowing me to serve you? May I enjoy the freedom of serving the One I was created to serve? Please send me."

What a privilege it is to serve Almighty God (Psalm 100:2). But the message is not always a joyous one and the service is not always a walk in the park (Acts 9:16). The harder it is, the more we are honored to expend our lives in His service. *⁹ And he said, "Go, and say to this people: "'Keep on hearing, but do not understand; keep on seeing, but do not perceive.' ¹⁰ Make the heart of this people dull, and their ears heavy, and blind their eyes; lest they see with their eyes, and hear with their ears, and understand with their hearts, and turn and be healed."* Isaiah 6:9-10 We usually focus on the first eight verses of this chapter, but these two verses are the ones emphasized in the New Testament (Matthew 13:14-15; Mark 4:12; Luke

8:10; John 12:39-41). The early believers faced fierce resistance to the gospel of grace. The gospel proclaimed melts hearts or hardens them. There's no in-between.

The final part of the call is the commission. Isaiah asked to be sent and God said, "Go!" Then God gave him the message. I think God waits till last to give us the message because we might not be so eager if we know what the message is. Isaiah's message was that the people of Judah had to go into captivity to be purified of their idolatry and prepared for the coming of the Messiah. Until they went into captivity, they would not yield to the message from God. If they repented, it would be short term and halfhearted, just to save them from calamity. But before long, they would be right back to their old ways. The healing would be short lived. It was better for them that they did not hear. This, too, is the grace of God.

Our message is the same and our nation is just as hard. The gospel is our message. We are sinners condemned to judgment (Romans 3:23). Jesus took the punishment we deserve. If we will acknowledge our wickedness, our selfish evil ways, truly repent, and ask God for forgiveness, then we can receive the grace and mercy of God made possible through the cross. Jesus paid our debt (Ephesians 5:2). All we need do is receive it. Then we can hear the Lord call to us. "Who will go for us?" You don't have to go, but it is a privilege to be sent. Isaiah recognized the freedom and joy of service.

In our Bible study we are learning that freedom isn't doing what we want. That often leads to bondage. Freedom is doing what we were made to do. It is living in accord with reality. God prepared good works in advance for us to do (Ephesians 2:10). There is joy in serving the One that loves us so much. There is peace doing what you know is pleasing to God. But you don't have to respond. You can live a boring life just trying to pay your bills and gathering toys that distract you from the reason God made you. If you have truly come to know forgiveness I don't think you will be content, but you can choose that.

Isaiah was a little concerned about the extent of this judgment and the length of the call. After all, it was a hard message he had to proclaim. Some people think that they will have to stand on a street corner and preach, or move to Africa as a missionary. Maybe. But God needs people right where you are to show people what it is like to live for Jesus as a clerk, or laborer, or business owner, or whatever occupation you have. Every part of society needs people who are ready to share the difference Jesus makes in our hearts and minds. The opportunities will present themselves because God has so planned it. We just need to be ready and committed to step into the opportunities when they come.

So Isaiah asked, *[11] Then I said, "How long, O Lord?" And he said: "Until cities lie waste without inhabitant, and houses without people, and the land is a desolate waste, [12] and the LORD removes people far away, and the forsaken places are many in the midst of the land.* Isaiah 6:11-12 I don't think that was the answer that Isaiah was hoping for. He probably would have preferred something like, "Three months." But the answer was that he would serve until the captivity came to pass. At least God didn't tell him the whole story by saying, "Until you are sawn in half by the people that remain in the land."

God rarely tells us the trouble we will face. He does give us the grace when we face it. The call of God is a lifelong call. There is no retirement. The message is a tough one. It's offensive, but it's gracious as well. We are investing in eternity, and you don't want to quit this short gig without being fully invested for the long term (Philippians 3:13-14).

Even the remnant that remained in the land would be purged again. *13 And though a tenth remain in it, it will be burned again, like a terebinth or an oak, whose stump remains when it is felled." The holy seed is its stump.* Isaiah 6:13 Judah would be refined and refined again. If only one out of ten people remained in the land, God would purge them as well. The cleansing fire of God would deal with their idolatry.

My wife and I cut down an oak that was shading our garden. The stump immediately started to sprout new shoots. We wacked them off, but we have to keep doing it. The life remains. Isaiah closed this chapter with a promise. The holy seed is the stump. The ancestors of the coming Messiah were being purged, and even though the nation would be decimated, the line of the Messiah would remain. Uzziah had died, but the line of David remained. God is faithful to His Word.

From Eve to Abraham, to David, to the stump that remained, God's promise was still active (Genesis 3:15). He can't deny His Word. This sad message of Isaiah had a golden lining. God was not done with Israel. The Messiah would be born. Our sins will be atoned. The call of God will go out to millions more who hear, "Whom shall I send, and who will go for us?" The testimony of God's goodness and His ways will go around the world. Every nation will hear of the gracious offer of salvation to all who will call on the Lord, and then the end will come (Matthew 24:14).

If you are a believer, you are somewhere in the process of this call. Have you been convicted of sin and humbled? Then did you confess and receive the atonement God offers in Jesus? Then have you heard Him ask if you would be His witness? We know His message for our day. Have you discovered the unique way and place in which God would have you deliver it (Romans 12:3)? This is freedom. This joy! This is the life that God is calling us to, as testified to by the life and words of Isaiah.

Questions
1 What was Uzziah's testimony?
2 Where is Jesus seated?
3 Why is there smoke in the Holy Place?
4 What did God do for Uzziah and Isaiah?
5 Why is this essential to our calling?
6 What should follow conviction?
7 How does the altar of sacrifice foreshadow the cross?

8 What is the choice then before us?
9 When do we retire from this calling?
10 Review each step of the call of God.
11 Who is the "holy seed?"

Immanuel - Isaiah 7:1 – 8:8

In the last chapter, Isaiah had a vision of the Lord. He was humbled by the contrast of God's holiness and his own uncleanness. After confessing his sin, it was atoned, and then he heard the call of God and volunteered to serve. The message God had him deliver was a harsh one that would be difficult for Judah to hear. Only a remnant would survive. They would be like a burned over stump in which the holy seed remained (6:13).

A little historical background will help us understand what has taken place between the last chapter and this one. Syria and Israel (the ten northern tribes) have both defeated Judah (2 Chronicles 28:5). Captives and treasure were taken. In one war with Israel 120,000 from Judah died and 200,000 were taken captive. Oded the prophet warned them that the wrath of God would come upon Israel if they took their brothers from Judah captive, so Israel released all the captives at Jericho (2 Chronicles 28:8-11).

Syria and Israel knew that Assyria was planning to conquer them, and they feared Judah would join Assyria making the war on two fronts, so they planned on defeating Judah again. The introduction in verse one tells us they won't succeed and then the passage proceeds into an account of Isaiah confronting the king Judah with the word of the Lord. *² When the house of David was told, "Syria is in league with Ephraim," the heart of Ahaz and the heart of his people shook as the trees of the forest shake before the wind.* Isaiah 7:2 King Ahaz of Judah and all the house of David heard that Syria and Israel were going to unite and attack again and replace him with a puppet king. They were still reeling from previous attacks, so Ahaz went into survival mode.

You know what that is like. You desperately try to think out every possible scenario. Who could possibly help and how? What if you do this or that? Every resource available, except God, is taken into account. In fact, you may say a little prayer, but you don't want to open your Bible or pause to be still because God might tell you to do something crazy, like just trusting Him and nothing more.

My old nature sympathizes with Ahaz. Look what happened before. He probably said a little prayer then and God didn't give them victory. He did see Israel return the captives, but they didn't get the treasure back! Is trusting God practical?

³ And the LORD said to Isaiah, "Go out to meet Ahaz, you and Shear-jashub your son, at the end of the conduit of the upper pool on the highway to the Washer's Field. Isaiah 7:3 God sent Isaiah along with his son, whose name meant "a remnant will return," to meet King Ahaz. The king was checking his water sources and planning his defense tactics. We don't know if it was before or after this that he had sent word to Assyria to come help him. One commentator said he was like a mouse about to be attacked by two rats and calling on a cat to help. After the cat ate the rats, he would have the mouse for desert.

The LORD God told Isaiah, *⁴ And say to him, 'Be careful, be quiet, do not fear, and do not let your heart be faint because of these two smoldering stumps of firebrands, at the fierce anger of Rezin and Syria and the son of Remaliah.* Isaiah 7:4 This was a gentle and encouraging instruction, but it was also a command. First, we should understand that God has promised the house of David that they would reign forever (1 Kings 8:25). If they believed God, they should never fear their annihilation. God is inviting King Ahaz to lean upon Him. He wants the king to have some faith and believe God.

When things seem desperate, this is great advice for us all. Be careful. Be quiet. Do not fear. Fear is the opposite of faith. And when we fear and give up faith in God, we can say and do some very counter-productive things. Be careful what you do and say in those times of testing. Don't act out of fear. Faith produces calm serenity (Proverbs 3:25-26).

What Ahaz feared would never happen. These two were smoldering tails of firebrands. Their fire had gone out. In spite of the past, what Ahaz feared was never going to happen, at least not from these two. And isn't that like much of what we fear. Someone has said that 90% of what we worry about never comes to pass and the other 10% isn't changed by our worrying. That is very practical advice, but what is more real for the child of God is that the Lord is with us no matter what comes. What should we fear or worry over when the all-powerful God is with us? We either believe that or we don't. Our true condition is evidenced by our disposition.

⁷ thus says the Lord GOD: "'It shall not stand, and it shall not come to pass. ⁸ For the head of Syria is Damascus, and the head of Damascus is Rezin. And within sixty-five years Ephraim will be shattered from being a people. Isaiah 7:7-8 In other words, what you fear will never come to pass. Rezin will stay in Damascus. The very next year Assyria would attack him (733 B.C.). In 65 years (669 B.C.) Israel (Ephraim) will no longer be a people. It didn't take that long before they were conquered, but in exactly 65 years other conquered people were brought into the land forever ending those who lived in the area of the ten tribes as the people of Israel. They became known as the Samaritans. We now call a part of that area the West Bank.

⁹ᵇ If you are not firm in faith, you will not be firm at all.'" Isaiah 7:9b Buck up Ahaz and advisors and have some faith. Get some backbone and believe, or fall on your face from doubt. "You" is plural in Hebrew, addressing those who witnessed him delivering the word from the LORD. Firmness comes from conviction. Unless we are firm in our faith in God, we cannot be firm. God is the only unchanging One (Malachi 3:6). All else we place faith in can and will falter and fail. Faith is the total commitment of

62

our heart and mind. Lean on Christ and we will stand. Trust in self or the world and you will crumble.

10 Again the LORD spoke to Ahaz, 11 "Ask a sign of the LORD your God; let it be deep as Sheol or high as heaven." 12 But Ahaz said, "I will not ask, and I will not put the LORD to the test." Isaiah 7:10-12 I see in this the gracious patience of God pleading with Ahaz to believe. Signs are needed for the weak in faith. It is God's gracious way of helping those who have not matured or perhaps have been confused by circumstances in life. The grace of God will give us a reason to have faith and overcome our doubt. But Ahaz refused, and did so with the hypocritical use of Scripture. It is God who is offering to help him overcome his doubt, but he refuses to ask. God put no limits on what he would do to help Ahaz believe, but Ahaz did not want to believe. He did not want to give control over to God and trust Him. God commanded Ahaz to ask for a sign and he refused to ask.

The verse Ahaz was quoting was about the Israelites demanding a sign from God to prove that God was with them (Deuteronomy 6:16). They were saying, "Prove it God!" Here God is saying, "I want to prove to your weak faith that I am God, so ask for a sign." The Jews in the wilderness were expressing a lack of faith, while God was asking Ahaz to stretch his faith. If you quote it, quote it in context.

To understand what is about to be said, we have to understand the flow of the passage. The last chapter ended saying the holy seed would remain. The line of the Messiah will not be destroyed. Threats come from the north, but God is telling King Ahaz this is not the time for the predicted captivity. God commands Ahaz to ask for a sign. He refuses. Then God will give the prophecy reassuring the coming of Messiah, the holy seed, but also warn of the eventual devastation of the land.

13 And he said, "Hear then, O house of David! Is it too little for you to weary men, that you weary my God also? Isaiah 7:13 Notice that God is speaking to the house of David from whom will come the Messiah. ("Hear" and "you" are plural.) They persist in their rebellion in spite of God's graciousness to give them any sign they asked. They are trying the patience of God, and He has patience in abundance! In verse ten Isaiah told Ahaz to ask "your God" to give you a sign. In verse thirteen Isaiah refers now to God as "my God." It appears Ahaz has now thoroughly rejected God as his Savior and refused to trust Him.

14 Therefore the Lord himself will give you a sign. Behold, the virgin shall conceive and bear a son, and shall call his name Immanuel. Isaiah 7:14 The "you" in this verse is again plural showing us that Isaiah is speaking to the house of David. Matthew quotes this verse as referring to Jesus (Matthew 1:22-23). Some would claim that this use of the passage distorts its meaning. They claim the word for "virgin" (*almah*) is simply a young fertile woman. Isaiah could have used a different word that definitely meant virgin. However, the word *almah* is never used of a married woman whereas the other word is (*bethulah* Joel 1:8). Isaiah's words were carefully chosen. This is the fulfillment of the "seed of the woman" from Genesis 3:15. Isaiah is addressing the house of David and telling them to have faith. The Messiah will still come through their lineage. God will be present with the nation to deliver us with a greater deliverance than that of Moses.

The critics of this interpretation point to the next chapter and say the boy that is born is the fulfillment. In a remote sense, that boy may have been a partial fulfillment, the Lord was still with them (8:10), but the particulars don't line up. First, verse fourteen says the woman names the child Immanuel. In 8:3 Isaiah, not the woman, names the child and secondly, he gives him a completely different name. Then in 8:8 Isaiah says Judah is Immanuel's land. Certainly, he is not referring to the boy. While the Lord said this virgin birth was a sign for the house of David, Isaiah says it is he and his boys who are signs for Ahaz about the immediate situation (8:18).

Finally, if this were the natural birth of a child to a fertile woman, how would it be a sign? How could any natural birth result in God being with us? The critics need to read on as this is the same child we will see in chapter nine that is called God (9:6).

15 He shall eat curds and honey when he knows how to refuse the evil and choose the good. 16 For before the boy knows how to refuse the evil and choose the good, the land whose two kings you dread will be deserted. Isaiah 7:15-16 Now the word "you" returns to the singular meaning that Isaiah is speaking to King Ahaz and referring to the son Isaiah brought with him. Before that little boy would come to what we call the age of accountability, those two nations would be deserted. Assyria decimated Israel the year after taking Syria (732 B.C.) (2 Kings 17:6).

The rest of chapter seven tells of the conditions in the land of Judah after the Assyrian invasion. *17 The LORD will bring upon you and upon your people and upon your father's house such days as have not come since the day that Ephraim departed from Judah—the king of Assyria."* Isaiah 7:17 When the northern ten tribes split off from Israel there was a civil war. Rehoboam, Solomon's son, had listened to his young counselors instead of the older men of wisdom (1 Kings 12:8). The nation was suddenly half of what it once was under David and Solomon because of one man's terrible and arrogant decision. It was happening again.

The land would be scraped of any good like a man shaves the whiskers from his face. If you can keep the milk animals from the invaders, their milk and wild game will be all there is to eat. Ahaz refused to ask for a sign and instead called on Assyria, and Assyria would come.

3 And I went to the prophetess, and she conceived and bore a son. Then the LORD said to me, "Call his name Maher-shalal-hash-baz; 4 for before the boy knows how to cry 'My father' or 'My mother,' the wealth of Damascus and the spoil of Samaria will be carried away before the king of Assyria." Isaiah 8:3-4 Isaiah's wife was a prophetess. Their second child was named "The spoil speeds; the prey hastens." By the time he is able to say "My father," or "My mother" Assyria will have taken Syria and Israel. In Hebrew these are very simple two syllable expressions (*avi* and *immi*). We learned already that was what took place.

6 "Because this people has refused the waters of Shiloah that flow gently, and rejoice over Rezin and the son of Remaliah, 7 therefore, behold, the Lord is bringing up against them the waters of the River, mighty and many, the king of Assyria and all his glory. And it will rise over all its channels and go over all its banks, 8 and it will sweep on into Judah, it will overflow and pass on, reaching even to the neck, and its outspread wings will fill the breadth of your land, O Immanuel." Isaiah 8:6-8 It is interesting to note that the Lord refuses to mention Pekah's name. It is a way of dismissing him as unimportant to call him the son of Remaliah. The people of Judah rejected the gentle water that sprang up for the city of Jerusalem. That is to say that they rejected the gentle goodness of God. They rejoiced over the destruction of Syria and their brothers in the north (Proverbs 24:17). The powerful Assyrian army, represented by the Euphrates, would sweep on past those northern nations up to the neck of Judah. Its wings would fill the land like a bird of prey. Judah would survive but only by standing on their toes to keep their head above water. They would go on as a people. The Messiah would come and change the world, while Assyria would disappear into history.

Once again, God was gracious to give Judah warning after warning. If there was any other way to turn them, God would do whatever it took. But they would continue to harden their hearts and look to man or other gods. Though they were faithless, yet God remained faithful to His Word (2 Timothy 2:13). The Messiah was coming. God would prepare a people for His arrival. If it meant captivity, then so be it.

What can we learn from this passage? Perhaps one of the most important points in our day is to see the desperate attempt to discredit and distort the truth of who Jesus is and the many prophecies about Him (John 15:18). And yet we see that it takes determination and careful examination to really understand them. God gives us enough so that those who are truly searching will find, but those who are looking for excuses can still manufacture them (Revelation 22:11).

At the same time, we see God's patience and love extended to King Ahaz. God would have done anything to get Ahaz to trust Him. Doesn't God do the same with every soul? He'll give them whatever they need to turn and trust in Him, if they are willing and desire the truth.

Another lesson we should take from Ahaz is that our fears are often unfounded. When our faith is in God we can do as God commanded Ahaz, "Be careful, be quiet, do not fear, and do not let your heart become faint." But most importantly of all, lean on the Lord. Trust Him. Believe His promises. Don't run off thinking you can handle everything. Fully trust in the Lord. Our gracious God will do whatever it takes to convince you that He is real and loves you. Are you willing to accept the sign He gives you?

We've all been given the greatest of signs, the life of Jesus, God with us. Some say Jesus was just a good teacher ahead of His time, not really God or a Savior. How else could He have rebuked the wind and commanded the waves, touched the lepers and made them whole, ordered demons to leave, or lifted a paralytic to his feet restoring his nerves and giving him muscle and balance? How else could He have fed thousands with a boy's small lunch, or spoke healing to a man's servant who was miles away, or predict the destruction of the temple? Who can turn water into wine, or cause one who was born blind to see, or call the dead to life? Who else has walked out of their own grave after three days? Who else could do these things and more but the One we know as "God with us?"

Who would say such things as, "I am the light of the world, whoever follows me will not walk in darkness but have the light of life (John 8:12)," or "I am the resurrection and the life (John 11:25)," or "love your enemies (Matthew 5:44)," or "no one comes to the Father but by me (John 14:6)!" Jesus said, "If you have seen me, you have seen the Father (John 14:9)." Immanuel is God's sign to you and me. Will you believe and trust Him? Or will you be like Ahaz, persisting in hardhearted rebellion? Jesus is God's sign to us.

Questions

1 Why was Ahaz so afraid?
2 What did God command Ahaz to do?
3 Why shouldn't we fear?
4 Was God's Word true? What happened?
5 What happens to those not firm in faith?
6 Why did Ahaz refuse God's command?
7 What was wrong with the verse Ahaz quoted?
8 Why is 7:14 about Jesus and not about Isaiah's son?
9 Would Assyria come to Judah?
10 Review the lessons?
11 What is the sign given for us to believe?

Nonconformity - Isaiah 8:9 – 22

God had spoken through the prophet Isaiah and told King Ahaz that his fear of Syria and Ephraim was unnecessary. Those nations would soon be conquered by Assyria, and then Assyria would stop just short of conquering Judah (8:7-8). Still, the Messiah from the house of David would come, born of a virgin (7:14). Ahaz refused to trust in God. His past experiences caused so much fear that he did not even desire a confirmation from God to prove the message true (7:12).

We pick back up in chapter eight verse nine with a short poem about the coming destruction of Syria, Ephraim, and other nations that Assyria would attack. *⁹ Be broken, you peoples, and be shattered; give ear, all you far countries; strap on your armor and be shattered; strap on your armor and be shattered. ¹⁰ Take counsel together, but it will come to nothing; speak a word, but it will not stand, for God is with us.* Isaiah 8:9-10 They could prepare for war and make their plans for defense, but the presence of God is the determining factor. If it was time for judgment, there was nothing they could do that would make a difference. God can be with us to defend us or to judge us. It all depends on our relationship with Him.

¹¹ For the LORD spoke thus to me with his strong hand upon me, and warned me not to walk in the way of this people, saying: Isaiah 8:11 Isaiah is not a person wondering if maybe God might be speaking to his conscience. This is a man under the strong hand of God hearing a clear word from the LORD. It is a warning, a warning that we should heed as well. Don't walk in the way of this people! God will elaborate on just what He means in the following verses. It has to do with the fear of man (Proverbs 29:25). In general, it has to do with the current of cultures that forsake God. Rarely is the majority following God (Romans 12:2). That means that, most of the time, fitting in with culture is to be in rebellion against God (2 Corinthians 6:17).

The way of Judah was to fear Rezin and Pekah, the kings that were planning another attack. The people of Judah were fearing another defeat by their enemies, a confiscation of their goods, and possible captivity. It wasn't coming from them. What does our culture fear? Perhaps it is pestilence or terrorism, economic collapse or an EMP destroying our electric infrastructure. But these are all temporal. If all of them were to happen, they wouldn't affect our eternal destiny. Societies live in disregard for God and His justice (Matthew 10:28). God is telling Isaiah and us to refuse to live like that. Don't follow the culture!

¹² "Do not call conspiracy all that this people calls conspiracy, and do not fear what they fear, nor be in dread. Isaiah 8:12 Name your conspiracy. They abound in our city, from cloaked space ships escorted to secret bases by black helicopters, to Obama's internment camps, we have conspiracies galore. Might one of the many conspiracy theories come to pass? Possibly, but what God is saying here is that the people of God are not to fear what the world fears. If God is for us, who can be against us (Romans 8:31). We aren't to dread what the world dreads. We should have total trust in the LORD and His ability to help us through whatever comes. Life is unpredictable, but God never changes (Hebrews 13:8). If we are in His hands, what do we have to fear?

Does our speech show that we do not fear what the world fears? I've been convicted about this. Start talking about our national debt and ballooning welfare and I join right in. I should be talking about being a citizen of the kingdom of heaven and not being worried about what comes. That would really bring up some opportunities to witness to the lost and help fellow believers set their priorities straight.

¹³ But the LORD of hosts, him you shall honor as holy. Let him be your fear, and let him be your dread. Isaiah 8:13 Eternity is a long time. Anyone who enters into eternity with a heart set against God will experience the greatest dread a person could ever know (Mark 9:48).

Should the believer fear God? If you are assured of salvation in Jesus, should you be in dread of Him? Though He calls you friend (John

15:15), if you honor Him as holy you will (5:16). That is because His holiness is expressed in righteousness. That means He deals with evil, especially in His children (Hebrews 12:6).

I liken it to fearing a good father's discipline. Your mother says, "Boy are you gonna catch it when Dad comes home." You live in dread of Dad's return because you know he loves you enough to discipline you so severely that you'll think twice before doing that deed again.

I fear discipline on my deceitful heart (Jeremiah 17:9). Humans can justify almost anything. We do need to trust the Lord to be our shepherd and to keep us from falling (Jude 24). I've seen too many pastors fall to take that protection for granted. God will not protect us from our own will. If my deceitful heart justifies sin, convincing my mind that it is really alright to act on it, I have one more line of defense. It's the fear of God. I know God won't let me get away with it. He has entrusted me with so much and expects me to be faithful (Luke 17:10). If I am not, the discipline in this life will be severe.

The unrepentant person doesn't fear the Lord or they would change their ways and seek forgiveness. They fear the temporal change in circumstance that keeps them from enjoying the moment. That is what God was telling Isaiah not to fear. Christ followers should be noticeably different in this regard. People who fear the Lord depart from evil (Proverbs 16:6).

14 And he will become a sanctuary and a stone of offense and a rock of stumbling to both houses of Israel, a trap and a snare to the inhabitants of Jerusalem. Isaiah 8:14 "He" refers back to the LORD of hosts. This is the God of angel armies. He is the One that spoke to Moses from the burning bush. He is different things to people depending on their relationship with Him. If He is your Abba daddy, he will be a sanctuary for you. That is a safe place and a place of worship (Psalm 27:5). I hope that is your relationship with Him. Even when He disciplines us, He is our sanctuary.

To the rebellious children of Judah and Israel who refused to believe the Word of God through Isaiah, the LORD of hosts was a stone of offense and a rock of stumbling. To the people of Jerusalem, He was a trap and a snare. Judah wanted to trust in Assyria, but Assyria was going to have them for dessert. Israel wanted to trust in Syria, but Syria would be defeated before Israel fell. Isaiah's call to repent and come and reason with God offended them (1:18), like a rock thrown at them. They stumbled over what Isaiah said because they didn't want to let go of their other gods or their trust in themselves.

It reminds me of attitudes in our day. Some say, "God would never bring calamity on us. He is a God of love. And besides, we are good people. You need to think positive." With the next breath they talk of conspiracies that they fear. The Jesus of the Bible is a rock of offense to them, a stone of stumbling. They hear the truth of His call to repent and receive Him as Lord, but they are offended that someone would think they need to repent. As we saw in a previous passage, they call good evil and evil good (5:20). So they can't see why they need to repent.

Jesus will be a sanctuary for you, or the stone over which you stumble. You will meet Him one way or the other. No one escapes an encounter with the Almighty! The stone of offense is declared by Peter (1 Peter 2:8) and Paul (Romans 9:33) to be Jesus, which means they believed He is *YHWH Saba,* the LORD of hosts.

The apostle Paul tells us it was the grace of Jesus that the people in His day stumbled over. Grace declares we are in need of forgiveness and God has made it possible. Pride says, "I don't need it! I'm just fine like I am, thank you." Was that what was happening in Judah? Absolutely! God invited them to come reason with Him, and to look to Him instead of Assyria. Recognize your sin, repent, and let God be your sanctuary. But they refused to give up their idolatry and their trust in themselves. They were stumbling over the grace of God. They were offended at the rock that is Jesus, the salvation of God.

How did Peter know this verse was about Jesus? Jesus told him. *⁴⁴ He said to them, "This is what I told you while I was still with you: Everything must be fulfilled that is written about me in the Law of Moses, the Prophets and the Psalms." ⁴⁵ Then he opened their minds so they could understand the Scriptures.* Luke 24:44-45 (NIV) Peter knew because Jesus opened his mind to understand the Scriptures, and Peter or the Holy Spirit explained it to Paul. It was grace the Jews were rejecting in the days of Isaiah and in the days of Jesus as well (65:2).

¹⁵ And many shall stumble on it. They shall fall and be broken; they shall be snared and taken." Isaiah 8:15 Man stumbles over grace because he thinks he is capable of doing something, of bringing about or participating in his own salvation. It is humiliating to recognize we are hopeless sinners in need of rescue. But that is the place we all must come if we are to know salvation and the peace of God in our lives. That is the only way we can live differently from our culture (Ephesians 4:1).

Jesus was probably referring to this passage when He said, *⁴⁴ And the one who falls on this stone will be broken to pieces; and when it falls on anyone, it will crush him."* Matthew 21:44 He changed the last part of the verse to line up with the Daniel two image, where a stone comes out of the mountain of God and strikes the image of man and fills the earth (Daniel 2:34-35; 44-45). "Snared and taken" was replaced with being crushed. The difference is that in the days of Isaiah, the nation was going to go into captivity, but Jesus saw Himself setting up the kingdom of God. To reject Him is to face the wrath of God.

If we throw ourselves upon the grace of God we will be broken, broken of pride and self-will. We will become dependent on another. If we reject the grace of God, we will face judgment for our rebellion and hardhearted response to His Word.

¹⁶ Bind up the testimony; seal the teaching among my disciples. Isaiah 8:16 The people of Judah who were not Isaiah's disciples won't hear the message, but a later generation will (Daniel 12:4). The disciples needed to carry the message into captivity and pass it on. This book of Isaiah became a favorite in Jesus' day just as Isaiah predicted. It was unsealed by Jesus as He explained to the disciples how the Scriptures pointed to Him. I imagine that Jesus had to wait until after the resurrection or they could not have accepted Him, as amazing and unique as He was, as really being the LORD of hosts incarnate. The resurrection was the convincing proof that they needed (Psalm 16:10).

17 I will wait for the LORD, who is hiding his face from the house of Jacob, and I will hope in him. Isaiah 8:17 Isaiah was content to not walk in the ways of the people. Though they would not hear the message, Isaiah believed it. Though there were no miraculous signs due to Ahaz' refusal, Isaiah would believe God and wait for Him. Will you? Will you trust the Word of God? Though He hide His face from America, will you place your hope in Him? Will you wait on Him to answer your prayers and fulfill His Word? We live in a time similar to that of Isaiah and we need to express the faith and hope that he exhibited. Just as he waited for the Messiah to come in God's time, so we wait for the Second Coming (1 Thessalonians 4:16).

18 Behold, I and the children whom the LORD has given me are signs and portents in Israel from the LORD of hosts, who dwells on Mount Zion. Isaiah 8:18 Before Shear-jashub would know right from wrong, Syria and Ephraim would be defeated. Before Maher-shalal-hash-baz could say "Mommy" or "Daddy" Assyria will have spoiled those countries (7:3; 8:3-4). What the people feared would not happen.

Those of you who are old enough remember the Bay of Pigs and the nuclear standoff with Cuba. We practiced "duck and cover" because we feared a nuclear attack. It never came to pass. Imagine if someone had told the press that we were doing all that practicing for nothing, that we needed to repent and trust the Lord. That kind of gives you a sense of what was going on in Isaiah's day.

19 And when they say to you, "Inquire of the mediums and the necromancers who chirp and mutter," should not a people inquire of their God? Should they inquire of the dead on behalf of the living? Isaiah 8:19 The multitude of spiritists is evidence of our nation turning its back on God. There have been TV shows of people supposedly speaking to the dead and giving living loved ones' responses. Should not the people inquire of God? Don't we want God's perspective? Don't we want truth? Like Ahaz, so many refuse it when it is offered to them.

20 To the teaching and to the testimony! If they will not speak according to this word, it is because they have no dawn. Isaiah 8:20 Some translations will have the word "law" instead of "teaching". Both are a correct translation of the word "*torah*." Testimony here means attestation or precepts. Isaiah is saying that if someone is teaching or sharing an experience that does not line up with the prophecy he has given, they have no light of dawn. Later in the book (60:1), he will speak of the dawn being the revelation of the Messiah. Though it was specifically a word for the people of Judah to not listen to false prophets, it is also a warning for all people to not listen to anything that does not line up with the Torah and the

70

writings of the Old Testament. Jesus may have been referring to this in his parable of the rich man and Lazarus. The rich man wanted someone to go back and tell his relatives about the cost of refusing grace. *²⁹ But Abraham said, 'They have Moses and the Prophets; let them hear them.'* Luke 16:29

Grace is a theme of the entire Bible. The message is the same throughout. We are sinners in need of the grace of God. If anyone says otherwise, Isaiah says, they don't have a genuine revelation. They are in darkness. They don't know Jesus.

²¹ They will pass through the land, greatly distressed and hungry. And when they are hungry, they will be enraged and will speak contemptuously against their king and their God, and turn their faces upward. Isaiah 8:21 When everything the people of Israel trusted in had failed them, in distress and hunger they would curse the king and God, shaking their fists in the air. Even calamity will not turn them.

²² And they will look to the earth, but behold, distress and darkness, the gloom of anguish. And they will be thrust into thick darkness. Isaiah 8:22 The things of the world only satisfy for a time. Seeking for them to fulfill you only leads to darkness of the soul. But the Light will still come. The next verse declares it (9:1). Grace comes even when we shake our fists at God. Even when we reject God's grace time and time again, He desires to bring us into the light. His desire is to lift us from our gloomy fallen condition and deliver us from stumbling in the dark by shining His light on us (John 8:12). The Messiah was coming. The next chapter tells of the wonder of the child that would be born of a virgin, the sign that we need so desperately (7:14). For us today, He has come. Will we humbly accept the grace He offers and place our hope in Him?

Questions
1 What is the way of the people?
2 What are we to do with conspiracies?
3 Why should we fear the Lord?
4 What are the two ways God can be toward us?
5 Why is the Gospel offensive?
6 How did Jesus use verse 15?
7 When was verse 16 unsealed?
8 What was Isaiah determined to do?
9 What does verse 20 teach us?
10 Where is this passage headed?

The Son Is Given - Isaiah 9:1-7

Today we have the privilege of examining one of the most glorious prophecies in Scripture. Isaiah has already pointed us to the holy seed being the stump of Judah (6:13). The promised Messiah's lineage would be a part of the remnant that would return from the refining fires of captivity. Then we saw Isaiah tell the house of David that the sign that God would keep His promise of a Messiah deliverer would be the virgin birth of this One that was coming (7:14). Our last passage ended with the gloom and darkness the land of Ephraim would experience when Assyria came to conquer them and set up another king (8:22). But now we come to chapter nine that paints a picture of the glorious hope for the future.

We should stop right at the beginning and observe that no matter what we face, even in the midst of the discipline of God, the promises of God are sure. The discipline of God is for our good. The judgments of God are necessary to reach the promised end. That glorious conclusion would not be what it should be without God's discipline and judgments. And while they may be hard to endure, they take us to greater heights (Hebrews 12:10).

The passage starts in stark contrast to the previous verse. *¹ But there will be no gloom for her who was in anguish. In the former time he brought into contempt the land of Zebulun and the land of Naphtali, but in the latter time he has made glorious the way of the sea, the land beyond the Jordan, Galilee of the nations.* Isaiah 9:1 When Assyria came to conquer Syria, the path led them right through this region of northern Galilee. On the return trip the Assyrian army conquered the land and set up another king who promised to pay tribute (2 Kings 17:3). Historical records show the huge tribute that was paid by the gloomy Israelites. But in our verse today, the picture totally changes. Instead of being the brunt of a conquering army, they would be honored with the light of the Messiah.

The land of Zebulun and Naphtali were the ancestral lands Joshua divided to those to tribes (Joshua 19:10; 32). They included most of the land in which Jesus lived and ministered in during His life until the last months of His ministry. What is truly amazing is the wording of this prophecy. It is called Galilee of the nations, but at the time it was inhabited by Israelites. Isaiah predicted in a short time they would no longer be a people. When the remnant returned, the land was full of Gentiles. Large Gentile cities like Sephoris, Bet Shean, and Tiberius were dominant. So in the days in which the prophecy would come to pass, it was truly Galilee of the Gentiles.

Even more interesting is the highway from Rome to Egypt which went through this region and came to be called the Way of the Sea. It passed over the Jordan through Capernaum and went to the coast of the Mediterranean and south to Egypt.

² The people who walked in darkness have seen a great light; those who dwelt in a land of deep darkness, on them has light shone. Isaiah 9:2 Jesus declared Himself to be the light of the world (John 8:12). Jews called the coming Messiah "the Great Light" (Ha'or Gadol) because of this prediction. Numerous other passages declared that the Messiah would be a light to the nations (Isaiah 42:6; 49:6). That is not only because Galilee was called Galilee of the nations, but other passages predicted His ministry to the world (Isaiah 51:5; Psalm 65:5).

These two verse were cited by Matthew as being fulfilled in Jesus' ministry (Matthew 4:15-16). The majority of Jesus' disciples came from the

72

region. Most of Jesus' miracles took place there. The people of the region who had looked to the earth for fulfillment saw the Light of the world, the glory of God, in the face of Jesus (2 Corinthians 4:6). Deep darkness was not only a spiritual condition of misunderstanding the Word of God and its promises, but also of Roman oppression, taxation and hard labor. When we consider the prophecy was given 700 years before Jesus fulfilled it in detail, we can truly marvel at the foreknowledge of God.

³ You have multiplied the nation; you have increased its joy; they rejoice before you as with joy at the harvest, as they are glad when they divide the spoil. Isaiah 9:3 It sounds like the Triumphal Entry and the feeding of the 5000. But it is multiplied even further in splicing in the Gentile branches as the gospel goes around the world (Romans 11:17). As a light to the nations, Jesus brings the joy of heaven when each soul comes into the Kingdom. It's Christmas! It's the joy of knowing our debt is paid and our eternity secure in the hands of our loving Redeemer.

Isaiah will prophesy again of the spoil being divided in the Suffering Servant Song of chapter 53. After the Messiah bears our iniquity and becomes a guilt offering He sees the light of life. That speaks of the crucifixion and resurrection. God promises to give Him His portion and He then divides the spoil among the strong, those He has made righteous (Isaiah 53:12). I take this to mean the gifts of the Spirit and the good works He prepared in advance for us to do. To be in His service and see His power at work through us gives us great joy.

⁴ For the yoke of his burden, and the staff for his shoulder, the rod of his oppressor, you have broken as on the day of Midian. Isaiah 9:4 The day of Midian is referring to Gideon's band of 300 taking on the hordes of Midian that oppressed the Israelites (Judges 7:7). Jesus, with His little band of 12 took on the hordes of evil much more numerable than the camp of Midian; and Jesus won! Think of it. A builder from the little town of Nazareth, under the subjugation of Rome, took some fisherman and other insignificant men and broke the power of sin and death! The Midian analogy was as close as the prophet could come to the glorious work of the Messiah.

⁵ For every boot of the tramping warrior in battle tumult and every garment rolled in blood will be burned as fuel for the fire. Isaiah 9:5 The day is coming when there will be no more war, no more bloodshed, no more need for battle gear or weapons. The coming King will cause such peace to reign that Isaiah's prediction of swords being beat into plowshares will come to pass (Isaiah 2:4).

How is that possible? Who is this One so mighty that with His little band He can transform this world of perpetual war and pain? Who can bring such joy from the hills of northern Galilee? Who is the great light that the Jews looked for at every Feast of Tabernacles who would bring light to the nations? *⁶ For to us a child is born, to us a son is given; and the government shall be upon his shoulder, and his name shall be called Wonderful Counselor, Mighty God, Everlasting Father, Prince of Peace.* Isaiah 9:6 He is the child born to the virgin predicted in 7:14. He is the One whom God told Eve would crush the head of the serpent (Genesis 3:15). He is the offspring of Abraham who would bless the world (Genesis 22:18). A baby! Imagine that! He would be born as a helpless baby to a virgin, but He is born *to* us. He isn't just this woman's baby. He is born for us.

To us a Son is given. The child is born to us, but also the Son is given to us. Does that remind you of another verse in which a Son is given? It should. For God so loved the world that He gave His one and only Son, that whosoever believes in Him would not perish but have everlasting life (John 3:16). John was using the language of this prophecy. Through the virgin the child is born to us, but He is the Son God gives to us. That is why we give gifts to one another on Christmas. It is to remind us that God gave the greatest gift ever given. We can't fathom the greatness of this gift we have so freely received. Nothing can compare!

This child will grow up to have the government placed on His shoulders. After every government of man has failed to bring peace and prosperity, we will finally have One who can reign in righteousness. We will finally have One who, unlike Moses, can indeed bear the burden of the people (Exodus 18:18). His shoulders are broad enough to bear whatever burden you face. I hope you realize that! If you are carrying a situation, an unresolvable problem, know that your shoulders are too small, but His are more than sufficient.

Hear His name. I can't emphasize enough the importance of a name to the Hebrews. The expression, "the name of the Lord" appears 109 times in the Bible. The various names the Bible ascribes to God and to Jesus are a wonderful study in the nature and character of God.

Isaiah is prophesying what this child will be called. The first name is Wonderful Counselor. Hope Cottage has an interesting way of helping homeless women. They go to the prayer room together and ask the Wonderful Counselor to reveal to the woman what is the real source of the problem. How does He want their life to change? In most cases the woman knows in her heart exactly what the Lord is counseling her to do. Why? Because He is a Wonderful Counselor. When we try to tell a person what to do they will rarely follow through, but when they believe the Lord who created them told them what they need to do to get their life back on track, they have a lot more conviction to carry through. The staff there believes in the Wonderful Counselor because He counsels them. Is He your wonderful counselor?

When I have a situation that I don't know how to handle, too often I try to reason in my mind how to best resolve it. The Wonderful Counselor is waiting for me to come and ask for the only advice that is perfect. And do you know why we so often look to Him only after our own ways fail? It's because we might not like what He tells us to do. It is usually humbling. It often costs. But it's always the best solution to the problem. Praise God for giving to us the Wonderful Counselor!

His most wonderful counsel of all is when He counsels us to repent of our sin and accept Him as the Lord of our life. That should be followed by us hearing that counsel daily, from His Word and His Spirit within us. I hope you know Him as your Wonderful Counselor.

The next name by which He will be called is "Mighty God". We have already seen Isaiah's prophecies that speak of the eternal God of Israel are applied to Jesus in the New Testament. We indeed call Him the Mighty God. He broke the power of sin and darkness. He took the keys of death and hell (Revelation 1:18). He conquered the grave! There is none so mighty as He. And when the Battle of Armageddon takes place, when the forces of the world gather to resist Him, He laughs (Psalm 2:4). He will single-handedly destroy them with the sword from His mouth (Revelation 19:15).

Sometimes we think of God the Father as the One with power and authority, but Jesus declared that to see Him is to see the Father (John 14:9). He is the Word, the instrument of creation. The Hebrew scribes that made the Aramaic translations of the Old Testament so closely associated the Word with God that they used "the Word" instead of the holy name of God. All things were made by Him (John 1:3). He is the image of the invisible God and preeminent over all. All authority comes from Him (Colossians 1:15-17).

Do you have a situation in your life that is too much for you to handle? It's not too big for the One called Mighty God. He can not only take care of it, but He can do something even greater. He can help you to walk through the difficulty triumphantly. I think that is what is meant by the expression of Paul, "more than a conqueror (Romans 8:37)." Consider how Jesus walked through the abuse and torture of that last day. He then rose victorious in spite of man doing his worst. That is what the Mighty God can do in your life as well, by His resurrection power at work within you (Ephesians 1:19-20).

This is where the prosperity gospel is so short-sighted. Real power is seeing joy in spite of hunger and physical need. It is seeing the martyr tell the persecutor, "Though He slay me, yet will I trust Him (Job 13:15)." Real power is putting our limited resources in the hands of the Mighty God and watching Him do the impossible. It takes the aid of the Mighty God to walk by faith and not by sight. We may not understand His hand, but He helps us to trust His heart, His wisdom, and to believe He is all-powerful.

Jesus is the Everlasting Father. We are accustomed to calling God our Father as Jesus taught us in the Lord's Prayer (Matthew 6:9). However, we can look to Jesus as the unchanging Father as well. Father, brother, head, Creator, husband, friend: it takes all of these descriptions and more to describe all He means to us. When I stumble and He graciously lifts me up and tells me to try again, I can see His fatherly care. When He provides my needs, I know Him as a father. When He protects me from danger, I see His father's heart. And it will forever be that way, for He is the Everlasting Father. Yes, we will be His bride, but does not the best husband have fatherly qualities of loving care for his bride?

I'm always impressed by the fact that the Bible's description of our relationship with God through Jesus is more wonderful than I could have ever come up with in my imagination. Everlasting means that will forever be so. We won't wake one morning to find He has tired of us, fallen out of love, or grown impatient and decided to move on. He is the same yesterday, today, and forever (Hebrews 13:8).

Jesus is the Prince of Peace. The word in Hebrew for prince can be translated in numerous ways: lord, keeper, master, etc. I'm reminded of Charles Cowman's first outreach in Japan. He found a minister who could translate for him and sent him around Tokyo to shout out, "If anyone is looking for peace come to the meeting at …" An elderly couple were sitting on their balcony and heard him and went to the meeting. The husband told his wife that all his life he had been seeking for peace in his heart. Maybe this man had the answer to finding it. Hearing the gospel for the first time, they received Jesus as their Lord and Savior. They found the peace they were seeking in the Prince of Peace. He is the only way for us to have peace in our hearts (Romans 5:1).

Maybe today you have come with some anxiety. You don't know where to turn. The situation seems hopeless, but there is One in Whom you can find peace. That is why He is called the Prince of Peace. He alone can give you peace with God. He alone has the shoulders that can carry our burden. He alone has the power to change the situation, or greater still, to see us through it.

7 Of the increase of his government and of peace there will be no end, on the throne of David and over his kingdom, to establish it and to uphold it with justice and with righteousness from this time forth and forevermore. The zeal of the LORD of hosts will do this. Isaiah 9:7 He will increasingly reign in more and more hearts. His peace will never be overthrown by some unforeseen event, for He is already in the future. There is no power that did not come from Him. In the words "everlasting", "forevermore", and the phrase "no end", we have a triple assurance that our relationship with Jesus will never grow old. His power will never wane. Unlike the rulers of this world, He will never be replaced by another, nor would we desire it.

The prophecy of the Messiah reigning on David's throne has depths we don't have time to go over now. Let me just say that David united the kingdom, conquered Israel's enemies, and planned for the building of the temple. His son was to build the temple and reign over David's great accomplishments, but it is the descendant of David, Jesus, who builds the eternal temple of living stones (1 Peter 2:5), conquers the Enemy of our soul, and unites Jew and Gentile in Himself.

The zeal of the Lord of Hosts is going to cause this Son given to us to be all these things to us. Zeal is a passionate personal desire. The disciples saw Jesus' cleansing of the Temple as a demonstration of this zeal (John 2:17). It was just a picture of us as His house of worship where we commune with Him. He is as passionate or more so about the reality of that shadow, you and me. He wants us to be His and His alone. He is all we could hope for and He wants us to understand that. The Son is given to us, but we must

76

receive Him (John 1:12). The most important decision you will ever make is to receive Him as your wonderful counsellor, your mighty God, your everlasting Father, and your Prince of peace. But next in importance is to experience Him as all these names imply every day.

Questions
1 How was verse one fulfilled?
2 What is the Great Light?
3 What is the joy of verse 3?
4 What is "the day of Midian"?
5 Why "child born" and "Son given"?
6 What is the first name by which He is called?
   Do you experience it?
7 What is the second name? Implication?
8 What is the third name? Implication?
9 What is the fourth name? How can you experience it?
10 How is all this possible?

Remedial Anger - Isaiah 9:8-10:15

Jacob, Israel, and Ephraim are all ways of referring to the northern ten tribes of what was once the twelve tribes of Israel. Samaria was the capital of the region. Our passage begins by declaring a word from the Lord has come to this nation. Verses eight to twelve tell of Syria and Philistine invasions that had destroyed the walls and hewn down the trees. This was a typical battle tactic. Trees were used to build siege ramps, and at the same time, it weakened the nation from rebuilding.

Everyone heard the message of God's judgments, though Israel did not think they needed to repent. In their pride and arrogance, they predicted a glorious rebuilding. *10 "The bricks have fallen, but we will build with dressed stones; the sycamores have been cut down, but we will put cedars in their place."* Isaiah 9:10 This begins a series of pronouncements of increasing judgments, but each ends with the sad declaration that God isn't done pouring out His wrath on their rebellion. *12b For all this his anger has not turned away, and his hand is stretched out still.* Isaiah 9:12b

We often hear that the angry God of the Old Testament is so different from the loving God of the New Testament, but this just isn't the case. God's anger is a result of His love and righteousness. God is bringing these judgments on the nation to turn them from the sins of idolatry and injustice which were destroying them. Someone who passionately loves another is naturally angry with whatever would destroy the one they love (Exodus 20:5).

The spouse who is watching their loved one destroy their body with a drug, hates that drug and the loved one's choice to take it. If they were to force their loved one into rehab, that loved one would be angry with their spouse for taking away their freedom and the comfort they derived from that drug. It would be an act of love that was misinterpreted.

That is exactly what we do with God's judgments and discipline in our life. Most of the time, the discipline of God is a natural result of our actions. If Israel had returned to the rule of the godly Davidic kings and the worship of YHWH, they would have been a stronger nation. The diseases that resulted from immoral practices of their false religion would not be afflicting them. In this immediate passage it is the sin of pride that is keeping them from a better future (Proverbs 16:18). It's the attitude that says, "We don't need God. We can do this ourselves without having to submit to God."

13 The people did not turn to him who struck them, nor inquire of the LORD of hosts. Isaiah 9:13 The anger of God expressed against their sin was to turn them back to the LORD. But they would not turn. They didn't even want to ask God what they should do. Instead, they dug in their heels. Have you been in those boots with heels? When we are afflicted, or we face loss, or difficulty, do we get angry with God, or do we seek His face and ask Him if what we are experiencing is a result of our sin (Psalm 139:23)?

Many Christians, myself included, will sometimes blame our difficulties on Satan. We'll claim it is a spiritual attack. But we had better be certain whether or not it is the Lord who is dealing with us before we make that claim. Those times of frustration and pain are times when we are in the greatest need of stopping to do a heart check (Psalm 26:2). Are we walking with the Lord? Are we rebelling in some area? Have we refused to listen and accept His leading in something (Leviticus 26:18)? You don't want to call the discipline of God the work of the devil. I often find the tension in my life comes from a lack of trust in the Lord and His sovereign reign over my life. I go about trying to deal with something in my own way and run into roadblocks and then get frustrated. As soon as I pray and ask God what it is about, I can see my own part in the problem.

The wife of Jonathan Edwards was experiencing physical afflictions of her own when she received news of his death. In this letter to her daughter, listen to her humble acceptance of whatever came from God's hand. "What shall I say? A holy and good God has covered us with a dark cloud. Oh, that we may kiss the rod [of discipline] and lay our hands on our mouths! The Lord has done it. He has made me adore his goodness, that we had my husband so long. But my God lives, and he has my heart. Oh, what a legacy my husband, and your father, has left us! We are all given to God; and there I am, and love to be." (Preaching the Word – Isaiah: God Saves Sinners. Originally from Iain Murray biography of Jonathan Edwards) May God help us be so accepting and count our blessings in our times of loss.

Israel was so set in their rebellion against God that they would not even ask God what they should do. In effect, they shook their fist at God while declaring they were just fine without Him. So, in love, or what one commentator put as "lovingangerkindness," God allowed the next round of trouble.

14 So the LORD cut off from Israel head and tail, palm branch and reed in one day— 15 the elder and honored man is the head, and the prophet who teaches lies is the tail; 16 for those who guide this people have been leading them astray, and those who are guided by them are swallowed up. Isaiah 9:14-16 Their leadership was cut off in one day. While they had the very leadership they deserved and desired, leaders are still accountable to God for their actions. We see this discipline of leaders many times in Scripture. Even King David suffered the loss of his child as the result of his adulterous affair. I wonder if the whole rebellion led by Absalom and resultant loss of life would have been avoided had David looked the other way when he first saw Bathsheba (2 Samuel 12:18).

We have the same problem with leadership in our homes, churches, and nation today. Where are the elders who will put God first and live godly lives of service to their congregation (1 Timothy 5:17)? Instead we have CEO men with charisma amassing fortunes and operating unchecked until some sin becomes public knowledge.

Where are the political leaders who will stand for Biblical principles in spite of the direction our culture is taking? Where are the voters that will put the godly in office? Only half of evangelicals bother to register to vote and only half of those vote in a presidential election. Only a quarter vote in the mid-terms. Don't blame the leaders if you don't vote. A nation without leaders is a nation drifting toward a reef of destruction.

17 Therefore the Lord does not rejoice over their young men, and has no compassion on their fatherless and widows; for everyone is godless and an evildoer, and every mouth speaks folly. For all this his anger has not turned away, and his hand is stretched out still. Isaiah 9:17 Israel had become a nation of godless evildoers. Every mouth spoke folly. I listen to conversations in the world, on the news, and passersby, and believe we are rapidly approaching this condition of every mouth speaking folly (Ephesians 4:29). When the Lord doesn't have compassion on the needy, it is because even the needy are rebellious toward Him.

18 For wickedness burns like a fire; it consumes briers and thorns; it kindles the thickets of the forest, and they roll upward in a column of smoke. Isaiah 9:18 This is what I was saying earlier. Sin brings its own judgment with it (Romans 6:23). Wickedness burns like a fire. It destroys homes, nations, churches, and every place it is allowed to go unchecked. It is adultery in the home, cheating in the workplace, greed in political office, and on and on. But it is also the effect of raunchy entertainment, gossip, and every form of moral compromise that we so readily excuse. Yes, some sins are more destructive than others, but all wickedness burns like a fire and spreads like one too (James 3:5).

21 Manasseh devours Ephraim, and Ephraim devours Manasseh; together they are against Judah. For all this his anger has not turned away, and his hand is stretched out still. Isaiah 9:21 When wickedness reigns, it is every man for himself. Selfishness and greed have everyone abusing and misusing one another. Prolonged military sieges in that time resulted in cannibalism, but I believe this passage also refers to the general atmosphere of fear that prevails in ungodly nations. When you can trust no one, and when crime is rampant, fear and uncertainty are in the hearts of the people. It is a terrible way to live. Five of the last six kings of Israel had come to power by assassination. The result of sin is the wrath of God (Galatians 5:15).

Chapter ten begins with a cry against the injustice of the land. Though the Lord has declared He no longer has compassion on them, it is still sinful to abuse the needy. God asks them, *³ What will you do on the day of punishment, in the ruin that will come from afar? To whom will you flee for help, and where will you leave your wealth? ⁴ Nothing remains but to crouch among the prisoners or fall among the slain. For all this his anger has not turned away, and his hand is stretched out still.* Isaiah 10:3-4 The poor had nowhere to turn. As Assyria invaded, the ones who oppressed the poor would have nowhere to turn. Their ill-gotten gains from oppressing the needy will no longer be theirs. All that will be left for them is servitude as a slave or death. And that is exactly what happened in 722 A.D.

Why is God's hand still against them? Even in slavery these people of the northern tribes are set on their idolatry and rebellion. Nothing would turn them. God's mercy is taking away every false thing they trust in, but they still will not repent. Is it possible to be so hardhearted? Once the fire is kindled, it can grow to that extent. Put the fire out while you are still able to hear the voice of God. You will never win a battle with God. You will never get Him to give in and allow your sin to remain. It must go or you will continue to find Him resisting you.

We tend to worry way too much about what other people think of us. We should be concerned about how God sees us. We will never find a love as great as the unconditional love of God. It is God who truly loves us. Only in learning to love Him in return and putting His Word above that of man will we find eternal value.

⁵ Ah, Assyria, the rod of my anger; the staff in their hands is my fury! Isaiah 10:5 Remember, whatever God is using to deal with you, it is a rod in His hand. It is not something out of His control. It is controlled by Him. He wields the staff. That should comfort us as the psalmist suggested (Psalm 23:4). Why? Because He wields it in love for our good.

Assyria was an evil nation, but God used it as a rod of judgment. He will deal with Assyria later. Though they were used by Him, it was of their own free will. The abuse of their power will be dealt with by another rod. This shows us the wonder of God's sovereignty. God does as He pleases (Psalm 115:3). He can use the evil intentions of man to do His bidding and still be just in judging the evil in their hearts. We are seeing this today as Sunni radicals fight Shia radicals. Both are killing anyone who worships Jesus, and God is using their evil mindset to judge one another.

Critics could ask how they could be judged by God for carrying out His will. God is judging the evil in their hearts. They have no intention of obeying Jesus as Lord, but they are serving Him without knowing it.

Assyria was a nation so evil that it enjoyed psychological warfare by the abuse of those they conquered. Surrender and give up all your wealth and you would not be abused; but resist and you would face torture.

⁶ Against a godless nation I send him, and against the people of my wrath I command him, to take spoil and seize plunder, and to tread them down like the mire of the streets. Isaiah 10:6 When the Israelites heard this they would surely have asked how in the world they could be considered godless compared to Assyria. But God doesn't judge by comparing the depth of our depravity (Acts 10:34). All sin is rebellion against God. The more we know of God and His will, the more heinous our rebellion is toward Him. Refusing to obey is to be in effect, godless. Israel had the prophets of God. They had received these warnings we have just read, and they arrogantly went on their prideful way refusing to turn (1 Peter 4:17). "God is able to use godless worldly powers to discipline his godless covenant people. Human oppressors don't even have to be aware of God to be useful for his purifying purpose." (John Ortlund Jr.- Preaching the Word – Isaiah: God Saves Sinners. p 107)

In spite of the evil in man's heart, God has His way in human history. When we are defeated, God is not defeated. It does not mean that God is on the side of the victor. God will judge the outworking of evil in man's heart even if it serves His purposes. God is never compromised by the evil.

¹² When the Lord has finished all his work on Mount Zion and on Jerusalem, he will punish the speech of the arrogant heart of the king of Assyria and the boastful look in his eyes. ¹³ For he says: "By the strength of my hand I have done it, and by my wisdom, for I have understanding; I remove the boundaries of peoples, and plunder their treasures; like a bull I bring down those who sit on thrones. Isaiah 10:12-13 When God deals with Judah through Assyria, then God would punish the king of Assyria. I have told you before how Assyria conquered all but Jerusalem and how God spared Jerusalem. Then how the boastful and arrogant king of Assyria was dealt with by man. That, too, was God guiding and orchestrating history while still allowing man to do as he pleases.

Historical records of the kings of Assyria show their prideful boasts that correspond with these verses. (ARAB 1:110) We all have the same old nature within us. When believers go astray it is often connected to them believing they have been successful because they were special in some way. Even if you were the perfect servant of God, your voice, your breath, your opportunities, your acquaintances, and your intelligence all came from God (1 Corinthians 4:7).

You and I are merely His instruments. He will take the willingness of a believer and use it for His glory, doing wonderful things through our lives, much of which we don't discern. He can also take the outworking of evil in the heart of those who rebel against Him and use it for His glory though they know not what they do or how God is using it.

¹⁵ Shall the axe boast over him who hews with it, or the saw magnify itself against him who wields it? As if a rod should wield him who lifts it, or as if a staff should lift him who is not wood! Isaiah 10:15 All glory to God! If anything is accomplished through the life a believer, all the glory goes to God. Every good thing you have comes from God (James 1:17). Every opportunity to serve Him was prepared by Him before you were born (Ephesians 2:10). He picked the time and place you were to be born to draw you to Himself and work through you for His glory (Acts 17:26).

I've have a couple chainsaws and a few cords of oak to cut up for winter, thanks to Jory hauling it out of the woods for me. The chainsaw didn't get me out of bed one morning and take me to the wood pile as it sawed up the logs as I hung on. It didn't move my hands to pile it up. Neither can I say a sermon comes from my own power. I can't tell God, "Look what a great job I did explaining these verses!" Nor can you say, "This week I won a soul to Jesus." It is God who works in you and me to will and to do His good pleasure (Philippians 2:13). Let's thank Him for letting us be His instruments. Let's joyfully yield to His guiding hand at every leading of the Holy Spirit. Let's give Him all the glory. It is joyful privilege to be a willing and cooperative instrument in His loving, powerful hands. In God's kingdom there is no place for pride.

At the same time, let's be sensitive to His correction and discipline. Let us be aware that our hearts can deceive us (Jeremiah 17:9). Let us be like Mrs. Edwards, graciously, with humility and reverence receive whatever God's hand might bring into our lives. Our ultimate example did just that in the Garden of Gethsemane. He yielded to the Father and did not resist wrath of man, but trusted God to work our salvation through it. Let us follow His perfect example.

Questions
1 Why does God become angry?
2 How did the people respond?
3 How should we respond to adversity?
4 What was the second judgment?
5 What does verse 18 teach us?
6 How do we devour each other?
7 What happened to the oppressors?
8 Why should the staff in God's hand comfort us?
9 How does the passage describe God's sovereignty?
10 What is Jesus example in accepting the will of God though painfully difficult?

The Coming King - Isaiah 10:16 – 11:4a

In our previous passage the Lord spoke of the coming captivity of Israel because of their pride and injustice. They boasted that they would rebuild their fallen bricks with dressed stones. It was defiance against God.

Amazingly, Tom Daschle quoted that verse on 9/12/01 on the senate floor saying it spoke to all Americans. He thought he was talking about rebuilding, but he was quoting a passage that spoke of the judgments of God coming on a prideful unrepentant nation.

After judging Israel, God began to describe what would happen to the nation that He used to punish them, Assyria. He spoke of the pride of the Assyrians and compared them to an axe boasting against the hand that wielded it (10:15). They were mere instruments in God's hand but spoke as if they were gods.

Our passage today picks up with how God was going to deal with the pride of Assyria. *16 Therefore the Lord GOD of hosts will send wasting sickness among his stout warriors, and under his glory a burning will be kindled, like the burning of fire. 17 The light of Israel will become a fire, and his Holy One a flame, and it will burn and devour his thorns and briers in one day.* Isaiah 10:16-17 Man has a tendency to look to his might and inventions for security. God's weapons make ours look like toys. What can man do against a category 5 hurricane? Or what can we do against a new airborne virus? We dream of stopping asteroids. Good luck with that.

In contrast with Assyria's pride and man's pride in general, the last part of this chapter ticks off various names of God. The Lord God of hosts is the God of angel armies. He calls Himself the Light of Israel, the Holy One, the Holy One of Israel, the Mighty God, and the Majestic One. Those names declare His supreme greatness and power, but also His covenant with the Jewish people (Genesis 17:7). While He was disciplining them severely, He was also holding accountable the tool with which He disciplined them. He was not forsaking them by any means, and it is the same for all who know Him. His discipline is His "lovingangerkindness" to purify us (Job 5:17). If the rod of His discipline in using their free will deals with others more severely than God intends, then God will hold them accountable.

18 The   glory of his forest and of his fruitful land the LORD will destroy, both soul and body, and it will be as when a sick man wastes away. 19 The remnant of the trees of his forest will be so few that a child can write them down. Isaiah 10:18-19 The Assyrian army is referred to as a forest which would be destroyed, both their souls and bodies. So few would survive that a child could count them. We often place hope in numbers, whether it is a nation or a church. But God has shown time and again that it is not the number of people that matter, but His presence with those people (2 Samuel 24:10). A single soul fully surrendered to the Lord can do more than we can imagine. The stories are numerous. Consider Noah, Abraham, Gideon, Jonathan, Sampson, Paul, but most of all the God/man Christ Jesus. Numbers are not important to God, but a humble, submitted spirit is His delight (Psalm 147:11).

God is using this little church to touch the world through giving to missions, the web, and your personal lives. We just need a few who are faithfully committed to putting God first, like those of you who explain the glory of the resurrection in that painting, or who are willing to run a storefront on 89a when the Lord opens the door, or give to mission needs. If God adds to our numbers, may we never boast in those numbers or natural talent, but rather may we always boast in the Lord who is our strength (Judges 7:2). Whether the culture comes against us as annoying thorns or as a forest like army, the fire of God is more than sufficient to deal with it.

[20] In that day the remnant of Israel and the survivors of the house of Jacob will no more lean on him who struck them, but will lean on the LORD, the Holy One of Israel, in truth. [21] A remnant will return, the remnant of Jacob, to the mighty God. [22] For though your people Israel be as the sand of the sea, only a remnant of them will return. Destruction is decreed, overflowing with righteousness. Isaiah 10:20-22 Sadly, only a few of those in Israel would survive and truly turn to the Lord and lean on Him in truth. That is because destruction was decreed, overflowing with righteousness. The righteous justice of God would come upon the idolaters and those who leaned on anything other than the Lord. They heard the truth through the prophets. They would see the prophecies come to pass. That was the grace of God extended to them in mercy to turn them from their ways. And yet they would not turn and be saved (45:22).

This is one of those prophecies in which we can see multiple fulfillments. This was true of the return to the Promise Land from captivity in Persia. It was perhaps more clearly fulfilled in the days of Jesus when only a few leaned on Jesus in truth and much of Israel was destroyed in 70 A.D. (Romans 9:27). It will be true in the last days in the time of Jacob's trouble (Zechariah 14:2) and when the 144,000 are chosen out of Israel to be witnesses to the world (Revelation 7:4).

[24] Therefore thus says the Lord GOD of hosts: "O my people, who dwell in Zion, be not afraid of the Assyrians when they strike with the rod and lift up their staff against you as the Egyptians did. Isaiah 10:24 After speaking to Israel, God addressed Judah. Since the rod God was using was for the purpose of refining a remnant and causing them to lean on Him and return to Him, they should not fear that discipline. Neither should we.

Is the diagnosis cancer? Be not afraid. If you are God's child, He will use it to take you home into His presence or purify you to trust more completely in Him as the Mighty God. Did you lose your job? Be not afraid. God is our provider. After we learn to lean on Him, He can work more powerfully through us, as we happily and humbly give Him all the credit.

The Assyrians would soon find themselves on the receiving end of God's justice, only it was not to refine them, but rather to destroy them. *[26] And the LORD of hosts will wield against them a whip, as when he struck Midian at the rock of Oreb. And his staff will be over the sea, and he will lift it as he did in Egypt.* Isaiah 10:26 Once again God refers to Gideon's defeat of the hordes of Midian (Judges 7:25). He also reminds them of the defeat of the Egyptian army when Moses stretched out the rod of God over the sea and it drowned Egypt's army (Exodus 14:27-28). The reason God reminds the Jews of these stories is that they knew that in each case the final outcome

84

was only because of the mighty power of God. If they had looked to their own strength or wisdom, they would have been utterly destroyed. In both cases God wrought a mighty victory because the people trusted in Him and leaned on Him. Though the people of Judah would later go into captivity and be decimated, God could bring a mighty victory that was beyond their imagination. Through their descendants would come the Messiah who will, in God's time, usher in the Kingdom of peace described in the next chapter.

We don't always live long enough to see what God is doing in and through our lives. Hebrews 11 of is full of people who died in faith not yet having received what God promised them (Hebrews 11:39). Most of church history is a record of people dying in faith looking forward to what God has for us. We experience it in part when we yield to the Holy Spirit, but the fullness is something we look forward to by faith (1 Corinthians 13:9-10). Dying in faith is coming across the finish line as a winner (2 Timothy 4:7-8). Our last breath here is followed by our first breath of the air of heaven, marveling at the countenance of Jesus in all His glory.

33 Behold, the Lord GOD of hosts will lop the boughs with terrifying power; the great in height will be hewn down, and the lofty will be brought low. 34 He will cut down the thickets of the forest with an axe, and Lebanon will fall by the Majestic One. Isaiah 10:33-34 The Assyrians as the axe in God's hand boasted in their pride, but the Mighty One would now wield an axe against them. The greedy, prideful powers of this world that wage war to conform the world to their liking will answer to the axe wielder. They will face the Prince of Peace and find He brings peace by bringing them low (9:6). The Majestic One will show who wields whom. You see, peace is not found by pretending the heart of man is good, but rather when evil in man's heart is confessed and forsaken or judged and brought low. It is the Prince of Peace who does both mighty works of grace for the good of those who choose life in Him.

Now all that is left is the stumps of Judah and Assyria. But God had already told us that the holy stump was the seed from which the Messiah would come (6:13). That stump includes another stump, the stump of Jesse. It was to Jesse's son, David, that the promise of the lineage of Messiah was given (Psalm 89:3-4). *1 There shall come forth a shoot from the stump of Jesse, and a branch from his roots shall bear fruit.* Isaiah 11:1 The roots go back through Jacob, Isaac, Abraham, and all the way back to Eve. God has always been seeking fruit that remains (John 15:16). Fruit trees have branches that will bear fruit and those that don't. Often the flowers will come in clusters and several will be pollinated. Sometimes you can see five small fruits beginning to grow from one flower cluster, but most of them will drop off and die. The one that remains is the fruit that endures to eternal life (Romans 6:22).

Jesus is the fruitful branch, the branch of promise. That is one of the names for the Messiah, the Branch (Zechariah 3:8). He is the One that bears lasting fruit to the glory of the Father. The difference between Him and all the other descendants of David is seen in the rest of the prophecy. *2 And the*

Spirit of the LORD shall rest upon him, the Spirit of wisdom and understanding, the Spirit of counsel and might, the Spirit of knowledge and the fear of the LORD. Isaiah 11:2 We are told that three pairs of qualities of the Holy Spirit will rest on Him.

The first set is wisdom and understanding. Jesus declared that One greater than Solomon was present, referring to Himself (Matthew 12:42). That would mean He is the wisest One to ever live (John 7:46). We see that wisdom not only in how He answered His accusers and critics, but in how He taught and dealt with people. His understanding came from His heavenly perspective (John 7:38). He knew what was in man's heart. He understood that being great is being the servant of all (Mark 9:35). He understood that to do the will of the Father was the only thing one should do. He understood the Scriptures like no one else (Colossians 2:3).

The second set of anointed qualities from the Holy Spirit is counsel and might. He is the Wonderful Counselor. When asked which was the greatest law or if it was lawful to pay taxes to Caesar, His counsel was always perfect. Though He veiled His true might, it came out in the power of His words. It was revealed in a small part when He told those who came to arrest Him, "I Am!" (John 18:6) But it was totally revealed when He walked out of the grave as Victor over death, hell, and all the forces of evil.

The third set consists of knowledge and the fear of the LORD. His knowledge of Scripture was perfect. He knew when a verse was spoken out of context and when another clarified the meaning (Luke 4:10-12). Knowing the Scriptures so perfectly and clearly meant He had knowledge to apply to every situation He faced.

We do not think of Jesus having a fear of the LORD, however, the fear of the LORD is what deters us from evil (Proverbs 16:6). He knew the righteous judgments of God. He was tempted in all points like we are and yet without sin (Hebrews 4:15). Why? It was not because he was incapable of sinning. It was because He had the perfect fear of the LORD. He shows us how important it is that we should have the same. He loved and trusted the Father and longed to return to His side, and yet He lived in the fear of the LORD. He demonstrated the perfect balance. These three pair of anointed attributes make Him the Wonderful Counselor and Prince of Peace. And we will now see how this anointing is expressed in the age to come.

In case the "fear of the LORD" seems out of place, the next verse tells us that He not only was anointed with it but He delights in it. *³ And his delight shall be in the fear of the LORD. He shall not judge by what his eyes see, or decide disputes by what his ears hear, ⁴ but with righteousness he shall judge the poor, and decide with equity for the meek of the earth;* Isaiah 11:3-4a Jesus delighted in the fear of the Lord keeping Him from the destructiveness of evil.

The world only has what it sees and hears to go by. Even when we want to do the right thing, we often make the wrong judgment. If you are in Christ, then the Spirit of God lives in you and can help you do as Jesus did, which is to listen to the Spirit who knows all things. Then you can judge a

86

righteous judgment (John 7:24). That is a result of delighting in the fear of the LORD. Because God is just, those who fear Him want to see justice in their decisions.

Injustice is most often directed toward the poor and the meek because one can get away with it. The poor and the meek don't have the resources to resist injustice, but Jesus does. He stands in their defense. The day is coming when He will be Judge over the whole earth. In the Millennial Kingdom Jesus will judge the world through His saints (1 Corinthians 6:2). There will be no more injustice.

Injustice was one of the chief complaints God had against Judah. Much of that injustice was to take advantage of the weak, but some of it was probably the limitations of man and our trust in ourselves. How often we go about our day never looking to God in our decisions but trusting in our own limited resources. "That is our greatest sin—to think and act as our own saviors and to disrespect the Savior of the world." (Ortlund Jr. - Preaching the Word – Isaiah: God Saves Sinners. p 115) Can you imagine the day when injustice will be no more? The leadership of man has failed time and time again, in every form and every way. We have tried to create utopia but failed because of what is in our own hearts (Jeremiah 17:9). But the day is coming when a pure heart will reign through others whose hearts He has made pure.

As a side note, this passage is why the soldiers blindfolded and struck Jesus and then asked who it was that hit Him (Luke 22:64). His claim to be the Messiah meant He could judge without seeing. They were mocking that claim. It was a demonstration of His meekness to not name each man and their ancestry.

We'll continue next week with this glorious description of the Kingdom we are all headed toward. Our great hope is not only that His work in us will be completed, but that He will reign in righteousness. Then we will experience life as He meant it to be in all its fullness. Every time we hear of injustice or face it ourselves, we should remember that the day is coming when the One who does not judge by what He hears with the ear or sees with His eyes will be the great Judge who reigns in righteousness with all power to enforce it. He is anointed with might and will be called the Mighty God. None will dare resist His righteous judgments. There will be no more politics, no more debates about which way things should be, no more indoctrination and religion, just the presence of the Majestic One who will make all things right (Ephesians 1:22). God has put this hope in our hearts and described it through the prophets. He will bring it to pass, for He is Mighty God, the Majestic One. Until that day come, let us lean on Him by learning His Word and listening to and obeying His Spirit.

Questions
1 What was God going to do to Assyria and why?
2 How can numbers be detrimental?
3 Go over the multiple fulfillments of 10:21-22.

4 Why fear the Lord but not fear discipline?
5 What examples were given in regard to the coming judgment on Assyria?
6 Why do we call Jesus "the Branch"?
7 Review the three pairs of anointing.
8 How can we judge the world?
9 Why would Jesus delight in the fear of the LORD?
10 Review the Orland Jr. quote.

Great Expectations - Isaiah 11:4-12:6

In the previous passage we saw God's prediction of the army of Assyria, as numerous as a forest of trees, would be reduced to the point a child could number them (10:19). Judah would be reduced to a single stump, but life was still in it. While great Assyria would come to an end, the future of the Davidic line was almost too glorious to describe. The Messiah was going to come, anointed with all the qualities a perfect king should have, wisdom and understanding, counsel and might, knowledge and the fear of the Lord (11:2).

This coming King would be able to judge in righteousness, for He would have the ability to see beyond the externals. Nothing but righteousness would influence Him. The poor and needy could expect Him to judge fairly. Is not this what man has waited for, longed to see, and tried to find a way to bring about? Communism and socialism stem from this desire to see all treated equally and fairly, but their rulers enrich themselves at the expense of the masses and distort justice. Democracy intends to give the people a voice in their governance, but neglect the fact that people can vote for their own ease while leaving future generations the bill. The leaders the people elect can choose to leave their campaign promises unfulfilled. Democracy could only work if the majority were godly. With all governments, the problem is the heart of man (Jeremiah 17:9). How can we make a world of fairness and justice where the good are protected and the evil are justly punished? We can try our best, but it will only be a reality when the Prince of Peace, the Branch from the stump of Jesse reigns (11:1).

We pick back up our study in the second half of verse four. There are numerous interpretations for the passage we are looking at today. Some believe it applies to the advancement of the gospel around the world and that the language is all figurative. Others believe this is describing the Millennial Kingdom. Still others think this is a description of the new heaven and new earth after the final judgment. I think they are all right to some extent. As we have seen before, prophecy can have intermediate and ultimate fulfillments.

4b and he shall strike the earth with the rod of his mouth, and with the breath of his lips he shall kill the wicked. Isaiah 11:4b We see this both at Armageddon (Revelation 19:21) and at the end of the Millennium (Revelation 20:9). When the world rises up against the King of kings, the

88

One anointed with might will slay them with the sword that comes from His mouth. Who can stand against their Creator? His Word created man and it can destroy evil men. This is absolutely necessary if there is to be peace. It will be completely clear just who these armies are resisting. They choose not to accept His love and mercy and would rather be in hell than to worship Jesus in heaven. These who are hardened in heart want only their own will and way and recognize that Jesus will not let their evil continue (Psalm 2:9).

⁵ Righteousness shall be the belt of his waist, and faithfulness the belt of his loins. Isaiah 11:5 The ancient people wrestled with a belt which each opponent tried to take from the other. To be girded with your belt meant you were ready for the match. Jesus is more than ready. It reminds me of the cleansing of the Temple (John 2:15). I can see Jesus waiting with anticipation for the day to come in which the Spirit of God told Him, "Now!" He waits for the day to rid the world of evil. His belt of righteousness and faithfulness can't be taken from Him, but He can certainly remove the belt of evil from the world. It is His righteousness and faithfulness that motivates Him to jump into the ring and finish the job (Revelation 21:5-8).

Verses six through nine are seen in the three ways I mentioned earlier. If we see Judah as the lamb and Israel as the fattened calf, the vicious nations that once threatened their existence will one day no longer be a threat to them but will be at peace. That could come through the Gospel transforming both nations as they accept Jesus as their Savior. It could come after the Psalm 83 war. There are prophecies of the conversion of these nations, but that may not happen until the Millennium (Isaiah 19:23-25).

If we are to read this literally, we could see it as the reversal of the curse to take place during the Millennial Kingdom or in the new heaven and new earth. It would seem to me it would have to be the latter as "none hurt or destroy in all" God's kingdom. At the end of the Millennium there is an uprising and every intention is to hurt and destroy (Revelation 19:19). My impression of the Millennium is that it will be a time when man is taught that even under the benevolent rule of our righteous and just Savior, man's heart must be changed. Even after experiencing a thousand years of perfect conditions, man will still choose evil, just as he did in the Garden of Eden (Genesis 3:6).

The verse that concludes the four-verse poem seems to indicate it is describing a general condition of peace that is greater than the world has ever experienced. *⁹They shall not hurt or destroy in all my holy mountain; for the earth shall be full of the knowledge of the LORD as the waters cover the sea.* Isaiah 11:9 When everyone knows the LORD, when His character and judgments saturate the heart and mind of all mankind, there will be no more pain or destruction. This also leads me to lean toward the interpretation that the ultimate fulfillment is in the new heaven and new earth. It is after every tear is wiped from our eyes (Revelation 21:4). It is when there is no more concern what another might do to you emotionally or physically. Nature will be restored to the condition before the fall of man (Genesis 1:29-

30). Even our most ancient of enemies, the snake, will not bite a child who plays with it.

This is our great expectation! Death and sorrow will be no more. The world and all that is in it will be in perfect harmony. Abuse and sickness will be unheard of. There will be no lack or anxiety. Even the most perfect Christian life experiences problems in this fallen world. Job did, and God said there was none so righteous as His servant, Job (Job 1:8). But one day, no one will face the fallen conditions of our world. It will truly be a new earth wherein dwells righteousness and only righteousness (2 Peter 3:13). Then we will know living as God meant it, abundant, loving, reverent, and ever grateful.

The passage goes on to describe the return of the people of Israel. We have seen this happen in the last hundred years. As Isaiah predicted this so eloquently in his final chapter, *8 Who has heard such a thing? Who has seen such things? Shall a land be born in one day? Shall a nation be brought forth in one moment? For as soon as Zion was in labor she brought forth her children.* Isaiah 66:8 God sovereignly restored a nation after almost 2000 years. There is nothing else like this in all of history. But that is the intermediate fulfillment. The ultimate one is when the redeemed who survive the tribulation are returned to Jerusalem to be with their Savior. *10 In that day the root of Jesse, who shall stand as a signal for the peoples—of him shall the nations inquire, and his resting place shall be glorious.* Isaiah 11:10 Jesus' physical presence as the King will be the signal for believers to come from the corners of the earth. There will be no more false religions. Truth will reign with authority. He will clarify all things. Our many interpretations of Scripture will be reduced to His perfect explanation. The Word will be clear. Truth will be known by all. The verse literally says that the place of His rest will be glory. If any are in doubt they simply need to go to see the glory shining from His throne.

11 In that day the Lord will extend his hand yet a second time to recover the remnant that remains of his people, from Assyria, from Egypt, from Pathros, from Cush, from Elam, from Shinar, from Hamath, and from the coastlands of the sea. 12 He will raise a signal for the nations and will assemble the banished of Israel, and gather the dispersed of Judah from the four corners of the earth. Isaiah 11:11-12 Paul tells us that in that day all Israel will be saved (Romans 11:26). That is those who survive the day of Jacob's trouble will all turn to Jesus as the Messiah. They will all return to Israel where Jesus reigns. We should note that in Isaiah's day, Israel was not dispersed anywhere near this extent. It was a prophetic indication that it would be the case. The first great return in our day saw Jews return from all these countries. I believe in the second return there will be in even greater numbers.

14 But they shall swoop down on the shoulder of the Philistines in the west, and together they shall plunder the people of the east. They shall put out their hand against Edom and Moab, and the Ammonites shall obey them. Isaiah 11:14 If any would resist the redeemed in Israel in that day, they will quickly be brought into line. David conquered all these enemies of Israel. The Son of David will reign over them, as well as the whole world.

^{16} And there will be a highway from Assyria for the remnant that remains of his people, as there was for Israel when they came up from the land of Egypt. Isaiah 11:16 Just as God led the Children of Israel through the Red Sea, He will dry up the Euphrates, so they can walk over in shoes as they migrate to Israel. Every impediment from keeping the Jews from receiving Jesus as their King and Lord will be removed.

^{1} You will say in that day: "I will give thanks to you, O LORD, for though you were angry with me, your anger turned away, that you might comfort me. Isaiah 12:1 The remnant that survives and returns will be thanking the LORD that His anger has turned away. Now they are comforted by the LORD. When we look at the history of Israel since 70 A.D. it would appear that God has been angry with them. While there are certainly many that seek to do the will of God their Creator, and who call on His name, YHWH, as a whole, they have been blinded to the fact that Jesus is their Messiah (Romans 11:8). But the day will come when they look on Him whom they have pierced and mourn (Zechariah 12:10). Then they will know Him as Savior and Lord.

The reason for this comfort is found in the next verse. *^{2} "Behold, God is my salvation; I will trust, and will not be afraid; for the LORD GOD is my strength and my song, and he has become my salvation."* Isaiah 12:2 We miss something when reading it in English. In Hebrew it says, "El – my Yeshua!" God – my Jesus! Now they can trust in Him and not fear judgment. That is what happens when anyone comes to know Jesus as their Savior. They recognize Jesus is God in the flesh (Romans 10:9). They trust in what He did for them and no longer fear God's judgment on their sin. Instead of running from Jesus, they run to Him. He becomes their strength. They no longer trust in their own ability to be good, but lean on the One who empowers them to live a new life.

God is the song they sing because He is their Yeshua (salvation). Jews and Christians are the most singing people of any of the world's religions. Jewish songs are usually in a minor key, and often mournful. But in that day, they will have a key change to the key of David (pun intended – see Revelation 3:8). They will be singing with us even as the messianic congregations do today. Our song is about Jesus and the salvation He has so freely and graciously given us (Exodus 15:2). So, we see this partially fulfilled even now.

You don't have to be Jewish to live this verse. You can live it today. You need never fear again. You can place your complete trust in Jesus and let Him be your strength, your song, and your salvation. You can do as the next verse invites. *^{3} With joy you will draw water from the wells of salvation.* Isaiah 12:3 Jesus is our well of salvation.

I think He was referring to this verse when He spoke to the woman at the well. *¹³ Jesus answered, "Everyone who drinks this water will be thirsty again, ¹⁴ but whoever drinks the water I give him will never thirst. Indeed, the water I give him will become in him a spring of water welling up to eternal life."* John 4:13-14 (NIV) To receive Him as our Savior is great joy for us, for other believers and even for angels in the heavenly realms (Luke 15:10). We find our sin burden lifted and are at peace with God. This is the joy that Isaiah foresaw when the people of Judah would turn to the Lord in faith and trust. It is the joy that will one day be manifest by everyone in that heavenly kingdom of peace that Isaiah was describing.

⁴ And you will say in that day: "Give thanks to the LORD, call upon his name, make known his deeds among the peoples, proclaim that his name is exalted. Isaiah 12:4 This certainly fits all three interpretations. If you have drawn water out of the well of salvation, you called on His name. You give thanks to the LORD. The earth is full of the knowledge of the LORD in that day, but it doesn't know your testimony. Make known His deeds!

When I spend any time with other believers I love to hear their story of the deeds of the LORD in their life. At Wheaton my wife and I went around asking individuals about the deeds of the Lord in their life. I heard the story of the stutterer from India who was instantly healed one morning and became a campus minister in the U.S. I heard the story of a Chinese man who found Jesus on the internet searching for truth. Ask fellow believers you meet about the deeds of the Lord in their life. Exalt the LORD's name by telling others those stories and ones from your own life.

Proclaiming that His name is exalted is to share the wonder of His attributes such as His grace, love, and faithfulness. His name is the essence of His being. When believers get together, we should quickly turn the conversation to what God is teaching us and what He is doing in our lives. It's all about Him, but we see Him through His Word and the ways He works in our lives.

⁵ "Sing praises to the LORD, for he has done gloriously; let this be made known in all the earth. Isaiah 12:5 The joy of sharing these testimonies and remembering the great things God has done for us should overflow into song. I don't understand how any believer could not desire to sing God's praises. There should always be a song of praise overflowing from our hearts. As I'm writing this I'm whistling We Declare Your Majesty. I don't think about it; it just is there from that fountain springing up in me. Has the Lord done a glorious thing in saving you? Has He met all your needs? Does He have a wonderful heaven awaiting you that is greater than we can imagine? If you really believe it, you'll want to proclaim it in all the earth. Did you ever put your testimony on Facebook? You don't have to be preachy. Just tell what God has done in your life. The Internet is a new way to proclaim it in all the earth. Let's use it for God's glory (Mark 8:38). Post those testimonies.

⁶ Shout, and sing for joy, O inhabitant of Zion, for great in your midst is the Holy One of Israel.” Isaiah 12:6 In the day that Isaiah is referring to, this will be quite literal. The Holy One of Israel will be enthroned in Zion. I'm sure there will be a lot of shouting and singing for joy then. But He is in the midst of the church today. When you get together with a brother and sister in Christ, He is there with you. He is in the midst of you personally, His temple (1 Corinthians 6:19). We should be shouting for joy and singing. That's Thanksgiving! It should be Thanksgiving every day for believers; thanking God for His presence in our lives, for His mercy and grace that saved us, and for the joy we have in Him. He is the song we sing with our lives and our voices.

By God's sovereign design we have come to this passage on Thanksgiving week. How appropriate! While we have many things in this life to be thankful for, they are only a glimpse of what is coming for those who have placed their faith and trust in Jesus. We should be living every day with this great expectation of seeing our Savior face to face and His transformation of our world. Our hope isn't in the governments of man; it is in these promises of God (Hebrews 10:23). We don't need to be discouraged as this world falls apart. It's to be expected. We are to keep our eyes on the world to come where nothing will hurt or destroy, and where the lion will lie down with the lamb. Righteousness will reign, and evil will be abolished. Jesus will be the glory in the midst of it all.

While we look expectantly for that day, let's keep drawing with joy that water out of the wells of salvation and making known His deeds among the nations. Let's keep sharing with all who will listen what great things He has done for us. Let the song overflow from your heart. He loves you!

Questions
1 Why must the wicked be slain?
2 What are the three interpretations of verse 6 -9?
3 Why do the nations come to Zion?
4 What will happen to the Euphrates? Why?
5 How can God's anger be turned from us?
6 What does 12:2a declare?
7 Who should be our strength? Our song?
8 How did Jesus use 12:3?
9 What do verse 4 and 5 tell us to do?
10 What should our response be to Jesus in our midst?

Sovereign Over Nations - Isaiah 13 – 20

We are entering into a new section of the book of Isaiah. Like Jeremiah 46-51 and Ezekiel 25-32, Isaiah grouped his prophecies to other nations together in one section 13 -27. We won't spend a lot of time on each, but we will instead draw out some relevant points for us today.

Once again, we come to a chapter in which the skeptics attempt to disavow Isaiah as the author. Because Isaiah is seeing into the distant future, long after his own lifetime, addressing the future kingdom of Babylon, the skeptics insist the passage must have been added by a later scribe. They claim it was either added, or the name of the country was changed to apply to their current situation. But the passage begins by declaring this is the vision of Isaiah son of Amoz. As the passage proceeds, it jumps back to Assyria, a nation that was no longer in existence in the time of Babylonian captivity of Israel. This shows us that it was written during Isaiah's lifetime. It was written in the same writing style as the first part of the book and only makes sense in light of the prophecies in that first section. The author also uses phrases that can be found in all three sections of the book.

I think the reason liberal scholars try so hard to discredit prophecy is that it would show divine origin (1 Peter 1:21). That would imply responsibility to hear and obey the principles, which is something they are unwilling to do. So, the attempt goes on, often in the face of historical and literary evidence.

The theme of next fifteen chapters is that God is sovereign over the nations. Though Judah will go into captivity, nothing can thwart God's plan of bringing the Messiah and His kingdom. All the rising powers and the tumult of the nations, as frightful as these may seem, were all under the control of Almighty God. As we have seen before, though these nations were violent in exercising their own free will, God directed the defeat of kingdoms for His own purposes. He could still judge the tool in His hand for the excesses that they chose to exhibit (10:12).

It has been argued that the violence in the Old Testament could be used to justify brutal acts of warfare today. It is one thing for us in our secure homes, who have never had our loved ones slaughtered simply because they are Christians, to speak of non-violence. But for many in the world today, having lost a loved one or be personally maimed because of your faith is a painful reality. What keeps us from retaliating in the same brutal manner? God's justice upon nations that are brutal should warn us against being like those nations.

We seek to imitate God's nature as much as humanly possible. When it comes to judging others, God tells us emphatically that vengeance is His, and He promises to repay (Romans 12:19). Sometimes we see it in this life. Most of the time it comes later. While we should oppose injustice and can't dispense justice on our own terms, what do we do when injustice prevails? What do you do when the con gets away scot-free and laughs at you? Where do we turn when our loved one is harmed, and the perpetrator gets away with it? Some of you have had to deal with this lately. This world is often inequitable in its dispensing of justice.

We have to turn to the fact that God is utterly just and He will give each one what he or she deserves (Deuteronomy 32:4). What peace this can give us in the face of injustice! God sees all and knows all and will see justice is served (Hebrews 4:13). The guilty will pay, unless they humble themselves and turn to the only available recourse for sin, Jesus. Our agony over injustice is often shortsighted. "The day of the Lord" is a day when even God's high standard of justice will be satisfied. In the New Testament it is referred to as the "day of our Jesus Christ" because He is the One through whom God will judge the world (1 Corinthians 1:8). He is the reason we don't take matters into our own hands. Only He can enable us to love our enemies (Matthew 5:44).

Isaiah is addressing that coming day for Babylon. Babylon is a type of all those systems and governments that exalt themselves against God. The prophets used Babylon to represent these anti-Christ systems because the first great organized effort to defy God was the Tower of Babel (Genesis 11). As with many of the prophecies we have seen, this one is also fulfilled in the immediate and distant future. The judgment that was coming against Babylon would take place by the hands of the Medes in 539 B.C., but Jesus quoted chapter 13 verse 10 when He spoke of His return. *29 "Immediately after the tribulation of those days the sun will be darkened, and the moon will not give its light, and the stars will fall from heaven, and the powers of the heavens will be shaken.* Matthew 24:29 It will be a day when the world's armies battle Jesus. While Babylon's defeat was a day in history, it was a preview of that ultimate day. And so too is every major war. John the Revelator speaks of a future judgment of Babylon, meaning the whole human effort of defying God and His people.

Throughout the prophecies to the nations, there runs a common thread that God is addressing. The pride of nations keeps them from God and from acting in a way that is acceptable to Him. Babylon is the first example because, of all the nations mentioned, it seemed to be the surest to succeed. From its hanging gardens to its immense fortified walls, they truly believed they were unbeatable. In fact, when they were attacked by the Medes, they threw a party to celebrate their gods, and brought out vessels they had taken from the temple in Jerusalem with which to drink wine (Daniel 5:23). They praised the gods of gold and silver as the Medes diverted the river that ran under the city, providing them an attack route which led to the city's downfall that very night.

They did not fear God. One of the points that God is making through Isaiah's prophecies is that He is no local area deity. He is the Creator of heaven and earth and every nation answers to Him. Every person will answer to Him. The nations will answer to Him in history. We will answer to Him at His throne of judgment (Romans 14:12).

Wars will continue until the final battle against God (Matthew 24:6). Wars throughout history are really just precursors. One side or both are fighting God, for they are treating those made in God's image as cannon fodder to obtain what they want. God will raise up nations to resist other nations in their greed and arrogance, but those nations will also be accountable for how they conduct themselves in warfare.

As with Isaiah's previous prophecies, there is inserted in the midst of these judgments a word of promise. *¹ For the LORD will have compassion on Jacob and will again choose Israel, and will set them in their own land, and sojourners will join them and will attach themselves to the house of Jacob. ² And the peoples will take them and bring them to their place, and the house of Israel will possess them in the LORD's land as male and female slaves. They will take captive those who were their captors, and rule over those who oppressed them.* Isaiah 14:1-2

Remember the three themes that Isaiah is addressing: the judgment of Israel, the coming captivity and return, and the coming Messiah. In the midst of telling of the judgments of the nations surrounding Israel, God reminds His people that His purposes are intact. They will return from captivity to the Promised Land. They will prosper again. In verse one there is a hint of the inclusion of the Gentiles as sojourners attach themselves to Israel. When we come to faith in the Messiah, we Gentiles are grafted in (Romans 11:17). While some from the captivity purchased slaves on their return, a greater fulfillment is found in the Gentiles becoming servants of the Lord.

I appreciate the way the Lord interjects these little rays of hope and promise. It tells us that life can be very hard at times, but God has a plan and His purposes will prevail. Like those in the hall of faith in Hebrews chapter eleven, we will probably die in faith not receiving the promises. Yet, we know God is at work and has something better in mind for us. The author of that passage says it was for the purpose of them attaining a better resurrection (Hebrews 11:35). God has the eternal perspective while we are focused so much on the temporal. That is why the grace of God keeps interjecting these words of promise into this book and into our lives. It helps us change our focus.

Chapter fourteen continues with the taunt that will be raised against fallen Babylon. Remember, Babylon is not even a nation yet and Isaiah is telling them the song they will sing after it falls. The reason for this is that Babylon will be the nation that takes captive what is left of Israel. It will seem that the plan of the coming Messiah and His kingdom has been thwarted. So God is telling them in advance what they will sing. Some believe this description of the fall of the king of Babylon parallels the fall of Satan or the Anti-Christ (2 Thessalonians 2:4). In a remote sense that may be true.

The taunt tells of five "I wills" that declare the pride of Babylon's kings. *¹³ You said in your heart, 'I will ascend to heaven; above the stars of God I will set my throne on high; I will sit on the mount of assembly in the far reaches of the north; ¹⁴ I will ascend above the heights of the clouds; I will make myself like the Most High.'* Isaiah 14:13-14 In Babylon's attempt to rule the world, they were voiding the promises of God, and that can't happen. It was Babylon or the Word. The Word will always prevail. These kings were as insolent and arrogant as one could be. Now they are worm food. Hell declares the depths to which they have fallen. Each of them became just another prideful but helpless soul in Hades unable to demand attention or control a single thing.

Prestige in this world often means nothing in eternity (Luke 16:15). In fact, God Almighty resists the proud (James 4:6). That is the message to these nations. For all the might they thought they possessed, each was told how they would be brought low. *⁶ We have heard of the pride of Moab— how proud he is!— of his arrogance, his pride, and his insolence; in his idle boasting he is not right.* Isaiah 16:6 These nations stand condemned because they ignored the God of Israel trusted their idols. They dare to boast before God.

Pride is the downfall of nations. They become so sure of their greatness that they think they are undefeatable. Then they lose the fear of God, become undisciplined, and unprepared, ripe pickings for another nation eager to take their place. We see the cycle again and again in history, yet we don't learn. But it will continue until the day of the Lord. The only difference is that prophecy seems to indicate that man will become increasingly anti-Christ (Matthew 24:12). How else would they dare to consider resisting His glorious appearance? And isn't it that way with individuals? God works on our heart time and time again and yet we keep looking to ourselves for direction and deciding on our own what we will do regardless of God's direction for our lives. Nations simply reflect the heart of man.

In chapter seventeen God tells us what it often takes for us to turn to Him. He describes the failure of crops that result in hardship. When we forget God, desolation is often the only thing that will force us to turn back to Him. *⁷ In that day man will look to his Maker, and his eyes will look on the Holy One of Israel. ⁸ He will not look to the altars, the work of his hands, and he will not look on what his own fingers have made, either the Asherim or the altars of incense.* Isaiah 17:7-8

God works through the hardship that is often a result of our sin to remind us of what we have lost. Sin always promises more than it can deliver and costs us more than we are willing to pay (Romans 6:23). When we have nowhere else to turn, we let go of the control of our lives and surrender. It doesn't have to be so hard, but we often insist that it be so by our choices. God doesn't want it to be so hard.

In the previous chapter Isaiah was crying over Moab (15:5). Though they had been enemies of Israel and refused to take their refugees in the day of calamity, his heart was broken over what the Moabites would face. That was the heart of God in Isaiah weeping for them. He longs that we see through the deceptiveness of sin and yield to Him.

In Dickson's talks on Freedom in the Ten Commandments he shared a personal illustration that helped him grasp the freedom found in following God's ways. He had been skiing for years but thought he would buy some lessons for his son and take a few himself. The teacher tried to tell him how to make a slight difference in his turns, doing a little hop and digging in a certain way. He struggled changing his longtime habit of how he went through a turn, but once he forced himself to change, he found it was so much better than the way he had done it. It added a whole new pleasure to skiing. It was a rule to which he conformed to find a new joy and freedom. That freedom is what Moab could have experienced had they come under the reign of the Davidic kings and worshiped with Israel. But they were not willing to make the change (16:5).

God goes through the list of the nations that surrounded Israel: Babylon, Assyria, Philistia, Moab, Syria (Damascus), and Egypt. Why did He bother to tell them when they weren't going to change? On the Day of Judgment, they will not be able to say that they didn't know God's will. Perhaps a few did hear and change. A hundred years later when Judah was taken captive they knew that their captors, the Babylonians, would one day fall. They knew the taunt they would sing. It encouraged their faith to read God was faithful to His Word. And if He was faithful to do that, then surely He would be faithful to bring the Messiah and the kingdom of God as well.

And what of us? Do we look back and see the faithfulness of God to fulfill His Word and allow our faith to be strengthened by the fact He did send the Messiah? Do we trust Him today and look to Him or to our own abilities and in our pride resist His directions to us? Do we lean to our own understanding or do we pray and seek His direction (Proverbs 3:5)? Are we anxious about situations or are we walking by faith in His goodness (Philippians 4:6)?

Chapter nineteen closes with surprise of which most people are unaware. It's a prophecy of which we have only seen a partial fulfillment. The Lord cuts off all which Egypt depends on; and the amazing result is that Egypt and Assyria begin to worship the Lord and bring offerings to Jerusalem. *21 And the LORD will make himself known to the Egyptians, and the Egyptians will know the LORD in that day and worship with sacrifice and offering, and they will make vows to the LORD and perform them. 22 And the LORD will strike Egypt, striking and healing, and they will return to the LORD, and he will listen to their pleas for mercy and heal them. 23 In that day there will be a highway from Egypt to Assyria, and Assyria will come into Egypt, and Egypt into Assyria, and the Egyptians will worship with the Assyrians. 24 In that day Israel will be the third with Egypt and Assyria, a blessing in the midst of the earth, 25 whom the LORD of hosts has blessed, saying, "Blessed be Egypt my people, and Assyria the work of my hands, and Israel my inheritance."* Isaiah 19:21-25

There have been Christians in these nations since the first century. However, right now, Egypt and Assyria are Muslim nations. But God is declaring that will change. I don't know if this is during the millennial kingdom or before. It is a fascinating prophecy. It speaks of God's desire that none should perish (2 Peter 3:9).

How could that possibly happen? We do hear of numerous conversions through dreams and visions, but it is still unimaginable. Egypt has booted the Muslim brotherhood but it has certainly not helped the

Christians. While many are converting, many Christians are still fleeing these countries as well. We'll have to wait and see how this unfolds.

In chapter twenty, Assyria defeated the Philistine town of Ashdod (20:1). Isaiah was told to walk naked for three years as a sign to Egypt and Cush that they would be the next slaves taken into captivity (20:2-3). I'm glad the office of prophet is over (Luke 16:16). I much prefer preaching the message than acting it out as a drama. You probably prefer receiving the message that way too, I hope.

We can't go over these messages to the nations without thinking of how it applies to us as a nation. Are we humbling ourselves before God and looking to Him? There have been 143 national calls to prayer, humiliation, fasting and thanksgiving from the office of the President of the United States, but they seem to be decreasing in frequency and attendance. Where are we looking for guidance? It all starts with each individual, then our homes, then as a church, and the community in which we live. If we are to change culture, we must individually change first. Jesus must become our life. We must let His love give us our priorities. Then as a church we must depend on God and be led by Him. Then we must let our light shine in our communities, unafraid and unashamed to show His love, to invite others to church, and to talk about issues of faith. Jesus invites us into an all-consuming relationship of faith.

Questions:
1 How can we tell Isaiah wrote this?
2 Where do we turn when evil wins?
3 What does Babylon represent?
4 What verse did Jesus refer to?
5 What was the word of hope?
6 Why did God give them the taunt in advance?
7 Why did God give them the taunt for Babylon so far in advance?
8 Review the five "I will".
9 What can it take to turn us back to God?
10 Why warn those who won't hear?
11 What is the surprise prediction?

Sovereign Over Nations part 2 - Isaiah 21-23

We are in the section of Isaiah that groups the prophecies to nations. This is our second of three sermons in that section. Last week we heard the prophecies to Babylon, Assyria, Philistia, Moab, Syria, and Egypt. We saw that God holds nations accountable for their actions and their pride. We learned that Babylon was a type of all world powers that defy God. We also saw that there are times when God allows calamity to turn us back to God.

Our passage today returns to addressing Babylon. *² A stern vision is told to me; the traitor betrays, and the destroyer destroys. Go up, O Elam; lay siege, O Media; all the sighing she has caused I bring to an end.* Isaiah 21:2 As we saw last week, this siege on Babylon came to pass long after Isaiah's life. It was important for the Jews to know that when Babylon took them into captivity, that it was only for a set amount of time. They would be restored as a nation, even though the reign of Davidic kings had come to an end. That did not mean the promises of God had failed. The line of David was keeping careful records of their lineage. One of those groups would settle in a town called Nazareth, meaning "the Branch," a messianic title referring to in a previous passage in Isaiah (Isaiah 11:1).

In Isaiah's vision, the nations that would destroy the coming kingdom of Babylon are specifically named, Media and Elam. This took place under King Darius in 539 B.C. Isaiah was so disturbed by the vision that he was doubled over and describes his pain as woman giving birth, and making his nights disturbing instead of restful. He grieved for the very people who would take His own people into captivity.

Verse five gives and amazing prediction of a detail that Daniel would describe over a hundred years after Isaiah. *⁵ They prepare the table, they spread the rugs, they eat, they drink. Arise, O princes; oil the shield!* Isaiah 21:5 The Babylonians were partying while the Medes were attacking (Daniel 5:1, 30).

⁹ And behold, here come riders, horsemen in pairs!" And he answered, "Fallen, fallen is Babylon; and all the carved images of her gods he has shattered to the ground." Isaiah 21:9 Darius the Mede did not destroy idols, but the defeat of the Babylonians who worshiped the god Marduke showed those idols to be mere stones (Jeremiah 51:47; 52). The idols were shattered to the ground in the sense that people no longer looked to them as a power that could protect them.

John's revelation sees this verse partially quoted by an angel in Revelation 14:8 and 18:2. Babylon had taken Judah captive and ended the Davidic dynasty. It threatened to put an end to the hopes of a coming Messiah. That is why it represents the forces of Satan in their attempt to stop Jesus from reigning in the hearts of men.

Babylon was a place of luxury and ease at the expense of all those they conquered who groaned under their oppression (see verse 2). Luxury and oppression are the two ways in which Satan attempts to reign, and luxury is usually more successful. The fall of Babylon therefore symbolizes the freedom that God's people will enjoy when people are no longer slaves of sin and when persecution and oppression of every kind ceases (John 8:32). (See next verse) "Babylon is fallen" is to say Christ has conquered. The world powers that deny God and persecute His people will one-day end. Injustice and oppression will cease. The fall of ancient Babylon foreshadowed the final fall of all nations that resist the kingdom of God.

10 O my threshed and winnowed one, what I have heard from the LORD of hosts, the God of Israel, I announce to you. Isaiah 21:10 Isaiah speaks to the future captives of Babylon. He calls them a threshed and winnowed one. The Israelites threshed grain by taking a board into which they had pounded sharp rocks and then dragging it over the harvested grain. Then they would throw it up into the wind to blow the chaff from the grain. We could say in today's vernacular, "raked over and tossed about." One hundred years later when the Jews in captivity felt that very way, they could look to this prophecy and know deliverance was on the way. That would encourage them to look the Lord and lean on Him.

In the rest of chapter twenty-one, Isaiah prophecies to Edom and Arabia using a play on words and prose. He switches a letter in the name Edom to make it the Hebrew word for silent, implying the silence of death. Just when they get a hint of dawn, the night comes again. That is a prediction that after these areas were no longer under the thumb of Assyria, they would be under the dark cloud of Babylon.

Hundreds of years later an Edomite would reign in Israel. His name was Herod the Great. In this season of looking forward to the coming of Christ we are reminded of Herod's choice to remain in darkness instead of coming to the light (Isaiah 60:1). He heard the prophecies of a coming Messiah, but instead of worshiping Him with the Magi, Herod tried to kill Him by executing the babies in Nazareth (Matthew 2:16).

Chapter twenty-two begins by addressing Jerusalem again. Isaiah predicted that the Babylonian siege on Jerusalem would see the Jews partying on their rooftops, eating their flocks and drinking up their wine. The spirit of Babylon was prevalent in Jerusalem. They used up their food supply and would die a death of starvation and pestilence (Lamentations 4:9). The leaders would try to escape but be caught and bound. All the rest who survived were captured and taken into captivity.

In Isaiah 22:5 Isaiah calls Jerusalem the valley of vision. *5 For the Lord GOD of hosts has a day of tumult and trampling and confusion in the valley of vision, a battering down of walls and a shouting to the mountains.* Isaiah 22:5 Though Jerusalem is on a hill, it is surrounded by mountains. From the mountain of Gethsemane, you actually look down on Jerusalem. They had the words of the prophets. That is why it was called the valley of vision. But because they did have revelation and still lived like Babylon, a day for the siege had been appointed by God.

8 He has taken away the covering of Judah. In that day you looked to the weapons of the House of the Forest, 9 and you saw that the breaches of the city of David were many. You collected the waters of the lower pool, 10 and you counted the houses of Jerusalem, and you broke down the houses to fortify the wall. Isaiah 22:8-10 The removal of their covering might refer to God's hand of protection or it may refer to Jerusalem as a woman who is shamed by her public nakedness (Nahum 3:5; Lamentations 1:8). There was no repentance. Instead there was just dependence on weaponry (1 Kings 7:2-6). The House of the Forest was an armory that was built by Solomon. When hearts are hardened to the message of God, they will always place trust in the things that cannot save.

¹¹ You made a reservoir between the two walls for the water of the old pool. But you did not look to him who did it, or see him who planned it long ago. Isaiah 22:11 They lived in the valley of vision, but they wouldn't receive the vision. They looked to the armory and water storage rather than to "look to him who did it."

How often we look for the worldly practical solution and forget that God is sovereign over all things? How many times in their history had God intervened in impossible situations? But God knew they would refuse to look to Him when this time would come. He knew this was coming when He called them to be His people. He knows prosperity often leads to spiritual decay. He knows we tend to trust in the flesh before we trust in Him. Yet, He purges us, allowing us to be winnowed and threshed by the world that we might be of eternal value (James 1:2-4). He teaches us that carnal ways won't meet our needs when times are difficult. Don't despise the chastening of the Lord or trials of life. Know that He is disciplining us for our good (Hebrews 12:5-6).

It's a sad prediction for the nation, but it is the mercy of God that is warning them of what is coming and telling them of the future hope. God is showing them they aren't different from those who will be their captors. They have the same priority of luxury at any cost. Worldly pleasure is their sole aim. Pleasure is their god regardless of what they claim. Their indictment is found in verses 12 and 13. *¹² In that day the Lord GOD of hosts called for weeping and mourning, for baldness and wearing sackcloth; ¹³ and behold, joy and gladness, killing oxen and slaughtering sheep, eating flesh and drinking wine. "Let us eat and drink, for tomorrow we die."* Isaiah 22:12-13

The siege was a chance for them to turn back to the Lord with weeping and sackcloth. Shaving the head was also a sign of repentance. Instead the people prepared to die in their sin. If the enemy was going to take their herds and wine storage, why not consume them now. This is what they lived for, so enjoy it and die. This is the attitude of the world, living for the temporal pleasures of this life (1 John 2:15-17). God meant for natural pleasures to be enjoyed in moderation as gifts from Him. Judah responded to the call to repent with defiance and rebellious revelry. The result would be prolonged starvation. This kind of defiant sin is self-defeating.

Paul contrasts the suffering that believers endure for the Lord with this attitude (1 Corinthian 15:32). He wrote that if our hope was in this life, we would have the same attitude. But instead we gladly endure because we know the resurrection is coming. We are living for the glory of God and eternity in His presence. By referring to this passage, Paul was shaming those in the Corinthian church who were still living for pleasure like the Jews before captivity and the Babylonians.

Chapter twenty-one closes with an example of why Judah was headed this direction. Under godly King Hezekiah there was an administrator name Shebna. Apparently he was not Jewish for his father's name is not mentioned and the name sounds Egyptian in origin. He misused his office and authority to try to make a name for himself. He wanted his tomb to be like that of the kings. He was a blot on Hezekiah's godly government.

Shebna made plans to be famous in Israel, but God made plans to hurl him out of the land. The same thing can happen in the church. Godly leaders try to act to exalt the Lord alone. However, some individuals crave recognition and honor. When our focus turns from glorifying God to being important and influential, we are in danger of being hurled out of the fellowship of the saints by the Lord Himself. Just as Shebna was a shame to Hezekiah's government, so we can be a shame to the church if we seek our own glory (John 7:18).

What Shebna labored for is given to Eliakim, whom God calls, "my servant." That is a title of high honor, for it will later be applied to the Messiah. Eliakim's fatherly heart of unselfish concern for the people is in contrast with Shebna's selfish ambitions. A fatherly heart is the heart every leader needs. It is a heart of genuine concern, protection, and provision. Isaiah predicted the key of David would be on Eliakim's shoulder. That means he would have the responsibility even though he did not hold the power.

Here again we have verses that are quoted in the New Testament. Jesus is said to hold the key of David and open what no man can shut, and shut what no man can open (Revelation 3:7). Eliakim's fatherly heart and faithfulness with his responsibilities was just a shadow of the coming Messiah. The contrast of the self-seeking Shebna and the fatherly heart of Eliakim is a picture of the contrast of governments of man and of the reign of Christ Jesus.

Though Eliakim is God's servant and given great authority over so much, the office Eliakim held would not last. The suddenness may imply an untimely death or simply that his position ended. Jesus on the other hand will reign forever (9:7). (Also see Hebrews 7:23-24)

Chapter twenty-three moves to the oracle of Tyre and Sidon. While Babylon conquered land by force, Tyre colonized and spread by trade. Nevertheless, Tyre was just as prideful as Babylon. Babylon worshiped power and oppression to attain what they desired. Tyre used trade to and commerce to obtain what their hearts lusted after. Neither looked to the Lord.

In verse eight the prophet asks who purposed this downfall of a nation that crowned kings. The next verse answers the question. *⁹ The LORD of hosts has purposed it, to defile the pompous pride of all glory, to dishonor all the honored of the earth.* Isaiah 23:9 All who seek their own glory, glory in fallen man, will face the ever true maxim, "God opposes the proud." James 4:6 Nations or individuals that exalt themselves against God, who walk arrogantly as if they had no need of God will find themselves facing reality (Psalm 9:17). That is the faithfulness of God to turn them. When believers forget their need of a Savior on a daily basis, we will have trials to remind us of our need.

James tells us that when God is so gracious as to give us trials, we should receive them with all joy. If we can see that the end result is patient endurance, maturity, and not lacking any good thing, then we can make this our new and honest way of seeing the trials we face (James 1:2-4). Unlike these kingdoms that will fade into oblivion because they would not receive God's message or repent, we can repent and be willing to change. Trials make us face the reality that God's love allows difficulty to come into our lives to perfect us. These nations could have been changed had they been willing to humble themselves and turn to God. We can change if we are willing to do the same. But it must be an unconditional surrender to the way God sees us and to His will for us. Humility is taking a backseat to God, and that is something these nations refused to do.

15 In that day Tyre will be forgotten for seventy years, like the days of one king. At the end of seventy years, it will happen to Tyre as in the song of the prostitute: Isaiah 23:15 Why was Tyre compared to a prostitute. E.J. Young tells us "For the sake of material gain men may sell their souls, as well as for the gratification of fleshly desires and appetites." This selling of our souls for temporal pleasure is like prostitution. This is the way of man and man's systems (Revelation 18:3).

The Lord told how short the memory of Tyre would be. One generation would pass and the glory of Tyre would be completely forgotten. I often think of this concept at funerals. I have done some funerals for wonderful, godly people, but even if they were the godliest saint I wonder how soon they will be forgotten? Depending on our calling, this could be true of us. How few names have endured?

Do you know of Charles Cowman? He was an amazing man of God whose labors for Christ resulted in every house in Japan receiving the Gospel. He took on Korea and started on China before world war broke out. He worked himself to heart failure. More than likely you never heard the name of this great servant of God.

The point I'm getting at is that what this world remembers doesn't really matter. It is what heaven will be talking about through eternity. Most of that talk will be about the grace of God that changed us and prepared good works in advance for us to walk in (Ephesians 2:10). We are only talking about Tyre because it is in God's Word. It is in God's Word to tell us that the memory of man is short and unimportant in eternity. What is highly esteemed among men is often an abomination in the eyes of God (Luke 16:15).

If the people of Tyre could have heard this message and received it, how their history would have changed. God gives us a preview of what that change looks like. *18 Her merchandise and her wages will be holy to the LORD. It will not be stored or hoarded, but her merchandise will supply abundant food and fine clothing for those who dwell before the LORD.* Isaiah 23:18 Initially, Tyre's purpose was still self-centered, and still

104

described as prostitution. But eventually she received God's invitation to do what lasts (Ezra 3:7). Change is possible. God can still bring Himself glory through your life.

This is God's invitation to us. Everything we do can be sacred (1 Corinthians 10:31). Everything we do can matter. Even our daily routine can be sanctified if we are living for the glory of God. Why do you get up each morning? Is it just for selfish, temporal pleasure or for the eternal glory of the One who made you?

Questions
1 What does Babylon represent? Why?
2 Why is the fall of Babylon and angelic cry?
3 How does the prophecy address God's people?
4 What is the application to Herod?
5 Where do the hardhearted turn?
6 How did Judah respond to God's plea for them to repent?
7 How did Paul use 22:13?
8 What/whom did Eliakim foreshadow?
9 How do we face trials with "all joy"?
10 Why was Tyre compared to a prostitute?
11 What is "forgotten in seventy years"?

End of the Word - Isaiah 24-27

In the chapters that preceded those we will look at today, we saw that God is sovereign over nations. He judges each nation in history. Each nation rises and falls, which shows us that man is incapable of building anything that endures. In the end, every system of man resists God, which means their inevitable decline to and final demise.

The cycle of nations rising and falling shows us two biblical truths. The first is that man needs government and leadership. It is a gift from God. But soon the second truth becomes obvious. Man has an evil heart (Jeremiah 17:9). Power gives opportunity for corrupt hearts to express what already lies within. We quote that phrase "power corrupts, and absolute power corrupts absolutely," but in reality power simply gives the corrupt heart of man opportunity to expose itself. How many times have we seen leaders think they were above the boundaries placed on them by their government's own rules? It happens in the church too. That is why equal and accountable eldership is so important, and why multiple branches of government are important. These checks and balances limit the opportunity for man to get away with his selfish tendencies.

Our chapters today do not speak of specific nations, but of the end of the reign of man, or as we saw in previous chapters, the fall of Babylon. This is a parallel to Daniel chapter two when the stone cut out of the mountain smashes the image of man and becomes a mountain that fills the whole earth (Daniel 2:44-45). Isaiah is seeing the grand conclusion of man's kingdoms.

¹ Behold, the LORD will empty the earth and make it desolate, and he will twist its surface and scatter its inhabitants. ² And it shall be, as with the people, so with the priest; as with the slave, so with his master; as with the maid, so with her mistress; as with the buyer, so with the seller; as with the lender, so with the borrower; as with the creditor, so with the debtor. Isaiah 24:1-2 We saw a little twisting of the earth during our recent earthquake. I've seen the ground roll like waves, but this sounds like all the plates of the earth shifting at once. The book of Revelation mentions an earthquake in six passages (Revelation 6:13; 8:5; 11:13, 19; 16:18). The last reference is mentioned in conjunction with the fall of Babylon.

Towards the end of this chapter in Isaiah God makes it clear that this is a physical earthquake. *¹⁹ The earth is utterly broken, the earth is split apart, the earth is violently shaken.* Isaiah 24:19 The result is the end of man's classifications and a great equalization. This great equalizing of men is something socialism and communism has tried to bring about, only to find their efforts resulted in loss of individual initiative. The only time this equality can be realized is in a body of Christ followers. Even then, we find weeds among the wheat (Matthew 13:24-25). Only the reign of Christ on earth will bring about true equality that maintains individual enthusiasm. That is because God will justly reward godly effort. While our heavenly rewards will vary, our standing before God is equal because we are all recipients of the righteousness of God (2 Peter 1:1).

The destruction will be so complete that few men will be left. *⁵ The earth lies defiled under its inhabitants; for they have transgressed the laws, violated the statutes, broken the everlasting covenant. ⁶ Therefore a curse devours the earth, and its inhabitants suffer for their guilt; therefore the inhabitants of the earth are scorched, and few men are left.* Isaiah 24:5-6 The Bible teaches us that God has nature respond to the sin of man (Numbers 35:33; Psalm 106:38). We are always looking for the empirical explanation for every natural disaster, but rarely do we do as the ancients and look for a spiritual cause. While pagans used natural disasters as an excuse to punish those they opposed, Christians have seen disasters as being allowed by God to bring us to repentance. There will be no doubt in the days of God's wrath on the earth that it is from the hand of God. We find a parallel in Revelation in the fourth bowl of wrath. *⁸ The fourth angel poured out his bowl on the sun, and the sun was given power to scorch people with fire. ⁹ They were seared by the intense heat and they cursed the name of God, who had control over these plagues, but they refused to repent and glorify him.* Revelation 16:8-9 (NIV)

Our chapter in Isaiah goes on to speak of the end of all the things that man delights in. All the things the carnal person lives for will be taken away. But strangely in the midst of all this devastation there are songs of praise rising from the earth. *¹⁴ They lift up their voices, they sing for joy; over the majesty of the LORD they shout from the west. ¹⁵ Therefore in the east give glory to the LORD; in the coastlands of the sea, give glory to the name of the LORD, the God of Israel. ¹⁶ᵃ From the ends of the earth we hear songs of praise, of glory to the Righteous One.* Isaiah 24:14-16 These who are praising God are the great number who have turned to the Lord and recognized that this judgment on the earth is the end of Babylon the great (Revelation 7:9, 13-14). That means Christ is coming to reign and righteousness and justice will prevail. The devastating results of sin will be removed for a thousand years. The earth will be filled with the knowledge of the Lord (Isaiah 11:9).

²¹ On that day the LORD will punish the host of heaven, in heaven, and the kings of the earth, on the earth. ²² They will be gathered together as prisoners in a pit; they will be shut up in a prison, and after many days they will be punished. Isaiah 24:21-22 Revelation chapters nineteen and twenty tell of the details of this event. The kings who lead the nations in the battle of Armageddon are killed. Hebrew people referred to the grave as the pit, because they kept the bones of ancestors in a pit for the day of resurrection (Psalm 28:1). Thus, gathered in a pit means to die, but also may mean a place of confinement. Satan will be bound for a thousand years after which time the dead will be judged and punished. That is the "many days" referred to in verse twenty-two.

²³ Then the moon will be confounded and the sun ashamed, for the LORD of hosts reigns on Mount Zion and in Jerusalem, and his glory will be before his elders. Isaiah 24:23 The glory of the sun and moon will be nothing compared to the glory of the Lord reigning on Mount Zion (Revelation 21:23). We can see the parallel in Revelation where the twenty-four elders are described as being around the throne (Revelation 4:4). This is the climactic end of man's governments and the beginning of the eternal reign of Jesus on the throne of David (Isaiah 9:7). While Isaiah will go on to prophecy to nations and tell of Jesus' suffering, he has already given us a glimpse of where it is all headed.

Chapter twenty-five begins with Isaiah joining the redeemed in praising God. *¹ O LORD, you are my God; I will exalt you; I will praise your name, for you have done wonderful things, plans formed of old, faithful and sure.* Isaiah 25:1 Isaiah can see that this end of man's kingdoms means the end of suffering and oppression. But He also sees that this was God's plan all along. God allowed man to see how depraved and helpless he is to bring about any good. How many thousands of years have we been striving for the perfect government? Even when we plan for checks and balances there is abuse and corruption and the real needs of the people are neglected.

God allowed man to try everything his imagination could conjure, and yet we refuse to learn from our experiences. We need God. That is the message of history. We need a Savior. We need a holy Leader who will reign in righteousness. The wonderful, faithful, sure, and ancient plans of God will come to pass. Man will reach the end of himself, as in the days of Noah (Matthew 24:37). Then Christ will come and put an end to our suffering and receive His own. That is why Isaiah is praising God in the midst of all the destruction he envisions. Before he was crying at the fall of nations (Isaiah 15:5a), but that is not the case at this final judgment. We cry when we see others reject the chance to turn to God. But during the pouring out of God's wrath, the choice will be so clear that we will know that those who face His wrath would never turn from evil. (See Revelation 16:9 on page 2.)

Isaiah foresees the feast of the Word that God will prepare for all those are willing to come into His presence. *⁶ On this mountain the LORD of hosts will make for all peoples a feast of rich food, a feast of well-aged wine, of rich food full of marrow, of aged wine well refined.* Isaiah 25:6 The rabbis saw in the prophecy to Judah that the Messiah's kingdom would have an abundance of wine (Genesis 49:11). That is why Jesus' first sign was turning water into wine (John 2:11). If you can make water into fine wine, you certainly could have an abundance of it. But the spiritual significance is the joy that wine represents. Isaiah will speak again of the wine and food that is rich, meaning joy in the Holy Spirit and spiritual nourishment (Isaiah 55:1-2; Psalm 22:26). We taste it now when we come to know Jesus as our Lord and feast on His Word, but our present experience is just the appetizer for what is to come (Revelation 19:9).

⁸ He will swallow up death forever; and the Lord GOD will wipe away tears from all faces, and the reproach of his people he will take away from all the earth, for the LORD has spoken. Isaiah 25:8 The Victor over death has taken away the power of our greatest fear. That means He conquered the one who had the power over death. That is why Christians have such hope. We don't mourn for our loved ones like the world does, because we know in a short time we will see them again (1 Thessalonians 4:13). Sorrow and crying will be no more. Don't you long for the hands of Jesus to wipe away forever the tears from your eyes? Every hurt will be gone. Every scar healed over (Revelation 7:17). Death is the result of sin, and sin will be no more!

The verse also speaks of the reproach of His people. The Jews have been and are still a reproach in the eyes of much of the world. Christians, in many countries such as Pakistan, are only allowed to have the most menial of occupations. In our own country, Christians are increasingly insulted and marginalized. We are mocked by the entertainment industry, but we haven't seen anything like that which many of our brothers and sisters around the world face. We will increasingly find we are the reproach of this world until Jesus reigns.

⁹ It will be said on that day, "Behold, this is our God; we have waited for him, that he might save us. This is the LORD; we have waited for him; let us be glad and rejoice in his salvation." Isaiah 25:9 The intermediate fulfillment of this verse came when Jesus was incarnated. The ultimate fulfillment will come when we meet Him in the air (1 Thessalonians 4:17). Everything we have longed for as believers will be realized. Every promise of God will be fulfilled. Those promises we did not receive in this life will be ours then. We will be like Him for we will see

Him as He is (1John 3:2). That is our reason to be glad and rejoice with super-abounding joy.

The prophecy turns next to the old enemy of Israel, Moab. *11b but the LORD will lay low his pompous pride together with the skill of his hands.* Isaiah 25:11b Those same gentle hands that wiped the tears from our eyes will powerfully lay low the pompous prideful ones who resist Him. This is what we have been reading about to this point in Isaiah. The prideful nations and individuals that have rejected the Lord, those who refuse to listen to His invitation to come to Him and find peace, will be brought low.

Chapter twenty-six is a song that will be sung in Zion. It welcomes the righteous nations that bring their tribute into the city (Isaiah 18:7; Revelation 21:24-27). The song also has a number of proverbs. Verse three is one everyone should memorize. *3 You keep him in perfect peace whose mind is stayed on you, because he trusts in you.* Isaiah 26:3 This has been a refuge for me personally. We will face times of difficulty when our mind is whirling with all the possible outcomes of a situation. That can bring on a lot of anxiety. But this promise is the antidote for all anxiety. Instead of worrying, we should fix our mind on the Lord, on all He has done for us, on how much He loves us, and on how we can trust Him. When our mind is on Jesus, the peace comes in like a warm blanket. We'll be tempted to shift our thoughts to the worries, but that is why the verse says our minds must stay there. This is not just any peace that is promised. It is perfect peace. To know God is all-powerful and more than sufficient to see you through anything is the source of this perfect peace. This peace puts an end to fear and worry. Whenever you start to be anxious again, you can know your mind needs to be pulled back to Jesus.

One reason for that perfect peace is found in the next verse. *4 Trust in the LORD forever, for the LORD GOD is an everlasting rock.* Isaiah 26:4 Our God is strong, secure, and eternal. He will never change. Everything else will change. The governments of man will come and go, but His reign will endure forever.

8 In the path of your judgments, O LORD, we wait for you; your name and remembrance are the desire of our soul. Isaiah 26:8 The path of the Lord's judgments is not only His punishment of evil but walking in His will. We should live in a way that is pleasing to God while we wait for Him to fulfill His promises. His name is the sum of His attributes. Remembering His great deeds and help in the past, along with reminding ourselves of His character, should be the desire of our soul (Psalm 73:25). What does your soul desire? If your first answer is anything other than a deeper walk with Jesus, you'll have a difficult time being at peace.

19 Your dead shall live; their bodies shall rise. You who dwell in the dust, awake and sing for joy! For your dew is a dew of light, and the earth will give birth to the dead. Isaiah 26:19 Many theologians tell us that the Old Testament did not teach of an afterlife. I'm not sure which Bible they are reading. Mine sure teaches it (Daniel 12:2; Hosea 13:14)! Keep in mind how this fits in with previous chapter. Isaiah is still speaking of the end of the systems of man and the reign of Christ on the earth. Death is not the end. For us it is graduation day.

Chapter twenty-seven again speaks of Israel as God's choice vineyard (Isaiah 5:7). God tells of His faithful care of it, and how He would contend with nations that would come against it (thorns and briars). God would rather those nations laid hold of Him for their protection. He would rather they made peace with Him. His love and favor is not only for Israel, but for all, as we often see throughout Isaiah.

This chapter tells of how God will deal with Israel through captivity and how they would respond by destroying their idols. We have an amazing promise in verse 6.

⁶ In days to come Jacob shall take root, Israel shall blossom and put forth shoots and fill the whole world with fruit. Isaiah 27:6 This is obviously speaking of physical descendants as well as spiritual fruit. However, it has been literally fulfilled as well. Israel has indeed been taken root again a second time. They are now the largest source of citrus fruit for all of Europe. If you go to Israel today you can see the large banana, orange, and grapefruit groves all over the land. In another sense, the entire world uses medicine manufactured in Israel. But the greater fulfillment is yet to come.

In these four chapters we've seen the end of the governments of man that comes about through the wrath of God on the earth. We've seen the great multitude that are saved during that period, and the eternal reign of Christ. We've been invited to God's great banquet, seen the end of death and how all tears will be wiped from our eyes. We learned that peace comes from keeping our mind on Jesus and trusting Him. He is the desire of our soul. And this last chapter showed us that God would indeed take Israel through captivity but would restore them as a people purged of idolatry.

This is real life. We know that trials purge us of worldly distractions. We know God has good plans for us and desires for us to be fruitful. We experience His peace when we keep our mind on our unshakable Rock. We rest in the promise of resurrection, knowing that Jesus is the Victor over death and has a victory meal prepared for us. I'm going! Are you?

Questions
1 How will God equalize all mankind?
2 Why will God use nature to punish man?
3 Why do people praise God in 24:14-16?
4 What prompts the praise of 25:1?
5 What is the victory feast of God?
6 What happens to death?
7 What will be the fruit of waiting on the Lord?
8 How can you stay in perfect peace?
9 What should our soul desire?
10 Does the Old Testament teach resurrection?

110

Worlds Apart - Isaiah 28

We are beginning the new year in a new section of Isaiah. Commentators see chapters 28 – 35 as God affirming that He is able to carry out the salvation that He promised in chapters 1-27. Ray Ortlund Jr. describes this section this way: God looks us right in the eye and claims that he can and will deliver on every single promise in the gospel. Do we believe him? Does Jesus rule over the mess called my life, or in unsparing realism must I despair? May I expect a new work of the Holy Spirit in my experience, or is my past the measure of my future? Isaiah now prompts us to rethink our lives with questions like these. They have the potential to help us break the faith barrier into a new sense of God's power and love. (Preaching the Word – Raymond Ortlund – Isaiah: God Saves Sinners p 152)

Chapter 28 is a call from God to the northern ten tribes referred to as Ephraim, and to Judah to recognize their true condition. When I first read the chapter and the ones that followed, I admit I was wondering what I could possibly preach that we have not already covered. Even after reading one of the most complete commentaries on this passage I was thinking of lumping all six woes that begin here and through the following chapters in one message. But after reading Raymond Ortlund's message on this chapter, I realized I was missing the richness of the passage. I begin by acknowledging the inspiration he received and I am borrowing for this message.

The chapter begins contrasting two crowns. There is the crown of the proud drunkards of Ephraim with its fading flower, Samaria. From other sources we know that Samaria had become a wealthy city with beds of ivory (Amos 6:4; 1 Kings 22:39). The other crown is that in verse five, a crown of glory, who is the Lord Himself.

Though the people of the northern tribes had long since turned to idolatry, there were some who had seen a brief revival in Jerusalem and defied their own government by going to celebrate the feasts in Jerusalem (2 Chronicles 30:11). But the nation as a whole was entrenched in idolatry. Their pride convinced them that Assyria would not prevail over them. They took their blessing of prosperity and used it as an excuse for excess. God was warning them that they were drunken with their pride, symbolized by their drunkenness from wine. Pride and luxury had blinded them to the reality at hand.

God presented to Ephraim, and presents to us, two types of crowns. There is the crown of self-reliance or the crown of the Lord Himself as our glory. When we put it that way, the choice looks so obvious, but in the midst of the threats we face, we fear that God's way of rescuing us will not be what we would choose. So, we turn to what we think is more predictable: our own ingenuity and cunning. Our cry is, "Yes, we can!" And God responds, "Not without me, you can't!" But we try anyway. And time and time again we find that God's way would have ultimately been the best way.

The suddenness of Ephriam's ruin was described as an overwhelming flood. Israel has flashfloods similar to our own. A torrential downpour could turn a dry wash into a raging torrent in seconds, sweeping away man and beast. That was the description of the coming Assyrian invasion. God also described it as someone coming upon a first ripe fig. It goes from the hand to the mouth in the blink of an eye, and down the hatch. It's devoured.

The remnant would choose the crown of glory in the Lord. These are *not* those that survive the Assyrian invasion, for we will see that Judah was just as bad if not worse. These are the ones who in the future will choose the cornerstone that God sets in the midst of Jerusalem. It includes all those who place their faith in God's provision of the Messiah. *⁵ In that day the LORD of hosts will be a crown of glory, and a diadem of beauty, to the remnant of his people,* Isaiah 28:5

Ephraim's condition shows us history was repeating itself. The goodness and patience of God prospers a nation. The nation starts to live for the material blessings and turn from God. "The fading flower of its glorious beauty" is phrase that can be applied to everything this world prizes. The beauty of youth is short lived (Ecclesiastes 11:10). Today's treasures belong to someone else tomorrow or they fade away and are rubbish (Matthew 6:19). Pride blinds us to the threats that surround us, as nations gather to take the blessings for themselves. Suddenly the nation that thought itself invincible is brought to its knees. Faith in man and his ingenuity is demolished (Jeremiah 17:5).

Malcom Muggeridge asks, "Can this really be what life is about, as the media insist? This interminable soap opera going on from century to century, from era to era, whose old discarded sets and props litter the earth? Surely not. Was it to provide a location for so repetitive and ribald a performance that the universe was created, and man came into existence? I can't believe it. If this were all, then the cynics, the hedonists and the suicides would be right. The most we can hope for from life is some passing amusement, some gratification of our senses, and death. But it's not all.... As Christians we know that here we have no continuing city, that crowns roll in the dust, and every earthly kingdom must sometime flounder, whereas we acknowledge a king that men did not crown and cannot dethrone, as we are citizens of a city of God they did not build and cannot destroy." (Malcom Muggeridge, *The End of Christendom,* Eerdmans 1980, pp 50-52)

You would think, living in the times that we do, that man could see more clearly now than ever before that we need God. If ever the gospel should ring true to man, this is the time. Communism, socialism, and every other ism of man has only shown the heart of man to be evil through and through. We are watching democracy prove the same point. Regardless of the system, those in power will prove themselves corrupt. Why can't everyone see this truth? Is it because they don't want the alternative, which is to place our trust in God?

Total trust in God is the great adventure of faith that always lies before us. Who else is utterly trustworthy? Certainly not any man or woman, including ourselves! Like Israel, we are invited to step out in faith and follow wherever He leads. We leave our little practical ways behind and head into the adventure He has for us. Because faith is what pleases God (Hebrews 11:6) He is always stretching our faith, inviting us to step out and trust Him. Unless we act on that invitation, we will never know the all-sufficiency of God. We'll never see the things He was willing to do through us. Of all the resources God has given us, He is by far the greatest but least tested. How the history of these nations would have been different had they received the message from God's prophet!

Isaiah's message moves to Judah and its capitol, Jerusalem. Though they lived in "the valley of vision," they were no better than Ephraim. *7 These also reel with wine and stagger with strong drink; the priest and the prophet reel with strong drink, they are swallowed by wine, they stagger with strong drink, they reel in vision, they stumble in giving judgment. 8 For all tables are full of filthy vomit, with no space left.* Isaiah 28:7,8

The priests and the prophets are so drunk on their own vain philosophies that they defile everything as they spew their ideas. This reminds me of the Jesus Seminar and so many other secular Bible teachers. Many seminaries today are so filled with vomit, what comes from inside their own minds, that there is no space left for the reality of the Word of God. The message is not simply unheeded, it is mocked.

These priests and prophets ask *9 "To whom will he teach knowledge, and to whom will he explain the message? Those who are weaned from the milk, those taken from the breast? 10 For it is precept upon precept, precept upon precept, line upon line, line upon line, here a little, there a little."* Isaiah 28:9-10 They are asking if Isaiah thinks he is teaching little babes. "Who does he think we are!" And then the Hebrew text sounds like baby talk, repetitive sounds, *ṣav lāṣāv ṣav lāṣāv qav lāqāv qav lāqāv.* They are mocking the message from God. It's not sophisticated enough for them. "Repent and trust in God. That's not the intelligent thing to do," they say. But it is the wise thing to do. The priests and prophets drunken on their own philosophies didn't realize how profound the Word of the Lord from Isaiah really is.

God turned it around on them and told them that if it sounds like babbling to them, he'll use the tongue of a foreigner to instruct them. The Assyrians will tell them how to do their tasks as slaves. *11 For by people of strange lips and with a foreign tongue the LORD will speak to this people, 12 to whom he has said, "This is rest; give rest to the weary; and this is repose"; yet they would not hear.* Isaiah 28:11-12

The apostle Paul quoted this passage to tell the church that God speaks clearly to those who will hear, but to those who refuse to believe He speaks in a way they cannot comprehend. Those enslaved by sin will only hear babbling. Those who believe will hear and receive the Word (1 Corinthians 14:20-22).

God offered them rest and repose, but they would not hear Him. God offers us so much more than the world could ever deliver, but many refuse to listen. That is the indictment against every rebellious soul. This why there is a place called hell. Many will insist that God is not trustworthy. They will insist on turning away from God, mock His Word, and reject His offer of rest. But the offer still goes out to all (Hebrews 4:11).

Jesus told His listeners that this rest is found in Him. *²⁸ "Come to me, all you who are weary and burdened, and I will give you rest. ²⁹ Take my yoke upon you and learn from me, for I am gentle and humble in heart, and you will find rest for your souls. ³⁰ For my yoke is easy and my burden is light."* Matthew 11:28-30 (NIV) To hear Jesus and receive Him is to receive God's Word and know the rest and repose God offers us. To receive Him is to follow Him wherever He leads (Luke 9:23). It's to place your *total* trust in Him.

Judah rejected the Word of the Lord from the prophet to the point of even mocking it. We see this today on a regular basis in our entertainment world. We live in a world where people perceive two very different realities. To us, the Word of God is rich and profound. It's like a feast. In it we find rest from striving to please God, for Jesus is our righteousness (1 Corinthians 1:30). We are accepted by God in Him. We no longer try to find a reason to feel of value, for we know God has adopted us into His family (Ephesians 1:5). We know where we are going when we die, and we know where our loved ones in Christ wait for us. We know that the all-powerful God loves us and will work all things together for good in our lives (Romans 8:28). We've entered His kingdom of righteousness, peace, and joy in the Holy Spirit (Romans 14:17).

Yet, to the rest of the world, we are ignorant fools bound by religion as if addicted to a drug, believing in a world that doesn't exist. To them there is no reason for hope or joy except in the fleeting pleasures this world offers. The destructiveness of sin is seen as pleasure to be indulged in, which they think we are missing out on. Selfishness is natural and immorality is self-actualizing. It's the same world viewed from completely different perspectives. One declares man's nature to be good, the other declares it is evil. What does the evidence show us?

What do you hear? When the Word of God is preached in a worship service, one person hears the voice of God speaking to their soul. They are thrilled to get His direction for their lives and can't wait till next Sunday to hear more (Jeremiah 15:16). The person next to them can hear the same sermon and think of it as simple moral lessons to make children behave. Does God's Word delight and change you or annoy you? Or do you care at all?

The leaders of Judah were making a secret deal with Egypt (30:1-2). God invited them to trust Him, but the leaders thought they knew better than God. God called this deal with Egypt a covenant with death. The leaders thought it would save them, but God knew it would destroy them. It does matter which one is true! Differing views don't change reality. There is your

114

truth and my truth, but the only real truth is God's truth! Assyria was going to deal with Egypt before it dealt with Jerusalem. The leaders were trusting in a false hope.

But God would bring a sure hope to Jerusalem in days to come. *16 therefore thus says the Lord GOD, "Behold, I am the one who has laid as a foundation in Zion, a stone, a tested stone, a precious cornerstone, of a sure foundation: 'Whoever believes will not be in haste.' 17 And I will make justice the line, and righteousness the plumb line; and hail will sweep away the refuge of lies, and waters will overwhelm the shelter."* Isaiah 28:16-17 God would bring salvation in spite of the failure of the leaders to turn to Him. Jesus is that tested stone, a precious cornerstone, of a sure foundation. Jesus is the cornerstone of the church. That is not of its history, traditions or rituals, but of the people who place their trust in Him. He is the plumb line. It is His righteousness that is the standard, and He freely credits it to those who place their faith in Him. (Romans 9:32-33; 1 Peter 2:4-5; Ephesians 2:19-20). While the leaders looked to Egypt, the people of faith look to God's provision. In Him they find rest and repose. Through Him they become a part of God's eternal city (Revelation 21:2).

Those who place their faith in the cornerstone will not be in haste. They won't be franticly running to the world for a solution. They will wait on the Lord (Psalm 27:14). Their spirits will not be agitated when times of testing come. I see this battle in my grandchildren and am reminded of my own times of testing. Something disturbs our world and we run to look for solutions here and there. But those of real faith are not in haste. Our trust is in an all-knowing, all-powerful God who allowed our circumstances and will work through the circumstances for our good (Isaiah 26:3).

Isaiah goes on to describe what is coming to Judah, to those who do not trust in God but instead in their own cunning and abilities. The scourge of Assyria was about to sweep through the land by day and night. Like a bed that was too short to stretch out on or a covering too narrow to cover oneself, so their false hopes would bring them little comfort. *21 For the LORD will rise up as on Mount Perazim; as in the Valley of Gibeon he will be roused; to do his deed—strange is his deed! and to work his work—alien is his work!* Isaiah 28:21 One of the references is to a time when David was anointed king over Israel, the Philistines rose up to try to defeat him. Instead he won an overwhelming victory and destroyed their idols (2 Samuel 5:17-21). The other reference is to Joshua's defeat of the armies of Canaan that allied against Israel (Joshua 10:5-11). In these cases, God was saving Israel. Now He is anointing Judah's enemies to save them from their own destruction. Judah's pride and self-reliance were their greatest enemy. Defeat is a strange work but a necessary one. There are times when God must take His children through times of difficulty to save us from our own ways.

The chapter closes with words of comfort. Those words start with a plea to listen. They wouldn't listen to words of instruction, but perhaps they would listen to God's purposes. *23 Give ear, and hear my voice; give attention, and hear my speech.* Isaiah 28:23 Just as God gives the farmer wisdom to plow enough and plant in ways that are best for each crop, as well as how to uniquely deal with each harvest, so God knows how to deal with His people. He is not utterly destroying them but bringing out what is of value while getting rid what is worthless. He won't plow them too long or thresh them too severely, but just enough to bring about the best harvest. *²⁹ This also comes from the LORD of hosts; he is wonderful in counsel and excellent in wisdom.* Isaiah 28:29

The same is true for our lives. We need times of plowing our hearts so that the Word can take root (Hebrews 13:6). We need a harvest time when the Word becomes productive. It is often followed by a winnowing when that which is worthless is removed. God knows how to transform us to the image of His Son (Romans 8:29). It's not an easy path, but it's incomparably better than the path the world has chosen. It requires that we listen to Him and be willing to let Him change us.

Questions
1 What is this section of Isaiah about?
2 What are the two crowns?
3 How fast can destruction come?
4 What can we call a flower of fading beauty?
5 What did priests and prophets of Judah do wrong?
6 How did they respond to Isaiah?
7 Who can't understand God's message?
8 Where can we find rest and repose?
9 How do people see life so differently?
10 Why is it so urgent that we hear?

Surprising Grace - Isaiah 28

¹ Ah, Ariel, Ariel, the city where David encamped! Add year to year; let the feasts run their round. Isaiah 29:1 This second woe (ah), is to Ariel. Ariel represents Jerusalem, the city where David encamped (2 Samuel 5:9). It is also the Hebrew word for the hearth of the altar where a fire was stoked to consume the sacrifices the Israelites offered to the Lord (Ezekiel 43:15-16). At the same time, it is a compound word composed of lion *(ari)* and God *(el)* (2 Samuel 23:20). This play on words seems to be the message of the entire chapter. The people were going through their cycle of religious feasts that God had appointed in a monotonous fashion. The Lion God doesn't tolerate lukewarm worship. He deserves much more than ritualized performance. False religions might believe their gods are appeased with ceremony and ritual, but the true God is worthy of whole-hearted devotion (Revelation 3:16).

² Yet I will distress Ariel, and there shall be moaning and lamentation, and she shall be to me like an Ariel. ³ And I will encamp against you all around, and will besiege you with towers and I will raise siegeworks against you. ⁴ And you will be brought low; from the earth you shall speak, and from the dust your speech will be bowed down; your voice shall come from the ground like the voice of a ghost, and from the dust your speech shall whisper. Isaiah 29:2-4 God was declaring He would distress Jerusalem and make it burn like an altar hearth. God doesn't even mention Assyria or Babylon, for this siege is God's work. As He declared in the last chapter, a "strange is His work – alien is His deed" (28:21). God was going to humble Jerusalem and put an end to hypocritical worship. The noise of the celebratory feast would be replaced with just the whisper of the dead.

The words are meant to be shocking. It was a wakeup call. What is it about human nature that turns vibrant heart felt faith into dry routine? How do we go from passionate faith to meaningless rituals? I think it has something to do with the deceitfulness of sin. We are steadily bombarded with the false promises of the world. How many thousands of commercials promise satisfaction and joy if you just use their product? But Israel didn't have advertisements. They did have the same old nature that is tantalized by the temporary pleasures of this passing world. In every age the temptation is the same. And when we listen to its "siren song," the flame of passion is doused, not all at once, but little by little. It happens slowly, almost imperceptibly. That is when God must do His strange and alien work.

He allows trouble to rattle our cage. We seem besieged all around with one problem after another. We are brought low with illness or financial problems or relational difficulties and find we don't have a solution. Then we turn to God and ask, "How could You let this happen?" But really, how could He love us so much as to get our attention and turn us around? How could He not let His bride know she is flirting with disaster? It seems strange or alien to us because we are so used to His abundant blessings. What we were really asking is, "Why didn't You let me go on in the delusion of lukewarm apathy and stray further from You?" Then the answer is obvious. Our trials may be an expression of His love (James 1:2). It's a slap in the face to wake us from our drug induced stupor and save us from spiritual death.

This is the point in marriages when people start talking about divorce. That's because the passion is gone. But why is it gone? We found satisfaction in other things or other people. We grew irritated at the response of our spouse who became distant or tried to wake us up. Fortunately for us, God has more grace than any spouse. He is our example of patience and love, and He knows just how firm to be. He never draws away. He just keeps pursuing us in spite of our unfaithfulness to put Him first (2 Timothy 2:13).

When we finally let go and without reservation throw ourselves on the Lord, He shows up. *⁵ But the multitude of your foreign foes shall be like small dust, and the multitude of the ruthless like passing chaff. And in an instant, suddenly, ⁶ you will be visited by the LORD of hosts with thunder and with earthquake and great noise, with whirlwind and tempest, and the flame of a devouring fire.* Isaiah 29:5-6 Isaiah's message takes on the flavor of an end-time prophecy. Jesus spoke of the time when Jerusalem would be surrounded by armies (Luke 21:20). But that was not in reference to this passage. Jesus told his audience to flee when those conditions came. That was Rome's conquest of Jerusalem in AD 70. In our present passage, it is a multitude of foreign foes that is not ultimately victorious. That language points us to the day of Jacob's Trouble (Jeremiah 30:7).

That will be a time when it will seem that Jerusalem has been lost and the Jewish people are on the verge of extinction. It is then the Lord will appear as they turn to Him as their Messiah (Zechariah 14:1-3). The enemy will vanish as if they were just a dream, like chaff blown away with the wind.

That is just like our troubles when we return to the Lord. We put our trials in His hands. Either He takes care of them, or shows us how to, or gives us such grace that we rise above them so that they do not oppress us as they once did. He loves to rescue us, but He'd rather we stayed passionately in love with Him, worshiping with our whole heart as we should.

At this point in the prophecy, God turns again to the present condition of Judah. The hardness of their hearts has caused them to be calloused toward the things of God. Rather than have them become even more accountable in their sin, God causes them to be unable to perceive the message. *⁹ Astonish yourselves and be astonished; blind yourselves and be blind! Be drunk, but not with wine; stagger, but not with strong drink! ¹⁰ For the LORD has poured out upon you a spirit of deep sleep, and has closed your eyes (the prophets), and covered your heads (the seers).* Isaiah 29:9-10 It reminds me of the work God did with Pharaoh. First Pharaoh hardened his heart (Exodus 8:32). Then God hardened Pharaoh's heart (Exodus 9:12). It's as if God gives us what we insist on. If we don't want to see, He keeps us from seeing. But that brings on the troubles that bring us to our knees.

It's interesting that God uses drunkenness as an analogy. I have several friends that were alcoholics. Their testimonies have several things in common. They couldn't see where they were headed until they were at rock bottom, had nowhere else to go but total surrender to God, and then they began to see. That is the same pattern for nations and individuals who turn from a vibrant relationship with God.

There are rare times in history when God sovereignly moves to stir hearts even when things are going well. We call these times "awakenings" or "revivals." But the most common pattern throughout the Bible and history is that we will not awaken unless we hit the bottom and have nowhere else to turn. This is where the nation of Judah was headed. They were receiving the leadership they deserved, prophets with closed eyes and seers that covered their heads.

It did not matter if one was a literate scholar or an illiterate laborer. All were in the same condition of being unable to see what was coming or hear the Word from God. *¹¹ And the vision of all this has become to you like the words of a book that is sealed. When men give it to one who can read, saying, "Read this," he says, "I cannot, for it is sealed." ¹² And when they give the book to one who cannot read, saying, "Read this," he says, "I cannot read."* Isaiah 29:11-12 God is emphasizing the blindness of the people to what is coming. They could not see or hear when it came to God's Word. I hear the same thing today. "I just don't understand it when I read it." You have to want to and be willing to hear what it says to us. It is like the parables the Lord used (Matthew 13:13-15). It really is a supernatural thing. For some people it is rich and meaningful, while for others it seems to say nothing. It doesn't matter how educated you are. It's the spiritual condition of your heart that matters (1 Corinthians 1:18-25).

¹³ And the Lord said: "Because this people draw near with their mouth and honor me with their lips, while their hearts are far from me, and their fear of me is a commandment taught by men, Isaiah 29:13 Every time I read this I feel I must pause and examine my heart. It is a stinging indictment. Jesus quoted it when the Pharisees confronted Him about the oral law. Jesus pointed out how they broke God's law and taught others to do the same. He told them this verse was prophesied for them (Mark 7:6-7). It is for everyone that puts rules and the sayings of their culture above God's Word.

If our mouth professes love for God and our actions show a lack of love for man, John declared that we are spiritually dead (1 John 3:14). One of the worst effects of this hypocrisy is that it turns others away from God. But just as bad is the chance that we have deceived ourselves. Religion can have a crippling effect on our spirit. If we think by coming to church and not using curse words and dropping some money in the plate that God is pleased with us, we've missed the point. God wants our whole heart, not just obligatory acts of duty (1 Chronicles 16:29). He is, after all, the Lion God!

The fear of God is a reverence for the glory and honor He deserves (Psalm 90:11). It is knowing that His holy nature requires justice and expects gratitude for grace received. It's knowing that if we are casual about our relationship with Him, He may deal with us to help us know how dependent we are on Him. It's not just an expression we recite.

Because of this hypocrisy and lack of the true fear of God, *¹⁴ therefore, behold, I will again do wonderful things with this people, with wonder upon wonder; and the wisdom of their wise men shall perish, and the discernment of their discerning men shall be hidden."* Isaiah 29:14 "Wonder" is the Old Testament word for the miraculous. God was promising miracle upon miracle in spite of their hypocrisy. The other way to wake people out of their lethargic spiritual condition is to show them the power of the Spirit, something so amazing the wise are dumbfounded and the discerning miss it.

I believe this is not only referring to the coming captivity and restoration, but also to the coming of the Messiah. God's response to our hypocrisy is grace. He will graciously intervene in our lives to wake us and change us. It seems that we have this opportunity in our own lives every time we hit a crisis. When we are up against a wall, we have a chance to take a new direction, to see God at work in our life. We can experience His grace to get us back on track. It may not feel like grace, and certainly may not be what we would have desired, but if it causes us to face the real condition of our heart and invites us to change, then it is certainly the grace of God.

15 Ah, you who hide deep from the LORD your counsel, whose deeds are in the dark, and who say, "Who sees us? Who knows us?" 16 You turn things upside down! Shall the potter be regarded as the clay, that the thing made should say of its maker, "He did not make me"; or the thing formed say of him who formed it, "He has no understanding"? Isaiah 29:15-16 It is ridiculous to think we can hide anything from God (Hebrews 4:13). It is ignorant to think we can avoid the justice of God on our actions. People try so hard to deny the existence of God because they don't want to believe that there is a day of reckoning.

We are seeing this hardness of heart now more than ever. As the evidence for a Creator becomes overwhelming, the explanations of man become more farfetched. The latest theory I've heard to try to explain away our existence is that ours is one of the infinite number of multiverses. The odds of life developing as we know it from what we know of the universe is so impossible that for it to be possible one must increase the possibilities. That does nothing to explain the origin of matter. It does reveal the desperation of man to avoid acknowledging a Creator. It is just as God predicted, the pot is telling the potter He is just part of the clay and has no understanding. But as God explained earlier, they just can't see it. It's sealed to them. The heavens declare the glory of God, but they can't read it (Psalm 19:1; 14:1).

God's viewpoint is right side up. It is to see things as they really are, unbiased truth! Turning things upside down is to make the temporal of greatest importance and the detestable things honored while dishonoring the sacred and eternal.

Again, despite the hardness of the heart of man, the grace of God comes in. The prediction is about the effects of God's intervention in our lives. *18 In that day the deaf shall hear the words of a book, and out of their gloom and darkness the eyes of the blind shall see. 19 The meek shall obtain fresh joy in the LORD, and the poor among mankind shall exult in the Holy One of Israel.* Isaiah 29:18-19 In contrast to those who just could not understand or receive the message, the day was coming when the deaf would hear the words of a book, and out of gloom and darkness blind eyes would see. The words "gloom" and "darkness" points us back to 9:1-2, which is clearly a prediction of the coming Messiah. Not only would Jesus fulfill this literally, but in an even greater way He would cause the spiritually deaf ears and spiritually blind eyes of mankind to hear and see.

The meek were those who could hear and receive the truth to which Jesus opened their eyes (John 9:39; Matthew 5:5). That was the source of their fresh joy. The spiritually poor will be blessed with the kingdom (Matthew 5:3). The physically poor were the bulk of the followers of Jesus, exulting in the Holy One of Israel. Their possessions did not hinder them from receiving His message of laying up treasures in heaven instead of on the earth (Matthew 6:19-21). Jesus' Sermon on the Mount used terms from this passage, showing the fulfillment had come.

These terms of "fresh joy" and "exulting" are contrasts to the vain worshipers who are focused on the commandments of men. It happens today too, doesn't it? Granted, we can go overboard in either direction. We can be so focused on the letter that we neglect the fruit of the Spirit, or we can be so focused on the fruits and feelings we neglect the good boundaries of the Word. We must always seek that balance of worshiping in Spirit and in truth (John 4:24).

In that day when hypocritical worship was normal, religious instruction was the commandments of men, when truth was turned on its head, and when the leaders thought God didn't see what they were up to, into all that gloom and darkness Jesus came. The deaf could hear the Word. The blind could see the truth. Light came into the darkness (Matthew 11:4-6). The poor and meek received the Messiah. Judah would get a preview of this when they returned from captivity and Ezra brought back the importance of the Word (Ezra 10:1; Nehemiah 8:1). But the fullness came with Jesus (John 1:14-17).

Even though it appeared that evil men prospered, yet *[20] For the ruthless shall come to nothing and the scoffer cease, and all who watch to do evil shall be cut off, [21] who by a word make a man out to be an offender, and lay a snare for him who reproves in the gate, and with an empty plea turn aside him who is in the right.* Isaiah 29:20-21 Where is Caiaphas? Where is Herod? Where are all those who predicted the demise of Christianity? Death feeds on them (Psalm 73:18-20). They will stand before the Judge and be asked to give an account. They will receive a just compensation for all their deeds.

The chapter closes with a promise of the greatest revival, the ingathering of the Jewish people to their Messiah. *[22] Therefore thus says the LORD, who redeemed Abraham, concerning the house of Jacob: "Jacob shall no more be ashamed, no more shall his face grow pale. [23] For when he sees his children, the work of my hands, in his midst, they will sanctify my name; they will sanctify the Holy One of Jacob and will stand in awe of the God of Israel. [24] And those who go astray in spirit will come to understanding, and those who murmur will accept instruction."* Isaiah 29:22-24 Anyone who accepts Jesus as Lord can come to understanding (Romans 10:13). The work of God in a child's life can pierce some of the hardest hearts. Though deaf and blind in Isaiah and Jesus' day, God encouraged Isaiah with the promise of a future day when all Israel would be saved (Romans 11:25-26)

Questions
1 What is "ariel"?
2 What question are we often really asking when faced with difficulty?
3 What is the prediction of future grace to Judah?

4 Can God do for us what He will do for Judah?

5 How does God use our stubbornness to turn us?

6 Has 29:13 ever been true of you?

7 How does God respond to our hypocrisy?

8 Why are the actions in verse 16 so common today?

9 How does man explain our world?

10 What is right side up? Upside down?

11 What are the promises that were yet to be fulfilled?

Surprising Ways - Isaiah 30

A good deal of our spiritual life is spent learning to turn from our previous resources to complete trust in the Lord. Jesus told us we needed to be like little children to enter the kingdom of God (Matthew 18:3). Little children know their parents have the answers and trust them for everything. As we get older, we start to think we know it all and wonder what's wrong with our parents. That is what has happened with Judah in this passage. They thought they had a better plan than God. They didn't want God's direction. Too often we find ourselves following this bad example. But we are going to see that God is patient and gracious, and though His ways don't seem to make sense, they are always best.

¹ "Ah, stubborn children," declares the LORD, "who carry out a plan, but not mine, and who make an alliance, but not of my Spirit, that they may add sin to sin; ² who set out to go down to Egypt, without asking for my direction, to take refuge in the protection of Pharaoh and to seek shelter in the shadow of Egypt! Isaiah 30:1-2 This is the fourth woe. The word "Ah" is the same word for "woe" (28:1; 29:1, 15), and this woe is to the stubborn children of God who insist on trusting in something other than God. The previous verses described those who accept the Lord's instruction. The people of Judah who are being addressed in this chapter stubbornly refused God's direction. They had a plan, but it wasn't God's. They had an alliance, but it wasn't with God. They sought direction, but it wasn't from God.

How often is this true of born-again children of God? Times of crisis come, and we learn where our faith is really placed. But it is also revealed in every day decisions. Is our plan God's plan and His direction? Are we looking to God or just operating out of our own whims? Where is our faith placed?

Consider how ridiculous it was for Judah to turn to Egypt. They had been slaves to Egypt in the past. God delivered them through plagues that showed the gods of Egypt were powerless. God showed His mighty power in parting the Red Sea, destroying the army of Pharaoh, providing for them in the wilderness, and defeating the Canaanites before them. Considering their history, what sense did it make to turn to Egypt for help?

Don't we do the same thing? It is so easy to forget how God met us before and showed us He is trustworthy. We forget all the times we looked to Him and found His grace and mercy delivered us from our situation. Instead we turn to the very things that have failed us in the past. We can see them. It doesn't take faith, because it is reasonable to us. But we have lost the faith of child that just runs to Daddy for the answer and help we need.

In verses three through seven Isaiah tells of the envoys that have gone to ask help from Egypt. He declares that instead of help, they will be their shame. The shame is that they were going to pay for help that would never come. It was also in the fact that they were trusting in the very nation they had been delivered from in the past.

God declared that Egypt would be like "Rahab who sits still." Rahab was the harlot that hid the spies, Joshua and Caleb. She did something. She took them up and hid them and later lowered them out her window and down the wall to safety. She risked her life in faith! But Egypt was just a harlot who would receive money but do nothing.

Egypt is a picture of the world system. We often look to its help and even spend our money on it (Mark 5:26). In the final analysis it does nothing lasting for us.

8 And now, go, write it before them on a tablet and inscribe it in a book, that it may be for the time to come as a witness forever. 9 For they are a rebellious people, lying children, children unwilling to hear the instruction of the LORD; Isaiah 30:8-9 The people of Judah were so hardened toward the Lord that God told Isaiah that his prophecy wasn't for this people but for a future people. That's because these people were unwilling to hear it. They were going through all the religious rituals but without any relationship with God or desire to hear His counsel (29:13).

They did have a desire to hear something though. *10 who say to the seers, "Do not see," and to the prophets, "Do not prophesy to us what is right; speak to us smooth things, prophesy illusions, 11 leave the way, turn aside from the path, let us hear no more about the Holy One of Israel."* Isaiah 30:10-11 Notice that they know they are asking for a lie. They don't want to hear from God or hear more about Him. Sometimes what God has to say to us is comforting. Sometimes it's a slap in the face to wake us up. *We go deep by making our hearts vulnerable to truths most offensive, yet most salutary and essential.* (Raymund Ortberg - Preaching the Word – Isaiah: God Saves Sinners p 173)

God had already told them He would deliver Jerusalem from Assyria. He also warned them that eventually they would go into captivity because of the hardness of their hearts. Who wants to hear that? We need to hear the truth, but we often desire to hear a lie. They didn't want to hear about the Holy One of Israel because He requires that we be holy as He is holy (1 Peter 1:16).

This goes back to the point at the beginning of the chapter. They wanted to do it their way and not God's way (Proverbs 14:12). We are so used to just following our whims when we really need to be looking to God for His plan for our daily choices. It is easy for a believer indwelt by the Spirit to stop for a moment and just check in your spirit if you believe what you are about to do is the Lord's direction or your own. The question is, are we willing? Judah wasn't willing, and that would be quite costly.

We see the same desire today to hear a happy message. Some churches preach a prosperity message that is all hope and happiness. There is no word of final judgment or of the fall of nations that turn from God (Psalm 9:17). "Hell" is an unmentioned word and even in some cases dismissed as an antiquated idea (2Timothy 4:3).

 ¹² Therefore thus says the Holy One of Israel, "Because you despise this word and trust in oppression and perverseness and rely on them, ¹³ therefore this iniquity shall be to you like a breach in a high wall, bulging out, and about to collapse, whose breaking comes suddenly, in an instant; ¹⁴ and its breaking is like that of a potter's vessel that is smashed so ruthlessly that among its fragments not a shard is found with which to take fire from the hearth, or to dip up water out of the cistern." Isaiah 30:12-14 The warning is to those who despise the Word of the LORD. The apostle John told us the Word was made flesh and dwelt among us (John 1:14). When we reject our relationship with Jesus, the natural repercussions are the damage resulting from our misplaced trust. The Jews had been oppressed by Egypt and now they are turning to Egypt for help. How perverse is that? The result is like a chunk of a high wall falling on your head. It's like a clay vessel so violently smashed that there isn't even a spoon size piece left. Nothing of any value remains. That is what we get when despise God's word and instead trust in man, which is to trust in oppression and perverseness.

 ¹⁵ For thus said the Lord GOD, the Holy One of Israel, "In returning and rest you shall be saved; in quietness and in trust shall be your strength." But you were unwilling, Isaiah 30:15 Isaiah uses numerous words that have double meanings. One of them was in the previous verse, "perverseness." He said they trusted in it. The word can also mean "to depart." They trusted in departing from the Lord. Now God says to return and rest in Him would mean salvation. They didn't need to pay off Egypt. They just needed to return to the Lord and the Lord would save them like He had in the past.

If they stilled their fears and quietly trusted God to be their strength, they could rest in Him. They could enjoy His salvation from Assyria. But they were unwilling. How often is this true of us? We run around trying to find solutions or some way we can resolve something or escape some problem but don't quietly put our trust in God. We have to first have a heart that is willing to trust and have faith in Him (Proverbs 3:5-6). That is the place of quiet rest. Whatever problems you face, this is the solution. Look to God. Trust Him. Get His plan and direction. Then quietly proceed in faith as you rest in Him. It won't always turn out like you hope, but God will always be faithful to work through it for your good (Romans 8:28).

The leadership of Judah responded with an alternative. They were going to get Egypt's help and if that failed, try to flee on horseback. They would be caught. And because of their rebellious heart that despised God's Word, when Babylon would conquer them, the following verse would come

124

to pass. *¹⁷ A thousand shall flee at the threat of one; at the threat of five you shall flee, till you are left like a flagstaff on the top of a mountain, like a signal on a hill.* Isaiah 30:17 It was the opposite of what God had promised them if they would obey His commandments. Five Israelites were supposed to chase a hundred of the enemy (Leviticus 26:8). God was on the side of their enemy. There would only be a small remnant left in the land.

¹⁸ Therefore the LORD waits to be gracious to you, and therefore he exalts himself to show mercy to you. For the LORD is a God of justice; blessed are all those who wait for him. Isaiah 30:18 The LORD is waiting for us to wait for Him. He is exalted in showing us mercy. He is a God of justice and must be just. He must have a reason to show mercy. God was greatly exalted in sending His Son to take our sin's just punishment that He might extend mercy to us. The promise is that those who wait for the Lord, instead of running of to solve problems in their own way, will be blessed. Are we waiting on the Lord (Psalm 27:14)?

Once again, God has declared the sin of Judah and then speaks of His unfailing love and desire for them. He is the same for all who would come to Him through His provision of His Son, Jesus (John 1:12). The prophecy pictures the distant future. There is partial fulfillment and an ultimate fulfillment. Some would say this is just prophetic language that shouldn't be taken literally. Sometimes that may be the case, but I believe the details of this prophecy will ultimately come to pass literally.

¹⁹ For a people shall dwell in Zion, in Jerusalem; you shall weep no more. He will surely be gracious to you at the sound of your cry. As soon as he hears it, he answers you. Isaiah 30:19 God is just waiting for them to turn to Him. This happened when the angel slew the Assyrians. It happened when Jews cried out for the Messiah under the oppression of Rome. It will happen again in the day of Jacob's Trouble (Jeremiah 30:7).

²⁰ And though the Lord give you the bread of adversity and the water of affliction, yet your Teacher will not hide himself anymore, but your eyes shall see your Teacher. Isaiah 30:20 In a remote way this was fulfilled as a shadow under Ezra at the time of the return to the Land (Ezra 7:10). It was definitely true when Jesus ministered in Israel (John 18:20). It will ultimately be true in the Millennial Kingdom. Imagine going to the city of God to bring a question to the King of kings!

²¹ And your ears shall hear a word behind you, saying, "This is the way, walk in it," when you turn to the right or when you turn to the left. Isaiah 30:21 While Ezra would teach them the Word of God which would serve this purpose, Jesus would send the Holy Spirit, the fullness of this promise (John 14:26). The Spirit was poured out to guide us moment by moment as we walk with the Lord. We have two extremes within the church today. One is looking only to the Word. The other is looking only to the Spirit. But the Biblical way is a balance of both. The Spirit will not contradict the Word. The Word is often the voice of the Spirit. The letter without the Spirit kills (2 Corinthians 3:6). The Word is only as good as it is

interpreted correctly, and for that we need the Holy Spirit to guide us (1 John 2:27).

While the chapter started with rebellious people that were refusing to listen and had a plan that wasn't God's plan, it ends with a people who listen to the Word and are obedient to His plan and direction. God is always offering us hope. He is always showing us that our fallen nature has a remedy.

22 Then you will defile your carved idols overlaid with silver and your gold-plated metal images. You will scatter them as unclean things. You will say to them, "Be gone!" Isaiah 30:22 The Spirit filled life abhors anything that gets in the way of devotion to Jesus. The temptations of the world are seen for the destructive things that they are and are forsaken.

There is another word play here. God chose the word "alliance" to describe what Judah desired with Egypt (see verse one). The same word can be translated "molten image." Egypt was their idol. When we are walking with the Lord, acting at His direction, following His plan, we will reject the idolatry of trusting in man (Jeremiah 17:5).

The passage continues with a description of the Millennial Kingdom's abundance. *25 And on every lofty mountain and every high hill there will be brooks running with water, in the day of the great slaughter, when the towers fall. 26 Moreover, the light of the moon will be as the light of the sun, and the light of the sun will be sevenfold, as the light of seven days, in the day when the LORD binds up the brokenness of his people, and heals the wounds inflicted by his blow.* Isaiah 30:25-26 Isaiah already spoke of the great earthquake in the end-time that will shake the world (24:19). It will usher in the Millennium and Jesus' reign on the earth.

Though the brooks may possibly be literal, Jesus spoke of the indwelling Spirit as a well of water springing up (John 4:14). Certainly, the brightness of light must be figurative because we'd all fry if the moon was like the sun. I take both of these expressions as meaning the Word of God and the teaching of Scripture is thoroughly known throughout the earth. Jeremiah predicted in that day no one will say, "Know the Lord," for all will know Him (Jeremiah 31:34). Isaiah predicted the earth will be filled with the knowledge of the Lord (Isaiah 11:9).

The rest of the chapter speaks of the Lord coming in judgment on the nations of the world and uses Assyria as an example. While the nations are defeated at Armageddon, the people of God will be celebrating. *29 You shall have a song as in the night when a holy feast is kept, and gladness of heart, as when one sets out to the sound of the flute to go to the mountain of the LORD, to the Rock of Israel. 30 And the LORD will cause his majestic voice to be heard and the descending blow of his arm to be seen, in furious anger and a flame of devouring fire, with a cloudburst and storm and hailstones.* Isaiah 30:29-30 Remember at the beginning of the last chapter there was a monotony to worship at the feasts. In this day to come when the Lord appears and saves Israel, worship will be sincere. There will be a song during such devastation, because evil is being defeated. All those who have set themselves against the goodness of God will be judged. The reign of the prince of this world will be over. The physical kingdom of Jesus on earth will begin.

How gracious of God to show this rebellious people the glorious future. But remember, God said it was written for those in the future who could learn from Judah's iniquity. Are we learning to look to God and trust Him rather than our own ingenuity and cunning? Are we trusting God or man? That does not mean God cannot use man. But where is your trust placed? Are you seeking His plan? Are you finding your strength in quietness and trust? Are you willingly listening for His voice of direction and following it? Man will fail you. God never will.

Questions
1 What is the message of the fourth woe?
2 How does it apply to us?
3 How is the world like "Rahab who sits still"?
4 Why was Isaiah writing this down?
5 Why didn't they want to hear?
6 What was the warning?
7 What are two of the words with double meanings? How are they used?
8 What was God's invitation? Why didn't they accept it?
9 What is God waiting for?
10 What are 3 fulfillments of verse 20?
11 What does the end of the chapter predict?

Trusting Man - Isaiah 31

Living in a fallen world with fallen people means inevitable difficulties. Trying situations and conflict are a part of human life that we simply can't escape. In these chapters, God addresses Judah and us so as to confront us about how we deal with these difficulties. He is asking us to take a look at where we really place our trust. Do we have idols that we depend on, idols like money, or human strength, or ingenuity, or the wisdom of others? Where do we turn first for help?
¹ Woe to those who go down to Egypt for help and rely on horses, who trust in chariots because they are many and in horsemen because they are very strong, but do not look to the Holy One of Israel or consult the LORD! Isaiah 31:1 This is Isaiah's fifth woe to Judah. It is the same message as the previous chapter. Have you noticed that when we don't get the message God is trying to teach us, He will often repeat it whether by bringing up the same message or difficulty again and again. The message bears repeating. Where is our trust placed? Is man the pinnacle of all things or is God?

The leaders of Judah thought they could defeat Assyria with the help of Egypt or escape by horseback if the situation got too bad. Why is it that we fail to look to the Commander of the armies of heaven? Perhaps it because we know He would tell us to repent and change our ways. David wrote, *⁷ Some trust in chariots and some in horses, but we trust in the name of the LORD our God.* Psalm 20:7 David trusted in the Lord rather than might, and he was victorious. That is why in his later years he was punished so severely for numbering his soldiers (2 Samuel 24:1). God pronounces a curse on all who trust in man, who make flesh their strength, whose heart departs from the LORD. (Jeremiah 17:5). Why would we put ourselves under that curse? Do we first consult with God or with man? Do we go to prayer or to the phone to call someone who might have an answer we seek?

This does not mean that God will never direct you to others for help or use natural means. Isaiah will tell Hezekiah of a natural remedy for an illness, but the direction to use it came from the Lord (2 Kings 20:7). Hasn't He given us common sense? Sure. But do you look to it first or to the LORD first? The LORD may direct you to use that common sense solution or He may not, but His answer is always best.

² And yet he is wise and brings disaster; he does not call back his words, but will arise against the house of the evildoers and against the helpers of those who work iniquity. Isaiah 31:2 God is all wise and knows what we need, even if it is disaster. The near total disaster brought by Assyria still did not save Jerusalem from defeat by the Babylonians. God has already said Judah's iniquity will not be atoned for until they die (Isaiah 22:14; Numbers 23:19). God knew they would not turn for long, but He speaks a word of warning for those in the future who read this, and possibly for a few individuals who did turn to Him.

³ The Egyptians are man, and not God, and their horses are flesh, and not spirit. When the LORD stretches out his hand, the helper will stumble, and he who is helped will fall, and they will all perish together. Isaiah 31:3 Egypt is symbolic of Satan and worldliness. Even if Egypt came in all its strength, what the Lord determines will come to pass. Nothing can stop Him from doing His will. How foolish to trust in man instead of God! We are so prone to walk by sight instead of by faith in our all-powerful, loving God.

⁴ For thus the LORD said to me, "As a lion or a young lion growls over his prey, and when a band of shepherds is called out against him he is not terrified by their shouting or daunted at their noise, so the LORD of hosts will come down to fight on Mount Zion and on its hill. Isaiah 31:4 Once again we come to a verse that has an immediate fulfillment and an ultimate one. What tips us off is the language that is used. First, intermediate fulfillments are often figurative and partial, whereas the ultimate ones are usually quite literal and conclusive. The Lord will send His angel to spare Jerusalem from Assyria (Isaiah 37:36), but only after all the other walled cities are taken. While the angel of the Lord may actually be the Lord Jesus,

Assyria is outside the city, not on Mt. Zion. So we see it doesn't match completely with the immediate events.

The second clue is often the language God employs. "As a lion" causes us to think of the Lion of the tribe of Judah, the Messiah, or of Ariel, the lion God. A band of shepherds reminds us of the evil shepherds in Ezekiel's prophecy and of those who convicted Jesus (Ezekiel 34:2). The lack of fear reminds us of Jesus before Pilate (John 19:10-11). We see Jesus as the Lord of hosts in Joshua 5:13-15. There we read of a man who is that commander who declares the ground where He stood was holy and commanded Joshua to take off his shoes just as God told Moses from the burning bush (Exodus 3:5-6). Joshua called this man "the LORD" (Joshua 6:2)

The ultimate fulfillment of verse 4, of *the LORD of hosts will come down to fight on Mount Zion and on its hill,* (Isaiah 31:4) is Jesus on Calvary of Mount Zion waging war against Satan and the fallen angels. Jesus was not daunted by the jeering religious leaders (Mark 15:29-32). He is the Lion of Judah, and the prize He has claimed is the souls of all who will come to Him. He covers, or makes atonement for, the city of peace (Jerusalem). They are those who have found peace in Him (Luke 2:14). He delivers them from the clutches of Satan. He covers us, as we will see in the next verse. That was the joy set before Him, for which He endured the cross (Hebrews 12:2)

Our Christmas message last year was about the Lord coming down to the womb of Mary to eventually wage war on our behalf on Calvary. The name "Lord of Hosts" means the Commander of the Armies of Heaven, but Jesus did not need His army (Luke 12:53). He overcame Satan with His sacrificial death, something Satan could not comprehend. Jesus is the super warrior of which all our hero stories are just a shadow (Jeremiah 20:11). He has already won the greatest battle through the most amazing means anyone could imagine.

5 Like birds hovering, so the LORD of hosts will protect Jerusalem; he will protect and deliver it; he will spare and rescue it." Isaiah 31:5 Like a mother bird spreading her wings over her chicks, so the Lord has come down to protect us from being Satan's prey. This imagery is used in Deuteronomy 32:11 to describe God's care for His people (Psalm 91:4).

"Spare" in the ESV is the Hebrew word that is also translated "passover." It reminds us of the blood-stained doors on the night of the last plague. The blood on the doorposts was the sign that God would hover over them and protect them from the plague of the death of the firstborn (Exodus 12:13). The language God gave Isaiah reminded the people of their beginnings and the love and care God had for them, and still had if they would just turn to Him. It is for us as well.

6 Turn to him from whom people have deeply revolted, O children of Israel. Isaiah 31:6 To turn is to repent. Salvation has always come to those who repent and trust in God. Jesus made it possible, regardless of whether it was before or after the cross. We are saved when we turn from our sins to God, from trust in self and self-rule, to the Lordship of Jesus. Though it is the Jews who were being addressed, it has always been true for all people who would turn to Him. Consider Jesus' example of the Gentiles to whom the prophets were sent (Luke 4:25-27).

The phrase, "From who people have deeply revolted," is such a sad expression. It breaks my heart to think of how we, as fallen beings, can so despise the One who loves us enough to die in our place. We can be so sin sick that we despise the greatest love of all. This verse is repeating the message in the previous chapter (Isaiah 30:15). Return and find God to be your rest and your salvation.

When we return to God we find our values were upside down. We detest the things we once sought after and love that which we despised. *⁷ For in that day everyone shall cast away his idols of silver and his idols of gold, which your hands have sinfully made for you.* Isaiah 31:7 Real help is found in returning to God to place our trust and reliance upon Him. He is the only place of true rest (Matthew 11:28). Quietly listening to His reassuring voice can become our strength.

This is a verse about the day in which the Jews would finally turn. As yet they were unwilling. The revival after the Assyrian army was slain was short-lived. The next king would dive headlong into idolatry (2 Kings 21:1-2). But those who would turn to the Lion of the tribe of Judah, to the One who would defeat our ultimate enemy, they would forsake all idols, all things that come between God and us.

⁸ "And the Assyrian shall fall by a sword, not of man; and a sword, not of man, shall devour him; and he shall flee from the sword, and his young men shall be put to forced labor. Isaiah 31:8 The angel of the Lord will wield the sword (2 Kings 19:35) and the Babylonian, Scythian, Chaldean, Medes, and Persian armies fulfilled the Word of God in this verse.

⁹ His rock shall pass away in terror, and his officers desert the standard in panic," declares the LORD, *whose fire is in Zion, and whose furnace is in Jerusalem.* Isaiah 31:9 Isaiah again uses the language of Deuteronomy 32. In that chapter, verse 31 tells us *³¹For their rock is not as our Rock; our enemies are by themselves.* There is no god with them. The gods they trust in aren't real. The previous chapter in Isaiah reminded the people of Judah that their Rock is the LORD (Isaiah 30:29).

Isaiah 30:33 told us a burning place was prepared for Israel's enemies and the breath of the Lord would kindle it. Once again, I believe we can see the double meaning. The Assyrians would flee in a panic when the sword of the Lord slew 185,000 of them. But Assyria as an enemy bent on destroying God's heritage represents another power. It's the power that would annihilate the lineage of David so that the Messiah would not come. It's the power that slew the children of Bethlehem (Matthew 2:16). The rock of this world will pass away in terror. His officers (fallen angels) will desert their standard in panic, for the Lake of Fire is prepared for the devil and his angels (Matthew 25:41).

¹ Behold, a king will reign in righteousness, and princes will rule in justice. Isaiah 32:1 If we weren't sure that the previous chapter (31) pointed

130

to the coming of Jesus, it becomes more clear when we see that Isaiah has moved on to the kingdom of the Messiah. The defeat of evil ushers in the reign of the Messiah. It's the pattern we have already seen, an intermediate partial fulfillment or shadow of what was to come, the coming of the Messiah and a spiritual fulfillment, and the total fulfillment in the Millennial Kingdom. The only righteous king is Jesus. The only princes that rule with total justice will be ruling under the King of Righteousness. If you don't get justice here, don't be surprised. No government of man can guarantee justice.

Some theologians are opposed to the idea of multiple fulfilments. The majority today believe prophecies were for the time in which they were written and not meant to be understood as Messianic. This goes against New Testament Scripture and Jesus' words (Luke 24:44). Others try to divide prophecies up as only for then or only for the future. My conviction is that prophecies of the Messiah are ultimately about the first coming or Messianic reign but may be foreshadowed in part by immediate events. We have seen this already in a number of prophecies by Isaiah.

2 Each will be like a hiding place from the wind, a shelter from the storm, like streams of water in a dry place, like the shade of a great rock in a weary land. Isaiah 32:2 What a relief it will be to know we can count on justice to always prevail in the day Jesus reigns on the earth. All leaders will be godly and appointed by Jesus. Though the freewill of man will still cause pain and loss, those living in that day can run to a godly ruler and know justice will prevail.

3 Then the eyes of those who see will not be closed, and the ears of those who hear will give attention. Isaiah 32:3 Though everyone will have an intellectual knowledge of God, the heart of man must still surrender to Him to have a relationship of submission to Him.

4 The heart of the hasty will understand and know, and the tongue of the stammerers will hasten to speak distinctly. Isaiah 32:4 In a previous chapter we saw those who trusted in the cornerstone would not be in haste (Isaiah 28:16). Many in the Millennial Kingdom will trust the Cornerstone. Those who have been given spiritual sight and hearing will continue to grow and not backslide, as opposed to those who did not want to see or hear and remained blind and deaf the things of God (Isaiah 30:10). And those who once had trouble sharing the Gospel and testimonies of what God had done in their life will become eloquent witnesses.

5 The fool will no more be called noble, nor the scoundrel said to be honorable. Isaiah 32:5 When the fool is exalted, and scoundrel is honored, society is in trouble. We have plenty of that, but so does every culture that turns from God. Imagine the day when that will no longer be a problem and every leader will be righteous and just.

6 For the fool speaks folly, and his heart is busy with iniquity, to practice ungodliness, to utter error concerning the LORD, to leave the craving of the hungry unsatisfied, and to deprive the thirsty of drink. 7 As for the scoundrel—his devices are evil; he plans wicked schemes to ruin the poor with lying words, even when the plea of the needy is right. Isaiah 32:6-

7 God is reminding them of what is wrong with their current social order, but He is also directing them to look to a future day when God will make sure that justice is served and the needs of all are met.

⁸ But he who is noble plans noble things, and on noble things he stands. Isaiah 32:8 His reign is coming. It is here now in the hearts of those who are surrendered to Him (Luke 17:21). This is God's noble plan. The Millennial Kingdom will be the final example for man to realize how much we need the Lord. The first couple had all they needed in the Garden of Eden but they still rebelled (Genesis 3:6). Jesus' reign on earth will show man a similar lesson.

The history of man has shown us man's governments of every sort fail eventually because the heart of man is evil (Jeremiah 17:9). The Millennial Kingdom will show us all that even if Christ reigns, and even if we are aware of the devil's schemes, many will still choose to rebel against God (Revelation 20:7-8) Nevertheless, it is God's noble plan that will prevail. How noble of God to go to such great lengths to show us how much we need Him and the greatness of His love for us.

Judah would not hear the message of grace and turn to God. Will we? They would once again face a siege that would result in captivity. I close with two quotes from Oswald Chambers' devotional. "What hinders me from hearing is that I'm taken up with other things." "The way in which I show God that I neither love nor respect Him is by the obtuseness of my heart and mind toward what He says." (Oswald Chambers, *My Utmost for His Highest,* February 13)

May the Lord help us to hear and receive God's Word in our mind and heart!

Questions
1 What problem is God addressing?
2 How did David's life demonstrate this?
3 What is more powerful, flesh or spirit?
4 How do we know verse 4 is Messianic?
5 How was it fulfilled?
6 What is the word "spare" in verse 5?
7 How does verses 6 and 7 go together?
8 Which "rock" is reliable?
9 Are you looking forward to 30:1-4?
10 What is wrong with our present culture? How will it change?

True Security - Isaiah 32:9-33:6

As we read the prophecies of Isaiah we need to keep in mind the overarching themes of the book: the coming captivity, the restoration, the coming Messiah and His kingdom. At this point in the text, the northern tribes had already gone into captivity (2 Kings 17:22-23). The southern tribes, referred to as Judah, were facing the powerful Assyrians. The questions on the minds of God's people were how would the dynasty of David continue and bring the Messiah if Assyria defeated them, and would they ever see the kingdom of God established? Our question today is, "Are we doomed to repeat the destructive cycle of the history of nations?"

When we read the text with these questions in mind, we can see God addressing both the sinners and the saints in Jerusalem. The sinners are warned of eventual judgment. The saints are encouraged with the promise of temporary relief and the ultimate coming of the Messiah and His kingdom.

God has already spoken to the men of Judah who trusted in Egypt (Isaiah 31:1). He has warned them of their rebellious refusal to hear from Him (Isaiah 30:9). He told them their effort to buy Egypt's help would just be to their shame (Isaiah 30:5).

Today our passage addresses the women of Judah. While the men are wringing their hands and trying to come up with a plan, the women went about complacent. God had already spoken to them quite sternly with a frightening warning in chapter three (Isaiah 3:24-26), but they did not listen. The loving faithfulness of God is warning them again and pleading with them to hear Him.

⁹ Rise up, you women who are at ease, hear my voice; you complacent daughters, give ear to my speech. ¹⁰ In little more than a year you will shudder, you complacent women; for the grape harvest fails, the fruit harvest will not come. Isaiah 32:9-10 The first warning to the women came quite a while before this one. Complacency had set in. While the men could see it coming, the women were at ease and just enjoying their worldly pleasures. But those pleasures were about to cease. To help end their complacency, God graciously gave them a timeframe. The physical things they looked to would fail them. Hardship was coming.

While God was about to rescue undeserving Judah, I imagine the crops and fields had been destroyed by the army of Assyria. It was the practice of invading armies to ruin the crops and cut the trees of a land they wanted to conquer. It was a way to destroy any future hope of the people they were fighting.

¹¹ Tremble, you women who are at ease, shudder, you complacent ones; strip, and make yourselves bare, and tie sackcloth around your waist. ¹² Beat your breasts for the pleasant fields, for the fruitful vine, ¹³ for the soil of my people growing up in thorns and briers, yes, for all the joyous houses in the exultant city. Isaiah 32:11-13 While the physical destruction of crops is still in the future, God is using it as an analogy of the bad soil of the people of Judah. They had a godly king, but they did not want to hear from God. They wanted the blessings of godly leadership, but they wanted to go their own way. They said, "Don't tell us anymore about the Holy One of Israel." Isaiah 30:11 They even mocked Isaiah's prophecies. God was telling the women that this is what they should be lamenting, bad soil and the bad fruit of the people of Judah. It's one thing to lose physical blessings, but it is much more ominous to lose a nation's spiritual health. That ends in a greater disaster both physically and spiritually.

How is the soil in the USA? How is the fruit of our nation? A vile film of perversion is a big hit this Valentine season. I won't even mention the name. It is simply soft porn and the Bible belt is where it's making the most money. The abortion industry receives federal funds. We hear on a regular basis how some expression of our Christian faith has come under fire. The majority of our states allow homosexual marriages. If we dare to comment on the destructiveness of that lifestyle we are labeled as bigots. Are we complacent? Are we at ease like the women of Zion? Perhaps it is we who should beat our breasts and don sackcloth as we cry out to the Lord for the hearts of people to have a desire to hear the Word of the Lord.

God said the people were growing up in thorns and briars. Jesus used this picture in the parable of the sower. You can always find that the expressions of Jesus have their source in the Old Testament. Don't think for a moment that it is not as every bit as valuable as the New Testament. Jesus explained to His disciples that the thorns and briars were the worries of this life, deceitfulness of wealth, and desires for other things that choked them and made them unfruitful (Mark 4:18-19; Matthew 13:22). Judah's prosperity was a blessing on King Hezekiah's obedience. But prosperity can tend toward complacency. This was the condition of Judah which was about to face a wakeup call from God. It was a message for the joyous houses in the exultant city.

14 For the palace is forsaken, the populous city deserted; the hill and the watchtower will become dens forever, a joy of wild donkeys, a pasture of flocks; 15 until the Spirit is poured upon us from on high, and the wilderness becomes a fruitful field, and the fruitful field is deemed a forest. Isaiah 32:14-15 God will deliver them, but eventually it will take captivity to turn their hearts back to God. The prophecy now looks forward and tells the people of Judah who are willing to hear, the saints, that even though God will rescue them in the immediate future, the day is coming when captivity must take place. But that doesn't mean the promises of God will fail. In fact, it is a fulfillment of the promises of God. God promised the Jews that if they ignored His Word and worshiped idols that they would end up in a foreign land (Deuteronomy 28:36). He warned through Isaiah earlier that God would speak to them through a people of a foreign language (Isaiah 28:11).

What is the solution to this cycle of blessing, complacency, rebellion, judgment, and repentance? It is the pouring out of the Spirit of God on those who come to the Messiah. Only the fire of the Holy Spirit can cause us to move forward in the process of sanctification (Isaiah 30:21). If left to our own strength, we will backslide every time. Only the Spirit of God indwelling us can convict us to repent and forsake sin. Only He can replace complacency with zeal. In Him we can enter into intercessory prayer for our nation and individuals caught up in the deception of sin's lying promises (Romans 8:27).

Thank God we live in a day in which the Spirit has been poured out. We live after the coming of Messiah who by His Spirit indwells all who come to Him. We can choose to move forward as a child of God. We are NOT doomed to a repeated cycle of apathy, fruitlessness, repentance, and restoration. To some extent we experience that cycle in a small measure day by day, but we don't have to go to the extremes the nation of Judah was experiencing.

When as a believer you find yourself slip into complacency and being at ease, build yourself up in your most holy faith (Jude 1:20). Turn on some praise music. Open your Bible. Sit down in prayer and tell God you aren't getting up until you hear Him speak to your heart. There are desperate prayer needs everywhere. Lift them up to God with your whole heart and you'll find the zeal you were lacking (2 Timothy 1:6).

The wording of the prophecy now takes on that of the Messianic Kingdom. *16 Then justice will dwell in the wilderness, and righteousness abide in the fruitful field. 17 And the effect of righteousness will be peace, and the result of righteousness, quietness and trust forever.* Isaiah 32:16-17 Unlike the kingdoms of this world, the Messiah's kingdom will be thoroughly just and righteous throughout. That will result in peace, quietness and trust forever. The Hebrew word for "trust" and "security" is the same *(betah)*. The women of Zion had a false sense of security. Our only real security is in the Lord.

These verses are true of any individual whose faith is placed in God. If, through your life in Christ, you are just and righteous, the effect on your life will be peace with God. When we are at peace with God, we have nothing to fear, for we know that He can see us through whatever we face (2 Timothy 1:7). The result is a life of quietness, trust, and security. We rest in knowing where we are headed and who and what awaits us.

The false security of the women in Zion was trust in their wealth and the warriors of Zion. They were no match for what was coming. The women's complacency would turn to horrible fear. But there would be those who trusted in God. Next week we'll see that the king trusted in God at first (2 Kings 18:7), but when things looked bad, he turned to wealth to save him (2 Kings 18:15-16). Finally, when wealth failed him, he turned to God as His last resort. God still graciously kept His promises, when He had reasons to abandon them.

18 My people will abide in a peaceful habitation, in secure dwellings, and in quiet resting places. 19 And it will hail when the forest falls down, and the city will be utterly laid low. 20 Happy are you who sow beside all waters, who let the feet of the ox and the donkey range free. Isaiah 32:18-20 "My people" in the Old Testament is a reference to the people of Israel. However, Hosea predicted that Gentiles would also be called "the people of God" (Hosea 1:10; Romans 9:26). Some commentators believe that only Jews will reign with Christ in the Millennial Kingdom. My personal opinion is that all the redeemed reign with Him. Thus, "my people will abide in peaceful habitations" would apply to all the redeemed who reign with Christ in the Millennium.

There is a contrast of words in verse 18 with those that describe the women in 9 through 11. The women are at ease and carefree because of a false hope. That is contrasted with the condition of those in the Messiah's kingdom who are at ease because of righteousness and true peace. The sense of being carefree can come from false security or from true security. The false sense of security will be dashed and make the fear and calamity even greater. The true security that comes through faith will never disappoint us.

Verse 19 jumps back to the warning of what must happen first. Before the Messiah's Kingdom is established, Judah must first be disciplined. Some think this is referring to the Assyrian capital while others, myself included, think this is a reminder that Jerusalem will eventually fall. They can't put their hope in the city. It must be placed in God alone if we are to dwell in peace.

Then verse 20 returns to the joy and abundance of the kingdom of God. Every effort will bring a good result. Every obedient act today will bear fruit too, when we are obedient to the leading of God through His Spirit. As waters are a picture of the people of the world in Scripture (Revelation 17:15), and as productivity has been related to spiritual condition, this may be a poetic way of predicting the joy of those called to missions. While in the Millennial Kingdom all will know of Jesus and the message of salvation, I believe there will still be the need of teaching and sharing faith with the nations of the world. The closing line of the free ranging ox and donkey is about the lack of concern for predators. The lion will lie down with the lamb (Isaiah 11:6).

The promise of the coming victory continues in the next chapter. 33:1 begins with the sixth and final woe. The first five were to Israel. This final one is to their enemy, Assyria. After Assyria accepted a fee of gold and silver to turn away from their attack, they went back on their promise and insisted on surrender. *¹ Ah, you destroyer, who yourself have not been destroyed, you traitor, whom none has betrayed! When you have ceased to destroy, you will be destroyed; and when you have finished betraying, they will betray you.* Isaiah 33:1 Sennacherib was a treacherous destroyer and he would meet his end in treachery by his own sons (2 Kings 19:37). Babylon would destroy the nation of Assyria just as Assyria had put an end to other nations. Even nations reap what they sow.

² O LORD, be gracious to us; we wait for you. Be our arm every morning, our salvation in the time of trouble. Isaiah 33:2 Seeing the gracious and merciful hand of God now turned against the enemy of Judah, Isaiah breaks out in a prayer for his nation. Be gracious! They didn't deserve it, but they certainly would welcome it.

In a previous passage God declared He was waiting on them to wait on Him. Now that every hope of man had failed, Judah was willing to wait on God (Isaiah 30:18). Isaiah is praying back to God what God had promised. God said He was waiting to be gracious and bless those who wait on Him. God didn't say, "Unless I'm their last resort." He had no such conditions. Isaiah seized on it and made it a petition.

"Be our arm," means to be their strength and deliverance. Later in Isaiah, God refers to the Messiah as "the arm of the Lord" (Isaiah 53:1). In the passage next week, we'll see how Jesus related to this passage as the divine warrior.

Even though it was a time of trouble, God was still willing to be their Savior. We can wait till the last moment, but why? Isn't it better to turn now? Only God knows if we will have another opportunity. The more we harden our heart, the easier it is to think we'll have another chance, when we just continue to grow harder until our end.

³ At the tumultuous noise peoples flee; when you lift yourself up, nations are scattered, ⁴ and your spoil is gathered as the caterpillar gathers; as locusts leap, it is leapt upon. Isaiah 33:3-4 Moses declared, *³ The LORD is a man of war; the LORD is his name.* Exodus 15:3 When He lifts Himself, which means to act, the nations are in tumult. He can take what He will from one nation and give it to another. Nothing and no one can stand against Him (Malachi 3:2)!

⁵ The LORD is exalted, for he dwells on high; he will fill Zion with justice and righteousness, ⁶ and he will be the stability of your times, abundance of salvation, wisdom, and knowledge; the fear of the LORD is Zion's treasure. Isaiah 33:5-6 God was the stability of Hezekiah's reign. While the people turned back to God, there was justice and righteousness. There was wisdom and knowledge. The fear of the Lord was their treasure. But like all nations and kingdoms of man, it did not last long. *Righteousness exalts a nation, but sin is a reproach to any people*. Proverbs 14:34

The next king would be the nation's tipping point. Each generation must have their own relationship with God. Though they would hear the story of God's miraculous deliverance, they would turn to other gods. Injustice would become rampant. Innocent blood would saturate the ground (2 Kings 21:16). And God would keep His promise to send them into captivity to purge them of the evil that threatened to end them as a people.

The message never changes. God is God and we are not. We so desperately need to hear Him for our good, but we seem to only turn as a last resort. There is a solution for this condition. The Spirit has been poured out. Your heavenly Father longs to fill you to overflowing (Luke 11:13). He invites you to ask Him, to wait on Him, and He will be your salvation. He will be the voice behind you saying, "This is the way. Walk in it" (Isaiah 30:21). Are you at ease in the world or in God?

Questions
1 What were the saints' fears?
2 What was wrong with the women?
3 Which passage did Jesus refer to?
4 What is the cycle? The solution?
5 What does righteousness yield?

6 What words were contrasted?

7 What might verse 20 refer to?

8 What is true security?

9 Why is the sixth woe different?

10 Go over Isaiah's prayer.

Just in Time - Isaiah 33:7-24

Why do we have to get to the very end of all our human resources before we will finally look to God? I suppose it is our fallen human nature. Oswald Chambers asked and answered a similar question: "Why are we so terrified lest God should speak to us? Because we know that if God does speak, either the thing must be done, or we must tell God we will not obey Him. If it is only the servant's voice we hear, we feel it is not imperative, we can say, 'Well, that is simply your own idea, though I don't deny it is probably God's truth.'" (Oswald Chamber, *My Utmost for His Highest,* February 12)

It's not as dangerous to listen to a sermon as it is to get quiet and ask God to speak to you through His Word. Or perhaps we could say it is easier to justify disobedience when there is a human messenger involved. But either way, the Holy Spirit is the One who is convicting us. It may be easier in our mind, but it is never justifiable to ignore Him.

Our passage begins just after God had promised a future when He would fill Zion with righteousness and justice. These prophecies go from rebuke to a future hope. God points out their sin, but then declares His grace. We'll see the pattern again in the remainder of this chapter.

7 Behold, their heroes cry in the streets; the envoys of peace weep bitterly. 8 The highways lie waste; the traveler ceases. Covenants are broken; cities are despised; there is no regard for man. Isaiah 33:7-8 Jerusalem was surrounded by the brutal Assyrian army. They were not unlike ISIS of today, and probably had the same dark territorial power of evil behind them. Daniel named one such power the Prince of Persia (Daniel 10:20). Throughout time, that fallen angel has been trying to destroy the people of Israel. He is still at it today. How else do you explain the fixation on destroying such a small territory and people group?

King Hezekiah trusted in God and rebelled against the new king of Assyria. The new king went out to reinforce his power among the subjugated nations and had come to Jerusalem. Hezekiah's faith wavered. He attempted to pay off the King of Assyria by stripping the Temple of gold and silver. Remember, he had already wasted a fortune trying to buy Egypt's help. But he didn't learn his lesson. Money can't always buy your way out of difficulty. We trust in God or mammon, one or the other.

The Assyrian's took the payoff money and decided they would use it instead to finance the siege. The covenant was broken. All the other walled cities of Judah were already conquered. The heroes of Jerusalem knew they were no match for Assyria and were preparing to die. The envoys realized they were lied to and had given bad advice. The Assyrian treachery is like ISIS recent attempt to trade a prisoner they had burned alive a month before? Now the people of Jerusalem were just waiting to starve to death. Human life meant nothing to the Assyrians.

⁹ The land mourns and languishes; Lebanon is confounded and withers away; Sharon is like a desert, and Bashan and Carmel shake off their leaves. Isaiah 33:9 The lands to the north, so beautiful and verdant were already conquered, a sad portent of what was almost certain to be Jerusalem's future. Isaiah had predicted a day when those proud lands to the north would be brought low (Isaiah 2:12-17), and it had come to pass. That prophecy predicted that that would be the time for the LORD alone to be exalted.

¹⁰ "Now I will arise," says the LORD, "now I will lift myself up; now I will be exalted. Isaiah 33:10 This was thirty years after a prediction of the LORD'S deliverance and exaltation. This verse shouts God's triple "now!" In our previous text, it was "in little more than a year," but that time has passed. Now, God would act. This shows us God has a set time to carry out His will. The New Testament calls it in Greek the *"kairos"* moment. It is God's appointed time, the perfect time.

We would have it come much earlier, but God's time is just the right time. Why did God wait so long to spare Jerusalem? It was because they were so hard. The harder our heart, the more desperate He must make us. Even this was not enough to avoid captivity. No one will be able to say that God did not do everything possible to bring us to Himself. When we ask why God waited so long, we should know it was either to stretch our faith or because we were so hardhearted.

"Lift myself up" and "arise" are words used when the LORD went to battle against the forces of man and the spiritual forces behind them. When the Ark of the Covenant set out each time the camp of Israel moved in the wilderness, Moses would pray that God would arise and scatter their enemies before them (Numbers 10:35, 36; Psalm 68:1).

As we have seen before, this attempt to wipe out Judah is a spiritual battle to doom mankind. Without the people of Judah, the promised line of a savior would be gone. There would be no hope for the salvation of mankind. That is why the prophecies of the defeat of Assyria at the hand of the LORD slips over into the defeat of Satan on the cross of Calvary. It was there Satan tried once and for all to keep mankind from being redeemed. In doing his worst Satan facilitated our salvation.

Jesus understood this parallel. That is why He spoke the triple "now" in John 12 and 13. When the Greeks came seeking Jesus, Jesus knew it was time. His hour had come. It was time for Him to be glorified. It is true that that means to be in the glory He had before with the Father before His incarnation (John 17:4). But it is also true that He was declaring He was going into battle with Satan, a battle in which He would be gloriously victorious. Jesus prayed that the Father's name would be glorified. He acknowledged that there was no way to escape this battle for it was this purpose that He was born (John 12:27-28). The Father answered in an audible voice that He had glorified it and would glorify it again.

Hearing that, Jesus responded, *31 Now is the time for judgment on this world; now the prince of this world will be driven out. 32 But I, when I am lifted up from the earth, will draw all men to myself."* John 12:31-32 (NIV) "Lifted up" is one of the many words with a double meaning. The Hebrew word means to lift, carry, forgive or exalt. Remember in Isaiah 6 that Isaiah saw the Lord "high and lifted up." What a perfect word for what Jesus was about to do. In being lifted up on the cross, He was going to bring forgiveness, and in the process be exalted, victorious over Satan. While John was correct in saying Jesus was speaking of the way Jesus would die, being lifted up on a cross, He was also lifting Himself to go into battle with the enemy of our soul (Isaiah 33:3).

You or I could never defeat that enemy. Many have tried and found eventually he finds our weakness and overcomes us. But there was One who could, One who had no weaknesses. When He raises Himself to do battle, He is the mightiest warrior of all. Thank God, literally, that He was fighting as a man on man's behalf.

Since God grieves with us and feels our pain, I can imagine the anticipation of the time of deliverance. If your child was struggling and destroying their life but you had to wait to intervene, imagine the excitement when the time of intervention finally came. Now! And so, God said through Isaiah, *10 "Now I will arise," says the LORD, "now I will lift myself up; now I will be exalted.* And 700 years later Jesus, with the same anticipation said, *31 Now is the time for judgment on this world; now the prince of this world will be driven out.* John 12:31 (NIV)

And the third "now" of Jesus came in chapter 13 as they left the upper room. *31 When he had gone out, Jesus said, "Now is the Son of Man glorified, and God is glorified in him.* John 13:31 The next morning He would be on the cross, lifted up, in the battle of the ages, and emerge victorious, glorified and bringing glory to the Father, sacrificing Himself to forgive you! All that is in the one Hebrew word *(nasa)!*

11 You conceive chaff; you give birth to stubble; your breath is a fire that will consume you. 12 And the peoples will be as if burned to lime, like thorns cut down, that are burned in the fire." Isaiah 33:11,12 Speaking now to the Assyrians, God says the fruit of their mighty army is just chaff and stubble, fuel for a fire. The words they spoke against the God of Israel would ignite the fuel and consume them. Be careful little mouth what you say. Mocking God never turns out well. There is a certain thorn bush in Israel that is used on the perimeter of fields to keep out unwanted animals. The plant produces an abundance of sap. To keep the plant in check, after harvest time, the plant is set on fire. It quickly burns to nothing. That is God's declaration of the future of Assyria and to all who oppose His goodness.

13 Hear, you who are far off, what I have done; and you who are near, acknowledge my might. Isaiah 33:13 And the world did hear that of all

140

the nations that rebelled against Assyria, only Jerusalem was able to withstand their attack. The Chronicles record that the nations brought gifts to the Lord and King Hezekiah when they heard what God had done (2 Chronicles 32:23).

The Apostle Paul may have seen the ultimate fulfilment when he invites those far and near to be at peace with God through the victory Christ obtained for us in the great battle of the cross (Ephesians 2:16,17; Isaiah 57:19). Those around the world today who have trusted Jesus for their salvation acknowledge what He has done for us and His mighty power to save us.

14 The sinners in Zion are afraid; trembling has seized the godless: "Who among us can dwell with the consuming fire? Who among us can dwell with the everlasting burnings?" Isaiah 33:14 Though God would come in power and judge the Assyrians, His righteousness would not spare the sinners in Jerusalem. There is a day of judgment. They would tremble when the saw the power and justice of God. The Scriptures tell us God is love (1 John 4:9), but He is also a consuming fire (Hebrews 12:29). Those who in previous chapters told Isaiah to quit speaking about the Holy One of Israel (Isaiah 30:10,11) would still answer to Him. There are many in churches every Sunday who mock God with their words and their life. When God shows up in power, they will tremble!

Here, the prophecy takes another turn. We began with the desperation of Jerusalem and the intervention of God to save them. Then the prophecy spoke to both the deliverance by grace then, and the ultimate deliverance from sin through the cross. Now we go forward even further into the future regarding those who will dwell in the Jerusalem of the Millennium.

The previous verses were about God coming to judge the Assyrians in battle, but that is a preview of the great battle called Armageddon. After that, who will dwell with Jesus on Mount Zion? The same question is addressed in Psalm 15 and 24. Who shall ascend into the hill of the Lord? Who will stand in His holy place? Only the priests were allowed to do that in days of the Psalmist. Who will share in the reign of Christ on earth? God's answer to His own question is similar to that in the Psalms. Only a righteous person can stand before a holy God.

That is why Jesus was thrown out of the Nazareth synagogue. It is why the disciples who would sit next to Christ in His kingdom. Jews debated who would reign with the Messiah. The debate still continues.

15 He who walks righteously and speaks uprightly, who despises the gain of oppressions, who shakes his hands, lest they hold a bribe, who stops his ears from hearing of bloodshed and shuts his eyes from looking on evil, Isaiah 33:15 That is to say only a righteous person. Whose life is righteous and only speaks what is right? There was One. If we are in Him, we will reign with Him on Zion.

16 he will dwell on the heights; his place of defense will be the fortresses of rocks; his bread will be given him; his water will be sure.

Isaiah 33:16 Those in Christ will dwell with Him on the exalted places. They will be secure. He is our Rock, our Fortress. He is our bread, the Bread of Life, and His Holy Spirit in us is a spring of living water continually refreshing us.

Now some would say that this is taking the text too far, that it was for that day alone. I don't know how they would explain the next verse. *17 Your eyes will behold the king in his beauty; they will see a land that stretches afar.* Isaiah 33:17 When Jesus is reigning on Zion, our eyes will behold Him! We could say it was true in an intermediate fulfillment of Simeon and Hannah in the Temple when baby Jesus was presented (Luke 2:25-38), but the overall picture is much greater than even they experienced. In the first coming we saw Jesus as a servant. In the next, we'll see Him as King of kings. His kingly beauty is as John saw Him in His glory (Revelation 1:12-16) Seeing a land that stretches afar is a view of His worldwide kingdom.

18 Your heart will muse on the terror: "Where is he who counted, where is he who weighed the tribute? Where is he who counted the towers?" Isaiah 33:18 I think we will be able to look back and think of all the things that had us trembling. We will recall the things we feared and realize all the time we were in God's all-powerful hands. We had no reason to fear. That which we feared came to nothing. The oppressor we were so angry with is no more. Satan is finished! His futile revolt is finally over!

20 Behold Zion, the city of our appointed feasts! Your eyes will see Jerusalem, an untroubled habitation, an immovable tent, whose stakes will never be plucked up, nor will any of its cords be broken. 21 But there the LORD in majesty will be for us a place of broad rivers and streams, where no galley with oars can go, nor majestic ship can pass. Isaiah 33:20-21 Again we see this could only be fulfilled in the Millennium. Though it gave them hope for the present, they would later find it was not for their time. Babylon would come as a result of their rejection of the Word. Rome would exile those who rejected the Word made flesh (John 1:14).

Though John describes a physical river flowing out from under the throne of God in Jerusalem in the Millennium (Revelation 22:1), this is not about a river one could navigate like the Nile. This is the river of God, the life giving water of the Word that slakes the thirst of the righteous (Matthew 5:6). The Word of the Lord will go out from Zion (Micah 4:2).

22 For the LORD is our judge; the LORD is our lawgiver; the LORD is our king; he will save us. Isaiah 33:22 This verse alone could be the source text for an entire sermon series. Let me just simply say that the LORD is the judge of all the earth. One day every soul will give an account to Him. He alone is our lawgiver. There are not multiple rules depending on your culture and the time you live and the tendencies of your physical nature. He makes the rules because right and wrong are based on who He is. He made the rules to help us all know what is best for us. He gives us laws for our good. His nature is good.

He is our King. He will reign through all eternity. His will will be done. He will save all who humbly come to Him and place their hope and trust in Him.

²³ Your cords hang loose; they cannot hold the mast firm in its place or keep the sail spread out. Then prey and spoil in abundance will be divided; even the lame will take the prey. Isaiah 33:23 While Jerusalem was like a ship so storm tossed there seemed no hope of salvation, at that very time, the Lord would deliver them. This would take place when the angel slew 185,000, but again in the day of Jacob's Trouble, just before the beginning of the Millennium begins (Jeremiah 30:7).

Instead of being the prey of the Assyrians and spoil taken from Jerusalem, Jerusalem will collect Assyrian spoil without fighting. Even the lame can hobble over and pick up treasures for themselves (Psalm 68:12). Jesus will divide the spoils of the victory over Satan with those who are His (Isaiah 53:12), even with the weakest believer.

²⁴ And no inhabitant will say, "I am sick"; the people who dwell there will be forgiven their iniquity. Isaiah 33:24 Once again, this is obviously the Millennial Kingdom. Sickness and uncleanness (sin) are related in Scripture. (Isaiah 1:5-6) Not all sickness is because of sin a person has committed (John 9:3), but it is from the sin of man that caused the world to be in its fallen state. So not only does this predict the removal of the curse on those in Zion but declares those who are there are the forgiven ones (Isaiah 1:26). They are the Jew (Jeremiah 50:20) and Gentile who have come to Jesus for cleansing. All who trust in Christ alone will be there. Will you? As the hymn writer put it, "What a day of rejoicing that will be. When we all see Jesus, we'll sing and shout the victory!"

Questions
1 Why don't we quietly listen to God?
2 What caused Hezekiah's faith to waiver? Lesson?
3 Review the three "now" of the LORD and Jesus.
4 Multiple meanings of "lifted up"?
5 How is verse 13 fulfilled then and now?
6 Who dwells with Jesus on Zion?
7 How do we know the last section of the chapter is about the Millennium?
8 What will we muse on?
9 Who is God to us?
10 How did this passage speak to you?

The Beautiful King - Isaiah 33:17

¹⁷ Your eyes will behold the king in his beauty; they will see a land that stretches afar. Isaiah 33:17 If you read the sermons from individual pastors you will notice that they tend to follow a certain pattern. Spurgeon used a single verse or part of a verse and would bring out several points and an application. Others pick a topic, start with a joke, and then bring out a few verses about the topic with an illustration. If you've been here awhile you know that I go through a book of the Bible one passage at a time explaining what it means and how it applies to our lives. Every pastor has a style or pattern and the Holy Spirit works within that personality. But sometimes the Holy Spirit can also interrupt that pattern. It makes preachers uncomfortable, but that is good, because then we tend to be more reliant upon God. This is one of those rare times. I just knew that I had to preach on this verse.

Your eyes will behold the King in His beauty! The cycle of godly and evil kings in Israel and their current state of hopelessness caused the people of Judah to wonder about the promises of God. Would this One who Isaiah predicted would to be called Everlasting Father, Wonderful Councilor, Prince of Peace, who would reign forever on David's throne ever come (Isaiah 9:6-7)? So to those with a Messianic hope, God promised their eyes would see Him. They would see Him at the right hand of God when they die, but their descendants would see Him physically walk the streets of Jerusalem.

We should first consider what is meant by "beauty." Jesus of Nazareth was not a handsome man. Another prediction of Isaiah tells us that the Messiah has no physical beauty that we should desire Him (Isaiah 53:2). He doesn't have the features of a movie star. Isaiah isn't contradicting himself. God is letting us know that there are different kinds of beauty. Perhaps God intentionally made Jesus' physical features unattractive so that people were attracted to something more than His physical being. His message and life were so important that physical beauty would have been a deterrent to the delivery of His message. It is the Spirit that makes alive, the flesh does not profit us (John 6:63). It is the heart of a person that makes a person truly beautiful, and there was never a more beautiful heart than that of Jesus (Isaiah 4:2). May the Lord help us to make this important distinction!

While Isaiah's prophecy speaks of the Messiah as King, Zechariah wrote that the King of Israel was coming humbly on a donkey (Zechariah 9:9). The first coming was not to force His kingdom on others, but rather to invite us to be His subjects. We can see the beauty of the King in both His first and second comings.

Let's look for a moment at how we see His beautiful heart expressed. He was certainly humble. In obedience to the Father, He submitted to the baptism of repentance even though He had no sin. This is when John the Baptist recognized He was the Lamb of God that takes away the sins of the world (John 1:29). Paul tells us that Jesus humbled Himself and took on the form of a servant (Philippians 2:8). His every action was service to the Father and to mankind. To the shock of His disciples, He even washed their dirty feet (John 13:5).

Jesus called men that longed to be servants of God but did not think they were worthy. Young boys in Galilee would study the Scriptures and learn to read and write Hebrew so they could take their turn in the reading of Scriptures in their local synagogue. Once they finished that education, they either went on to learn a trade, or, if they showed a capacity to memorize and understand the Scriptures, they could continue their education in the Scriptures. All of Jesus' disciples had gone on to a trade. One was a despised tax collector. Many were fishermen. One was a zealot. They were all rejected from continuing study of the Scriptures to become spiritual leaders, but Jesus chose them.

Think of it this way. What if in your heart you longed to be an Air Force pilot, but you failed the exams? Then, after going on to another career, a general came and asked you to go into flight training. You'd be elated. Jesus knew these men's hearts. Even though the culture said they couldn't do it, the beauty of Jesus' heart is that He could see their hearts' desires and called them to follow Him. Did you know that same beautiful heart is for you as well? If you long to serve Him, He has a place for you. He says to you what He said to them, "Follow me" (Matthew 4:19)!

We see His beautiful heart in how He treated women. Within the ranks of Jesus' followers were women disciples (Luke 8:1-3). He allowed them to sit in on His teaching and welcomed them to follow with the apostles. That was scandalous to the religious elite of that day who would never consider doing that. But Jesus' heart is for every soul, man or woman, and even the outcasts like the tax collectors, Samaritans, and so called "sinners."

He was so beautiful in loving the least, that He was called "a friend of tax collectors and sinners" (Luke 7:34). Jesus cared more about the broken hearts of men and women than He did about the respect of men. He showed the beautiful heart of the Father for sin sick souls and explained to the self-righteous leaders that those who were sick needed the Physician. Jesus is our soul doctor (Matthew 9:12).

Don't you love the beautifully patient but persistent way He deals with us? We see an example of it with Nicodemus, with the woman at the well, with the rich young ruler, and in His parable about the Good Samaritan. I could tell you how beautiful His patience and persistence has been in my life, but each of you can tell the story of how He's been with you.

If I was god dealing with someone like myself, I would never have called me to ministry. I wouldn't have bothered at all to even think of a person like me. Or even more likely, I'd have struck me dead. The numerous times I had close calls in car accidents, well a god like me wouldn't have bothered to spare a person like me. Let him crash, and good riddance! But that is because without Jesus I don't have the unconditional love of God. Can you recall the great patience and love God has had toward you throughout your life? Isn't that beautiful! (Song of Songs 5:16)

We are talking about the beauty of the attributes of God which Jesus demonstrated so clearly in His earthly ministry. God's patience, grace, and mercy are so beautiful. As the eyes are the windows of your soul, I can't imagine more beautiful eyes than those of Jesus (1 Samuel 16:12; Song of Songs 5:12).

The greatest display of that beauty was the cross. It was there we see the glory of God manifest most clearly. In the midst of all that brutality and suffering we see God's great love for us, bringing us forgiveness, as Jesus' paid a debt we could never pay. Outwardly it was horrific, but the unseen reality of what was taking place as the Divine warrior took on the forces of hell on our behalf, that was magnificently beautiful! We'll be talking about that throughout eternity. And wasn't it beautiful the way Jesus walked with the two on the way to Emmaus and opened the Scriptures to them (Luke 24:45)? And the way He restored Peter on the shores of Galilee (John 21:15-17), and the way He restores us when we fail, is so beautiful.

In Isaiah, the beauty of God is paralleled with His glory (Isaiah 28:5). His attributes are beautiful, and His attributes are His glory displayed. Isaiah saw the beauty of the LORD in chapter six (Isaiah 6:5). The train of His robe filled the Temple with glory. In that account He called Him the King, the LORD of hosts. It must have excited Isaiah to know that the day was coming when the eyes of others would see the King as he had seen Him. The revelation of His beauty puts us on our faces and reveals the areas of our lives that don't conform to His beauty.

The psalmist wrote that the heavens declare the glory of God (Psalms 19:1). How beautiful the night sky is where city lights do not hinder. Remember, that was written long before telescopes revealed an even greater beauty than we can imagine. The Hubble has sent us pictures of galaxies that amaze us with their beauty. As one of our satellites passed Venus, we learned that the outer ring was braided. How beautiful must be the God who created such beauty where no human eye could see.

My wife and I watched a TV special on a family that inherited the world's largest insect collection. The variety and colors were incredible. A stick bug was over a foot long. Beetles donned iridescent colors. Butterflies of all sizes were so beautiful in their patterns and colors. How beautiful must their Creator be!

We only have to look out our windows here in Sedona to see the beauty of this earth's topography. The red rock cliffs and formations, with thousand-foot sheer walls, and layers of color, capped with grey basalt, the Grand Canyon, the Painted Desert. Then there are the Tetons, the Himalayas, and beautiful oceans with their colorful reefs. How beautiful must be their designer and maker!

There is another beauty that may not have crossed your mind. It is the beauty of the body of Christ, His church. She is His bride (Song of Songs 1:15). Though the work is not completed, we can see glimpses of what she is becoming. When people give of themselves to serve like Jesus did, we see the beauty of Jesus in them. When you sacrifice your time and energy to do something for others just because there is a need, we see that beauty. Someone wants to stand out at our entrance and read the Word aloud as people pass by. Another person asked if they could just hand out an invitation to the church service to passersby. Another volunteered to cook men's breakfast. How beautiful is Jesus who inspired them to give of themselves without recognition!

I went to Rainbow Acres a few weeks ago and saw the beauty of Jesus in some of the staff who so graciously love and serve the Ranchers. And the Ranchers, well they have their own beauty of simplicity and love that reminds me of Jesus' beauty. Wherever we see unselfish love and service that does not seek recognition, we see the beauty of Jesus (Matthew 20:28).

Jesus said that Mary's act of anointing Him with precious oil and her tears was a beautiful thing (Matthew 26:10). To worship Him is to worship what is truly beautiful. To share the knowledge of His beauty by sharing the Good News is described as having beautiful feet (Isaiah 52:7). To ignore or despise Him is to shun what is truly beautiful. We should ask ourselves if we have a developed a taste for what is truly beautiful or if our sense of beauty is fixed on that which is fading.

Our verse today told the Jewish people they would see the King in His beauty. The first coming of Jesus was a preview of the glory that will be seen when He reigns on the earth (Revelation 22:22-24). During His first coming He only unveiled His glory briefly on the Mount of Transfiguration. There Peter, James, and John saw Jesus shining like the sun, whiter than any white they had ever seen (Matthew 17:2) Later Peter wrote about that experience and said it was a glimpse of Jesus' majesty (2Peter 1:16). Majesty is the King's beauty.

God was telling the faithful in Judah that though the Assyrian siege would be costly, it would not end the promises of God. No man or army or even spiritual powers can stop the promises of God. Those Jews would one day stand before the throne of God and see His glory. Their descendants would one day see Him reigning on Zion in all His beautiful glory, in a similar scene to what the three disciples saw on the Mount of Transfiguration.

We have a natural fear of such an all-powerful ruler, because every man that obtains such power becomes unaccountable to others and soon falls into a depravity. We look at the Caesars, and some of the popes, and other world leaders, and shudder to think of the devastation of an all-powerful ruler. Only Jesus can be a beautiful ruler. The rule of man is often ugly and brutal. The rule of the beautiful One will be just but also merciful and kind. He is the kind of ruler man has longed for, one that will truly be a servant of all, and yet who will deal with evil swiftly and in righteousness (Isaiah 32:1). The good will be honored and the evil will be dealt with. That is beautiful! And so we say, "Come quickly Lord Jesus!" (Revelation 22:20)

What is beautiful to you? What do you ask of the LORD? What are you seeking after? King David was a man after God's heart (Acts 13:22). He was a sinner, like the rest of us, but God honored him by calling the Messiah the son of David, and having the Messiah come from his lineage. That was God's sovereign choice, but I think it had something to do with David's great passion. He wrote, *4 One thing have I asked of the LORD, that will I seek after: that I may dwell in the house of the LORD all the days of my life, to gaze upon the beauty of the LORD and to inquire in his temple.* Psalm 27:4

David understood that all beauty came from the Beautiful One. He wanted to live in the Tabernacle and just gaze upon the beauty of the LORD. He wanted to just ask questions and hear His beautiful answers. Everything that conforms to our Creator is beautiful. Everything that does not is ugly. We say that beauty is in the eye of the beholder, meaning that each of us considers beauty uniquely. While that may be true of the passing beauty of this world and personal taste, it is not true of eternal things. The eternally beautiful is beautiful because it conforms to Christ and His attributes. That which does not is ugly.

We are deluded if we think there are grey areas in our hearts and minds. Our affections and thoughts are beautiful or ugly. This is why we must be born again (John 3:3).

To be born again means we acquire a taste for what is truly beautiful, and we begin to be uncomfortable with, and even detest what is truly ugly. Our society is telling Christians that they need to conform to the present standards and tastes of this world. Those who are born again are unable to develop a taste for it. Compromise sickens us, for our hearts are after one thing, to behold the beauty of the LORD. For us who are subjects of the King, God has given us a promise through the prophet Isaiah. *17a Your eyes will behold the king in his beauty;*

Questions
1 Was Jesus handsome? Why or why not?
2 When does Jesus come as King?
3 How did Jesus' actions express beauty?
4 Has He been beautiful toward you?
5 What was His most beautiful action?
6 How does creation speak of God's beauty?
7 What beauty might we overlook?
8 When did the disciples see His beauty?
9 When will all Jews see His beauty?
10 What was David's desire?
11 What is your desire?

Super Saved - Isaiah 35

You may have noticed that I skipped Isaiah 34. That is because I believe it very well may have something to do with what some see as an intermediary fulfilment referred to as the Psalm 83 War. Pastor Ken has done a lot of research on it so in a few weeks we will switch pulpits so he can share it with you. The ultimate fulfilment is the wrath of God upon the world in rebellion against Him. Then, chapter 35 which we will look at today gives the promise of the future for those who place their hope in God and His Messiah.

I enjoy this cooperation between churches with those who do not feel we are in competition, but one body with one purpose in different branches of the same tree. And that purpose is to teach and preach the Word faithfully so that we grow in the knowledge of Jesus and His power to save all who come to Him by faith (2 Corinthians 4:5; 1 Corinthians 3:6).

Our passage today I've entitled Super Saved. That is because I see four different types of salvation that are suggested in the passage, all of which lead to the ultimate salvation in the Messianic Kingdom and eternity as the bride of Christ. I'll try to bring out each so that you can see the depth and glimpse some of the power in the Word of God.

As we have seen throughout Isaiah, the prophecies go from condemnation of sin, impending judgment, the intervention of God, captivity, restoration, the Messiah, and then to the Messiah's kingdom. Chapter 34 is on the judgment of the nations, so it follows then in order that this chapter would be on the restoration of the people of God and their salvation. The first verses describe the healing of the land.

¹ The wilderness and the dry land shall be glad; the desert shall rejoice and blossom like the crocus; ² it shall blossom abundantly and rejoice with joy and singing. The glory of Lebanon shall be given to it, the majesty of Carmel and Sharon. They shall see the glory of the LORD, the majesty of our God. Isaiah 35:1-2 When God brings the people out of captivity, He will restore His blessing upon the land. I'm not sure to what extent this happened in the return of the remnant from Babylon (Haggai 2:19), but we do know it has been true in these Last Days' return of Israel as a nation to the land. Swamps were drained, and forests were planted. Israel has become the largest exporter of citrus fruit to Europe. Israel's invention of the drip system has made the deserts literally bloom. I've personally witnessed the flowering deserts in spring.

This is a theme that is picked up again later in Isaiah describing the effects of God's Word performing His purposes (55:12-13). I believe we can also look at this in spiritual sense. The Word made flesh came to Israel and there were spiritual streams in the desert (John 1:14). Jesus told the woman at the well that He could give her living water that would spring up within her (John 4:14). He was speaking Isaiah's language. Water in the desert is life and refreshment. It has a transformative power. The blossoms and expressions of God's majesty are the transformation of lives by the power of living water within.

This certainly took place in the lives of Jews and Gentiles who came to know Jesus as their Messiah in the first century to today. Messianic congregations are springing up in Israel as Arab and Jew come together in faith in Christ Jesus. On one trip to Nazareth I met an Arab pastor who told me how Arab and Jewish Christian pastors are breaking down the walls between them and worshiping together.

Brothers and sisters, we are living in the Last Days! The "Time of the Gentiles" is ending (Luke 21:24). The stirring and turmoil in the nations is no accident. Muslims are coming to know Jesus through revelations and risking their lives to tell other Muslims. We must be about our Father's business. Amen?

Are you experiencing the joy and fruitfulness of God's restoration or do you relate more readily to the dry and barren desert? The only source of living water is the One who invites all to come to the water and drink freely (Isaiah 55:1-2). All our fresh springs are in Him (Psalm 87:7). He waters our desert like hearts so that they overflow with life.

3 Strengthen the weak hands, and make firm the feeble knees. Isaiah 35:3 One thing we need as we go through life is encouragement to take the next step, to keep on keeping on. Just before beginning to work on this sermon I read the March 6th devotion in My Utmost for His Highest. It begins with this paragraph: *"It takes Almighty grace to take the next step when there is no vision and no spectator—the next step in devotion, the next step in your study, in your reading, in your kitchen; the next step in your duty, when there is no vision from God, no enthusiasm and no spectator. It takes far more of the grace of God, far more conscious drawing upon God to take that step, than it does to preach the Gospel."* (Chambers, Oswald, *My Utmost for His Highest,* March 6) We forget the grace that is needed to just continue marching forward each day. Chambers' solution to sinking into drudgery and becoming a desert is to keep our spiritual eyes open to the risen Christ. That will confirm our feeble knees and strengthen our weak hands.

The author of Hebrews quotes this verse in Hebrews 12:12. A few verses earlier in that chapter the author tells us to keep our eyes fixed on Jesus and consider how He dealt with His life on earth, how He endured (Hebrews 12:2-3). Then he tells us to appreciate God's corrections in our lives. It is for our good. So lift up your weak hands and strengthen your weak knees.

4 Say to those who have an anxious heart, "Be strong; fear not! Behold, your God will come with vengeance, with the recompense of God. He will come and save you." Isaiah 35:3-4 How we need to do this to help our brothers and sisters in Christ who have anxious hearts! We all need reminders at times to look at how Jesus did it. He looked to the Father. He spent time in prayer. He had His priorities straight. He trusted the Father even upon the cross. So, buck up! Pull it together. Rely on the Holy Spirit. Capture those thoughts that are pulling you down and bring them to foot of the cross (2 Corinthians 10:5). Remind yourself who wins this battle. God will deal with all evil and reward all good. That is His just recompense. Your labor in the Lord is not in vain (1 Corinthians 15:58). Those who resist and slander you because of your commitment will have to answer to Him.

He will come and save you! For those surrounded by Assyria it was an amazing one-night deliverance. For those in captivity it was a long 70 year wait. For those living after the return it was a 400 year wait until the coming of Messiah. And for us in the church it has been a 2000 year wait. Yet, in a very real sense we have already experienced salvation. He spoke to our anxious hearts and brought us the salvation He gained for us on the cross. He has dealt with the enemy of our souls. We have heard His words in our hearts, "Be strong! Fear not!" Nothing can separate us from the love of God (Romans 8:39).

Be strong in the Lord! Don't let the fallen condition of this world bring you down. You are citizen of heaven and have nothing to fear (Philippians 3:20). If God is for us, who can be against us. Do not fear those who kill the body but have no more that they can do. Fear not, for unemployment or economies of man. God is your provider. Fear not physical problems for the Lord will be your strength and see you safely home. Fear not that you will stand before the judge of the whole earth for you are clothed in the righteousness of God in Christ Jesus your Lord (2Corinthians 5:21). We need to remind one another of these things and how great the God we serve truly is.

This verse will come alive in the day of Jacob's trouble. When Israel finally turns to God in the midst of calamity, Jesus will be their Messiah and become their strength and salvation (Zechariah 13:1).

5 Then the eyes of the blind shall be opened, and the ears of the deaf unstopped; 6 then shall the lame man leap like a deer, and the tongue of the mute sing for joy. For waters break forth in the wilderness, and streams in the desert; Isaiah 35:5-6 For those in captivity, it meant seeing and hearing what they were previously unable to see or hear of the faithfulness of God. For those in the days of Jesus' ministry it meant that too, but it was manifest in very literal signs that demonstrated the spiritual reality. When the man born blind could see (John 9:18), it was a spiritual message to everyone that they had been born spiritually blind but now, through faith in Jesus, they could see. When the paralyzed walked (John 5:8-9) it was a message that the leaders were spiritual cripples and needed to hear Jesus to truly serve their people instead of themselves.

As we saw in the end of Isaiah 33, in the Kingdom of the Messiah there will be no illness and the truth will be plain for all who are willing to see (Isaiah 33:24). The key word is willing, just as it is today and was in the days of Jesus' ministry.

I addressed water in the wilderness and springs in the desert in the first verses but let me add that this was especially irritating to the Jewish leadership in Jesus' day. When they saw His miracles, the association with this passage would imply that they had led the nation into a wasteland that was spiritually dry as cracker dust ten miles from a glass of water. Jesus cried out, *37 On the last day of the feast, the great day, Jesus stood up and cried out, "If anyone thirsts, let him come to me and drink.* John 7:37

That is what is happening today as well. We deplore the adulteration of the Word of God and the abandonment of His moral principles given to us for our good. But, we should also see that it is creating spiritual thirst (Jeremiah 2:13). Nothing in this world can slake that thirst. Lots of things can distract from it, but nothing can quench it other than the fountain of living water, Jesus!

⁷ the burning sand shall become a pool, and the thirsty ground springs of water; in the haunt of jackals, where they lie down, the grass shall become reeds and rushes. Isaiah 35:7 This arrival of life giving water was way more than they experienced upon the return from Babylon. We so greatly undervalue the abundance of life giving water that came from Jesus' three years of ministry. It's still flowing today through the recorded Word.

The description here reminds me of our recent storm. A boulder had come down off the mountain and smacked the Nicolella's van, so I decided to hike up to see where it came from. The ground was so saturated that as I tried to make my way back to the house even the rocks I stepped on would sink and slide. A dirt wall beside our house was oozing with water. This is the kind of abundance Isaiah is describing, saturation! How we need to be saturated with the Word of God! How few are grasping the opportunity before us.

I hope you know and have personally experienced that in Jesus there is more than enough for your heart's every need. There is a song entitled *More Than Enough* by Chris Tomlin that says it so well. *"All of You is more than enough for all of me, For every thirst and every need, You satisfy me with Your love, And all I have in You is more than enough. You are my supply, My breath of life, And still more awesome than I know. You are my reward, worth living for, And still more awesome than I know."* That is just a meager effort to describe the abundance we have in Jesus. Our problem is that we so seldom tap into that abundance! We settle for a few drops when we could be swimming in His love.

⁸ And a highway shall be there, and it shall be called the Way of Holiness; the unclean shall not pass over it. It shall belong to those who walk on the way; even if they are fools, they shall not go astray. Isaiah 35:8 And Jesus said, "I am the Way!" John 14:6a He is the highway to heaven. He is the Way of Holiness. That is why the early church was called, The Way (Acts 9:2).

If you are in the Way you are clean because of His shed blood for your sins. The unclean can't pass over it, they must go through Jesus, and if you go through Jesus you become clean (1 Peter 1:2).

That Way is ours and we are His. It's just as the lovers in the Song of Songs declares, *"I am my beloved's and my beloved is mine!"* Song of Songs 6:3 What a glorious truth this is: Jesus gives Himself to us when we give ourselves to Him. Every believer should take time to revel in that on a regular basis. I belong to Jesus. He has given Himself to me.

As for the last part of the verse, *even if they are fools, they shall not go astray*. I can personally relate to this verse. I have been a fool. I have fallen for stupid lies that creation should be more sought after than the Creator. I was a fool when I thought I was in some special end-time movement. I could go on, but you get the idea. Yet in spite of my foolishness, I was in the Way and God was using it all to direct me to a closer relationship with Him. He was keeping me from stepping out of the Way, and from going too far from His path. What grace and mercy (2 Timothy 2:13)!

⁹ No lion shall be there, nor shall any ravenous beast come up on it; they shall not be found there, but the redeemed shall walk there. Isaiah 35:9 The Great Shepherd won't allow the lion to come up onto the Way (1Peter 5:8). When we start to step off the Way, He allows him to nip at our heels. But He keeps a close eye to see that that the old lion does not go too far (1Corinthians 10:13).

I thought of the wolves among the sheep that Paul warned about (Acts 20:29), yet they are in the organizations, not *on* the Way. There is a big difference between the church, and organizations. The church is the called out believers who have placed their faith in Christ. They can't be a wolf. The organizations of man with its gatherings of people often have wolves among the sheep (Acts 20:29). The Way has no threatening beasts. And this Highway never ends. There is no end to Christ. The redeemed walk in Him. The penalty for their sin is paid. They are His and He protects what is His. We are safe in the arms of Jesus (John 10:27-29).

¹⁰ And the ransomed of the LORD shall return and come to Zion with singing; everlasting joy shall be upon their heads; they shall obtain gladness and joy, and sorrow and sighing shall flee away. Isaiah 35:10 It was true of those who returned from captivity, at least for a time. It is true of those who are ransomed by the blood of Christ. At least it should be true. Some still sigh, waiting to be delivered from this body and given our eternal one (2Corinthians 5:2). We still sorrow for the lost, especially loved ones who have not entered the Way. We sorrow for suffering sin causes in this world. Yet, we have an abiding joy that no sorrow can dampen.

That leads us to the conclusion that this is ultimately about entering our eternal abode. Small saved – from Assyrian siege, Medium saved – from captivity, Large saved – by Jesus from or sins, Super saved – is His work in us completed in our eternal home. This is our call upward to the wedding feast of the Lamb. Every tear will be wiped away (Revelation 21:4). Misunderstandings and old animosities and regrets will be gone forever. We have taste of it now with our joy in Jesus, but then it will be complete. The former things will pass away. Come Lord Jesus!

Questions
1 What was water to Israel?
2 Review the literal and spiritual fulfillment.
3 Why do we need Almighty grace daily?
4 What do we say to the anxious hearts?
5 Give two interpretations of verses 5&6.

6 How did Jews interpret Jesus' healings?
7 Is Jesus enough?
8 Are you on the Way of Holiness?
9 What are the promises on the Way?
10 What joys await us?

Mighty One - Isaiah 36-37

We have been studying the prophecies of Isaiah to the people of Judah, many of which have been pointing to the events in these two chapters we are looking at today. There is a similar account in 2 Kings 18. I'll briefly summarize what had previously taken place. Judah and the surrounding nations were subjugated to Assyria. When a new Assyrian king rose to power under some turmoil, the vassal nations rebelled. Hezekiah, king of Judah, believed the prophecies of Isaiah which told of God's deliverance from Assyria (Isaiah 10:26), so he too rebelled. All the other nations were subjugated again by warfare, Judah being one of the last to be attacked. According to the Taylor Prism, forty-two walled cities of Judah had fallen and only Jerusalem remained. Hezekiah tried to pay off the king of Assyria, but the king took the money and reneged on his agreement and continued the siege (2Kings 18:15-16). This is where our passage begins.
¹ In the fourteenth year of King Hezekiah, Sennacherib king of Assyria came up against all the fortified cities of Judah and took them. ²ᵃ And the king of Assyria sent the Rabshakeh from Lachish to King Hezekiah at Jerusalem, with a great army. Isaiah 36:1-2a Lachish was just to the south of Jerusalem and was one of the last strongholds between the Assyrian army and Jerusalem. There is a great deal of archeological information on the attack on Lachish. Ostraca, pieces of pottery with carbon inscriptions, have been found in the ruins. One of them tells of not being able to see the signal fire of Azekah. Jeremiah 34:7 tells us that Lachish and Azekah were two of the last cities to fall to Sennacherib. This was most likely written at the same time the Rabshakeh was sent to demand Hezekiah's surrender. Azekah had fallen and the conquest of Lachish was concluding. A relief of the battle was found in Assyria and is now in the British Museum.

Hezekiah's lack of faith in God is seen in his sending the temple gold and silver to buy off King Sennacherib. It failed to spare them from the siege. Hezekiah's attempt to buy Egypt's help had failed too (Isaiah 30:4-5). Now he had no choice but to trust God. When the money fails, I guess there is nothing left to do but trust God. How sad is that! "I guess we'll just have to trust the Lord." Why is that the last resort? Why don't we start with trusting God? Isaiah prophesied that it would be to their shame that Judah looked to Egypt (Isaiah 30:3). It was, and the Rabshakeh called them on it. *⁶ Behold, you are trusting in Egypt, that broken reed of a staff, which will pierce the hand of any man who leans on it. Such is Pharaoh king of Egypt to all who trust in him.* Isaiah 36:6

The world loves to point out our lack of faith and remind us how our trust in man has failed us. But what the world is saying is that we should trust a different man. The Rabshakeh (a title of representative of the king) went on to ask them to trust him (Jeremiah 17:5). God's message is we should trust in God and look to Him alone to guide us (Proverbs 3:5).

What the Rabshakeh then said showed that he misinterpreted the intelligence he had gathered. *7 But if you say to me, "We trust in the LORD our God," is it not he whose high places and altars Hezekiah has removed, saying to Judah and to Jerusalem, "You shall worship before this altar"?* Isaiah 36:7 Hezekiah was one of the few kings that had the spiritual conviction to remove the high places where other gods were worshiped (2Kings 18:4). He even destroyed the bronze serpent Moses had made because people had been worshiping it (Numbers 21:9). The Rabshakeh thought this was limiting the worship of YHWH, but on the contrary, it was refining the worship of YHWH and doing what God had commanded.

The Rabshakeh told Hezekiah and everyone on the walls that it is no use to look to YHWH. No other gods were able to withstand the assault of the Assyrians. Then the Rabshakeh said it was YHWH that told Assyria to destroy these lands. *10 Moreover, is it without the LORD that I have come up against this land to destroy it? The LORD said to me, Go up against this land and destroy it.'"* Isaiah 36:10

The enemy of our soul works in partial truths. God did use Assyria to bring judgment to the nations and to most of Judah, but that isn't the whole story. God was preserving a remnant in Jerusalem from which would come the Savior.

Consider this half-truth. "You are a sinner and a failure." Yes, but that isn't the whole story. The rest of the story is that I have a mighty Savior who has a plan for my life and wants me to spend eternity with Him (Jeremiah 29:11). Hezekiah could have said, "You know, the guy is right. God gave them the power to destroy those nations and most of our cities and now we're next." But that is not what God promised earlier. Beware of the devil's half-truths (John 8:44). Always respond to your doubts with what God has declared. He has the final say!

The enemy of our soul also likes to use faulty logic. *19 Where are the gods of Hamath and Arpad? Where are the gods of Sepharvaim? Have they delivered Samaria out of my hand? 20 Who among all the gods of these lands have delivered their lands out of my hand, that the LORD should deliver Jerusalem out of my hand?'"* Isaiah 36:19-20 The Rabshakeh was telling the people that YHWH was no more able to protect them than the gods of other nations. But wait a minute! Didn't he just say YHWH sent him? One minute he says YHWH is his power and the next that YHWH is unable to defend the Jews against the power of Assyria.

He is saying that the God of Israel is no greater than any other god. Just because Assyria defeated the other nations does not mean they can defeat YHWH. Israel has a long history of God delivering them from nations that appeared to be more powerful. This was really Assyria's undoing. You don't mock the holy One of Israel and get away with it (Psalm 74:22).

We should also notice that the Rabshakeh tried to discourage the people along with the king. He spoke in their language so that everyone could hear. But Hezekiah had given them a godly word of wisdom. Don't answer. *²¹ But they were silent and answered him not a word, for the king's command was, "Do not answer him."* Isaiah 36:21 The best way to keep from losing an argument with the devil is to not consider him worthy of a response. Unless you have word from God, be silent. You can resist the devil by ignoring him.

Hezekiah's representatives tore their clothes as a sign of grief and took the message to him. *¹ As soon as King Hezekiah heard it, he tore his clothes and covered himself with sackcloth and went into the house of the LORD. ² And he sent Eliakim, who was over the household, and Shebna the secretary, and the senior priests, covered with sackcloth, to the prophet Isaiah the son of Amoz.* Isaiah 37:1-2 What do you think God may have done if Hezekiah did this before sending money to the Egyptians and then to the Assyrians? We'll never know, but it would have spoken loudly of Hezekiah's faith in the words of the prophet and the power of God to be true to His Word. Where will you turn first when difficulty comes into your life (Luke 1:79)? Will you look to the Lord and His Word or to your bank account?

Hezekiah has finally done the right thing. Even though it was his last resort, God will still honor it. Don't think that because you waited to the last second to pray that God will not hear you. It may be that God allowed you to be in that situation so that you would finally look to Him. In that age the prophet was the voice of God. Today we turn to the Word of God and the leading of the Holy Spirit. We can also ask godly people who know the Scriptures for counsel (Proverbs 11:14). They told Isaiah, *⁴ It may be that the LORD your God will hear the words of the Rabshakeh, whom his master the king of Assyria has sent to mock the living God, and will rebuke the words that the LORD your God has heard; therefore lift up your prayer for the remnant that is left.'"* Isaiah 37:4 In other words, "I sure hope God heard what that guy said, because if He did, those of us who are left will be saved."

Hezekiah's torn robes and sackcloth tell us he was repentant as he should have been. Though he had removed the idols, the people had not really turned back to YHWH. It would be as if only Phoenix survived and the rest of the cities of Arizona were destroyed. We'd be in mourning for all those who died, but we'd also wonder how great our sin was that God would judge us so severely. The churches would surely be filled. I think these servants of the king were hoping that God would judge Assyria for the Rabshakeh's words, because there was little sign of citywide repentance in Jerusalem.

⁵ When the servants of King Hezekiah came to Isaiah, ⁶ Isaiah said to them, "Say to your master, 'Thus says the LORD: Do not be afraid because of the words that you have heard, with which the young men of the king of Assyria have reviled me. 7 Behold, I will put a spirit in him, so that he shall hear a rumor and return to his own land, and I will make him fall by the sword in his own land.'" Isaiah 37:5-7 Sennacherib did hear that the king of Cush had come against him and so Sennacherib put off the siege of Jerusalem. He sent a message to Hezekiah. *10 "Thus shall you speak to Hezekiah king of Judah: 'Do not let your God in whom you trust deceive you by promising that Jerusalem will not be given into the hand of the king of Assyria.* Isaiah 37:10 The message went on to remind him of all the other nations that were conquered and assured him Assyria would return to take Jerusalem. Once again, Hezekiah made the right choice, even though it may have been the only alternative. He took the message to the LORD.

Hezekiah prayed a short but to the point prayer. Remembering that Sennacherib represents Satan's attempt to stop the salvation of men, let's stand and say this prayer together. *16 "O LORD of hosts, God of Israel, enthroned above the cherubim, you are the God, you alone, of all the kingdoms of the earth; you have made heaven and earth. 17 Incline your ear, O LORD, and hear; open your eyes, O LORD, and see; and hear all the words of Sennacherib, which he has sent to mock the living God. 18 Truly, O LORD, the kings of Assyria have laid waste all the nations and their lands, 19 and have cast their gods into the fire. For they were no gods, but the work of men's hands, wood and stone. Therefore they were destroyed. 20 So now, O LORD our God, save us from his hand, that all the kingdoms of the earth may know that you alone are the LORD."* Isaiah 37:16-20 God alone is Creator and Lord over all the earth. Hezekiah first acknowledged the greatness of God. That would have reassured his own heart. Then he acknowledged that God had allowed Assyria to conquer all the other nations (Isaiah 14:24). He acknowledged what was true in the letter. But he also recognized what wasn't true. Those nations did not have real gods. Their gods were nothing. He asked God to look at how Assyria was mocking the one true God and asked that God deal with them to show the world that YHWH alone is God in all the earth. He didn't plead their own righteousness. He didn't even bring up past promises. He asked for God to reveal His greatness in the earth. That kind of prayer is powerful, because God's heart is to make Himself known to mankind.

That is why God sent Jesus. He was revealing Himself and His great love for us (John 12:45). He was showing us that He is just but loving, holy but merciful. He won't compromise with sin, but He would in love provide a way to be forgiven if we would come to Him and recognize how desperately we need the salvation He offers us (Acts 16:31).

As we have seen in chapter 33, this battle is a preview of Jesus the Divine Warrior going into battle for our souls on the cross of Calvary. This prayer is a prayer of salvation. We aren't saved just for our sakes. We are saved because God is showing the world that He is the one true God and desires that we come to Him in faith. He is showing the world that the gods of fame, fortune, and pleasure are no gods at all (Jeremiah 14:10). Only He can deliver us from the lie that those things will save us or bring any meaning to our lives.

God sent an answer to the prayer in the form of a poem through Isaiah. It began by saying that God was going to deal with Assyria because Hezekiah prayed. I wonder what would happen if our national leaders humbled themselves and prayed this kind of a prayer regarding radical Islam? Perhaps God would hear their prayer, not because our nation was repentant, but because they prayed that the world would know that He alone is God. Unfortunately, many of our leaders don't know that essential truth.

God's answer basically said that Sennacherib had mocked the wrong God. He was so lifted up in pride that, though he said YHWH sent him, he took full credit for all his victories. It was God who let him defeat his enemies and God who would now defeat him (1Corinthians 10:12). God was going to put a hook in his nose and pull him back to Nineveh.

33 "Therefore thus says the LORD concerning the king of Assyria: He shall not come into this city or shoot an arrow there or come before it with a shield or cast up a siege mound against it. 34 By the way that he came, by the same he shall return, and he shall not come into this city, declares the LORD. 35 For I will defend this city to save it, for my own sake and for the sake of my servant David." Isaiah 37:33-35 And that is what happened. Sennacherib returned with his army to lay siege on Jerusalem, but before he could attack, the angel of the LORD slew 185,000 warriors. Sennacherib departed with what remained of his army and was killed by his sons as he worshiped his god. Now whose god could not deliver? How ironic! For "David's sake" refers to the promise to David that a descendant would reign on his throne forever (1Chronicles 22:10).

Before his death Sennacherib had a prism made that told of his victories. He named city after city that he conquered, and then wrote that he "shut up Hezekiah like a bird in a cage." This artifact is known as the Taylor Prism. It, too, is in the British Museum. Like the Egyptians' war records, he didn't tell of his loss of men or why he did not conquer Jerusalem. After all, it was written to commemorate his victories, not tell of his defeats.

Hezekiah's prayer was answered. The chronicler recorded, *23 And many brought gifts to the LORD to Jerusalem and precious things to Hezekiah king of Judah, so that he was exalted in the sight of all nations from that time onward.* 2Chronicles 32:23 This was Jerusalem's chance to share with the world the message of the one true Creator of heaven and earth (Psalm 9:11).

Can we pray that God will do such amazing things that the world will see He is the one true God? Not only can we, but we should be constantly. The events of the end-times are filled with just such wonders. The wonder of your transformed life is the same message. How could you change from a selfish individual to being wholly devoted to God and serving others in love? Only God can transform a heart! It is a sign that God is just as powerfully active in the world today. He has won the greatest battle, the battle for our souls. The Divine Warrior has conquered hell and offers new life to all who, in the desperation we saw in Hezekiah, trust solely in Him (Psalm 34:5).

Questions
1 Review the political background.
2 What false hopes did Hezekiah trust?
3 Have you heard Rabshakeh's message?
4 What was Rabshakeh's contradiction?
5 How do we respond to a liar?
6 Where do you turn first in difficulty?
7 What did the messengers hope?
8 What was the promise?
9 What was the fulfillment?
10 What is the archeological verification of this account?
11 What can we apply from the account?

The Appropriate Response - Isaiah 38

We have previously studied God's miraculous deliverance of Jerusalem from Assyria. We read from Chronicles how the nations brought gifts to the Lord and to Hezekiah after hearing what God had done (2 Chronicles 32:23). The testimony of God's intervention was going out to the surrounding nations and they were impressed. But in our passage for today, things seem to take a turn for the worse. Hezekiah becomes ill. Isaiah told him his affliction was fatal. *¹ In those days Hezekiah became sick and was at the point of death. And Isaiah the prophet the son of Amoz came to him, and said to him, "Thus says the LORD: Set your house in order, for you shall die, you shall not recover."* Isaiah 38:1

What do we do when our time is up? Hopefully our life is hidden with Christ in God (Colossians 3:3). Hezekiah had lived an amazingly godly life. He is referred to as the godliest king ever to reign in Israel. (2Kings 18:5-6) Yes, his faith faltered when Assyria was conquering the cities of Judah, but we have not yet discussed just how godly he had been. When he came to power at the age of 25 (2 Chronicles 29:1), one of the first things he did was restore the Temple. His effect on the nation was something like the reformation. Even the remnant of the Jews from the Assyrian conquest of the northern tribes came for the greatest Passover celebration since the times of Solomon (2 Chronicles 30:26). The people were so stirred to return to the faithful worship of YHWH that they destroyed the idols throughout Judah.

Hezekiah even gave from his own wealth the sheep for the daily sacrifices. The singers and musicians were put in place. The priests and Levites were again supported by the people. The offerings to the Lord were so great that they had to use storerooms for it all (2 Chronicles 31:10-11). That is revival. But revival rarely lasts for more than a generation.

Hezekiah had not yet had a son. His father was previously told of a sign from the Lord that the house of David would not end. The Messiah would indeed come. A child would be born of a virgin and a son given who would have the very names of God. He would reign forever on David's throne (Isaiah 9:6). Hezekiah seemed to be at the height of his reign, with nations honoring Him. Could he not do more to establish faith in Judah and possibly live to see a son born who might be the one in the promise? (Jesus did come from the line of David but through another branch, though Jesus' step-father Joseph was of Hezekiah's line.)

² Then Hezekiah turned his face to the wall and prayed to the LORD, ³ and said, "Please, O LORD, remember how I have walked before you in faithfulness and with a whole heart, and have done what is good in your sight." And Hezekiah wept bitterly. Isaiah 38:2-3 God's grace had covered the errors of trusting in wealth in a time of panic. I believe Hezekiah's weeping can be interpreted as a sign of repentance for his failures, but it may also include the fact that he has no son to reign after him. He pleaded with God to remember the good he had done and how he had wholeheartedly lived for the LORD. He was one of the very few kings to remove the high places where foreign gods were worshiped (2Kings 18:22). Hezekiah's prayer does not say he asked for a longer life, but to be heard for the good had done. His poem, however, indicates he was asking for more time. He was asking for mercy to not die yet.

If we heard we were about to die, how many of us would ask God to remember all the good we had done and our wholehearted life for God? Thank the Lord that we know we can simply ask the Father to look upon the Son who is our righteousness (2 Corinthians 5:21). Amen?

God immediately had Isaiah turn around and tell Hezekiah his prayer was heard and he would have fifteen more years. The account in 2 Kings 20:5 tells us that God also promised that on the third day Hezekiah would be able to go up to the Temple and worship. Not only that, but God would continue to defend Jerusalem from Assyria.

Now we jump to the end of the chapter to see what happened next. *²¹ Now Isaiah had said, "Let them take a cake of figs and apply it to the boil, that he may recover."* Isaiah 38:21 God directed Isaiah to use a natural remedy. This is fascinating to me for this reason, God can heal supernaturally or He can direct us to natural means. A cake of figs was a bunch of figs that were dried and pressed together. There must have been something to the quality of figs that drew out the toxin. Recent research has shown that is true and has also shown fig leaves can inhibit the growth in certain types of cancer cells. There are natural remedies and God has also given man the wisdom to develop compounds to deal with certain illnesses. The important thing is that we look to the Lord for the solution to which He would direct us (2 Chronicles 16:12).

²² Hezekiah also had said, "What is the sign that I shall go up to the house of the LORD?" Isaiah 38:22 Hezekiah wanted something to bolster his faith. We can see doubt creeping in again. God promised but Hezekiah wants more than a promise. Could he really recover in three days and go up from the palace to the Temple on his own two feet? Archeology shows us there was a staircase of over hundred steps up and that was after going down from the palace about forty steps to where those stairs to the Temple began. Hezekiah was asking for a sign that in three days he would be well enough to climb those steps and worship in the Temple. The grace of the LORD was willing to give it.

   [7] "This shall be the sign to you from the LORD, that the LORD will do this thing that he has promised: [8] Behold, I will make the shadow cast by the declining sun on the dial of Ahaz turn back ten steps." So the sun turned back on the dial the ten steps by which it had declined. Isaiah 38:7-8 Heroditus in 440 B.C. wrote that the Syrians had created the sundial. The Odyssey by Homer written in 900 B.C. mentions some device for measuring the movement of the sun, so King Ahaz who was threatened by the Syrians very well may have installed such a structure in the palace. It may be the stairs mentioned in Scripture that led from the palace to the Horse Gate and from the Horse Gate up to the Temple. Ahaz altered the steps that went up to the Temple and may have done so in a way so as to use them to keep time (2 Kings 16:18). The shadow of the palace on those steps may be what is referenced as the sun would cast the palace pinnacle's shadow on those steps. Apparently, the king's bed was in sight of those steps.

   While the poultice of figs seems like a natural remedy, this seems like an unexplainable miracle. Attempts have been made to explain it as meteorological event. Under certain climatic conditions clouds of minute ice crystals can form at a great height in the upper reaches of the air; the apparent result as seen from the earth is the appearance of a band of light passing through the sun, and two additional suns, one on either side of the true sun. This effect, which is known as *parhelia,* or "mock sun" is due to the refraction of the sun's light as it passes through the prismatic ice crystals on its way to the earth. If now a cloud, at a much lower altitude, should obscure real sun and the western "mock sun" over a certain district, the only light reaching that district is from the eastern "mock sun," and the effect is as if the sun had receded eastwards by a certain fixed amount (always equal to one and a half hours of our time). Two occasions when this actually happened are on record; one was on 27th March 1703 at Metz in France, when the shadow on the sundial of the Prior of Metz was displaced by one and a half hours. The other occasion was on the 28th March, 1848 over parts of Hampshire when the same effect was observed. (http://www.biblefellowshipunion.co.uk/2008/May_Jun/Sundial.htm)

   It has also been suggested that the Shekinah appeared from the Temple and its light erased the shadow of the palace on the steps. That would certainly encourage Hezekiah to believe. Perhaps it is what was meant in his poem when he expressed his previous concern for his impending death, *[11a] I said, I shall not see the LORD, the LORD in the land of the living;* Isaiah 38:11a

It was such a notable event that Josephus wrote of it as an historical event in which the shadow that had gone down ten steps actually moved back up ten steps. (Antiquities 10,2,1) However God brought it about, the surrounding world heard of the sign and of Hezekiah's recovery (2 Chronicles 32:31). Nothing is too hard for God. He can encourage our faith in our hour of desperation. He can assure our faith with a miracle or a natural phenomenon that He times perfectly to convince us.

God could have used a natural phenomenon or have performed a miracle. It really doesn't matter which. What is important is that He answered Hezekiah's prayer and encouraged his faith. Hezekiah would pen the songs of ascent or "songs of the steps" written about those steps on which the Lord gave him the sign of a longer life, Psalms 120 through 134. Pilgrims in Jesus' time would sing these songs as they went up to the feast days in Jerusalem.

God answered Hezekiah's plea in spite of its results in the next generation, which we'll see in next week's sermon. Answered prayer isn't always a blessing. Extending life isn't always a benefit.

After his recovery, Hezekiah penned the poem in this chapter. Most of the Old Testament saints did not have an understanding of life after death (Psalm 88:11-12). Hezekiah thought only the living could praise God. Later revelation would show that the afterlife is filled with praise from the redeemed to God (Revelation 5:13).

Hezekiah referred to his body as a tent, an image picked up in the New Testament by the Apostle Paul (2 Corinthians 5:1). *[12] My dwelling is plucked up and removed from me like a shepherd's tent; like a weaver I have rolled up my life; he cuts me off from the loom; from day to night you bring me to an end;* Isaiah 38:12 We do well to consider the temporary nature of the body we inhabit. While we should care for it as the temple of the Holy Spirit, but we should not overemphasize it, recognizing how fragile and short this life is.

Verses 10 through 16 express so clearly the human struggle of illness. The pain and suffering we endure can cause us to be bitter, for we know God has allowed it but we often cannot understand why. (See *Why Suffering?* by Ravi Zacharias) Ezra was so insightful and honest when, in the psalm just before those of Hezekiah's in our Book of Psalms, he declared that it was in faithfulness God had afflicted him (Psalm 119:75). He declared that it was good for him to be afflicted so that he might learn God's statutes (Psalm 119:71). But most of us are more like Hezekiah. We ask, "Why me God? Haven't I tried to serve You with my whole heart?"

We should have the faith that Ezra expressed trusting that God knows what we can endure and allows things to come into our lives for His own reasons, reasons we may never understand in this life. The difficulties will refine us and deepen our trust if we will refuse to allow bitterness to take over our soul (Hebrews 12:15).

Hezekiah poem confesses that he was bitter, and perhaps that is the root of the spiritual weakness that will result in the failure we'll see next

162

week. Nevertheless, he realized he was a recipient of grace in spite of it. *17 Behold, it was for my welfare that I had great bitterness; but in love you have delivered my life from the pit of destruction, for you have cast all my sins behind your back.* Isaiah 38:17

The love and mercy of God toward Hezekiah delivered his physical life for fifteen more years and his spiritual life for eternity. Why? Because God cast all Hezekiah's sins behind his back. While Hezekiah first pleaded on the basis of his own good works and passion to please God, his afterthought is that it was just the love of God that put away his sins. The only way that would be possible is that one day the promised One would bear Hezekiah's sins and yours and mine and take the punishment we deserve (1Peter 2:24). Hezekiah didn't know how that was possible, but he believed that if God could save his physical life, He could save his eternal soul as well.

19 The living, the living, he thanks you, as I do this day; the father makes known to the children your faithfulness. Isaiah 38:19 While at the moment Hezekiah was filled with praise and vowed a life of thanksgiving, this fervor would wane for a time. He would not even adequately convey God's faithfulness to his son. His own mouth could condemn him if it were not for the grace of God upon his life. God help us never to forget what God has done for us, His many answers to prayer (Psalm 103:2-3). The nation would not forget what God did for Hezekiah, but somehow the passion of gratitude will fade for a while in Hezekiah's heart.

This fading gratitude of man must baffle the angels. Here is fallen man, graciously warned of the approaching end of life, pleading for more time and repenting for his lack of faith. God's love forgives his sin, gives him fifteen more years, promises to keep superpower off his back, and gives him a sign to assure his faith. Hezekiah writes a poem promising God he will show gratitude in numerous ways. But from the start of it all, God knew Hezekiah would not follow through and would have a period of backsliding into pride.

How do we keep gratitude from fading in our own lives? Hezekiah tells us but does not follow through on his own vows. He writes of giving praise, of telling his children, and of playing praise music with instruments. But it must be for more than just a season. It must be our life (Psalm 146:2).

20 The LORD will save me, and we will play my music on stringed instruments all the days of our lives, at the house of the LORD. Isaiah 38:20 He did write those songs of ascent. He promised this "all the days of our lives at the house of the LORD." But sadly, he would respond to the blessing of prosperity with pride (2 Chronicles 32:25). Over and over man responds to blessing with pride.

I want to conclude with the thought of our appropriate responses to bad news and to the answers to prayers. Hezekiah was right to go to God with tears when he knew his life was about to end. He probably had concern for the future of the nation, but his poem also reveals he was bitter about his illness. What is the right response to times of testing?

First, we should acknowledge that God owes us nothing (Romans 11:35). If we were perfect servants of God, He would still owe us nothing, for all we are and have is from Him. Anything short of praise and thanksgiving for everything from His hand is sin. Our appropriate response is to thank Him for all the undeserved blessings we have received (1 Chronicles 16:34). Be sure you have truly repented and are in Christ as you prepare to stand before God. Make sure there is no assignment He has given you that is left undone (John 17:4).

Jesus gave us quite an example of preparation for death. He taught the most impacting lessons with illustrations during His last week. From the cross He forgave those who had wronged Him (Luke 23:34). He took care of the obligation of His mother (John 19:26). He witnessed to the thief next to Him (Luke 23:43). Then when He was finished doing everything assigned by the Father He put His life in the Father's hands (Luke 23:46).

What is the appropriate response if God graciously answers your prayers, whether for longer life for yourself, your children, or a loved one? He certainly has done that for me, more than once. Hezekiah gave us a good outline even if he didn't follow it completely through.

Thank God daily for the rest of your life as you live daily in a vital relationship with Him. Remember His mercy to you. That will help to keep you from pride. It reminds us how dependent we are on Him. Don't let the joy of answered prayer fade. Tell your children of God's faithfulness. Make sure they hear the testimony again and again. And give praise with the people of God with your voice or on an instrument "all the days of our lives, at the house of the LORD."

The house of the LORD was the Temple. Today it is the fellowship of believers. Don't forsake the assembling of yourselves together (Hebrews 10:25). The body of believers can be a pain at times, but it is partially through our learning to have patience with one another that we grow, remembering that others are patient with us. Let us have the appropriate response to answered prayer out of gratitude to the LORD for our own spiritual life, for our family, for our congregation, and nation. Amen?

Questions
1 What had Hezekiah accomplished?
2 What were Hezekiah's concerns?
3 What can we learn from the remedy?
4 What was a sign of Hezekiah's lack of faith?
5 What was the miracle?
6 Who heard about it?
7 What should we learn about our tent?
8 How should we respond to illness?
9 How did Jesus demonstrate preparation for death?
10 How should we respond to graciously answered prayers?

Tend the Flame! - Isaiah 39

Our last study in Isaiah was about the miraculous healing of Hezekiah and the sign that God gave to encourage his faith. We saw how godly Hezekiah had been in bringing about a restoration of true worship in Israel, and even removing the high places where idols were worshiped (2Chronicles 30:1). But we ended with a hint that something was amiss in Hezekiah's heart, for he demanded a sign to be sure God had really spoken through Isaiah (Isaiah 38:22; John 2:18).

After Hezekiah's prayer was answered and the sign of the sun's shadow going backward came to pass, Hezekiah seemed to be on fire for the Lord. He wrote a poem promising to give thanks and praise the LORD. He promised to teach his children of God's faithfulness. He declared that he would make music to the LORD in the temple for the rest of his life (Isaiah 38:18-20). He was experiencing the high of a divine encounter.

Have you ever had a time when God seemed to be so real and near that you knew you *should* never be the same? I can recall a number of those times. As a young teenager I thought my mother was dying and prayed all the way to the hospital and made vows to God. There was a time in church when the text the pastor chose just grabbed me and wouldn't let me go. Another time was in a Bible study with some school friends who all knew Jesus was in our midst. When I was called into ministry was another time. You can't forget those encounters. They are a gift of God's grace to help strengthen our faith. Think for a moment of your own encounter. They are not necessary but help those of us whose faith is weak (Judges 6:17). The reality of our faith is seen after we come down from the emotional high.

Hezekiah was so moved that he wrote the psalms of ascension. He first wrote down in a poem how he should have responded. But sadly, he allowed the fire of passion for God to grow cold. That joy of answered prayer with its promise of fifteen years of life and protection to boot, slowly faded like a coal removed from a fire.

It doesn't happen all at once. Those psalms were probably penned over a number of years. But the cycle we have seen before with nations came to pass in his life. Blessing often brings financial prosperity. Prosperity can result in pride. We can begin to think that we are pretty clever and forget it all came from God's merciful hand. We begin to trust in the wealth instead of looking to God. The more we do so the more we take the glory for the accomplishments and blessings in our lives. As we do so we move further and further from that passionate fire we once had for the God we know spared us and showed us His greatness and His love (Isaiah 38:17).

We forget the vows we made and the earnest commitment we had to keep them. Before long our life begins to look like it did before our encounter with the living God, before His Word captured our minds and grabbed our hearts. Let's call it the cycle of the untended fire (2Timothy 1:6).

Just this morning Sandy Richards forwarded Spurgeon's morning devotion for today. He writes, "It is the incessant turmoil of this world, the constant attraction of earthly things which takes away the soul from Christ. While memory preserves a poisonous weed too well, it permits the Rose of Sharon to wither. Let's charge ourselves to bind a heavenly forget-me-not about our hearts for Jesus our Beloved, and, whatever else we let slip, let's hold fast to Him!"(1Corinthians 11:24)

Hezekiah was the only king to stave off the Assyrian assault. The other defeated nations brought gifts to the LORD and to Hezekiah (2Chronicles 32:23). Later when word got around of his miraculous healing and the sign from God, the king of Babylon sent letters and a present to Hezekiah. These kings wanted powerful allies and to be on the side of the allies whose god or gods were most powerful.

¹ At that time Merodach-baladan the son of Baladan, king of Babylon, sent envoys with letters and a present to Hezekiah, for he heard that he had been sick and had recovered. Isaiah 39:1 Babylon was one of the up and coming powers. If anyone could stop the Assyrians, it would be this great power. The honor bestowed on Hezekiah was a real ego booster. But remember, God had already promised to protect Hezekiah from Assyria and given him a sign to assure him (Isaiah 38:6).

So, what did Hezekiah do? Did he tell them how great YHWH is? Did he tell them how the angel of the Lord slew 185,000 Assyrians when Judah was helpless to do anything against them? Did he tell of how the Lord was the One who told him how to cure his illness? We don't have record of that. Instead we see him showing them how his wealth had returned and all the treasures of his fathers. *² And Hezekiah welcomed them gladly. And he showed them his treasure house, the silver, the gold, the spices, the precious oil, his whole armory, all that was found in his storehouses. There was nothing in his house or in all his realm that Hezekiah did not show them.* Isaiah 39:2

The words "all" and "nothing" are used in three sets. Hezekiah showed them *all* the treasures in his storerooms and there was *nothing* in his house that he did not show them. This seems so strange, and yet I can see how pride would lead down this path. These envoys had come because they saw God had been with Hezekiah. Instead of sharing the testimonies of God's greatness, he shows how great he is by showing his wealth (2Chronicles 32:25).

The last day of our vacation an elderly lady walked up to us and said we looked like lovebirds. She asked how long we'd been married. We told her almost 40 years! She then proceeded on a monologue to tell us of the vacation clubs she belonged to, the places she and her husband were going next year and the year after that. I went away thinking how wealthy they were, which is exactly what I think she wanted us to go away thinking. Our value is not in our wealth! It is in our relationship with God! How often the Scriptures address this. A man's life does not consist in the abundance of the things he possesses (Luke 12:15).

166

We can brag of wealth, or knowledge, or position, or fame, or any number of worldly things, but let the person who boasts boast in the Lord (1Corinthians 1:31). I wonder how history might have changed if Hezekiah focused his conversation with the Babylonians on the greatness of YHWH. Maybe they would have feared attacking Judah in the future instead of being incentivized by the wealth of Judah.

We saw that weakness in Hezekiah before when he tried to buy Egypt's help and again when he tried to pay off the Assyrians. Both attempts at leaning on money to save the nation failed. God alone could protect them. Now we see him falling back to faith in wealth as giving him meaning and value. Instead of tending the fire of passion and gratitude toward God, he is slipping back into his old weaknesses.

This is a repeated Biblical lesson. We see it in the judges Samson and Gideon (Judges 8:27). We see it in the kings David and Jehoshaphat (1Kings 22:48). We see it in the New Testament with Demas (2Timothy 4:10) and Diotrephes (3John 1:9). We see this in our neighbors who once attended church and had a vibrant relationship with Jesus, but now no longer have any desire for fellowship. The pride of life and the lust of the things of the world capture our thoughts (1John 2:15-17). Once our imagination is given the freedom to roam, our flesh promises more than it can deliver. It won't be long before our feet will follow, and then we end up in bondage to that from which we were once delivered (Galatians 1:6). It can happen to any of us if we don't tend the flame of passion and gratitude toward God.

How do we slip away from such great satisfaction and joy? We don't pay the price of time. A real relationship is a two-way street. If we don't put anything in, we grow distant and our eyes begin to roam. In our carnal nature, we look for something that can satisfy our emptiness without costing us. "Won't somebody worship us? Won't some pleasure fulfill us?" No! The hole in our spirit is too big to be filled with anything other than God, but we know He places demands on our lives (Matthew 16:24).

Our hearts need to feast on God's Word. We need to be in fellowship with Him and one another. We need to be with Him in prayer. We need to listen to and obey the Holy Spirit. These are vital to keeping the flame burning. The way to keep our eyes from wandering is to be constantly filled with Jesus, overflowing and grateful.

Isaiah confronted Hezekiah. *³ Then Isaiah the prophet came to King Hezekiah, and said to him, "What did these men say? And from where did they come to you?" Hezekiah said, "They have come to me from a far country, from Babylon." ⁴ᵃ He said, "What have they seen in your house?"* Isaiah 39:3-4a Don't you think Hezekiah knew he was in trouble? I'm sure he had that uneasy feeling that he had failed God, but when Isaiah showed up he knew it. When Isaiah asked about the men, I would guess that conviction told him what Isaiah was about to say. At least, that is how it happens to me. When we disobey the Holy Spirit, we can run but we can't hide. Sooner or later "the hound of heaven" catches up with us and we know we have to answer to God and face the consequences.

Hezekiah answered, "They have seen all that is in my house. There is nothing in my storehouses that I did not show them." Isaiah 39:4b At least Hezekiah was honest in his answer. Here is the second "all" and "nothing" I mentioned earlier. He was so eager to show them his greatness rather than God's greatness that he had to show them every treasure he possessed. When I'm talking about myself, I'm probably not talking about God. That is unless I'm telling you how weak I am to show the mercy and greatness of God by contrast. If someone tells you of all their gifts and all the many ways God uses them to do incredible things, the red flags should go up. Pride is one of the most enslaving and destructive sins.

The serpent is subtler than any beast of the field (Genesis 3:1). He'll convince you that it is ok to brag -I mean "explain"- how great a servant of God you are because it really shows how great God is. Or maybe it's good to tell how much you have because it shows God's blessings on your life. But really, when you are talking about yourself, it's not about God. It's about you.

Then Isaiah told Hezekiah the consequences of his sin. *⁶ Behold, the days are coming, when all that is in your house, and that which your fathers have stored up till this day, shall be carried to Babylon. Nothing shall be left, says the LORD.* Isaiah 39:6 There is the last set of "all" and "nothing". All in his house would be taken and nothing would be left. It was the utter captivity of Judah and all the physical blessings they so highly esteemed. If that is what it takes to humble us and get us to turn from our idols to the everlasting God, it is an act of mercy.

Was Hezekiah's sin really so bad? Well, the more we know and experience, the more accountable we are (Luke 12:48). It would really be the fruit of Hezekiah's apathetic end of life that would assure captivity for the nation. While he would be remembered as one of the best kings, his son would go down as one of the worst (2Chronicles 33:9).

⁷ And some of your own sons, who will come from you, whom you will father, shall be taken away, and they shall be eunuchs in the palace of the king of Babylon." Isaiah 39:7 Hezekiah may have once hoped to father the messiah, but now is told some of his descendants will be eunuchs in the palace of Babylon.

While Hezekiah had promised to relay God's faithfulness to his children, his son Manasseh was one of the worst kings in the history of the nation. It was written that captivity of the nation had to come because of Manasseh's great sins (2Kings 24:3). Manasseh was born during the fifteen extra years of life that God promised to Hezekiah.

The Chronicles tell us that captivity was held off during the life of Hezekiah because when he heard this word from the Lord, he humbled himself (2Chronicles 32:26). He recognized his fault and again repented.

⁸ Then Hezekiah said to Isaiah, "The word of the LORD that you have spoken is good." For he thought, "There will be peace and security in my days." Isaiah 39:8 When I first read this I thought how selfish and heartless he must have been. But considering that the Chronicles tell us he had repented, I read it differently. I think he saw this promise to hold off on captivity as God's mercy. He must have thought they deserved to have it come sooner, considering his ingratitude and prideful behavior. Perhaps he was saying God is gracious and just and more merciful than I deserve (Lamentations 3:22). It is a good word from God in that it showed an extension of the time of mercy.

I wonder if we, as a nation, aren't in a similar situation. Look at all the times God has intervened for this nation, saved us from destruction, and shown Himself mighty to save. What has been the nation's response? We take pride in our wealth, but we have such a huge debt no one expects it will ever be paid. Have we responded with the appropriate gratitude and fanned the flames of passion toward God to keep them burning strong?

While we may not be able to respond for our nation, we can certainly respond for ourselves as individuals. Will we humble ourselves like Hezekiah did? Is it too late to spare our children? Is our next president a Hezekiah or a Manasseh? We will see. We don't have to wait to humble ourselves before God and acknowledge our own ingratitude and failure to fan the flames of passion for Him.

I am convicted of my own ingratitude. I've been blessed with so much and yet I whine about the littlest things. I have a new motto to help me apply my repentant heart. "Ruthlessly deal with whining!" God help us quit whining and start rejoicing. Instead of talking about the petty complaints, let's talk about how blessed we are in the Lord. Maybe more people would consider Christ if they heard us talking about the joy we have in Him rather than all the things that don't go just like we'd like them.

Let us commit to doing those things Hezekiah meant to do. Let's keep praising and thanking God. Let's not stop telling our children and grandchildren about God's faithfulness to us (Deuteronomy 6:7). Whatever God has planned for the coming years, our children will be better off if they know they can rely upon God. We may have unintentionally given them the message that money is the answer, but from now on let's tell them the truth. A relationship with Jesus is all that matters.

Do you want to prepare your children for what is coming? Tell them about the faithfulness of God. Tell them how He has met you in your need. Tell them how important it is to fan the flames of gratitude when God meets them in their need and answers their prayers so that they don't slip away and again trust in things that can't help them.   TEND THE FLAME OR IT WILL DIE!

Questions
1 What is the hint something is wrong in Hezekiah's heart?
2 Have you had a God encounter?
3 What is the cycle of nations and many lives?
4 What did Hezekiah tell the envoys and why?
5 How do we slip away?
6 How do we keep the flame burning?

7 Review the three "all" and "nothing" uses.
8 Why did captivity not come sooner?
9 How should we interpret verse 8?
10 How have you responded to God's intervention in your life? How will you respond?
11 When will you share God's faithfulness to you with your children?

The Comfort of God - Isaiah 40:1-11

We are entering into the second section of Isaiah. In the first thirty-nine chapters, we read of God pleading with Judah to turn back to God (Isaiah 1:18). God warned of the consequences of continuing to practice injustice and the worship of idols. He spared the city of Jerusalem from the Assyrian army. But in the last chapter God warned the nation that captivity was inevitable (Isaiah 39:7).

This new section begins by speaking to those in that future captivity. It would come to pass by the very nation Isaiah predicted (Isaiah 39:5-7), but the grace of God would put it off one hundred years (586 BC). Most seminaries today teach that this section is written by a second Isaiah. That is because they don't believe the first Isaiah would have written to those people who would eventually go into captivity. That would be prophetic, and they don't believe in miracles. When conservatives respond that the apostles quoted from this portion and attributed it to Isaiah (Matthew 8:17), those learned men say, "It was simply the convention of that day." In other words, they weren't inspired. Could it be that the scholars' skepticism is a convention of our day? But then, rarely do they apply their reasoning to themselves.

The pastors' group was talking about the increasingly obvious fact that the universe had a beginning and that science is showing the world is designed. One pastor thought eventually the world would have to admit there is a creator. I don't think so. Mankind just comes up with ever more farfetched ideas to explain it away (Psalm 14:1). The odds of a planet like ours in this universe is so infinitesimally small that it is statistically impossible, so there must be multiverses to increase the odds. Now that is faith, or perhaps being obstinate!

Design is so obvious in nature that a prominent evolutionist has said that we must constantly remind ourselves that what we see is the product of time and chance. At the same they can't tell us how time and chance can produce information necessary for the design.

Here in Arizona we have the yucca plant. It can only be pollinated by the yucca moth. The moth then lays its eggs in the flower it has pollinated. The larvae will eat about half the seeds leaving the rest for reproduction. Which came first? The both had to exist at the same time. Each organism is dependent on the other.

Those who insist on being their own lord will find ever increasingly absurd explanations for the reality that is plainly in front of us. This is partially due to an idea of God being the judgmental, finger wagging, nagging old man they perceive to be described in the Old Testament. However, the previous thirty-nine chapters are not a demanding, mean spirited God who insists on His way, but rather a merciful God warning of the consequences of going the wrong direction (Isaiah 45:22).

We see a father warning his children not to ride their tricycle into the street as a loving request to spare them from injury. But those who see God as a tyrant see the same thing in their life from a teenager's perspective. You know what I mean. "What does dad know (Psalm 73:11)? He's so demanding!" And such were all of us until we responded to the Spirit of God moving upon our hearts with His love.

Captivity to a greater power, whether a nation or sin, is not God's desire. His desire is for us to know His love and wonderful plan for each of our lives (Jeremiah 29:11). That is why this section begins with a word of comfort.

¹ Comfort, comfort my people, says your God. ² Speak tenderly to Jerusalem, and cry to her that her warfare is ended, that her iniquity is pardoned, that she has received from the LORD's hand double for all her sins. Isaiah 40:1-2 Right up to the captivity of Jerusalem the people continued to rebel against God. Nevertheless, God still calls them His people. His heart is for them to learn from their sins and change direction. That is His heart for us as well. When we are dealing with the consequences of our idolatry, or our selfish choices, or refusal to heed God's warnings, He comes to us with tender words of comfort (Romans 5:8).

The world can be a very discouraging place. That is because of its fallen condition. We are all on our way to death. Our loved ones will die. Man's inhumanity to man is ever finding new ways to express itself. Corruption in government is reaching new heights. Our prisons are overcrowded. Our seminaries are producing liberal pastors who don't have faith in God's Word. Our education system is telling our children there is no such thing as truth. I could go on and on. But in the midst of it all, God declares comfort to us. There is an end to the struggle. There is hope in Christ.

Why should we be comforted? Judah would hear this prophecy when her seventy years of captivity were about over (Jeremiah 25:11). The consequences of her sins were dealt with. A new generation had risen. The nation would miraculously be restored. The line of David had survived. The Messiah was still coming. That is where this passage is leading us. It is the underlying theme of Isaiah. And for us today, He is waiting for us at the end of our stubborn resistance. When we finally bow our head and cry out for help, we are ready to see He has been there all along.

³ A voice cries: "In the wilderness prepare the way of the LORD; make straight in the desert a highway for our God. Isaiah 40:3 All four gospels tell us that this became the message of John the Baptist (Matthew

3:3; Mark 1:3; Luke 3:4; John 1:23). The Holy Spirit inspired John to see this as his appointed message proclaiming the coming of the Messiah. Notice that by using this passage, John the Baptist was declaring that Jesus is God. The highway he asks us to prepare is for our God.

The wilderness and desert are not physical locations but the condition of the heart of man. Without God, our hearts are barren and dry. Our thoughts are like hyenas in that desert barking out their selfish demands. The call is to get ready for things to change. We are commanded to make a highway there for our God. John declared that we do that by repenting (Matthew 3:2). We must see ourselves as God sees us. We need to see how desperately we need the water of life (Revelation 22:17). We have to choose life over death and hope over apathy. God can change us, but we must make that highway for Him to enter by agreeing with Him about our condition. Until we do that there is no entry point into our hearts.

The goodness of God leads us to repentance (Romans 2:4). He spares us from our own foolishness time and time again, and we begin to see His mercy, grace, and love for us. Our thoughts of Him start to shift from that of a demanding tyrant to that of a patient, loving Father. The more we see of His heart and agree with it, the more the highway is opened up until the next verse comes to pass within our hearts.

⁴ Every valley shall be lifted up, and every mountain and hill be made low; the uneven ground shall become level, and the rough places a plain. Isaiah 40:4 This is what citizens would do to the main highway when a king was coming to visit their area. They would go out and improve the road and make repairs to places that had flooded or collapsed. It showed they honored him and welcomed his visit. And this is what we need to do if we would have the King of kings at home in our hearts. We welcome the King by removing the obstacles in our hearts.

⁵ And the glory of the LORD shall be revealed, and all flesh shall see it together, for the mouth of the LORD has spoken." Isaiah 40:5 John the beloved tells us that Jesus manifested the glory of God (John 1:14). To some extent the world is seeing it as the Gospel is published in the languages of the world. As Christians let the life of Christ in them shine, the world sees Jesus' glory. But as we have seen before, there are intermediate and ultimate fulfillments. Certainly, Jesus' first coming and our lives are just an intermediate fulfillment.

In several prophetic passages regarding the Second Coming in great glory, every eye is said to see Him (Matthew 24:30; Revelation 1:7). The eyes of all who ever lived will see Jesus' unveiled glory as He returns to judge the earth. Some will repent at the sight of Him (Zechariah 12:10) while others seek to hide from His presence (Revelation 6:15-16).

In verse two a voice cries that the time of captivity is almost over. In verse three the voice cries out regarding preparing the way for the LORD. Now in verse six a voice cries out regarding the frailty of man and the permanence of God's Word. *⁶ A voice says, "Cry!" And I said, "What shall I cry?" All flesh is grass, and all its beauty is like the flower of the field. ⁷ The*

172

grass withers, the flower fades when the breath of the LORD blows on it; surely the people are grass. Isaiah 40:6-7

When we look at the three cries together we see a message to all humanity. 1. We are in bondage to sin, but that time of bondage can end. 2. Prepare your heart for the coming of the LORD. 3. He is the only One that gives our frail flesh eternal purpose. Without Him we will perish (John 3:36). That is the Gospel in three short declarations.

Man tends to think he is invincible, especially in his youth. As we age we increasingly see how fragile life is. Loved ones die. Illness strikes. We have some close calls, and we begin to see what God was saying through Isaiah. Get right with God while you have time. Our life has been compared to a dot that begins a line that goes on forever. If we knew how brief this dot of a life is, we'd certainly invest it in the line that is before us. This is the cry of the as yet unidentified voice. Life is short. Get serious about it. Think about what matters, about what is eternal. Act with wisdom (James 4:14).

[8] The grass withers, the flower fades, but the word of our God will stand forever. Isaiah 40:8 We look on the brevity of life and realize that we should be preparing the way for the Word to enter our hearts. This Word of the Lord is forever. The so-called scholars can redefine it any way they want, but it doesn't change its beauty or power. Their little wooden hammers of man's ideas are hammering on the granite mountain of the enduring Word of God. A billion of their hammers will wear away without any effect on the mountain of God's Word.

The emergent church is based on the philosophy of evolution being the source of this world. Therefore, they conclude that the Bible is a collection of good stories. We can't know which are allegories and which are true, but certainly the miraculous is all allegory. Bang, bang, bang, go the little wooden hammers as they wear themselves out. Philosopher and theologian go to their graves like withered grass, but the Word of God is unchanged. They do influence young minds, that is, until the Spirit of God moves on those young hearts and they begin to see the power of Almighty God and His own intervention in their lives. Then the veil is lifted and suddenly everything from nothing sounds absurd. Intelligence from non-intelligence sounds unintelligent. Then the Christian they once thought believed in fairytales is now their brother or sister in the faith. Sound familiar? It is the story many of you share.

[9] Go on up to a high mountain, O Zion, herald of good news; lift up your voice with strength, O Jerusalem, herald of good news; lift it up, fear not; say to the cities of Judah, "Behold your God!" Isaiah 40:9 These verses can also be translated, "O herald of good news to Zion," and "O herald of good news to Jerusalem." I think that fits the context better. Zion and Jerusalem are the people in captivity, but God still calls them His special city. Again, this was true when Jesus came to Jerusalem and people could see God (John 14:9). It will be ultimately true when He comes again in glory. It is then the Jewish people will finally recognize Jesus is their God (Zechariah 13:1).

Zechariah tells us this will happen during a time of distress for Jerusalem. It will appear that they are doomed, just as it did when Pharaoh's army closed in on Israel at the waters of the Red Sea. The LORD will fight for them as they mourn over their past rejection of their Savior (Zechariah 14:2-3). While some are quietly declaring the Good News today in Israel, in that day it will be shouted from the mountaintops.

¹⁰ Behold, the Lord GOD comes with might, and his arm rules for him; behold, his reward is with him, and his recompense before him. Isaiah 40:10 Jesus came as a Lamb the first time. He is coming as a Lion to rule and reign the next time. He is coming in power and great glory. Isaiah refers to Jesus as "the arm of the Lord" (Isaiah 53:1). Jesus will reign on Zion (Isaiah 24:23). Evil will be swiftly dealt with. All the voices that have asked why God doesn't wipe out evil will have their answer and be out of excuses. The Millennium will show once and for all that the real problem is not how God acts, but how we act (Revelation 20:7-9).

Jesus will bring His reward and recompense with Him. Some will be justly compensated for a life of service to Jesus. Others will be punished for their evil actions toward others. In my message *Rewards* I explained that these words, "reward" and "recompense" mean both blessing and punishment. Jesus promised to reward us for service rendered to Him. It is His sense of justice. We know that any good thing we accomplish is because of Him, yet His justice and grace assure we will be rewarded (Matthew 10:42).

The chapter began as a word of comfort. It is the introduction for the rest of the book, for the coming of the Messiah is the most comforting hope the world had. Now that we know He has come, we look back on what He accomplished as our hope of eternity in His presence.

I close on another word of comfort. *¹¹ He will tend his flock like a shepherd; he will gather the lambs in his arms; he will carry them in his bosom, and gently lead those that are with young.* Isaiah 40:11 He is the Shepherd of Psalm 23, our LORD. He declared He is the good shepherd in John 10:11 and explained that He knows each of us by name (John 10:3).

Shepherd's make sure to lead their sheep to pleasant pastures. He gives us the Word of God for our spiritual sustenance and the Holy Spirit to help us digest it. He looks after our wounds. He protects us from the predators. He guides us through life. He tends to us like no other. He is the Good Shepherd to whom none can compare.

Those who are young, immature in the faith, He carries in His bosom. Some of us remember that honeymoon time when we first came to Christ and He seemed to intervene constantly. We weren't strong enough to face adversity, so He protected us by holding us in His arms. Don't you love the imagery!

The shepherd is different from a cattleman in that he leads instead of drives. For those with little lambs that would have a hard time keeping up, that is a person who is discipling a new believer, He will lead at a pace that both can maintain. He is concerned about each and every sheep in His flock.

174

He knows you. He knows your need. He knows how fast you can go (Genesis 39:13-14). He'll steer you away from the poisonous weeds and lead you to good pasture and calm water if you'll just keep following Him (Psalm 23:2).

This is what the people of Judah in captivity were told to look forward to. The line of David was intact. A Savior would be born; a Son would be given (Isaiah 9:6). The answer to our sin debt was the Lamb of God (John 1:29). They could look forward in hope. We can look back in assurance. It is the reason for their souls and ours to find comfort. Our shepherd will lead us through this fallen world and on to glory.

Questions
1 Why is it so hard to believe in miracles?
2 How is God like a good father?
3 What was John the Baptist's message?
4 What is verse 4 about?
5 How are the 3 cries connected?
6 How fragile is life? What is eternal?
7 How can people see the truth?
8 When will Israel be saved?
9 Who will see Jesus' return?
10 In what ways is Jesus a good shepherd?
11 What is the comfort for us today?

The Greatness of God - Isaiah 40:12-26

This new section of Isaiah began with Isaiah addressing the future exiles in Babylon. The time of their captivity would come to an end and they would be restored to the Promised Land. The Temple would be rebuilt and the worship of the nation would be purified.

The problem with the nation had been idolatry. Joshua had challenged them when they first came into the Promised Land to choose who they would serve. After all God had done for them, they still had idols carried with them from Egypt (Joshua 24:14). They could worship those or the gods of the Ammorites. Joshua declared that he and his house would worship YHWH, the eternal God of Israel, the great I Am (Joshua 24:15).

As time passed their real choice became clear. They adopted the various gods of the people they had expelled from the land. There were occasional revivals such as the one under Hezekiah, but the nation would soon revert to idolatry. Moses warned them in his farewell address that they would choose idolatry and go into captivity because of it (Deuteronomy 31:29; 28:41). Eight-hundred-years later it came to pass. Isaiah is writing to the future captives, but the first readers were still one-hundred-years away from the prophecies of Moses and Isaiah coming to pass.

Isaiah was telling the people something similar to the message of Moses. They will cling to their idolatry and suffer because of it. But like Moses, Isaiah has already spoken of their future change of heart, the promise of being restored to the Promised Land (Deuteronomy 30:1-3), and most importantly the coming of the Messiah. Our passage today is addressing the banality of idol worship. It is similar to Moses' exhortation. He reminded the people that the gods of the nations through which they passed were powerless against YHWH, so why would they ever worship these gods? In one passage he refers to these gods as demons (Deuteronomy 32:17).

God had Isaiah take a different angle. He began with the greatness of the Creator and compared that to the irrelevance of an idol. *12 Who has measured the waters in the hollow of his hand and marked off the heavens with a span, enclosed the dust of the earth in a measure and weighed the mountains in scales and the hills in a balance?* Isaiah 40:12 Isaiah may have had access to the account of Job. In it, God asked Job a similar question. *4 "Where were you when I laid the earth's foundation? Tell me, if you understand. 5 Who marked off its dimensions? Surely you know! Who stretched a measuring line across it?* Job 38:4-5 (NIV) Job wanted to confront God with what he perceived to be the injustice of his situation. The Jews under King Manasseh thought that if they didn't get the answer they wanted from YHWH, then they'd try other gods. Man has a tendency to seek instant gratification at any cost.

It is mankind's dilemma. We are the crown of creation and yet we are broken. We were created to be the lords of the earth (Genesis 1:28), but our fallen condition has perverted our desires. We were to have our way in the earth in conjunction with our fellowship with God. That loving relationship was to guide our desires, but the fall of man destroyed that communion. We still want to reign but for the wrong reasons (Jeremiah 17:9). Our desires are rarely in-line with God's. That is why we turn to other gods to justify our choices of self-gratification.

Even a narcissist looks outside himself or herself to find satisfaction and approval. When we look to something other than God, we become idolaters like Israel. We create a god we can direct rather than yield to a God who directs us. More often than not that God is our self. Because our communion with God is so broken, we can't even recognize what is good for us. God allows circumstances to come into our lives to turn us back to trust and depend on Him alone. Our response is often to run away to find another solution that will change our situation. With King Hezekiah it was to trust in the idol of wealth (2Kings 18:15-16). With his son Manasseh, it was to look to other gods (2Kings 21:11). The only real difference is that Hezekiah repented and humbled himself. This was the message to Job and to the nation of Judah: humble yourself and recognize the greatness of your Creator. He is the One who has allowed you to be in your situation for His purposes.

If you think you are so smart as to know what is best for you, what the future holds, and how to deal with your circumstances, then just answer

176

these basic questions. What do you know about the creation of the very earth you stand on?

Astronomers discovered comets that were going the wrong way. It completely messed with their idea of how the solar system formed. If their theory was right, the comets should all go in the same direction. The first one discovered that was going against traffic was considered to be mistaken data. When the second one was confirmed they had to acknowledge it.

The earth is so perfectly engineered for human life that, as one astronomer put it, all these factors coming together by chance would be like shooting at quarter a hundred million light years away and hitting it dead center. The earth is the perfect distance from the sun with just the right speed of rotation to avoid temperature extremes. The magnetic poles shield us from solar radiation. The giant planets of Jupiter and Saturn reduce the possibility of comets colliding into earth. Our sun is just the right size and type and the earth in a narrow band of a circular orbit that enables water to exist (called the Goldilocks zone). We are in the right area of the galaxy. Too far in and we would have too much radiation. Too far into the spiral arm and we couldn't see other galaxies. The moon is just the right size and distance to stir the oceans to even out water temperatures but not too much to cause massive tidal fluctuation. How great is the God that put that all together with a numerous other physics and chemical constants that had to each be within an extremely narrow range?

God asks us, "Who has measured space?" We have no idea how big the universe is. Three days ago a galaxy was found to be thirteen billion light years away. We can see quite far but still don't know if there is an end or if there is more beyond the farthest lights the Hubble can capture.

[13] Who has measured the Spirit of the LORD, or what man shows him his counsel? [14] Whom did he consult, and who made him understand? Who taught him the path of justice, and taught him knowledge, and showed him the way of understanding? Isaiah 40:13-14 Is it even imaginable to measure the Spirit of the LORD? Would any creature dare counsel their Creator? Job was foolishly asking to do just that (Job 31:35). That is what we do as well when we look to created things for answers or fulfillment instead of looking to God. We are expressing our conviction that we have a better idea. How foolish! The God who knows the shape and weight of every grain of sand, of every cell in your body, of the details of eternity, what we would call past and future, doesn't need our input. We can't inform Him of anything. And yet we argue with Him instead of accepting what comes from His hand.

Recently a mental image has helped me to have a change of attitude about what comes into my life each day. I see myself in God's grip (Psalm 139:10). Those fingers that hold me are in a certain position, and that hand takes me where He knows best. If I allow myself to conform to the way He is holding me, I'm at peace. I can fight in vain to change His grip and direction, which represent my present circumstances, but I just make myself uncomfortable, even miserable, in the process. It shows I'm not trusting that all things work together for good to those who love God and are called according to His purposes (Romans 8:28). Resisting shows I think I know better than the God who created all and knows everything.

It's about trust and having faith that God means what He says. Can we believe Him? Can we trust Him? Then why do we keep squirming in His hand? I have started noticing what makes me squirm: traffic, human responses, unexpected interruptions, whenever things don't go like I think they should. That tells me I'm pretty big headed and need to relax, let go, and trust God in these areas of life. He does have the whole world in His hands. When we realize the greatness of God, how can we turn to idolatry of self-will?

15 Behold, the nations are like a drop from a bucket, and are accounted as the dust on the scales; behold, he takes up the coastlands like fine dust. 16 Lebanon would not suffice for fuel, nor are its beasts enough for a burnt offering. 17 All the nations are as nothing before him, they are accounted by him as less than nothing and emptiness. Isaiah 40:15-17 When Satan tempted Jesus with the kingdoms of the world (Matthew 4:8-9), the temptation was not that of the power obtained by ruling. Those national powers are nothing to the LORD. The resources of those nations are things He spoke into existence. It was the opportunity to exchange unjust rule for righteous rule that would meet the physical and emotional needs of man. It was a chance to eliminate most of the world's suffering. But there cannot be a good solution brought through evil means. Meeting our needs will not heal our hearts. Worship is for God alone.

God doesn't need our offering. We are blessed to give it. He doesn't need our service, but He graciously gives us the privilege of serving Him. God doesn't need our fellowship, but He offers it to us because He is love (1John 4:8).

Considering the little we can comprehend of the greatness of God, what can we compare Him to? *18 To whom then will you liken God, or what likeness compare with him?* Isaiah 40:18 Though man is made in the image of God, we should not compare man to God (Psalm 40:5). We are creation; He is Creator. Everything we do is imperfect. Everything He does is perfect. There are no heavenly beings that compare with the LORD (Psalm 89:6). God is the eternal Spirit. Nothing compares! So when we turn to things, instead of God, we are being like the idolaters of Judah.

19 An idol! A craftsman casts it, and a goldsmith overlays it with gold and casts for it silver chains. 20 He who is too impoverished for an offering chooses wood that will not rot; he seeks out a skillful craftsman to set up an idol that will not move. Isaiah 40:19-20 Whether it was made of precious metal or wood, it is just a piece of matter that is shaped by the hand of man. So are the solutions and answers of man, products of our limited ability. How can we compare that with an infinite God who inhabits eternity? We think how foolish the people of Judah were to look to some carved piece of wood, but in essence, we do the same by looking to man's solutions to our situations (Jeremiah 2:13).

21 Do you not know? Do you not hear? Has it not been told you from the beginning? Have you not understood from the foundations of the earth? 22 It is he who sits above the circle of the earth, and its inhabitants are like grasshoppers; who stretches out the heavens like a curtain, and spreads them like a tent to dwell in; Isaiah 40:21-22 Remember that this was written around 700 BC. It declares several truths that are more recent discoveries. The earth is round. It had a beginning. The heavens are still being stretched out. In fact, astronomers have now concluded that the universe we can observe is expanding at an increasing rate of speed. That can't be accounted for by the Big Bang theory.

23 who brings princes to nothing, and makes the rulers of the earth as emptiness. 24 Scarcely are they planted, scarcely sown, scarcely has their stem taken root in the earth, when he blows on them, and they wither, and the tempest carries them off like stubble. Isaiah 40:23-24 All our great leaders of history lived for a moment and then perished. The most powerful of men are like a blade of grass that springs up in the springtime and dries in the summer and blows away in the fall (James 4:14). They boast in their arrogance of the power that God has granted them, but before long it is left to others. They think their influence will last, but the next person in power quickly undoes all the good or evil of those before them. I heard of an interview with college students recently, the majority of whom did not know who Ronald Reagan was.

Along these lines, Malcom Muggeridge wrote the following: I've heard a crazed, cracked Austrian (Hitler) announce to the world the establishment of a Reich that would last a thousand years. I have seen an Italian clown (Mussolini) say he was going to stop and restart the calendar with his own ascension to power. I've heard a murderous Georgian brigand in the Kremlin (Stalin), acclaimed by the intellectual elite of the world as being wiser than Solomon, more humane than Marcus Aurelius, more enlightened than Ashoka.

I have seen America wealthier and, in terms of military weaponry, more powerful than the rest of the world put together–so that had the American people so desired, they could have outdone a Caesar, or an Alexander in the range and scale of their conquests. All in one lifetime, all in one lifetime, all gone! Gone with the wind!

England, now part of a tiny island off the coast of Europe, threatened with dismemberment and even bankruptcy. Hitler and Mussolini dead, remembered only in infamy. Stalin a forbidden name in the regime he helped found and dominate for some three decades. America haunted by fears of running out of those precious fluids that keeps their motorways roaring, and the smog settling, with troubled memories of a disastrous campaign in Vietnam, and the victories of the Don Quixote's of the media as they charged the windmills of Watergate. All in one lifetime, all in one lifetime, all gone! Gone with the wind!

Behind the debris of these solemn supermen, and self-styled imperial diplomatists, there stands the gigantic figure of One: because of whom, by whom, in whom, and through whom alone, mankind may still have peace–the person of Jesus Christ. I present him as the way, the truth, and the life. Do you know Him?"

²⁵ To whom then will you compare me, that I should be like him? says the Holy One. ²⁶ Lift up your eyes on high and see: who created these? He who brings out their host by number, calling them all by name, by the greatness of his might, and because he is strong in power not one is missing. Isaiah 40:25-26 Who created the universe with its incredible beauty where no human eye sees (Genesis 1:16)? How many stars has God stretched out like a tent? There are 300 billion stars in our galaxy and 100 billion galaxies the Hubble has discovered, but only God knows how many more. He has named each and every one of those stars (Psalm 19:1).

What is God trying to tell us through his servant Isaiah? God is so great our finite minds cannot begin to fathom Him. We needed the incarnation to get just a tiny sense of the wonder of who He is. Why would we look to anything or anyone else for solutions to our situations? Why would we hope in anything else? Why would we want any other to direct our lives? Can we trust in His grip of grace on our lives? If you can't trust Him, there is no hope. You certainly can't trust man, especially yourself. The end of idolatry begins when we start to see the greatness of Christ and His love and welcome that love into our hearts. I join with Muggeridge in asking, "Do you know Him?"

Questions
1 What was Judah's big problem?
2 What is man's dilemma?
3 How can we relate to idolatry today?
4 What are a few ways in which the earth is fine tuned for us?
5 What was the temptation in Satan's offer of the kingdoms of man?
6 Why is God incomparable?
7 What can we now add to Muggeridge's words?
8 What is the message to us?
9 Are you conforming to God's grip of grace?
10 Why would we turn to any other?

Source of Strength - Isaiah 40:27-31

Isaiah warned of the coming captivity in the previous chapter. In this chapter he began to address those in the future who would experience the captivity. He encouraged them that it would be a purifying experience for the nation. God would bring them back to the Promised Land, and the glory of the LORD would be revealed (Isaiah 40:5).

God reminded them how short human life is. To waste one's life on an idol's lying promise of prosperity was a complete waste of one's life. Idolatry was a main reason for the coming captivity. The difference between

God and idols was quite a stark contrast. A mere piece of wood that is overlaid with a precious metal is still just a hunk of wood and some metal. While the Israelites believed idols could represent a spiritual power, and the Torah tells us they do represent demons (Deuteronomy 32:17), those powers are nothing compared to the God who created the heavens and the earth.

The chapter began with a comforting word. It continued with a reminder of the stupidity of trusting idols, and went on to speak of the greatness of God. Our passage today tells of how that all plays out in our daily life.

27 Why do you say, O Jacob, and speak, O Israel, "My way is hidden from the LORD, and my right is disregarded by my God"? Isaiah 40:27 God uses both names of their namesake to remind them of their two natures. Jacob is the unredeemed nature. It is the carnal side of the people of Judah that would be crying out that God couldn't see their suffering. During the captivity they wrote songs of woe, missing their homeland (Psalm 137:4). They whined about their condition without acknowledging that they were responsible for it. They should have been singing songs of repentance. While crying about God not seeing their suffering, He was right there in their midst offering the comfort we see at the beginning of the chapter (Isaiah 40:1). That comfort was not only that things were about to improve, but that the Messiah was coming to redeem their souls.

It took them awhile to get the message, though it was written a hundred years before that captivity. It takes us awhile too. Haven't you thought, "Come on God! Why are you letting this happen? Can't you see what is I'm going through?" I know I've whined like that in the past. I told you a couple of weeks ago that I had decided to ruthlessly deal with my whining. Chambers wrote, *May God not find the whine in us anymore, but may He find us full of spiritual pluck and athleticism, ready to face anything He brings.* (Oswald Chambers, My Utmost for His Highest, May 15th) It is quite a task since it is so engrained in our old nature. The only way to ruthlessly deal with whining is to walk in the Spirit and crucify the flesh with its affections and desires (Galatians 5:24). Only when we choose to walk in the Spirit can we be victorious. It's a moment by moment decision of which life we will yield to. My flesh says God doesn't care about my situation. The Spirit says God is right here with me helping me go through it for His purposes which always end up being good (Romans 8:28).

The second half of their complaint asked why my right is disregarded by my God. What is your right? Do we have a right to anything? Do we expect God to intervene whenever there is injustice done against us? Be careful what you wish. God may intervene against you. They were going to receive their right, which was captivity. That is what we rightfully get when we become slaves of sin. It takes us captive (John 8:34). We try to stop because we see it destroying our lives and find we can't stop by our own power. They thought they had rights as children of Abraham, but they also had rights as people of the Mosaic covenant to be judged for their idolatry (Deuteronomy 29:17-19).

I've heard people declare, "I have rights! I'm and American!" Often what they were demanding was a twisted sense of justice. God cannot do anything that is not right. Man can be counted on to be unrighteous. So when the sins of men affect your life, or justice for your own sins catches up with you, be careful about what you demand of God. If you ask for justice, you just may well get it. God asks why we would say those things as if to suggest He was somehow clueless.

Then God tells us what we were missing. *28 Have you not known? Have you not heard? The LORD is the everlasting God, the Creator of the ends of the earth. He does not faint or grow weary; his understanding is unsearchable.* Isaiah 40:28 He isn't clueless. We are! He inhabits eternity. He knows the end from the beginning (Isaiah 46:10). He sees all time in the present. He made it all and knows every detail about it all. He never wears down or wears out. You could spend a trillion years trying to learn what He knows and find you had just begun. How can we possibly suggest God is unaware or unconcerned about our situations? If you got an email from God completely explaining all that was involved in the trial you are experiencing today, it would take you the rest of your life to read it all. As believers, we have to let go of the idea that we can comprehend what God is doing in a given situation. Sure, He might give you a bit of insight, but only a miniscule bit, like one byte in a terabyte.

God is continuing to drive home a point from the previous verses. He is so great that we simply will never fathom His greatness. So why would we say something as stupid as, "God doesn't see what's happening here, and if He does, He's not being fair"? It's because we are in the flesh and seeing things from our limited view. We need to step back into the Spirit and know it's all in God's hands and will all glorify Him in the end (Jude 25).

I ask why this political scandal or that crime of Isis isn't dealt with by God. I don't need to know the answer. I need to know that God knows and the day will come when He will balance the books. It may be on the Day of Judgment or it may come in this life, but it will come (Romans 14:10). It will come because He is the Almighty Creator whose understanding is unsearchable.

In the meantime, injustice wears on us. Life can beat us down. How can we endure life in this fallen world? Why not go to the One who doesn't faint or grow weary?

29 He gives power to the faint, and to him who has no might he increases strength. Isaiah 40:29 God is the source of power and strength. Why do we look to ourselves as if we could somehow buck up and pull ourselves up by our own bootstraps? When you come to the end of yourself, you can turn to the source of strength and power, the LORD. Notice that the verse tells us this power and strength go to the faint and to the ones who have no might.

We wonder why God takes us right down to the last second or the end of our resources. Here is why: Only then will we totally rely on Him and give Him all the glory. It is lesson after lesson on our inability and God's all sufficiency. I often have people come to me when they just don't think they

182

can get the victory over something in their life, or their situation seems hopeless. It's then that God can show them His greatness and love for them. When we give up and throw ourselves upon God with no other hope but Him, then He supplies the strength and power. Hopefully we learn this lesson and lean on Him continually, but it often seems we need a refresher course. And all the honest people said, "Amen!"

30 Even youths shall faint and be weary, and young men shall fall exhausted; Isaiah 40:30 The strongest and healthiest find they don't have what it takes to face difficulties in life. Why should we think we are any different? Mankind just needs to realize what God said in the previous verses. We are like a blade of grass that springs up, dries out, and blows away. We think if we just eat the right food, avoid this or that, exercise, get enough education, somehow, we can have what it takes to face any challenge that may come our way. Those aren't bad things, but they aren't the answer. The only thing that will get you through is a relationship with the source of strength.

What is the best way to prepare for the inevitable difficulties you will face in life? It is to walk in complete submission to the Spirit of God in your life today. That includes getting rid of anything that hinders your communion with the Lord (1Peter 2:1). That often means an attitude toward someone in your life. Loving God will result in loving your fellow man. Men, God tells us that not living with our wives in an understanding way can hinder our prayers (1Peter 3:7). We eat certain things to boost our immune system. How much more important is it to live in fellowship with God for this life and the next?

31 but they who wait for the LORD shall renew their strength; they shall mount up with wings like eagles; they shall run and not be weary; they shall walk and not faint. Isaiah 40:31 The Hebrew word translated "wait" also means "to look for" or "expect." I think of it as that quiet time in prayer when you ask the Lord if He has something to say to you. Wait for Him to speak. Expect His direction. Look for His guidance. Inspiration can come to your mind to pray for certain people or to encourage someone with an email. A verse will often come to mind to consider. Sometimes I'm convicted to forgive and pray for a person I'm upset with. Other times I just sense how great God's love is for me and sing a song praising Him for that love.

It doesn't take a lot of time. But if we will do that regularly, then when the difficulties come, and they will come, it is just natural to go to the Lord and receive the strength He gives to get through the trial. The lines of communication are clear.

This is one of those habits that we should develop because Jesus set the example to show us how. He arose before dawn and went to an isolated place to pray. When the disciples found Him, they told Him the village was waiting for Him. But Jesus had received different directions from the Father. He wasn't going to respond to the demands of men, which is what we tend to do. Instead He went on to other villages He had not yet visited (Mark 1:35-38).

Another example for us in Scripture is Philip. He was experiencing a revival in Samaria. Peter and John came to assist and then returned to Jerusalem. Philip would no doubt think it was important to stay and disciple all these new believers. Instead, an angel of the Lord told him to go to a lonely road in the wilderness where he met a man whom he led to Jesus as Savior (Acts 9:26). That man took the Gospel to Ethiopia, which became the beginnings of the Coptic Church. I'd be surprised if the angel just appeared in the middle of Philip's busy day. It was no doubt during his time of prayer.

Peter's vision of going to the Gentiles was a revelation he received when he went up on a rooftop to pray (Acts 10:9). The Apostle Paul is an example of thinking he should go one way, but by being attuned to waiting on the LORD, he had a vision that gave him the direction he needed (Acts 16:9). These all waited, expected, and looked to the LORD and He gave them the strength to soar like eagles.

This is such an amazing promise; it is incredible that more of us don't apply it to our lives. Who doesn't want to soar like an eagle, run and not be weary, walk and not faint? We either don't have faith in the promise, have other priorities, or there is something we have not surrendered that we fear may be addressed.

Is it possible that our greatest hindrance is that our life is all about "me"? Do we tolerate the Jacob nature? "Lord, you can be my god as long as you supply my needs like I expect and keep me happy and healthy (Genesis 28:20-22).

If you can relate to Jacob's prayer, let me suggest that you step out in faith and experience the joy of submitting to and serving the Lord. It far surpasses anything the world has to offer. It is joy unspeakable and full of glory (1Peter 1:8). Don't let the world deceive you into thinking that it has anything of real substance to offer you (1John 2:17). We were made for the glory of God, and every substitute will eventually disappoint us.

We may avoid being still before God because we realize there is something in our life that we know God will address, and we just aren't ready to give it up. For those who feel this way, let me remind you that God has your best interest at heart (Jeremiah 29:11). He only asks things of you that are for your good (Deuteronomy 10:13). We only hurt ourselves when we refuse to hear His instructions and cling to something that is detrimental to our spiritual health.

What does it take to get up early enough to take ten minutes in God's Word and ten minutes in prayer? Twenty minutes! I guarantee you if you do that you'll want to take thirty minutes. Then you'll want to take more, and you'll find a way to do it. It's a matter of priorities. If a television show the night before, or Facebook in the morning, or whatever keeps you from that time is more important, then you won't take the time. Decide to live according to your priorities (Matthew 6:33). Refuse to let your old nature be your default mode!

Waiting on the Lord can also be to expect Him to answer. Sometimes we pray, and the answer comes and we don't connect the answer with our prayer. We might ask for an opportunity to share our faith with a person, and that very day we end up in the company dining room at the table with that person. What do you think the Lord wants you to do? Or we ask God for work and someone invites us to help with a job, but it was not what we were hoping for. Maybe we should think again. When you pray, wait and watch for the Lord to answer.

If you will develop this life pattern of looking to the Lord each morning and as you go through your day, He promises that you will mount up on wings like eagles. You will be able to soar high above your situations and see them from a heavenly perspective (Isaiah 55:6).

Dr. James Kennedy gave a sermon once on soaring on wings of eagles. He told of watching eagles as a boy and how they would so rarely flap their wings. Even when taking off from the ground they would wait for the wind and let it lift them. The word for "wind" and "spirit" is the same in Greek. We can ride on the Spirit by spreading our wings of faith. When we sense Him moving, directing, answering prayer, we respond and go with it. It's not a lot of our effort. It's all about waiting for the wind of the Spirit to blow and take us where we need to go (John 3:8).

Did you notice that the verse goes from soaring to running to walking? The soaring can be a special time when God seems so near and present with us. Those times are rare. There are times when just running without growing weary is what is needed. It reminds me of some weeks I call a marathon. There is so much to prepare and do that I feel like I run all week long. If I try to do it in my own strength I will grow weary. But when I wait on the Lord it is a joy.

Perhaps most needed of all is the strength to walk and not faint (James 5:11). That is just to persevere. We know what God has called us to do and we keep plugging away day after day. Routine can cause us to be so tired we feel as if we may faint, just quit trying any more. But when we wait upon the Lord, there is strength to endure. His encouragement, inspiration, and love renew us again and again. There is a freshness even in routine. Why would any believer not want to take hold of this promise and experience it every day (2Peter 1:4)?

Questions
1 What are two complaints in verse 1?
2 What big factor do we often miss?
3 Will justice prevail? How do we know?
4 Who does God assist with power?
5 Why aren't we strong enough?
6 How can we prepare for trials?
7 What are other translations for "wait"?
8 Give Biblical examples of waiting?
9 Why don't we wait on the Lord?
10 Elaborate on the three promises.

God Over All - Isaiah 41:1-20

A recent poll showed an 8% decline in Christianity in the USA in just 7 years. The news media informs us on an almost daily basis of a new political scandal. Racial tension is on the rise. Our debt is reaching incomprehensible numbers, while the stock market is reaching record highs. What's wrong with this picture? We are waiting for the next terrorist plot to unfold. The Middle East is in complete turmoil as a genocide of Christians in that area of the world is underway. It's not a rosy picture. That is what we see. But what does God see? What is heaven's perspective?

God's address to the people of Israel and future captives was a challenge to them see what was actually happening. Many of the first readers of Isaiah's prophecy probably felt like we do about the condition of the world in their day. The turmoil and national conflicts were just as frequent if not more so. The reign of Manasseh was a sudden decline in the worship of God. Those in power were literally getting away with murder on a frequent basis. Idolatry filled the land. Just imagine how the true believers felt as they watched all that take place then.

It was in such a setting that these words came through Isaiah. [1] *Listen to me in silence, O coastlands; let the peoples renew their strength; let them approach, then let them speak; let us together draw near for judgment.* Isaiah 41:1 The coastlands of that day included Philistia, Egypt, Tyre, Sidon, as well as distant lands. God asks them to draw near and quietly listen. Listening to God renews our strength (Isaiah 40:31). God wants even these gentile lands to hear him and find true strength in Him (Isaiah 42:6).

This is an invitation to all people. God is always speaking. Will we come near and quietly listen (John 10:3)? We often run to God in time of need, but we can't stop talking and sit in silence to hear God's solution (Habakkuk 2:20). Instead, we dictate to God what we think He should do. Should it not be the other way around? If your strength is sapped away and you don't know what to do, go listen to God and find your strength renewed (Psalm 27:14).

The next word in the verse is "then." Then you can speak. Hear God first. Wait on Him. If we hear what He has to say first, it may change our requests. I'm as guilty as anyone in bringing my laundry list of things for God to fix before I will stop and listen. Good thing God is patient. This verse has taught me there is a proper order to prayer. Listen first. Let His words strengthen you by giving you a proper perspective. Then speak according to what you have heard.

God speaks; you are strengthened; you approach and then speak. That is when you can hear God's verdict on what you are asking. "Judgment" is not referring to a sentence for guilt, though it can include that. Judgment is a verdict. It may be, "Go ahead and be blessed." It may be, "Don't do it, for if you do, it will cost you dearly." Or it may be to wait for another time. Sometimes there is no answer at all, and that is the answer of "not now."

² Who stirred up one from the east whom victory meets at every step? He gives up nations before him, so that he tramples kings underfoot; he makes them like dust with his sword, like driven stubble with his bow. ³ He pursues them and passes on safely, by paths his feet have not trod. Isaiah 41:2-3 God's question sets us on the right course by asking "who" instead of "what"? We make the mistake of looking to conditions or individuals instead of God who is behind it all. We should search out what He is doing, instead of crediting circumstances alone with any power to direct our course or the world's direction.

As they listened in silence God asks, "Who stirs up future conquerors?" God is predicting one hundred years in advance how He will raise up Cyrus to return the Jews to the Promised Land. Who gives kings their power and determines the outcome of wars? It is God Almighty (Romans 13:1). He sets up kings and removes them. He often gives a people a king like themselves. We have a difficult time understanding that God can put a murderous despot on a throne. God has His divine purposes. It is often in difficulty that people turn back to God and become serious about faith. We cannot know all God's reasons, but we can still trust Him.

⁴ Who has performed and done this, calling the generations from the beginning? I, the LORD, the first, and with the last; I am he. Isaiah 41:4 The second question they were to hear is even more inclusive. Who has planned every generation? God had preordained Cyrus and every life and the length of each before the world began. He is before all things and never changes throughout eternity (Hebrews 13:8). In the fulfilling this prophetic word we should be convinced of the omniscience and sovereignty of God.

This expression of being the first and the last is seen three times in Isaiah (Isaiah 44:6; 48:12). It is also seen three times in Revelation (Revelation 1:17; 2:8; 22:13) where it is applied to Jesus. The first of each set of three contains the "I am he" reference to God's name. Both sets contain the phrase, "Do not be afraid." John's writing is clearly saying that Jesus is the "I am." He uses the same words (*eigo eimi)* as the Greek version (LXX) of Isaiah. John's letters also apply "he who is from the beginning" to Jesus (1 John 1:1; 2:13-14).

Jesus sets up kings and removes them. Jesus has determined the generations of man. He is the first and the last, the alpha and the omega (Revelation 1:8).

⁵ The coastlands have seen and are afraid; the ends of the earth tremble; they have drawn near and come. Isaiah 41:5 When we do draw near and hear of impending judgment for rebellion, of the need for God to take away that which our culture depends on so that we will turn to God, we fear and tremble. Last week I told you how we prepare for those times. Get close to God! Be in the center of His will. Tune your ear to the Holy Spirit.

Rebels against God do just the opposite. They turn to idols. *⁶ Everyone helps his neighbor and says to his brother, "Be strong!" ⁷ The craftsman strengthens the goldsmith, and he who smooths with the hammer him who strikes the anvil, saying of the soldering, "It is good"; and they strengthen it with nails so that it cannot be moved.* Isaiah 41:6-7 People within a society can unite together to rebel against God. They come up with human ideas to avoid God's judgments. There is a kind of anti-god comradery. We see it in the rebellions in the wilderness wandering and during the period of the Judges when everyone did what was right in his own eyes (Judges 40:25). We saw it under the northern ten tribes and some of the kings of Judah. We saw it demonstrated against Jesus. History has seen it against the church numerous times in different lands. Today it is evident in the western education system and entertainment. They strengthen one another and boast about how well their idol is welded together and influencing culture.

Isaiah is using a bit of tongue in cheek when he tells us they use nails to fasten it. One little bump and it might fall over. What a contrast with the God who is the beginning and the end. As beautiful as their manmade schemes appear, as convincing as their rhetoric may seem, they have to try hard to secure it against one little bump that will knock down their idolatrous house of cards. Their remark, "It is good," is quite a contrast with the marvel of creation of which God said, "It is good." (Genesis 1:25) Do you see the huge difference in what God does compared to man's pathetic efforts?

Next week we will go into greater depth on the vanity of idols. These first seven verses of the chapter have declared God to be sovereign and His decisions final. He moves kings to carry out His will and the efforts of man to stop Him are nothing. Now God turns to His plan for Israel.

⁸ But you, Israel, my servant, Jacob, whom I have chosen, the offspring of Abraham, my friend; ⁹ you whom I took from the ends of the earth, and called from its farthest corners, saying to you, "You are my servant, I have chosen you and not cast you off"; Isaiah 41:8-9 Remember that this is for those captives that have yet to return to Jerusalem. He reminds them of who they are. They are God's servants. That is how the prophets referred to themselves. It is an honor to be a servant of the most high God. And though they had fallen into idolatry that led to captivity, God had not forgotten them or His promises to the patriarchs. They thought they were cast off, but God had not forsaken them. He was just refining them for what was to come. They needed to recognize the destructiveness of idolatry.

God will take us through whatever it takes to prepare us for the calling He has on our lives. I would never suggest my path for anyone else. Nor would I want your path. We each have the path we need to show us what we need to see and reveal to us what we need to understand to serve our good God.

He hasn't cast you off. It may be tough, but He is preparing you. You are Abraham's heir if you are a person of faith (Romans 4:16). You are chosen to be God's servant, to represent Him in the earth. But we all need to experience God's preparation and hear His words of encouragement. *¹⁰ fear not, for I am with you; be not dismayed, for I am your God; I will strengthen*

188

you, I will help you, I will uphold you with my righteous right hand. Isaiah 41:10 If Almighty God is with us, do we have anything to fear? I'm concerned about the process, but I don't fear the outcome.

Someone told me they had a dream that I jumped off a high cliff diving down into a little pool of water. They said it looked real risky. I immediately knew it was abandoning oneself to God that looks risky to the world (1Corinthains 2:14). We leap out in faith telling God we'll go wherever He says and do whatever He tells us regardless of the cost. That looks risky. But if you have faith, it's a sure thing. If God is with you, you may lose your life but you will win (Matthew 10:39).

If God is your God you should not be dismayed regardless of the circumstances that come your way. You can know He is the One that allowed them to be what they are and that He already has a plan to see you through. Dismay is a sign of a lack of trust in His power and sovereignty.

He promises to strengthen us, help us, and uphold us with His righteous right hand. The right hand is the hand of power and authority. What a promise to cling to when we feel like the end of our captivity will never come. This is a verse we should all memorize for those times when we are tempted to fear and be dismayed.

¹¹ Behold, all who are incensed against you shall be put to shame and confounded; those who strive against you shall be as nothing and shall perish. ¹² You shall seek those who contend with you, but you shall not find them; those who war against you shall be as nothing at all. Isaiah 41:11-12 Justice sometimes happens quite quickly, and other times it may only come on the Day of Judgment. But it will come. If you stand for righteousness and act as you are led by the Word and the Holy Spirit, if you lean upon the Lord and are upheld by His righteous right hand, you will prevail in the end. The righteous judge will rule in your favor because of Jesus' sacrifice. The mouth of liars will be stopped. The motivations of their hearts will be revealed (Psalm 44:21). Their self-serving agendas will be clear for all to see. If they have not repented and trusted in the sacrifice of Jesus, they will be as nothing and perish. You will never have to face them again. They will never harm another godly soul.

¹³ For I, the LORD your God, hold your right hand; it is I who say to you, "Fear not, I am the one who helps you." Isaiah 41:13 God promised to uphold us with His righteous right hand, and here He promises to hold our right hand (Psalm 139:9-10). This is the Creator of the universe telling us how intimate and caring He is with us. I was thinking about how He upholds us with His righteous right hand while holding our right hand. My granddaughter walked up to the front of the church during the Call to Worship and sat down by me. I put my arm around her and then she held my other hand. There it was! After a few minutes she got up and went back to where she was sitting. Thanks Lord! What an intimate picture!

While He directs the nations and sets up kings, He is right here with you and me, right arm around us while holding our right hand. He is transcendent and immanent. He is everywhere in space and time, and right here with you and me this very moment. This is the God who tells us we don't need to be afraid. He will finish what He started in us. He will see us through the battles and pain that are a part of life in this world. And He will see us safely home to glory. Don't be afraid. In Christ we have nothing to fear. His grace will always be sufficient for our every experience (2Corinthians 12:9).

If Almighty God is the One who helps us, can we ever lack the strength or assistance we need to endure? Would you let this verse be the voice of the LORD to you right now? *13 For I, the LORD your God, hold your right hand; it is I who say to you, "Fear not, I am the one who helps you."* Isaiah 41:13 What a comfort this must have been to the captives in Babylon.

14 Fear not, you worm Jacob, you men of Israel! I am the one who helps you, declares the LORD; your Redeemer is the Holy One of Israel. Isaiah 41:14 In case we didn't hear the "fear not" in verses 10 and 13, He repeats it for the third time, reminding them that if God is for them, who can be against them (Romans 8:31). He is the Redeemer, the Holy One of Israel. He took on the gods of Egypt and Canaan and showed them to be powerless. He has all power and knows all things. If He is the One that helps us, why would we fear?

This is the first mention in Isaiah of God being our Redeemer. There are two words in Hebrew for "redeemer." The one used here is used for the duty of a kinsman. You might recall how Boaz became the kinsman redeemer for Ruth, buying her dead husband's property and marrying her (Ruth 4:9-10). It can encompass avenging a wrong done to a kinsman or redeeming them from a debt. The choice of words here looked forward to the Word becoming flesh so that have God as our kinsman redeeming us from our sin debt that held us captive.

When God asked Job a few questions about creation and revealed some of His glory to Job, Job said he was of small account (Job 40:4). God acknowledges that we are pretty insignificant compared to Him. He calls Jacob/Israel a worm, a little dirt eating slimy food for birds and fish. That should help us deal with our pride. But God holds the right hand of us little dirt sucking worms. He tells us He is for us and not against us. That makes us treasured little worms indeed. So treasured are we that He would send His Son to be a worm like us. That is how Jesus saw Himself on the cross (Psalm 22:6). God helps us and strengthens us. And one day He'll transform us into the butterflies He intends for us to be.

15 Behold, I make of you a threshing sledge, new, sharp, and having teeth; you shall thresh the mountains and crush them, and you shall make the hills like chaff; 16 you shall winnow them, and the wind shall carry them away, and the tempest shall scatter them. And you shall rejoice in the LORD; in the Holy One of Israel you shall glory. Isaiah 41:15-16 A threshing sled is several boards fastened together on the bottom of which are inserted sharp rocks every few inches. It is dragged through the grain to break it up and loosen the kernels. Armageddon will be such a day when those who hate God will be on the receiving end of justice.

Then when the books are settled, and evil is purged from us by an act of God, we will rejoice at the outworking of this plan we have watched unfold. Good will prevail. Evil will be punished. Righteousness will reign. We will not glory in man or his passing illusion of power and wealth (Proverbs 23:4,5), but in the Holy One of Israel.

[17] When the poor and needy seek water, and there is none, and their tongue is parched with thirst, I the LORD will answer them; I the God of Israel will not forsake them. [18] I will open rivers on the bare heights, and fountains in the midst of the valleys. I will make the wilderness a pool of water, and the dry land springs of water. Isaiah 41:17-18 Israel can be a very dry land. It often rains in November and February with very little rain the rest of the year. There is a constant battle over water. Animal husbandry and agriculture compete for every drop that comes from the few springs and the Jordan River. Like our own area, a sudden cloud burst can have the arroyos (wadis) raging, only to be dry in a week's time. While God is speaking of a future blessed time of an abundance of water, He is primarily addressing the spiritual thirst of the people. At the well in Samaria, *[13] Jesus answered, "Everyone who drinks this water will be thirsty again, [14] but whoever drinks the water I give him will never thirst. Indeed, the water I give him will become in him a spring of water welling up to eternal life."* John 4:13-14 (NIV) Jesus was speaking of life giving water for all who would come to Him and drink (John 7:37). He is the fulfillment of the promise in Isaiah.

[19] I will put in the wilderness the cedar, the acacia, the myrtle, and the olive. I will set in the desert the cypress, the plane and the pine together, [20] that they may see and know, may consider and understand together, that the hand of the LORD has done this, the Holy One of Israel has created it. Isaiah 41:19-20 This passage is also a physical promise that has a spiritual analogy. It has come to pass in our day. Look at these before and after pictures just one hundred years apart. The very trees mentioned here fill what was once a barren land.

Previously we saw trees refer to people such as the forest that represented the Assyrian army (Isaiah 10:18). Not only is Israel bursting at the seams with residents, but Messianic Jews and Arabs are increasing in the land. No one thought that was possible.

Do you see and know, do you consider and understand together, that the hand of the LORD has done this, the Holy One of Israel has created it? He told us before it came to pass so that we might know and believe.

The jump is not risky. God has proven He knows the end from the beginning. What is risky is going the way of the world. Do you recognize that you are poor and in need of the Redeemer? Is your spiritual tongue parched with thirst? Jesus says, "Come to me and drink!" Let him uphold you with his right hand and take hold of your right hand. Know that the One who is the first and the last has all things under His control.

Questions

1 What does the passage suggest is the first thing we should do when we pray?
2 Who appoints kings and decides the outcome of wars?
3 How are "first and the last" sayings in Isaiah and Revelation similar?
4 What do these sayings show us?
5 How does Isaiah mock idols?
6 What are the first 7 verses about?
7 What is the focus of the rest?
8 Why should we be fearless?
9 What wonderful promises are here?
10 Who is a worm? How is that good?
11 What proofs has God given us that He can be trusted?

Same Plan Different Outcome? - Isaiah 41:22f

It has been said that doing the same thing and expecting a different outcome is the definition of insanity. As I read over the passage for today, that seemed to be the point that God was driving home. The nation of Judah had seen the northern tribes of Israel fall from trusting in idols. Now Isaiah has prophesied that Judah will go into captivity too. What is it about idolatry that seems to irresistibly draw us despite the terrible past track record? If you had a surgeon that botched your last operation, you wouldn't try him or her again. Yet, our mind seems to be stuck on stupid when it comes to trusting in idols.

You might be thinking, "Wait a minute; I don't have any statues that I place my faith in." Recently I read a commentary that succinctly summed up present day idolatry. "The Baals of the Old Testament are 'the world' in the New." John defines the world as the lust of the flesh, the lust of the eyes, and the pride of life (1John 2:15-16). We've become a little more sophisticated, at least in our own minds. Most people realize a statue can't do anything for them. But what most people don't realize is that trusting in the world to satisfy your heart is fallen man's new form of idolatry. John Calvin said the human heart is a perpetual idol factory. We set our hearts on one thing after another that we think will make us happy. This is the reason that God speaks so clearly against idolatry. Idolatry takes the rightful place of God in our hearts. John Ortberg writes, *"Our faith in him is so unimaginative. Our expectations of him are so low. We run from him to stuff ourselves full of counterfeit pleasures and empty salvations. What we need every day is to taste the goodness of the Lord all over again."* (John Ortberg, *Preaching the Word, Isaiah*, p.268)

When people worshiped graven images, it was because they thought the images promised prosperity. The images represented local deities that were believed to make their worshipers successful. Success means getting what you want, whether it is a full pantry, health, or a new cart (Colossians 3:5). Things really haven't changed because the heart of man hasn't changed. The thing we devote ourselves to may be different, but it is for the same purposes. When you consider it that way, you realize religion can be idolatry. I can tithe, attend worship service, spend time in prayer, and other religious activities to get what I want regardless of God's will.

God, on the other hand, invites us to enter a relationship where we trust Him to see us through whatever He allows to come into our life for His good purposes. Idolatry is an attempt to manufacture a god who will give me what I want. True faith is to surrender to God to become and do what He wants. The world never delivers what it promises, costs more than we expect, and leaves us empty. God has more for us than we can comprehend (Isaiah 64:4), will never leave us (Matthew 28:20), and brings us to a glorious and eternal union with Him (1Thessalonians 4:17).

Let's see how God conveyed these concepts to Judah. *21 Set forth your case, says the LORD; bring your proofs, says the King of Jacob.* Isaiah 41:21 The chapter opened with God telling Judah to come listen in silence and then speak. They were to listen while God asked a few questions that showed how little they knew and how great God is. Who knows the end from the beginning? Who determines who will reign over kingdoms and win wars? Who knows the name of every one of the billions of stars? Certainly, the answer is not our little pathetic local deity that you have made an image of and have to secure so it doesn't fall over. After they considered that, God, their King, said it was their turn to speak. Lay out the case for idolatry, for trusting in something other than Him. Bring out the proof that your way is better, or that these gods do anything of value.

When we relate this to the present idolatry of the world, we can ask the same questions. Has the lust of the flesh ever done anything of lasting value for you? Has it delivered what you hoped? Has the lust of the eyes ever helped you through a time of difficulty? Has the pride of life ever spared you from the results of your own ignorance? What lasting good has the worship of the world ever done anyone? If your goal is to die with the most toys and enter eternity embarrassed about your misplaced emphasis, I guess you could say it got you what you wanted. If it is to have so many broken relationships you can't remember them all and know you will stand before God to give an account for your wasted life and the pain you caused others, the world will certainly deliver.

God has put eternity in our hearts (Ecclesiastes 3:11). We know there is more. I watched an agnostic proclaim how ecstatic she was that agnosticism was on the rise in America and how that could change our culture for the better. I wondered at her blindness in not realizing the decline we see already. And as I wrote this I wondered if she would feel the same if thieves break into her home and rob and violate her because there is no moral reason not to. Will she feel the same when she stands at the threshold of eternity and her philosophy has failed to deliver what she imagined it would? Lay out your case for man being his own god? Tell me if that has ever worked in the past (Psalm 14:1). What happens when a man gains such power that he can do what he wills?

²² Let them bring them, and tell us what is to happen. Tell us the former things, what they are, that we may consider them, that we may know their outcome; or declare to us the things to come. Isaiah 41:22 What? Are there no great examples of man trusting in himself, being his own benevolent god? We look back at the debauched Caesars, the depraved popes, Hitler, Stalin, Mao, Pol Pot, and many more, and we wonder that we have not understood the nature of man's heart. Our founding fathers understood and so created three equal branches of government to try to keep man's insatiable lust for power in check. When man has such power, he executes his rivals. When Jesus realized all power was in His hands, He washed dirty feet (John 13:3-5).

God went on to ask about the future. If they couldn't give a good past example, perhaps they could see into the future. God had just told them he was raising up someone to deliver them from captivity, a captivity that was still in the future. What could their idols tell them about the future? And so it is today. We make plans to deal with threats and contingencies for different potential problems and suddenly what we never imagined or foresaw comes out of nowhere and threatens our existence. Yet, we refuse to look to the One that knows the future.

²³ Tell us what is to come hereafter, that we may know that you are gods; do good, or do harm, that we may be dismayed and terrified. Isaiah 41:23 If your idols are worth trusting, let them tell you what is to come. If your faith in the world is properly placed, let the fortune tellers tell you what will happen tomorrow, not in some vague terms that could apply to anything or a generality that is inevitably going to happen someday. Have them give you some specifics like God does. There are dozens of specific predictions about Jesus' first coming given hundreds of years before His birth. The prophets told of His conception in a virgin (Isaiah 7:14), His birth place (Micah 5:2), the area of His ministry (Isaiah 9:1), His manner, the response of people to Him (Isaiah 53:3), His torture (Psalm 22:14-18), when He would die (Daniel 9:26), the details of how He would die before the invention of crucifixion (Psalm 22:16), His burial conditions (Isaiah 53:9), His resurrection after three days (Hosea 6:1-2), and His message going to the entire world (Matthew 24:14). And there are many more. That is specificity! Can what you place your faith in do that? No? Then why are you continuing to trust in it?

Idols can't do good or harm. They can't help you or harm you or anyone else. They are powerless. If what you trust in doesn't know what is happening in the next moment, and couldn't do anything about it if it did, how ridiculous it is to place faith in whatever it is. And for most of us it is ourselves. But God says you don't know what will happen tomorrow. Your life is like a vapor that is here for a moment and gone (James 4:14). How stubbornly rebellious of us to continue to trust in ourselves. How just plain foolish to ignore a loving God who does know the future and can help us.

194

24 Behold, you are nothing, and your work is less than nothing; an abomination is he who chooses you. Isaiah 41:24 Here is God's estimation of everything we trust in outside of Him. It's nothing. We are trusting in something that is less than nothing. Not only will it fail to help, it will leave us without hope or recourse.

I have called choosing an idol or trusting in man "foolish." God uses a harsher term, "an abomination." That means someone who is morally disgusting. God has explained why it is the height of stupidity to trust an idol, but here He describes the morality involved in trusting idols, or in our case, the world.

I believe the Scriptures declare that everyone will be confronted in the way that God is confronting Judah in this passage. We will all see the failure of idolatry and recognize there is a God who is calling us to surrender to His love. But when we have that encounter with the Holy Spirit, we know that means giving up control. It is the King that is confronting Judah. He is the ruler. It is the King that confronts us. Unlike powerful earthly leaders, He has all power but uses it with grace and love. However, accepting that love means submission. And there is the line many are unwilling to cross. Despite knowing idolatry is nothing, it lets them remain to be their own little god. That is moral abomination. It is to accept a lie so that selfishness might be maintained. God has rendered His judgment (41:1).

The invitation and response foreseen in the first verse of the chapter has concluded. Now God continues to draw the contrast with idols by telling them what would come. *25 I stirred up one from the north, and he has come, from the rising of the sun, and he shall call upon my name; he shall trample on rulers as on mortar, as the potter treads clay.* Isaiah 41:25 In verse two God stirs up one from the east, repeated here as "from the rising of the sun," and now He says from the north. We have to wait till chapter 44 for the revelation of the name of this one (44:28). Cyrus did come from the north, but his nation was in the east. He had a meteoric rise to power and dominance. No one else predicted it. When the children of the first readers of this prophecy saw it fulfilled, the message to forsake idolatry and trust in the Lord would be clear.

Some commentators have made a case for this referring to Abraham instead of Cyrus. (Targums, Torrey, and Kissane) Remember that from chapter 40 God is speaking to those in captivity to comfort them. He is telling them the things to come so that they will know the difference between idols that know nothing and God who knows the future. For that reason, I agree with those who see this as Cyrus.

26 Who declared it from the beginning, that we might know, and beforehand, that we might say, "He is right"? There was none who declared it, none who proclaimed, none who heard your words. Isaiah 41:26 God predicted the coming of Cyrus by name a hundred years before he came on the scene. No idol could do that. In fact, no one foresaw Cyrus sudden rise to power. Besides, idols can't speak. How could a mute idol predict anything?

On the other hand, from the time of the expulsion from the Garden of Eden, God was predicting the coming of a Savior (Genesis 3:15). You could say that all Biblical prophecy culminates in Christ, for the prophetic words to Israel, such as these we are reading in Isaiah, are to keep the lineage of David intact until the Messiah comes. Some prophecy that is yet to be fulfilled deals with preparing Israel for His Second Coming. It is all about Jesus. He is the lodestar.

27 I was the first to say to Zion, "Behold, here they are!" and I give to Jerusalem a herald of good news. Isaiah 41:27 Before they had gone into captivity, before Cyrus was born, God was already saying the Persians are coming to rescue them and return them to their homeland. Persia would even pay for some of the cost. The comfort in the beginning of the previous chapter is being proclaimed long before the intended readers were born (Isaiah 40:1). What an amazing God!

While Israel was unique in that God was bringing the Messiah through them and had chosen that nation to be the recipients of the words of the prophets, God works with us in a similar way. He tells us He has good works planned in advance for us to do (Ephesians 2:10). He tells us He has chosen us to be a nation of priests (1Peter 2:5). He promises to return for us and finish the work He started in us (Philippians 1:6). That is comfort! Amen? And though we may have hard times before we see the fulfillment, when it comes to pass we will look back like they did and declare that God knew the end from the beginning (Isaiah 46:10). We'll say that He alone is God, for He told us in advance so that when it came to pass we would believe and understand that there is none like Him.

28 But when I look, there is no one; among these there is no counselor who, when I ask, gives an answer. Isaiah 41:28 God has challenged Judah and all who trust in idols. He has invited us to tell why we should trust them, or trust ourselves. He has asked us to tell Him what is coming. What does your idol or the prognosticators of the world tell you? I remember the world telling me when I was young that the work was going to go down to 30 hours. They were right, but not because they foresaw political workings. They thought machines would do so much for us we'd have lots of free time. Instead, the machines take up all our time and we run faster than we ever did before. No one in Judah had a good answer for their idolatry, but that didn't stop them. Selfish morally abhorrent behavior reigned supreme.

29 Behold, they are all a delusion; their works are nothing; their metal images are empty wind. Isaiah 41:29 A delusion! That is what we see all around us. There is the delusion of fortune telling, mystic healers, aura photos, and on and on. You can even purchase a good old fashion Buddha to put in your entryway to declare your rebellion against God. Buddha tells everyone they can do it on their own by just trying to eliminate desire. What do you do with the desire to eliminate desire? It's all empty wind. None of it brings productive refreshing rain. As God said a few verses earlier, "They are less than nothing."

All this is leading up to the verses that open the next chapter. The Servant of the Lord is coming (42:1). You want something you can see? Alright! He's coming, but you might not like what you see, for He doesn't lead you to worldly satisfaction in selfish pleasures. He leads you to a life of selfless service. He demonstrated laying down your life for others. There is none like Him. He could tell them their glorious Temple would lie in rubble (Matthew 24:2). He could predict the manner of His humiliation and death (Matthew 20:18-19). And He would do it to save us from the bondage of sin and the justice it deserves. While idols are less than nothing, we can say He is more than everything, for He created everything. He is the One who upholds us with His righteous right hand. He is the only One we should trust with our very lives and follow all the days of our lives. He is the incomparable One.

Questions
1 What is the idolatry of today?
2 How can religion be idolatry?
3 How is the passage connected with the opening verses?
4 How does God mock idols in this passage?
5 What would happen to a nation that abandoned its moral foundation?
6 What can an idol do?
7 Why would anyone place faith in idols?
8 Who does God call an abomination?
9 Why is this Cyrus and not Abraham?
10 What does God call delusional?
11 What is the chapter teaching us?

Look! My Servant - Isaiah 42:1-9

As we begin this important passage we should remember the setting and a few points in the preceding chapters. Isaiah is prophetically speaking to the future people of Judah in captivity. He has told them that they should take comfort for God will raise up a ruler who will return them to their homeland (Isaiah 40:1-2). God will also send a Redeemer (Isaiah 41:14).

In this passage, just as we have seen with previous prophecies, we can see an intermediate fulfillment or foreshadowing of an ultimate fulfillment. It very well may have been taken one way when the captives read it, but a deeper and more complete way by those who returned. The captives may have thought this servant that God was speaking of was the ruler that would come from the east and allow them to return to Jerusalem. While those who returned read it as speaking of the Messiah who was to come. Today we may even see another application.

¹ Behold my servant, whom I uphold, my chosen, in whom my soul delights; I have put my Spirit upon him; he will bring forth justice to the nations. Isaiah 42:1 While Cyrus may have been God's servant in financing the return of the Jews to Jerusalem (2Chronicles 36:23), and may have had the Spirit of God upon him to do so, we can't say he brought justice to the world. The rest of the passage goes on to describe someone much greater than Cyrus. The only one to bring justice to the nations, the only one in whom the soul of God delights is Jesus. As God said two different times in an audible voice from heaven, *[17b] "This is my beloved Son, with whom I am well pleased."* Matthew 3:17b (Matthew 17:5) Jews and Christians call this the first of the Suffering Servant Songs. While later Jews interpret this as referring to the Jewish people, the early rabbis and the Aramaic notes on these passages declare this to be about the Messiah. (Babylonian Talmud, Sanhedrin 98b) The other Suffering Servant Songs in Isaiah make this quite clear, but to avoid losing adherents by conversion to Christianity, Jewish rabbis began to point to several verses to show the servant is the Jewish nation. *[1] "But now hear, O Jacob my servant, Israel whom I have chosen!* Isaiah 44:1 (Also see 41:8)

I remember overhearing a Christian and some young Jewish boys talking about Isaiah 53, which is another Suffering Servant Song, while on an El Al flight. The Christian tried to tell them it was about Jesus. The boys showed him several verses that declare God's servant is Israel. Both sides were fully convinced. Both sides were unaware of the multiple use of the same term being used in different ways. For example, in Malachi 3:1 there are two distinct persons called "messenger." One was John the Baptist preparing the way. The other was Jesus, the messenger of the New Covenant. The servant in the passage we are looking at, can't be the servant of the second half of the chapter who is blind and deaf to the things of God (Isaiah 42:19). There are two messengers and two servants. If you press a Jewish person about the prophetic details of the servant in the Suffering Servant Songs, they would find difficulty holding to the opinion that it is about the Jewish people. Would they agree that the Spirit of God is upon them, that they have brought justice to the world, or that they don't lift up their voice in the streets? You'll smile at that one if you've been to Israel. Looking at the details of the songs show the servant must be a righteous individual who suffers for the sins of the world making many righteous (Isaiah 53:11). In addition, Matthew quotes these verses saying they were fulfilled in Jesus (Matthew 12:18-20).

Understanding this servant is Jesus of Nazareth, let's see what God has said about Him in this first verse. God upholds Him as He does all those who trust in Him (Isaiah 41:10). God has chosen Him, as He has chosen all who come to Him by faith (John 15:16). God's soul delights in Him, as He does to a lesser extent all who fear Him and hope in His steadfast love (Psalm 147:11). God puts His Spirit on Him as He does with His servants (Joel 2:29). But bringing justice to the world is an act of God alone (Isaiah 2:4). All these descriptions together point us to the ultimate servant of God.

[2] He will not cry aloud or lift up his voice, or make it heard in the street; Isaiah 42:2 Jesus was a teacher. He wasn't a rabble rouser or the kind

198

of leader who incites people. He invites people. Gentleness is a fruit of the Spirit. The way of the world is pushy and forceful. But Jesus just leads and invites us to follow. He blazed a trail of holiness with the scent of heaven as He loved the sinner and healed the leper. Unselfish love was never demonstrated so graciously as in the life of Jesus.

3 a bruised reed he will not break, and a faintly burning wick he will not quench; he will faithfully bring forth justice. Isaiah 42:3 The bruised and broken were embraced by His words and actions. The isolated woman at the well found a love that wouldn't use her (John 4:28). The widow who lost her son found compassionate power that raised the dead (Luke 7:15). The berated tax collector found the acceptance that transformed his life (Luke 19:9). It reminds me of a line from the song, Untitled Hymn. "Weak and wounded sinner, lost and left to die, come raise your head for love is passing by. Come to Jesus and live."

He is not only mercy and grace, for that would mean injustice would reign. He will faithfully bring forth justice. Injustice is more than a political dysfunction. "It is a spiritual evil, a denial of God." (John Ortberg, *Preaching the Word – Isaiah: God Saves Sinners* p 273) The user and abuser will answer to Him. The selfish and merciless will give an account. Justice will be meted out upon Jesus or should they refuse Him, on them. If it were not so, heaven would be no different from this sick world.

4 He will not grow faint or be discouraged till he has established justice in the earth; and the coastlands wait for his law. Isaiah 42:4 Chapter 40 told us that those who wait on the LORD will walk and not faint (Isaiah 40:31). In His steady plodding toward worldwide justice He will not stop until every wrong is righted and every debt is paid. I can't imagine how discouraging it would be to face unrepentant soul after soul and recount all their sins and the righteous justice upon each one. What all the worldly judges have to hear and decide in a lifetime of service is miniscule compared to the justice that Jesus will deal out upon mankind at the Great White Throne (Revelation 20:11-12). But if that never was to take place, how hopelessly wrong would our existence be? *22 The Father judges no one, but has given all judgment to the Son,* John 5:22

The world will wait for His law. His law is love (John 15:12). Until justice is meted out, His law will not prevail in the world. The Hebrew word for law is "torah." It can also mean "instruction." The coastlands speak of the people of the world that long for this broken world to be fixed. Man hasn't come up with the answer in his thousands of years of history. All we have proven is that we don't have the ability to fix the mess we created when we turned from God and decided to play gods (Genesis 3:17). That is why we wait for Jesus to come and give us His law.

Around the world today the broken hearts of men and women are made whole when they hear and receive the law of Jesus. Hope is renewed and guilt is removed. Joy and peace are experienced for the first time. Imagine the expectation when Christ comes to reign on the earth!

⁵ Thus says God, the LORD, who created the heavens and stretched them out, who spread out the earth and what comes from it, who gives breath to the people on it and spirit to those who walk in it: Isaiah 42:5 The One speaking through Isaiah introduces Himself. He is *El.* The Creator of heaven and earth. He is *YHWH*, the eternal God. God reminds us He stretched out the incredible universe with its incomprehensible size and is still stretching it out (40:22). He made this amazing planet and everything in it, animal and plant life. The verse ends with a parallelism. He gives breath to people on the earth which is repeated in different terms as "spirit to those who walk in it." This is Genesis one abbreviated. God created the heavens and the earth, the plant life, the animal life, and the crowning of His creation was man and breathing into him the breath of life (Genesis 2:7). God is telling Isaiah's readers that He is the God of Genesis chapter one, from whom and to whom and for whom all things exist (Romans 11:36).

⁶ "I am the LORD; I have called you in righteousness; I will take you by the hand and keep you; I will give you as a covenant for the people, a light for the nations, Isaiah 42:6 Who is the one who is called? Once again, we can read this as the mission of the Jewish people to bring the laws of God to the world through the Torah. Those in the captivity may have read it that way. But they would not come close to completing that mission. However, through the lineage of Abraham, Judah, and David would come the One Jewish person who would live a life of righteousness (Isaiah 53:11). The Father would keep Him from Satan's attempt to destroy Him at His birth (Matthew 2:16) and Herod's attempts on His life, that is, until His time came to become a covenant for the people.

Jeremiah and Ezekiel predicted the days of a new covenant that was unlike the Mosaic covenant written in stone (Ezekiel 36:26). This new one would be written in our hearts. That is what Jesus proclaimed Himself to be at the Last Supper (1Corinthains 11:25). He made a new covenant with His own blood that fulfilled the old. It is He, who became the light of the world, as Jesus proclaimed Himself to be (John 8:12).

Jesus' life and words have made the greatest impact on the world for good. No one comes close to affecting the world like Jesus. While our culture keeps pointing to the wrongs done using the name of Jesus, few will acknowledge the great good done by Christianity. Books have been written on the way Christianity was the chief cause for the end of the serfdom and feudal lords. It was the chief cause of the end of slavery. Capitalism with private property ownership can be traced back to Christian influence. That alone has done more to raise the quality of life than any other single factor. Personal responsibility and an honorable work ethic stem from the Christian faith. Our legal system and its effort to see that right prevails is traced to Jewish roots.

Jesus is a light in a practical sense but even more so in a spiritual sense. It is by His power alone that we are freed from guilt and enslaving patterns of sin (John 8:32). It is through Jesus alone that we have the hope of heaven (John 14:6).

Jesus is a light to the nations, *⁷ to open the eyes that are blind, to bring out the prisoners from the dungeon, from the prison those who sit in darkness.* Isaiah 42:7 Without Jesus and His teaching we are blind to spiritual reality. "Our salvation will never come from our own self-assertion; it will only come from the gentle servant of the Lord. Our idolatries can do nothing but corrupt, because they're the magnification of our proud self-salvation. That's why our good intentions end up unleashing more evil. Everything we do is laced with poisons we cannot detect in time." (Ibid) The upside-down way of the world has us chasing after our own destruction, but Jesus illuminates our understanding so that we can see where sin actually leads (John 3:20-21). Our eyes are opened to what is worthy of our attention and what is vanity. We were blind to what was of real value, but now in His light we can see.

This is one reason Jesus healed the blind. The man who was born blind illustrated for us our spiritual condition (John 9:30). We were all born spiritually blind. Jesus did what was impossible in the physical realm to show us He can and does do what is impossible for us to do without Him in the spiritual realm. The man's physical blindness was not nearly as consequential as our spiritual blindness.

Bringing out the prisoners from their dungeons and those in prison who sit in darkness is saying the same thing in a different way. Sin enslaves. It isolates us. It keeps us in darkness so that we can't see. The chains the sinner wears are forged by his or her own fallen desires. In Christ our chains are gone and we are free to live to righteousness (Romans 6:22).

⁸ I am the LORD; that is my name; my glory I give to no other, nor my praise to carved idols. Isaiah 42:8 *YHWH* is the name of the eternal God. He doesn't give His glory to an image. There is nothing to compare Him. The only way we could see that glory was the incarnation. We have seen His glory in the only begotten of the Father (John 1:14). He didn't have to share His glory with another for He is one with the Son. (John 10:30).

⁹ Behold, the former things have come to pass, and new things I now declare; before they spring forth I tell you of them." Isaiah 42:9 God is reminding Judah that their idols don't know the past and can't predict the future. God can because He is *YHWH.* He lives in eternity. He is in the past and the future right now. He is declaring to them their Messiah is coming. He will be the new covenant, not bring an agreement but be the agreement. He will bring light into the darkness. He will cause the physically and spiritually blind to see. He will release us from our bondage to sin. This is the glory that will come to Judah, to the city of Jerusalem, the very glory of God. And He did come. As Matthew declared, these verses came to pass in Jesus.

I want you to look at this passage again in a way that I have already been hinting. If you abide in Christ and He abides in you, then you will represent Him wherever you go. His prayer is that you be one with Him and with the Father. *²¹ that they may all be one, just as you, Father, are in me, and I in you, that they also may be in us, so that the world may believe that*

201

you have sent me. John 17:21 Remember that Paul declared it was no longer he that lived but Christ who lived in Him. That is the desire of the born-again believer, that the life of Christ be manifest in our mortal bodies (2Corinthians 4:10).

Just as the Father called the Son the One He upholds, the chosen, on whom He puts His Spirit, so are we to be His chosen ones, His servants in the world, upheld by Him, with His Spirit in us. Just as He was gentle and gracious, befriending the hurting, loving the needy, so are we, by His grace, to be the friend of sinners, gently leading them to wholeness and spiritual life in Him. While we cannot bring justice like He will, we can seek justice in the society in which we live. We can bring His law of love to the coastlands, to the hungry souls who see there is more than this world.

He has called us in righteousness and will take us by the hand. We saw that in the previous chapter (Isaiah 41:13). He will even make us a light to the nations, as Jesus said, "You are the light of the world!" (Matthew 5:14)

As we bring the new covenant in Jesus' blood to the world, we open the eyes of the blind and loose prisoners from their chains. Through the Gospel we bring them up out of the dungeons of despair and into the promises of God in Christ Jesus.

In Christ, this Suffering Servant Song is our song too. Jesus declared as much when He said, *"As the Father has sent me, even so I am sending you."* (John 20:21) You can sing this song in praise to Jesus, and you can sing it as a reminder of your calling in this fallen world.

Questions
1 What are several ways to read this passage?
2 Why can't the servant be Cyrus?
3 Who do Jews think the servant is? Why do Christians think He is Jesus?
4 How does God describe the servant?
5 How did Jesus demonstrate verse 3?
6 What is God's self-description?
7 How does Jesus open blind eyes?
8 Why can't an idol represent God?
9 Why can we apply some of this passage?
10 What specifically does this tell us to about our calling?

The New Song - Isaiah 42:10-25

Isaiah 42 has returned the theme of a deliverer who will do for Israel what they had not been able to do, bring justice to the nations and be a light to the world. He is the true Israel, One who prevails with God. It was the first of four Suffering Servant Songs. The theme carries on into the next passage. The song is by no means over. There is still more.

[10] Sing to the LORD a new song, his praise from the end of the earth, you who go down to the sea, and all that fills it, the coastlands and their inhabitants. Isaiah 42:10 The response God calls for from the Servant Song is for the ends of the earth to praise the LORD with a new song (Psalm 33:3). In fact, "all that fills it" is to sing this song of praise. The new song we are to sing is found in Revelation 5:9 -10 (NIV). *[9] And they sang a new song: "You are worthy to take the scroll and to open its seals, because you were slain, and with your blood you purchased men for God from every tribe and language and people and nation. [10] You have made them to be a kingdom and priests to serve our God, and they will reign on the earth."* That is a song that is about the Suffering Servant and the result of His suffering. The song Isaiah wrote promised an individual would become a covenant and light for us. We saw that it was Jesus, who made the covenant in His own blood, and who is the Light of the world (John 8:12).

Everyone who comes to Christ and is brought out of their dark dungeon of sin sings a similar new song. God's heart is that the entire world of men and women sing it. How many songs have been written to praise Jesus for all He has done for us? Fanny Crosby alone wrote 10,000. It is new song after new song as we see the glory of Jesus more fully. New songs come from new revelations and intimate times with the LORD.

When the curse is lifted from the earth even the plants and animals will sing a new song. Isaiah declares in another passage *[12] "For you shall go out in joy and be led forth in peace; the mountains and the hills before you shall break forth into singing, and all the trees of the field shall clap their hands.* Isaiah 55:12 It is probably from passages like this that C.S. Lewis created the talking animals of Narnia.

While the captives in Babylon may have seen this passage as a return to Jerusalem and restoration of the land, that is but a shadow of what I believe God has in mind. The message of Isaiah often includes the whole earth as in this first verse. The return of the captives was but a faint foreshadowing of the whole earth being brought out from captivity. The Apostle Paul pointed to this in Romans 8 when he wrote the following. *[19] The creation waits in eager expectation for the sons of God to be revealed. [20] For the creation was subjected to frustration, not by its own choice, but by the will of the one who subjected it, in hope [21] that the creation itself will be liberated from its bondage to decay and brought into the glorious freedom of the children of God.* Romans 8:19-21 (NIV) That is the ultimate fulfillment of which we sing the new song recorded in Revelation (Isaiah 2:4).

But right now we sing a new song too. The life of every unrepentant person is the blues or a country western song at best. But life in Christ is a praise and worship song. We know where we are going and how greatly we are loved (Isaiah 54:8). We know whatever comes our way will be used by God who will walk with us through it as He holds our hand and upholds us with His righteous right hand (Isaiah 40:11; 41:10). Our song is a song of victory. It's always fresh and new because we keep seeing more of God's great love for us. When we do see it we are to shout it from the mountaintops.

The subject of the passage then changes to the LORD coming to deliver and judge. *13 The LORD goes out like a mighty man, like a man of war he stirs up his zeal; he cries out, he shouts aloud, he shows himself mighty against his foes.* Isaiah 42:13 Let us not miss the connection with the previous passage. The servant of the LORD does not cry aloud or lift up His voice or make it heard in the streets (42:2). But now, it's a different story. Is the LORD and the Suffering Servant the same? The next verse makes it clear by saying that He has restrained Himself for a long time, but now He's letting it all out.

We can see that this might have been read by the captives as God using Cyrus to defeat the Babylonians, but the reality is the victory over Satan on the cross. There Jesus cried with a loud voice, "It is finished!" (John 19:30) The mighty warrior took on the forces of hell with our sins upon Him. He showed Himself mighty against His foes.

There is yet another fulfillment. The Apostle Paul tells *16 For the Lord himself will descend from heaven with a cry of command, with the voice of an archangel, and with the sound of the trumpet of God. And the dead in Christ will rise first.* 1 Thessalonians 4:16 The Lord will give a cry of command. He calls our bodies to rise, but it's also a battle cry against all who refuse His love and mercy, and against all the forces of hell (Joel 2:11). The One who came as the Lamb of God will return as the Lion of the tribe of Judah (Revelation 5:5).

14 For a long time I have held my peace; I have kept still and restrained myself; now I will cry out like a woman in labor; I will gasp and pant. Isaiah 42:14 Imagine our Creator watching this sin sick world and all the pain and suffering, the abuse of women and children, as He waits for the last soul to accept His salvation (2Peter 3:9). That is restraint! Finally, it is time to end all this evil that has permeated His good creation. It's been a long time! But now He's going to clean up the mess that generations of sinful selfishness have created. If you were with your wife when she delivered a baby, you know the picture God is painting. You don't want to be in His way.

15 I will lay waste mountains and hills, and dry up all their vegetation; I will turn the rivers into islands, and dry up the pools. 16 And I will lead the blind in a way that they do not know, in paths that they have not known I will guide them. I will turn the darkness before them into light, the rough places into level ground. These are the things I do, and I do not forsake them. Isaiah 42:15-16 For the captives in Babylon this sounded like God's promise to return them safely to Jerusalem. Most of them were children of the original captives and had never made the journey. God cleared all obstacles and made it possible for them to return. In fact, the conquest of Babylon was made possible by the diverting of the river that ran through the city so that the Medes and Persians could enter the city by the dry river bed, as seen in verse 15.

But there is a much deeper meaning. We are all blind, sitting in darkness, until we come to the Light. (See verses 6 and 7.) This verse also connects the Suffering Servant with the LORD. Man doesn't know His way, Jesus. Jesus is the path, the Highway of holiness (Isaiah 35:8).

The way to righteousness was impossible for us to travel. To us, it was rough, with rivers to cross, and dark. We had no map and no hope of ever reaching our destination. But Jesus came to take us by the hand and led us to Himself, and He became the way (John 14:6). He dried up the rivers and made the rough places smooth by prodding us with His Holy Spirit and then taking our sins upon Himself. This is what He did for us. He did not forsake us, nor will He ever. *⁶ So we can confidently say, "The Lord is my helper; I will not fear; what can man do to me?"* Hebrews 13:6

When you look back on your old life after coming to Christ, you often wonder how you could have been so blind. But when you consider how blind you were, you wonder how you made it to faith. Here is the answer. He took you and me by the hand and led us into His light (Isaiah 42:6). He leveled out the rough places and became the way when there was no way. He became the way by taking our sins upon Himself and paying our debt.

As for the seemingly all-powerful Babylonian gods and those who trust in this world, *¹⁷ They are turned back and utterly put to shame, who trust in carved idols, who say to metal images, "You are our gods."* Isaiah 42:17 The Babylonians faith in their idolatry stood in stark contrast with the kings who, through Daniel's influence, saw YHWH as the Lord over all (Daniel 4:2). Remember that in the account in Daniel, they were praising these gods represented by idols when the Babylon fell (Daniel 5:4).

¹⁸ Hear, you deaf, and look, you blind, that you may see! ¹⁹ Who is blind but my servant, or deaf as my messenger whom I send? Who is blind as my dedicated one, or blind as the servant of the LORD? Isaiah 42:18-19 Israel is invited to hear and see what God is doing. "Servant" returns to its meaning, Israel, as in the previous chapter. The servant, Israel, is told to see that God is sending them back to Jerusalem so that the Suffering Servant can come to them to redeem them from their sins and bring them into the light that they might no longer be blind.

The history of Israel seemed to be such a repeated cycle of sin and rebellion followed by the consequences of decline that we wonder why God had chosen them to be the recipients of the Law and the bloodline of the Messiah. But then we look at the world around us and realize He doesn't have much to choose from. Sin blinds us to what is harmful and deafens us to the voice of God. God is telling them words of comfort and grace that they will not hear until they end up captives in Babylon. Something often has to tragically interrupt our lives before we slow down and look and listen to what God is trying to convey to our deaf ears and blind eyes (Psalm 119:75).

²⁰ He sees many things, but does not observe them; his ears are open, but he does not hear. Isaiah 42:20 This makes clear that the blindness and deafness are spiritual. God is at work all around us and is always speaking, but we tend to let the world drown out our hearing and fill our vision. We should be watching and listening for Him (Hebrews 12:2).

I have found that when you expect God you are much more likely to see God at work (Deuteronomy 4:29). If you are expecting Him to speak, you are much more likely to hear that still small voice. We are always looking for the big things when God is working in our personalities and the multitude of daily details. Oswald Chambers wrote, *"We have the idea that God is going to do some exceptional thing, that He is preparing and fitting us for some extraordinary thing by and by, but as we go on in grace we find that God is glorifying Himself here and now, in the present minute."* (Oswald Chambers, *My Utmost for His Highest*, May 4) Are we looking and listening?

The tendency of Christians in affluent societies is to go the way of the Jews in Isaiah's time. We are so busy with work, entertainment, hobbies, and gadgets that we can miss God amid it all. What really matters are what He is doing and saying. Jesus set the example of always having an ear open to His heavenly Father and of always watching for Him. Jesus said, *[49] For I have not spoken on my own authority, but the Father who sent me has himself given me a commandment—what to say and what to speak.* John 12:49 Jesus' ears and eyes were always open to the Father. It is the outworking of His love for Him. As our love for God increases, our attention will be more continuously directed toward Him (John 12:26).

[21] The LORD was pleased, for his righteousness' sake, to magnify his law and make it glorious. Isaiah 42:21 I think there is an intentional contrast presented here between the Servant of the first nine verses and the servant in this last portion. The LORD'S soul delights in the Suffering Servant. He is pleased for His righteousness sake to magnify His law. Jesus is that law in the flesh (John 1:14). But the servant Israel does not see or hear the law. John's prologue puts it this way, *[11] He came to his own, and his own people did not receive him.* John 1:11 God exalted the Word that He delivered to Israel, but they would not hear. He laid it out for them in black and white, but they chose to turn away from it and go into exile.

[22] But this is a people plundered and looted; they are all of them trapped in holes and hidden in prisons; they have become plunder with none to rescue, spoil with none to say, "Restore!" Isaiah 42:22 That was the condition of the people when this prophecy of comfort came to them. It is the condition of the sinner when the Gospel reaches into their heart. But it is so because they have rejected the Word of the Lord that would rescue and restore them (Psalm 107:20). For Judah it was a physical oppressor. For mankind it is the oppression of our hearts' wickedness (Jeremiah 17:9). We are plundered, looted, and trapped by our own misguided desires. It is the Suffering Servant that sets the prisoners free from their dungeons. Jesus is the answer to our spiritual condition.

[23] Who among you will give ear to this, will attend and listen for the time to come? Isaiah 42:23 Who will hear the message of repentance and

salvation? Who would take this word of comfort into captivity with them? Most of you are here this morning because you do want to hear. You do want God's direction now so that you can follow the LORD through whatever is to come.

²⁴ Who gave up Jacob to the looter, and Israel to the plunderers? Was it not the LORD, against whom we have sinned, in whose ways they would not walk, and whose law they would not obey? Isaiah 42:24 It is not some unguided, accidental flow of circumstances that powers rise and fall. God has made it abundantly clear that He is the One who directs the course of human affairs. He is the One who will send Judah into captivity as He promised to do if they turned away from His law and worshiped other gods (Deuteronomy 29:26-28).

²⁵ So he poured on him the heat of his anger and the might of battle; it set him on fire all around, but he did not understand; it burned him up, but he did not take it to heart. Isaiah 42:25 The servant, Israel, was dealt with severely to turn them back to God. It was grace that dealt this harsh blow, and it is righteous anger. All the words of the prophets, all the godly priests and kings, the special interventions of God on behalf of the nation, and they still turned to idolatry. Their enemies laid siege and took them into captivity and yet they still did not take it to heart. How hardhearted is that?

Don't we see something similar in the decline of our nation? Our nation's blood and treasure was poured out to save a people from a tyrant only to watch a far more tyrannical people fill the void. Scandals fill the headlines day after day and no one seems to notice any more. Practical solutions are offered but fear of not being re-elected won't allow them to even be considered.

But we should also look within to our own house. If God brings desperation into our lives, it is to cause us to turn from our idols and hear Him for our good. He invites us to give ear and listen for a time to come. Will we let the Suffering Servant, Jesus, guide us by the hand into his leveled way, or will we insist on going our own rough way? That is the choice set before Judah, and it is the same choice set before us. We can join the chorus that sings the new song of praise or remain a captive of our own design (John 8:34). Choose this day whom you will serve. The gods of the culture that make promises that are vain, or the LORD of all creation who gave Himself for you. As for me and my house… (say it with me) we will serve the LORD!

Questions:
1 What is the new song? Who sings it?
2 Why is it a victorious song?
3 When does Jesus come as a warrior?
4 Why is God so angry?
5 How did God make a way for us?
6 Why is verse 19 a different servant?
7 When are we more likely to see and hear God?

8 What really matters?

9 What is God pleased with?

10 Why does man not take to heart God's discipline?

11 What are the choices God has presented in this passage?

I Am He! - Isaiah 43:1-15

God has a great plan for your life. It's not because of who you are, but because of who He is and the destiny He has given you. The previous passage in Isaiah ended with God describing how He had judged the people, taking them into the fire, and yet they still did not take it to heart. We are often too hardhearted to see what God is doing. But the overall message of *this* portion of the book of Isaiah is of comfort to the captives, to point to a hope and a future. This chapter begins by declaring that even though they don't respond to God's discipline, He still calls them, as He does all believers, His own people. *¹ But now thus says the LORD, he who created you, O Jacob, he who formed you, O Israel: "Fear not, for I have redeemed you; I have called you by name, you are mine.* Isaiah 43:1

God identifies Himself as YHWH, their Creator. He again calls them by both names, (Jacob) "one who deceives" and (Israel) "one who prevails with God." (Genesis 32:28) It speaks of the duplicitous nature of man (Galatians 5:17). We are so prone to selfishness and yet by God's grace we are capable of godliness, of being who we were created to be.

I've been reading The Light and the Glory by Peter Marshall. The Puritan pilgrims were no different from ancient Israel. They would have such dedication to one another and the cause of Christ, and yet in one generation they would exhibit such greed and dismissal of the need for God and fellowship. It is a cycle consistently repeated throughout human history.

Even though we fail so miserably to show the gratitude we should for all God blesses us with, He has still redeemed us and called us by name. That is why we need not fear. He will not forsake us, even though we so often fall short of His glory and operate in the Jacob nature instead of the Israel nature. As I read this passage it occurred to me that the redemption God is speaking of is judgment. We'll see that in the next verses. They were redeemed from Egypt by judgment on the gods that Egyptians worshiped. We are redeemed from sin by the judgment of that sin falling on Christ on the cross (Galatians 3:13).

Calling us by name is a wonderful and repeated message in Scripture (1 Samuel 3:7). It is true of nations and individuals. It is right for us to invite people to put their own name in John 3:16. He knows your name. He gave you your name. And He has a new name for those who will overcome by His grace (Revelation 2:17). Because of that redemption and personal relationship of calling us His own, by name, we have no need to fear anything. Are you redeemed? Have you answered when He called your name?

² When you pass through the waters, I will be with you; and through the rivers, they shall not overwhelm you; when you walk through fire you shall not be burned, and the flame shall not consume you. Isaiah 43:2 The nation of Judah would have thought of their captivity as they read this, but also of God's deliverance through the Red Sea (Exodus 14:22) and crossing the Jordan at flood stage (Joshua 3:17) when they had entered the Promised Land. Though Daniel's companions had not yet faced the fiery furnace, this passage was written to the people of that future time. They surely thought of this verse. God is speaking of calamity and danger. Whatever we go through, He promises to be with us. We won't lose everything because our treasure is in heaven (Matthew 6:20-21). Your body may drown or burn but God will be with you and your soul will suffer no loss.

We know at times this is fulfilled literally, and we know there are times when it is figurative of God delivering us spiritually. We have testimonies of the saints who have died with confidence of God being with them as they were burned at the stake or faced painful loss of loved ones. God's grace is sufficient to see us through whatever we face. As the three facing the furnace said, "Our God is able to deliver us, but if not, we still won't bow!" (Daniel 3:16-18)

If you read the book, *Killing Christians* by Tom Doyle, you know that God is doing the same today. He can deliver you from a blood thirsty mob, or He can be with you in death as a testimony. I recently heard a testimony from YWAM leaders in the Middle East. An ISIS jihadi wanted to speak to them. Would you meet with a jihadi? They did, and he told of his past pleasure in killing Christians. But one believer had told him that he was going to give him his Bible before he was martyred. The jihadi took the Bible and began to read it. He had dreams of Jesus asking him why he was killing God's servants. Shortly after, his pleasure in murder turned to disgust. He needed to know who this man in white who appeared in his dreams was. Was He the Jesus in the Bible? The jihadi became a child of God! Some are delivered and some go home to glory, but either way, we are redeemed and God is with us.

³ For I am the LORD your God, the Holy One of Israel, your Savior. I give Egypt as your ransom, Cush and Seba in exchange for you. Isaiah 43:3 Here is the connection with the deliverance from Egypt. If God would deal with an entire nation to free His people, is He not capable of dealing with your situation? Do you think ISIS is a surprise to God? Do you think whatever you are going through is out of the reach of God? His hand is not short that it cannot save (Numbers 11:23). God delights in taking the worst and turning them into His saints. Nothing is too hard for God!

He is our Savior. The word used here implies deliverance and freedom. We were captives of sin and destined for judgment, but we have a Savior, a liberator. We don't have to live in selfishness and destructive passions.

⁴ Because you are precious in my eyes, and honored, and I love you, I give men in return for you, peoples in exchange for your life. Isaiah 43:4

This is spoken to the captives, but it is also spoken to you. For God so loved you, you were so precious in His eyes, so honored, so loved, that He gave His only Son. As the Apostle Paul wrote, *32 He who did not spare his own Son but gave him up for us all, how will he not also with him graciously give us all things?* Romans 8:32 He gave His only begotten Son in exchange for your life! That is how precious we are to Him. I know it is hard to believe. It is hard to accept that kind of love, but it is true. He came for you. What a shame it would be if you do not receive that great a love (Romans 8:39)!

Our hearts long for this great a love, but when it is presented to us we draw back in fear. That is because we are afraid we may get so caught up in it that we lose ourselves. Jesus said that won't happen. Instead, you will find your life (Matthew 10:39). You will lay aside the old deceptive pleasures you once valued because of this all-encompassing love, but that will be because you see He is more than worth your all.

Fellow believers, I want you to hear this and let it sink into your heart. Jesus sees the finished product, the beautiful bride that He is making out of us. We see that in the analogy with Rebecca (Genesis 24:16), in the Song of Songs (Song of Songs 6:4-5), and in the Revelation (Revelation 21:2). The love your heart longs for, the love you've sought all your life, is a reality in Jesus who loves you so much. He sees you as beautiful, precious, and honored. Meditate on that and I guarantee you that you will love Him more.

5 Fear not, for I am with you; I will bring your offspring from the east, and from the west I will gather you. 6 I will say to the north, Give up, and to the south, Do not withhold; bring my sons from afar and my daughters from the end of the earth, Isaiah 43:5-6 Once again God tells the captives they have no reason to fear because He is with them. God said that to numerous individuals in Scripture (Genesis 26:24; Exodus 3:12; Deuteronomy 31:23). He says it to us. He promised to make His home in the one who believes and places his or her trust in Jesus (John 14:23). I want you to think for a moment just what it is that you fear. Have you identified something? Loss of income? Financial collapse? Illness? Death of a loved one? Is Jesus with you (Hebrews 13:5-6)? Then why are you afraid? It amounts to us not trusting that He can see us through whatever we fear.

The Jews feared they would not return to their Promised Land. God said He would do it and He did it. God is always faithful to His Word (Titus 1:2). But that was only a partial fulfillment. He did it more exactly according to the wording of this passage about 65 years ago, and the return continues to this day.

7 everyone who is called by my name, whom I created for my glory, whom I formed and made." Isaiah 43:7 This was prophesied to Israel, but again we see wording that is more encompassing. Who was created for God's glory? Who did God form and make? Everyone! But only believers are called by His name. If you have taken the label "Christian" then you should be living for the glory of God. People ask why God created us in the first place. It is for His glory. How glorious is God? He is so glorious that

He could take wretches like you and me and transform us into the bride of Christ with His likeness in all we say and do. The work is not done, but that will be the conclusion of what He has started (Philippians 3:21).

⁸ Bring out the people who are blind, yet have eyes, who are deaf, yet have ears! ⁹ All the nations gather together, and the peoples assemble. Who among them can declare this, and show us the former things? Let them bring their witnesses to prove them right, and let them hear and say, It is true. Isaiah 43:8-9 God is revealing the immediate and distant future. Now we can look back and see it was true. He brought back His servant, Israel, who was deaf and blind to the things of God.

The nations can't look back on their gods and say, "See this was predicted in detail and it came to pass." God is declaring that prophecy is proof that He is God of all. None can compare. It is an open invitation throughout time. He alone inhabits eternity and knows the end from the beginning (Isaiah 46:10).

¹⁰ "You are my witnesses," declares the LORD, "and my servant whom I have chosen, that you may know and believe me and understand that I am he. Before me no god was formed, nor shall there be any after me. Isaiah 43:10 We can read this two ways. The people of Judah are God's witness and they are His servant, His chosen ones. OR we could read it as saying that the people of Judah are His witnesses, and so is His Servant, the Suffering Servant, His chosen One. The Jews are witnesses to the world through the Word delivered to them and God's dealing with them. The Servant is the One who will help the witnesses know and believe that "I am He!"

It is Jesus who convinces us that God is real and loves us, that He is the I Am. Twenty-two times in John's gospel Jesus declared, "I am He!" Jesus said to know and believe Him is to be saved (John 17:3; 11:26). It is the only way to know the Father. He is the One who convinces us that there is but one triune God. His miraculous life and words convince us. The way He lived out this passage should convince us.

Jesus demonstration of this passage is recorded in John 6. Notice in this Isaiah passage YHWH tells them not to fear. When they pass through the waters He will be with them. In verse 3 He tells them He is their Savior. In verse 5, He says, "Do not fear, for I am with you." And in verse 10 He declares, "I am He!"

Listen as I read each of those expressions in the account in John 6:16-20 (NIV). *¹⁶ When evening came, his disciples went down to the lake, ¹⁷ where they got into a boat and set off across the lake for Capernaum. By now it was dark, and Jesus had not yet joined them. ¹⁸ A strong wind was blowing and the waters grew rough. ¹⁹ When they had rowed three or three and a half miles, they saw Jesus approaching the boat, walking on the water; and they were terrified. ²⁰ But he said to them, "It is I; don't be afraid."* Or we could translate it, "I am He! Do not be afraid." (YLT) Do you see the parallel? As they passed through the water He was with them. He is their Savior. He tells them not to fear. Why? I am He! We might add that this Isaiah passage seems to refer to the crossing of the Red Sea in which it was a dark night with a strong wind blowing, just as in this passage, John 6.

¹¹ I, I am the LORD, and besides me there is no savior. Isaiah 43:11 And to this the Apostles agree. *¹² And there is salvation in no one else, for there is no other name under heaven given among men by which we must be saved."* Acts 4:12 YHWH and Jesus are one (John 10:30). It is so obvious in Scripture that we wonder how the cult of Jehovah's Witness could continue.

Man looks for salvation in others and in things because we know God's love demands a total surrender (Mathew 10:38). Anything or anyone other than Jesus who claims to offer you salvation from your fallen nature, from God's justice upon sin, is a liar and can never deliver. Jesus is our only hope. Thank God He loves us so!

¹² I declared and saved and proclaimed, when there was no strange god among you; and you are my witnesses," declares the LORD, "and I am God. ¹³ Also henceforth I am he; there is none who can deliver from my hand; I work, and who can turn it back?" Isaiah 43:12-13 Look throughout the history of man. Only God can miraculously save, whether from the flood in Noah's day, or from the fire that fell on Sodom. He delivered a nation from Egypt and gave them victory over nations (Psalm 60:6-8).

He has saved us as well. Remember the day you brought your sins to the cross and knew you were forgiven, made right with God, an heir of eternal life. And so we are His witnesses as well. That is why He gave us the Holy Spirit, to have the power to be a witness by the transformed life that is ours in Jesus (Acts 1:8).

Again God declares, "I am He!" What He decides is what will happen. You can't escape Him. You can't change His course. He has determined all things. He alone has all power and authority.

In our day there are so many deceptions. So many claim to be god. So many claim another god. Put them up alongside these claims of the one true God and you will see they are nothing compared to Him who alone can save. They are nothing compared to Him who inhabits eternity and knows the end from the beginning. He alone has delivered, does deliver, and will deliver us in the future.

¹⁴ Thus says the LORD, your Redeemer, the Holy One of Israel: "For your sake I send to Babylon and bring them all down as fugitives, even the Chaldeans, in the ships in which they rejoice. ¹⁵ I am the LORD, your Holy One, the Creator of Israel, your King." Isaiah 43:14-15 God is promising that even though He brings Babylon to punish them for their idolatry and turn them back to Him, He will destroy Babylon like He destroyed Egypt. How is that possible? Is God so great that He can plan the details of the future and raise up and bring down mighty nations? He already has (Daniel 2:21). He did just as He promised for He is the Creator. He is the Holy One, our King. I hope you know Him as your King.

Questions

212

1 Why does the chapter start, "But now"?
2 Why should we not fear?
3 What is the promise of verse 2?
4 Why did the jihadi convert?
5 Who is precious, honored, and loved?
6 How do you know He means you?
7 Why did God make you?
8 How can we know YHWH alone is God?
9 What is the relationship with John 6?
10 What is the significance of "I Am He!"?

God's Solution to Failure - Isaiah 43:16-44:5

I have a friend who thought he had fallen too far from grace. For a time, he felt he had denied the Lord by his life to the extent that he had forsaken his salvation and was beyond hope. If you've ever felt that way or know someone who does, our passage today is for you!

The first half of this chapter promised deliverance for those who were going to be in captivity. God declared that none could stop Him from His plan (Isaiah 43:13). That plan was for Israel to be His witnesses in the earth, along with the Suffering Servant who would come from among them (43:10). God was going to bring deliverance and salvation so that the world would know "I am He." That is to say the God of Israel is the one true, eternal, and sovereign God of all creation (43:15).

The chapter continues with God declaring His ability to bring the remnant of Judah back to the Promised Land. *16 Thus says the LORD, who makes a way in the sea, a path in the mighty waters, 17 who brings forth chariot and horse, army and warrior; they lie down, they cannot rise, they are extinguished, quenched like a wick:* Isaiah 43:16-17 YHWH parted the Red Sea (Exodus 14:21-22) and the Jordan at flood stage (Joshua 3:16-17). Could we not also see in verse 16 Jesus walking on Galilee as appears to be the case in the first half of this chapter (John 6:19-20)? How rich is God's Word that it speaks in so many ways at once!

God is comforting the future captives by reminding them what He has done before when their ancestors were captives in Egypt. If God could make a way for a nation to cross a sea and destroy the army of Pharaoh that pursued them, why shouldn't they have faith that God could do the same with Babylon? Why shouldn't we have faith that He can set us free from the captivity of sin?

In fact, God liberated the captives by making a path for the army of the Persians to enter Babylon by inspiring the Persians to divert the river that ran under the city. God literally made a way in the mighty water's river bed. Babylon's army was defeated by a tidal wave of Persian soldiers. Whether supernatural or natural, it is all God, the sovereign One.

^{18} *"Remember not the former things, nor consider the things of old.*
Isaiah 43:18 The captives in Babylon will not have to look back on the
exodus from Egypt for inspiration. They will have their own exodus from
Babylon that will be just as miraculous. We look back on God's work in our
lives in the past to encourage us, until He does something new and greater.

^{19} *Behold, I am doing a new thing; now it springs forth, do you not
perceive it? I will make a way in the wilderness and rivers in the desert.*
Isaiah 43:19 In the deliverance from Egypt they fled from a rebellious
Pharaoh. God provided a miraculous solution to an impossible situation.
Now God would provide deliverance from Babylon by raising up a heathen
king who would fight for them and even finance their return.

Which is more miraculous, the parting and closing of the Red Sea,
or moving the heart of a king to do God's will? Seems like a toss up to me.
Both are impossible with man. If you've struggled with your own heart in
serving the Lord, imagine the miracle it would take to move the heart of a
king to serve anyone other than himself! God made a way in the wilderness
of a king's heart and streams in the desert of his soul.

^{20} *The wild beasts will honor me, the jackals and the ostriches, for I
give water in the wilderness, rivers in the desert, to give drink to my chosen
people,* Isaiah 43:20 Just as God provided for the Jews that wandered forty
years in the wilderness, so God would provide for those Jews returning to
the Promised Land. He would move the wild beasts of heathen people to
honor God. They would, by a king's edict, give tax money for the restoration
of Jerusalem against their will (Ezra 6:3-5; 8-10). Where there seemed no
way and no provision, God provided from their bestial enemies and from the
heart of heathen king.

You may not see any way for God to bring you out of your captivity
to sin (John 8:34). You may think your desert is too dry to have any hope of
surviving spiritually. You can't do it. You don't have the resources, but God
does! We'll see how at the end of the passage. Just like He miraculously
provided for them, He can provide for you, if you will look to Him and cast
yourself completely on Him.

Follow Jesus' lifelong example of surrendering His will to the
Father. It wasn't a sudden decision in the Garden of Gethsemane that caused
Jesus to say, "Not my will but yours be done (Luke 22:42)." That was His
daily life. If it's your daily life, when that crucial moment comes in your life,
by God's grace you will continue to follow your life's pattern.

^{21} *the people whom I formed for myself that they might declare my
praise.* Isaiah 43:21 Why was God being so merciful to this people whose
fathers had been so rebellious? They were His chosen. He formed them for
Himself that they might declare His praise. Is that not who you are? (John
15:16) Is this not what we are called to do, to declare His praise (Isaiah
42:10)? But are we? Having experienced His deliverance from the
destructive bondage to habitual sins (John 8:36), let your heart be filled with
gratitude for saving you from that life by seeing where it would have led

you. Declare His praise to others. That gives them hope that they can be set free as well.

I hope you all understand what I'm referring to. The Apostle Paul writes of being delivered from this present evil age (Galatians 1:4). If you are a servant of sin in your life, it will rob you of the relationship you could have with Jesus. It will keep you from the joy you could know. In the end, it will destroy you physically and spiritually. Don't believe the lying promises of sin. They never deliver and will cost more than you know. God formed you for Himself, so that you could declare His glory. If any human asked you to declare their glory, we would know it would be from a heart of selfishness. But when God says it, we know it is only right and comes out of a heart of love that desires our best.

22 "Yet you did not call upon me, O Jacob; but you have been weary of me, O Israel! Isaiah 43:22 The Jews had the history, the writings, and an abundance of opportunity and yet they would not call upon the Lord and be saved (Romans 10:13; Joel 2:32). Instead they grew weary of God through their ingratitude and indifference. What a warning for us! I meet people who are tired of going to church. That is because they are just going to a building. How can you grow tired of fellowship with believers and sharing testimonies of God at work in your life and hearing testimonies from others? How can you grow weary of worship of the One who loved you enough to die for you, who has plans for your future that are so great He says you can't imagine it (1 Corinthians 2:9)?

Religion can become a ritual when our hearts are not involved. Israel grew tired of their offerings because they would not consider what the offerings represented. They lost a heart of gratitude for deliverance from Egypt, for a land of their own, for fields they did not clear and houses they did not build, for victories over their enemies, for the revelation of God through the prophets, and for being the guardians of the Word of God and His promises to man (Deuteronomy 6:10-12).

The lack of offerings just represented their lack of gratitude for all God did and was doing. The same can be true with us. Some people are excited to give. Others give grudgingly. Our attitude toward giving is directly related to our understanding of what God has done for us and our willingness to respond from a heart of gratitude (2 Corinthians 9:7). Have you ever just spontaneously emptied your wallet into the offering out of sheer gratitude? Some people have realized it really is more blessed to give than receive (Acts 20:35).

23 You have not brought me your sheep for burnt offerings, or honored me with your sacrifices. I have not burdened you with offerings, or wearied you with frankincense. 24 You have not bought me sweet cane with money, or satisfied me with the fat of your sacrifices. But you have burdened me with your sins; you have wearied me with your iniquities. Isaiah 43:23-24 God declares that He had not burdened them, but they had burdened Him. Instead of offerings of gratitude, there was rebellion, sin, and iniquity. This was the history of Israel to this point, but grace was still being extended to them (Psalm 89:30-34).

This may be your history to this point, but if you are still breathing, God is extending grace to you this morning. Repent! Call on the name of the Lord and be saved. Like Israel, you can go from being a burden to God to become a witness of His glory. He made you for Himself. Nothing else will fill the void in your heart.

25 "I, I am he who blots out your transgressions for my own sake, and I will not remember your sins. Isaiah 43:25 Only the one offended can offer forgiveness to the offender. God can forgive because He provides justice for our sin through Jesus' sacrificial death in our place. It is not only love that sent Jesus, it is for God's own sake. He must be consistent with His perfect nature and that includes grace and mercy. He is also preparing a bride for His Son (Ephesians 5:31-32). We receive forgiveness and are transformed. He gets a pure and spotless bride for Jesus. She is the redeemed people of God.

Notice that God said He would remember our sin no more. Only God can choose to forget! We try to forget, but He does (Isaiah 38:17)! If you bring up your old sins which you have repented of and forsaken, He won't know what you are referring to! Hallelujah! Maybe you don't have an ugly past and can't say, "Hallelujah!" as heartily as some us. You can thank God for that (Luke 7:47)! In reference to the idea that someone can have a good heart without Jesus, Chambers wrote in today's devotion: "If I have never been a blackguard, the reason is a mixture of cowardice and the protection of a civilized life; but when I am undressed before God, I find that Jesus Christ is right in his diagnosis." (Oswald Chambers, My Utmost for His Highest, July 27)

26 Put me in remembrance; let us argue together; set forth your case, that you may be proved right. Isaiah 43:26 It's not because of your holiness or anything you have done that caused God to redeem and forgive you (Ephesians 2:8-9). Like the Jews, we come from a long line of rebels, as the following verses point out.

27 Your first father sinned, and your mediators transgressed against me. 28 Therefore I will profane the princes of the sanctuary, and deliver Jacob to utter destruction and Israel to reviling. Isaiah 43:27-28 The first father may be Adam or Abraham, either way, both sinned. Every mediator transgressed: Abraham, Moses, David, priests, every single ancestor.

While God is speaking to future captives, verse 28 shows they have not gone into captivity yet. Those who think it was written by a later author during the captivity have to explain this fact away.

The passage would find a second fulfillment when the Jews reject the Suffering Servant. And yet, there is still hope. The next chapter begins with what Jesus referred to as "the promise of the Father" and looks forward to the pouring out of the Holy Spirit who can change our hearts so that we can live for the purpose for which we were created, the glory of the Lord and to declare His praise (Isaiah 43:7).

¹ "But now hear, O Jacob my servant, Israel whom I have chosen! ² Thus says the LORD who made you, who formed you from the womb and will help you: Fear not, O Jacob my servant, Jeshurun whom I have chosen. Isaiah 44:1-2 Jeshurun is another name for Israel (Deuteronomy 32:15). In spite of their just punishment of captivity for the sins of generations of rebellion and ingratitude, God has chosen to show mercy *again* and help them. He has not forsaken those whom He has chosen and that is why they need not fear.

It was God who selected your specific DNA according to the good plan He has for your life (Ephesians 2:10). He reiterated in these verses that Israel is a chosen people. Someone has said that everyone who chooses to be chosen is chosen. The mystery of God's sovereignty and freewill is deep, but that simple idea bears consideration. If you choose to be chosen, then you must be chosen for everyone who asks receives. Everyone who seeks finds (Matthew 7:8).

³ For I will pour water on the thirsty land, and streams on the dry ground; I will pour my Spirit upon your offspring, and my blessing on your descendants. Isaiah 44:3 What the Jews were unable to do, the Holy Spirit would give them the power to do, to be the witnesses God intended them to be, to live for God's glory (Acts 1:8). This is the promise of the Father for which Jesus, before He ascended, told the disciples to wait in Jerusalem to receive (Acts 1:4).

Peter could have quoted this verse in his first sermon to explain to the crowd at Pentecost what was taking place, in addition to Joel 2:28-32. Isaiah is clearly predicting the time when the Spirit is poured out to empower us to be the witnesses God meant us to be and to change our hearts.

⁴ They shall spring up among the grass like willows by flowing streams. Isaiah 44:4 New life! Born again (John 3:3)! Flourishing like the tree in Psalm One by the rivers of water that brings forth fruit. As Jesus said, *¹⁴ but whoever drinks the water I give him will never thirst. Indeed, the water I give him will become in him a spring of water welling up to eternal life."* John 4:14 (NIV) This is the promise to those who meditate on God's Word and receive His Spirit, not just life, but vibrant, fruit bearing, abundant life (John 10:10)!

⁵ This one will say, 'I am the LORD's,' another will call on the name of Jacob, and another will write on his hand, 'The LORD's,' and name himself by the name of Israel." Isaiah 44:5 Well, is there anyone who will boldly declare it? "I am the Lord's!" My life belongs to Him! Does anyone here call on the name of Jacob? By that I believe God means that you recognize you were a deceiver but know that if God could change Jacob into one who prevails with God, then He can do it in you? If He could take the rebellious line of Israel and bring about the Messiah and twelve Apostles and the early church, there is hope for any and all!

Will you write on your hand, "The LORD's"? If you have to have a tattoo, how about this one right on the top of your right hand? To be named

Israel means more than just a given name but can mean faith to be a new creation in Jesus (2 Corinthians 5:17).

In this chapter we've gone from depths of the sins of generations to declaring by faith in Jesus' atonement that we prevail with God. We've gone from the depths of the past that God will forget, to become the bride of Christ. Glory to God! We've gone from realizing we are Jacob to knowing we are Israel. We've gone from the depths of hell to the heights of heaven, from being God's enemy to being the bride of Christ, all by His mercy, all by His grace, because He loves us so! Now declare His praise by your life and your words. Glory to God!

Questions
1 Why is God reminding them of the past?
2 Why does He then say forget the past?
3 Why did God make us?
4 What were the Jews weary of?
5 How was that expressed?
6 Why did God forgive our sins?
7 Why did God send Jesus?
8 Who can choose to not remember?
9 Why do we need the Holy Spirit?
10 What's on your hand?

Wise or Foolish - Isaiah 44:6-28

We live in a time when it is difficult to tell who is telling the truth. In fact, our culture questions if truth exists at all. With personal bias affecting everything from scientific data to polls to the analysis of language, where can you turn to find the truth? In our passage for today, God was laying down the challenge to all comers to stand before Him and give a reason why they should be considered at all. Then He goes about proving His absolute trustworthiness.

First, God declares who He is, something we have already seen in previous chapters but reiterated here for comparison to all who would claim the right to define reality. *6 Thus says the LORD, the King of Israel and his Redeemer, the LORD of hosts: "I am the first and I am the last; besides me there is no god.* Isaiah 44:6

God repeatedly reminds Israel who He is. YHWH - the eternal God. The King of Israel - the real King that reigns over the kings of the earth (Psalm 89:27). It is His sovereign will that prevails. He declares that He is the only God. The gods of antiquity did not claim exclusivity. Worshiping several was preferred and not seen to be disloyal to any of them. It is this claim to be the only God that challenges us to accept or reject Him.

"The first and the last" is also used multiple times and repeated in Revelation as a description of God and of Jesus (Revelation 1:8; 22:13. There is no other God than this triune God who inhabits eternity.

⁷ Who is like me? Let him proclaim it. Let him declare and set it before me, since I appointed an ancient people. Let them declare what is to come, and what will happen. Isaiah 44:7 Some people do claim to be a god, but in doing so they only show their spiritual ignorance. The God of verse six appointed a people group to declare His praise and transmit His words. Who can make that claim? Can they predict the future in detail? God is about to name the one He has chosen to return the future captives. Has anyone named a person yet to be born and told of the way they would be used by them to fulfill their purposes? No! And there never will be, for only the One who inhabits eternity already abides in the future (Isaiah 46:10).

If someone tells you they are God or a god, take them to this verse and let them answer God's challenge. Then let them know the real God will have mercy on their ignorance and forgive them if they will humble themselves and repent.

⁸ Fear not, nor be afraid; have I not told you from of old and declared it? And you are my witnesses! Is there a God besides me? There is no Rock; I know not any." Isaiah 44:8 Once again we have the command to "fear not, nor be afraid." This time the reason is that God has declared their return to the Promised Land. In the Law He promised that if their hearts turned back to Him that He would bring them back from captivity (Deuteronomy 30:1-3).

God alone can promise and with all certainty fulfill. He is the Rock, unchanging, steady, and sure. There is no other. All other so called gods are like shifting sand. You can't depend on their promises, because they don't have the power to fulfill them. What have they done compared to the God of the Bible? Where is the nation they have raised up and directed? What ocean have they parted? Can they walk on the waves of the sea? Can they command nature and it obeys (Mark 4:39) or can their words create matter (Genesis 1:3)?

Verses nine through seventeen declare the foolishness of the idol maker. In nine through eleven God explains why idols are not comparable to Him and can't predict the future. First, look at their makers. Can people make something better than themselves? While the people of Israel are God's witnesses and have God's Word, the witnesses of the idol maker don't see or know anything. When the idol fails to do anything advantageous, they will be ashamed of their ignorant efforts to make a god.

Verses twelve through seventeen describe the production process. The ironsmith and carpenter are merely men who try to make a god, but look how weak they are. Unlike God whose strength never fails and who never has a need outside Himself (Isaiah 40:28), the ironsmith gets tired and needs water to go on. The carpenter makes a god like he would make a house. His tools and materials are all created things that are used for other trivial things as well. Is there any logic in making a god out of something you use as fuel?

It is no different from the gods of this age. We tend to worship what our hands have made, the mere products of the hands of men, the latest gadget, the coolest car, the nicest home, or the entertainment box. They all fail to meet the need of the human heart. They can distract us for a time, but we will eventually realize there is no real satisfaction in them. They are not worthy of our devotion, of the commitment of our time. How we spend our time and money says a lot about what we idolize.

Recently with the crisis in several lives within our congregation I have heard one often repeated theme. "How do people get through something like this without a relationship with Jesus?" An idol can't get you through tragedy. No idol will deliver you from judgment, or from the captivity of sin, or give us an eternal hope (Acts 4:12).

[18] They know not, nor do they discern, for he has shut their eyes, so that they cannot see, and their hearts, so that they cannot understand. Isaiah 44:18 The idol maker and idolater can't see what is right before their eyes. Why would God shut their eyes and hearts? Because that is their desire (Psalm 106:15).

The following verses are so contemporary and applicable to today. *[19] No one considers, nor is there knowledge or discernment to say, "Half of it I burned in the fire; I also baked bread on its coals; I roasted meat and have eaten. And shall I make the rest of it an abomination? Shall I fall down before a block of wood?" [20] He feeds on ashes; a deluded heart has led him astray, and he cannot deliver himself or say, "Is there not a lie in my right hand?"* Isaiah 44:19-20 What happened to reason? Logic has been abandoned, and God says it is because He shut up their ability to see and understand. Of course, that is what they desired, and God gave them up to their desire. (2 Thessalonians 2:10-12) So when you point out that in accusing the Christian of being bigoted because of our moral convictions, they are condemning themselves, as they are expressing a moral conviction. You can't say calling something a sin is a sin. That is self-contradictory.

On the one hand people will convict someone of a double murder when a fetus is killed along with his or her mother, and on the other they will condone abortion right up to the time of delivery. On the one hand they will insist global warming deniers are flat-earthers, and then predict a coming mini-ice age because of sun cycles. They cannot deliver themselves or say, "Is there not a lie in my right hand?"

When we believe what we want to believe in spite of the facts, in spite of logic and solid evidence, when we manipulate the data or the polls to make the outcome conform to our predetermined conclusions, God shuts our eyes and hearts to the truth (Romans 1:25-26). No one can make a person believe against their own will. "A man convinced against his will is of the same opinion still." There are truth seekers and there are idol makers (2 Corinthians 4:3-4). There are those who pray, "Lead me in the way of truth." And there are those who say, "Leave me alone, for I have *my* truth and don't want facts to interfere."

Here's the facts. Drug abuse will destroy your body. Immorality will destroy your home and your soul. Un-forgiveness will make you bitter. What you sow you will reap. Pride guarantees a fall. Only Jesus can set you free. In Him alone is life. He is the only one to conquer death. You may not like the facts, but that doesn't make them untrue.

21 Remember these things, O Jacob, and Israel, for you are my servant; I formed you; you are my servant; O Israel, you will not be forgotten by me. Isaiah 44:21 God is reminding the nation of Judah in captivity that idolatry has failed them. They willingly accepted a lie. Now they are facing the reality of God's intervention and miraculous deliverance once again. If they are to be the servants of God and witnesses He has called them to be, they must constantly put themselves in remembrance of their Creator and His Word to them. They must continually remember that an idol is a lie that only deluded hearts will follow. God will not forget the Jews. He has a covenant with Abraham (Genesis 17:7).

We see the parallel in our lives. Idolatry failed us. The gods we looked to, whether drugs, money, fame or position let us down. We found God's miraculous deliverance. If we are to be the servants of God and witnesses He has called us to be, we must constantly put ourselves in remembrance of our Creator and His Word to us. We must continually remember that an idol is a lie that only deluded hearts will follow. God will not forget us. He has a covenant with us through the precious blood of Jesus (Luke 22:20). He empowers us with His Spirit.

What a privilege we have! Do you realize how blessed you are that Jesus would choose you, make His home in you (John 14:23), and have His life manifest through you (2 Corinthians 4:11)? That's over the top incredible. Why would we ever debate when it comes to flesh or Spirit? We are blessed beyond measure. Compromise should be utterly repulsive to us. We should be so in love with Jesus for all the love He has shown to us that we thank Him unceasingly for each time He shines through us. Every enticement of an idol should cause us to laugh at the pathetic little promises of temporal satisfaction, for the King of kings and Lord of eternity is living in us!

22 I have blotted out your transgressions like a cloud and your sins like mist; return to me, for I have redeemed you. Isaiah 44:22 Their idolatrous past was forgiven. Their sins were blotted out. A new start was waiting for them if they would return to God. He redeemed them. Like Boaz paid for the property of Ruth's dead husband and took her for wife, so God was now claiming to be Judah's kinsman redeemer (Ruth 4:9-10). That is a Jewish application of the Hebrew word "redeemed." He would take them as His own and care for them. He was taking responsibility to care for them and the land.

God has blotted out our sins and become one of us to be the kinsman redeemer of mankind and to prepare a bride for Jesus. He has taken back claim to the earth which Adam lost (Genesis 1:28) and accepted those who come to Him by faith as His bride. The price was precious, so steep that no one else could pay it. It was His own sinless life. That is how precious you are to Him. If He was so patient and merciful with Israel, won't He be the same with you. He calls to us, "Return to me, for I have redeemed you."

23 Sing, O heavens, for the LORD has done it; shout, O depths of the earth; break forth into singing, O mountains, O forest, and every tree in it! For the LORD has redeemed Jacob, and will be glorified in Israel. Isaiah 44:23 Time for that new song that was mentioned in a previous passage (42:10). Believer, this is the foreshadowing of what Jesus has done for us. Jesus has redeemed us, taken us for His bride. He has paid our sin debt, and He promises to care for us. He is determined to be glorified in creation and that includes us! You should be shouting a joyful "Hallelujah!"

24 Thus says the LORD, your Redeemer, who formed you from the womb: "I am the LORD, who made all things, who alone stretched out the heavens, who spread out the earth by myself, Isaiah 44:24 YHWH, your kinsman redeemer is the One who formed you in the womb. He designed you for His purposes. He fashioned you just like He intended. He is the creator of all things (a declaration of Jesus and YHWH being one). He stretched out the heavens in the vastness of the space He created all by Himself (Genesis 1:1). He spread out the earth by Himself. All the wonder we see in creation came from His hand. The Bible declares that the LORD did it and that Jesus did it (Hebrews 1:2). That is because they are one.

25 who frustrates the signs of liars and makes fools of diviners, who turns wise men back and makes their knowledge foolish, Isaiah 44:25 God frustrates the signs of liars. The false prophets that arise are eventually shut down by God. God orchestrates events to show the diviners to be fools. They might guess right a time or two, but God will see that the truth seeking honest heart will see the foolishness of diviners. God will show the knowledge of the wise men to be foolish. On the one hand you have the lying spiritual seers and on the other the practical wisdom of men. Both will be shown to be foolish compared to the wisdom and knowledge of God.

26 who confirms the word of his servant and fulfills the counsel of his messengers, who says of Jerusalem, 'She shall be inhabited,' and of the cities of Judah, 'They shall be built, and I will raise up their ruins'; Isaiah 44:26 But when God's prophets speak, He brings it to pass (1Samuel 3:19). At the time of captivity, it seemed impossible to expect the ruins of Judah to be inhabited. Yet, it came to pass to show the Jews and the world that God alone knows the future.

27 who says to the deep, 'Be dry; I will dry up your rivers'; Isaiah 44:27 God is again alluding to the miraculous deliverance from Egypt, but also hinting at the way Cyrus would defeat Babylon through a dry river bed. It is also a spiritual analogy of God removing the obstacles for the return.

28 who says of Cyrus, 'He is my shepherd, and he shall fulfill all my purpose'; saying of Jerusalem, 'She shall be built,' and of the temple, 'Your foundation shall be laid.'" Isaiah 44:28 God, for the first time, names the king He would use to bring it to pass before he was even born. The edict of Cyrus returned the Jews to Jerusalem and laid the foundation of the Temple.

It is so very specific. The foundation was laid in the time of Cyrus (Ezra 3:11) but the rest of the Temple was not finished until a following king's reign (Ezra 6:14-15). In doing so God proved to Judah, the world, and to us today that He knows all things. The future is in His hands. Your future is in His hands. You can trust Him.

Questions
1 What are two readings of verse 6?
2 What is God's challenge to those who claim to be divine?
3 What was the old promise?
4 What is wrong with an idol?
5 Why would God keep idolaters from seeing and understanding?
6 Why are some people so illogical?
7 Apply verse 21 to us.
8 What do we have to be grateful for?
9 What does the kinsman redeemer mean to us?
10 How does God deal with false prophets? Why?
11 How was verse 28 precisely fulfilled?

God's Amazing Ways - Isaiah 45:1-13

In our passage for today we have two verses that are frequently misused. We also have several theological concepts that are hotly debated. But the main point that God is conveying to us is often overlooked. We can have peace in whatever situations we face because we know that God is all-wise, loving, and just. The Apostle Paul's description of everything working together for good for those who love God (Romans 8:28) comes from the Old Testament concept we find in our verses for today.

¹ Thus says the LORD to his anointed, to Cyrus, whose right hand I have grasped, to subdue nations before him and to loose the belts of kings, to open doors before him that gates may not be closed: Isaiah 45:1 God introduced the name of this future leader who would liberate the Jews from Babylonian captivity in the previous verse. Cyrus is God's anointed and God takes hold of his right hand to defeat physical kings. God does the same with us. He anoints us (2 Corinthians 1:21), holds our right hand (Isaiah 41:13), and opens doors for us (Revelation 3:8).

The difference is Cyrus was a secular leader used by God to do God's sovereign will with the physical powers of this world. For believers, we come to Christ in repentance, are born again, and join Him in His work. He anoints us spiritually, takes hold of our hand to comfort, encourage, and direct us. He opens doors for us to minister to others (Ephesians 3:10). We fight a spiritual battle and advance an eternal, spiritual kingdom.

² "I will go before you and level the exalted places, I will break in pieces the doors of bronze and cut through the bars of iron, Isaiah 45:2 The Lord was going to go before Cyrus, preparing the way for his conquests. We can imagine the nations he was going to conquer having their own internal difficulties and strife that prepared the way for Cyrus armies to conquer them more easily.

We can see a spiritual parallel with our battle. Isaiah predicted that God would make the mountains low and fill the valleys for the Messiah (Isaiah 40:4). Jesus told us the gates of hell would not be able to withstand the spiritual assault of believers (Matthew 16:18). The strongholds of Satan are broken because the Lord goes before us (Isaiah 52:12).

Drug addiction, lust, pride, co-dependence, whatever the sin, we don't have the power to break free, but Jesus goes before us when we look to Him. He busts the gates of hell down and sets the prisoners free. We get to cooperate in that by sharing the love of Jesus with others and telling them what great things He has done for us. They have to realize they are enslaved before they will listen to us, but when they do, Jesus is the One who sets them free. He goes before us and prepares hearts. Watch for those hearts that are ready to hear and know they have a need.

³ I will give you the treasures of darkness and the hoards in secret places, that you may know that it is I, the LORD, the God of Israel, who call you by your name. Isaiah 45:3 For Cyrus these were physical treasures hidden in palaces and secret storehouses. Archeologists still come upon some forgotten stash now and then. God did this for Cyrus so that he would know God was the true God. Historically, Cyrus was a king who honored all gods of all the different lands. We don't know what happened when he was shown this prophecy, but it had to have a profound impact on him. It was huge leap of faith in that day to accept that there was only one God, Creator (2 Chronicles 32:15).

Believer, there is something for you here too. He calls us by name too, just as He called the Jews by name (Isaiah 43:1). Eye has not seen, nor ear heard, the things that God has prepared for those who love Him (1 Corinthians 2:9). There are secret treasures for us beyond our ability to imagine. As you go through life serving the Lord, He is laying up those treasures for you as your reward for serving Him (Matthew 6:20). Jesus tells us those treasures can't rust or be stolen.

⁴ For the sake of my servant Jacob, and Israel my chosen, I call you by your name, I name you, though you do not know me. Isaiah 45:4 He called Cyrus by name for the sake of Israel. Here is a spiritual truth. God will use the physical realm to advance the kingdom of God. He can cause the secular to bless the spiritual. Sometimes it comes through favors of rulers, and other times it comes through persecution. When the early church delayed going into the world to proclaim the gospel, Jewish persecution caused them to obey (Acts 8:1). Whether we need the blessing of government or its persecution depends on our situation. In different parts of the world today both are taking place. Persecution often brings the most fruit.

⁵ I am the LORD, and there is no other, besides me there is no God; I equip you, though you do not know me, Isaiah 45:5 This was the witness to

Cyrus. There is only one God! He equipped Cyrus to conquer the world though Cyrus didn't know Him. One God is our claim today as well. The world is still trying to push the philosophy that all roads lead to God. God loved Cyrus enough to demonstrate to Him that was not true. Jesus was the ultimate demonstration to the world the truth of God's claim in this verse. He declared, "No man comes to the Father except through me" (John 14:6).

The great difference between false religions and Christianity is works versus grace. Christians don't place faith in man's ability to pay for their own sin, to do more good than evil, or to do enough good to earn God's favor. We don't even believe in learning the right doctrines to attain grace, as important as that is. Our hope is solely placed in what Jesus did for us. It is trust in God to save us as demonstrated in both the Old and New Testaments.

⁶ that people may know, from the rising of the sun and from the west, that there is none besides me; I am the LORD, and there is no other. Isaiah 45:6 God wanted Cyrus to know so that the world would know. He was the ruler of a world empire. His testimony could reach the world if he was willing to testify to it. This prophecy is a testimony to the world today. When people read about the prophecy fulfilled 100 years later, it should convince them of the truth of one God Creator. That is why so many want to believe Isaiah 40 - 66 was written after the return of the Jews, in spite of the contrary evidence. YHWH is God and there is no other!

This repeated theme of prophecy belonging to God alone in Isaiah would just be a flat out lie to the first readers who would have known better if this was written after the fact. Someone could say they discovered an ancient book, when they forged it. But think about why they would have wanted to do it in that day. The theme of Isaiah is salvation through a coming Messiah and the glory of the Messianic age. Would an author try to bring a spiritual message that declared idols were a lie and that the Messiah would not speak deceit while his whole book was a deceptive lie? Sure, it is possible, but does that make any sense?

The same argument is true for the Gospel of John. Because John's message is as powerful as Isaiah's and clearly says Jesus is the way to God, critics say John made up the stories. But it is John's Gospel that declares Satan to be the father of lies (John 8:44). Would the author who penned those words then make up stories that were a lie? Again, it is possible, but is it sensible? Both these books have been an inspiration through the ages, encouraging life transformation and hope. The issue some take with these books is the declaration of only one God and one way to Him.

⁷ I form light and create darkness, I make well-being and create calamity, I am the LORD, who does all these things. Isaiah 45:7 The first recorded words of God had to do with the forming of light (Genesis 1:3). The Hebrew word for forming is the word used earlier in Isaiah for the potter shaping his clay. Physicists could have fun with these differing Hebrew verbs "forming," "creating," and "making."

Before the light there were the heavens and the earth, but no light (Genesis 1:1). That absence of light is darkness. To create space before photons is to make darkness possible. It is not a created thing, but the absence of a thing; that thing being photons. (John 3:19-21).

The second part of the verse has two possible translations, one of which has caused some confusion. The word for calamity can also be translated "evil." The Hebrew word is used for both moral evil and calamity. KJV translates it evil. Bible critics will ask why God created evil, and draw from it that all evil comes from God. The proper translation is calamity as we can see demonstrated in the many Biblical accounts. James 1:13-14 tell us God can't be tempted by evil and tempts no one. Temptation to evil comes from the misguided desire of the human heart.

Let us dwell on the issue of calamity for a moment. Death, disastrous storms, and plagues, are forms of calamity. Is death from God? Yes! He brought death as a punishment for sin (Genesis 3:17). Otherwise, we would live forever in this fallen world with no fear of the Day of Judgment (Genesis 3:22). That was part of the problem of longevity in the pre-flood world. God may also be sparing those who die young from something that would have been even more detrimental to their eternal state (Isaiah 57:1).

Job endured the worst kind of calamity, but his children were in heaven and he ended up with a deeper relationship with God. If calamity turns us to God, it is a blessing, not a curse. The same calamity that brings judgment to one can bring salvation to another. Calamity for Babylon meant the deliverance for the Jews. My son got a better position where he works, but was concerned for his friend who applied for the same job. To which of them was it a blessing and to which one was it calamity? Only time will tell. They both may be in the process of being blessed. When viewing what we perceive to be calamity we should keep in mind God's attributes and His desire for our eternal good.

[8] *"Shower, O heavens, from above, and let the clouds rain down righteousness; let the earth open, that salvation and righteousness may bear fruit; let the earth cause them both to sprout; I the LORD have created it.* Isaiah 45:8 The commentator Oswalt wrote of this verse: "Just as the sky that God has created cannot help but pour forth rain, and the earth that God has created cannot help but bring forth plants, so God the Creator can only pour out on his people right dealing and mighty deliverance in all his relations with them" (Oswalt, Isaiah 40-66, p 206).

Righteousness is right dealing in every aspect. That is not always what we desire. Of course God's righteousness includes His grace and mercy. The more we conform to His attributes, the more we act in that perfect balance of justice and mercy, as well as equity and grace. That brings forth the fruit of righteous living just as the rain brings fruit on the earth. The fruit of righteousness is called a peaceable fruit that comes from being disciplined in Hebrews 12:11 and James 3:18. This kind of fruit comes through Jesus Christ according to Philippians 1:11.

[9] *"Woe to him who strives with him who formed him, a pot among earthen pots! Does the clay say to him who forms it, 'What are you making?'*

or 'Your work has no handles'? [10] *Woe to him who says to a father, 'What are you begetting?' or to a woman, 'With what are you in labor?'"* Isaiah 45:9-10 Things are not always as they appear. I have talked with the caretakers of the disabled and heard about the amazing spiritual lessons they learn from them. Their simple relationship with God is a lesson for us all. And haven't you ever wondered about the nearly perpetual smile on some of those with Down's Syndrome?

I've told you my story of how God stopped my questions when my grandson was born with a cleft lip and palate. The Spirit of God directed me to Exodus 4:11 where I read, "Who made man's mouth?" Certainly we should study and try to understand all that we can. But we must also recognize that God wants us to trust Him in things we can't understand. That was the message to Job. What do we know of the deeper things of God? We must trust in His attributes and accept by faith that all things work together for good to those who love Him.

[11] *Thus says the LORD, the Holy One of Israel, and the one who formed him: "Ask me of things to come; will you command me concerning my children and the work of my hands?* Isaiah 45:11 This is another verse in which the KJV translation has caused some confusion. The context is clearly about trusting God's work in the world even when we don't understand. The Creator has a better plan than we can imagine, even when we don't understand. Perhaps it is better to say especially when we don't understand. The second half of this verse in KJV is, "Concerning the work of my hands, command thou me!" For years I went around commanding God to do what I thought best. The verse is saying just the opposite. God is in heaven. We are created beings of earth. If we could command God, the results would be chaos. God is saying that we are invited to ask Him about the future, our direction, His will for us, and the good plans He has for us. But we shouldn't be so arrogant to think we know what God should do for us or the world.

[12] *I made the earth and created man on it; it was my hands that stretched out the heavens, and I commanded all their host.* Isaiah 45:12 The Creator is the one who gives the commands the trillions of stars. Now that we know so much more about the universe, this statement should have an even greater impact. We know of a hundred billion galaxies each averaging a hundred billion stars, and God directs and orders each and every one. That is probably how many factors there are in any given situation we experience. That should humble us, like our size in the universe should humble us. How arrogant is it to tell God what to do?

[13] *I have stirred him up in righteousness, and I will make all his ways level; he shall build my city and set my exiles free, not for price or reward," says the LORD of hosts.* Isaiah 45:13 What's this all about? It's about God deciding when and how to bring the Jews back to the Promised Land and bring the conditions that were ripe for the Messiah. If He chose to use a heathen king to do so, then that was as it should be. He could cause that king to send the Jews back to Jerusalem of His own desire. Not only was he not paid to do it, but he financed it!

Today we can look at the latest miraculous return of the Jews to Jerusalem and its rebuilding after an even longer exile which came about because of their rejection of the Messiah. Just as the predicted return and rebuilding we are reading about was preparation for the first coming, so this second return is preparing for the Second Coming. There are eternal things that far outweigh the trials of this life. Are you trusting your Creator? Isn't that the most reasonable thing to do?

Questions
1 How are we like Cyrus?
2 Why are our treasures better?
3 What was the message to Cyrus?
4 Why does the world struggle with it?
5 Why does the world try to reject the authenticity Isaiah and John?
6 Why is their argument unreasonable?
7 How is verse 7 mistranslated?
8 Why would God create calamity?
9 When do we need to just trust?
10 How is verse 11 misinterpreted?
11 What is God teaching us in this passage?

The Only God - Isaiah 45:14-25

Today's passage tells us who God is, mankind's great problem, God's invitation to save us, and the final conclusion of all things. It is the Gospel of Jesus. Paul quotes part of this passage in his letter to the Philippians. While presidential contenders tell us their solutions for the nation, God is telling us the ultimate solution for the world.

14 Thus says the LORD: "The wealth of Egypt and the merchandise of Cush, and the Sabeans, men of stature, shall come over to you and be yours; they shall follow you; they shall come over in chains and bow down to you. They will plead with you, saying: 'Surely God is in you, and there is no other, no god besides him.'" Isaiah 45:14 As God crushed Egypt before, so He would again crush those who held the people of Judah back from returning to the Promised Land (Isaiah 43:3). The enemies of the Jews would recognize their gods had failed them and that Israel's God is the only God.

This may also predict a future time in which North Africa is conquered by Israel (Isaiah 19:23-24). Even now there are conversions from underground missions and direct revelations from God through dreams and visions. The more sharia law is applied, the more the people realize it is not the answer. This is what is happening in Iran today.

They will say, "God is in you!" That can be read as God in the nation, but also as God making His home in each individual. This is what Jesus predicted would take place after His ascension. *23 Jesus answered him,*

"If anyone loves me, he will keep my word, and my Father will love him, and we will come to him and make our home with him. John 14:23 Perhaps Isaiah was seeing into the millennium after the Jewish people have accepted Jesus as their Messiah.

[15] Truly, you are a God who hides himself, O God of Israel, the Savior. Isaiah 45:15 The concept of hiding Himself is one of not answering prayer or not helping in a time of need. God is always present, but in the Jewish way of thinking, He can turn His face away and let us deal with the consequences of our sins. It is the opposite of the Aaronic blessing that includes God turning His face toward us (Numbers 6:24-26). To hide Himself is to withdraw His protection and favor so as to discipline us. God's face is toward us in revelation, protection, and direction, or He conceals Himself as we face the consequences of our sin which may be catastrophic.

The God of Israel is the God of the Jews, but what of the Jewish people who reject Him as their God and turn to idols? God will not forget His covenant with Abraham. He will keep His promises. The day will come when all Israel will be saved (Romans 11:26). Before that day comes, not all Jews will choose to place their faith in God. It is evident today in Israel and here in the USA. There are secular Jews like there are secular Christians. They follow traditions but those traditions have little to do with how they think or act the rest of the time. The Apostle Paul declared, *[28] For no one is a Jew who is merely one outwardly, nor is circumcision outward and physical. [29] But a Jew is one inwardly, and circumcision is a matter of the heart, by the Spirit, not by the letter. His praise is not from man but from God.* Romans 2:28-29

Verse 15 calls the God of Israel "the Savior." The New Testament refers to Jesus as the Savior. Those cults that call Jesus the Savior but think He is separate from God will have trouble with this verse. Titus refers to both God and Jesus as the Savior (Titus 1:2-4). In Luke 1:46-47 Mary says God is her Savior and a few verses later (2:11) an angel declares the Savior is born! Numerous other passages in the New Testament declare that Jesus is the Savior (1John 4:14; 2Peter 1:11; Philippians 3:20; Ephesians 5:23; Acts 5:31; John 4:42).

[16] All of them are put to shame and confounded; the makers of idols go in confusion together. Isaiah 45:16 This is true in every age. Before we think of idols as little carved or metal images, let me share the way Kyle Idleman describes idols. "One of our problems in identifying the gods is that their identities not only lack the usual trappings of religion, but they are things that often aren't even wrong. Is God against pleasure? Sex? Money? Power?These things are not immoral, but amoral; that is, they are morally neutral until they are not. You could be serving something that is in itself very commendable. It could be family or career. It could be a worthy cause. You could even be feeding the hungry and healing the sick. All of those things are good things.

The problem is that in the instant something takes the place of God, the moment it becomes an end in itself, rather than something to lay at God's throne, it becomes an idol (Matthew 7:22-23). When someone or something replaces the Lord God in the position of glory in our lives, then whoever or whatever that is has by definition become our god." (from God's at War p. 21-22)

Verse 16 tells us that those "do it yourself" gods will always lead to shame and confound their worshipers. That is true during a life span, but also an eternal condition for those who will not turn away from their idolatry to the one true God. When we speak out against sin, it isn't because we want to condemn the sinner, but save them from the consequences of sin. We want to share the freedom we have found in Christ.

[17] But Israel is saved by the LORD with everlasting salvation; you shall not be put to shame or confounded to all eternity. Isaiah 45:17 This is the Israel the Apostle Paul described. They are those whose hearts have been transformed from Jacob the deceiver to Israel, one who prevails with God. They have put to death their old nature with their Savior's death and risen with Him to resurrected life (Romans 6:4)! Our salvation is not just a victory in our present circumstance, but everlasting salvation. This promise declares that we will not be put to shame or confounded to all eternity.

The Apostle Paul quotes the same thought from Isaiah 28:16 LXX. *[11] For the Scripture says, "Everyone who believes in him will not be put to shame."* Romans 10:11 Imagine standing before the glorious Lord of eternity and telling Him how you spent the life He gave you chasing things that no longer existed. How shameful would it be to explain why you ignored His many interventions in your life? And once you realized how many times He pleaded with you to come to Him, and yet you rejected His loving pleas, how confounded would you be? The only way to avoid that is by faith to accept His grace, to repent and surrender your life to Him.

[18] For thus says the LORD, who created the heavens (he is God!), who formed the earth and made it (he established it; he did not create it empty, he formed it to be inhabited!): "I am the LORD, and there is no other. Isaiah 45:18 God is declaring Himself alone to be the Creator and only god. Genesis 1:1 is quite profound. Heavens is not the stars and planets. Those were created later (Genesis 1:16). Heavens are space and dimensions. It is difficult for the mind to conceive, but it is quite logical. God as a spirit does not need space or dimensions. For physical things to exist there was the necessity to create space, dimensions, and matter. That is what the first verse of the Bible declares. In modern terminology we would say that the first acts of the eternal God's creation were space, dimensions, and matter.

The earth was uniquely formed to be inhabited.[3] Scientists marvel at the precise tuning of fundamental physical constants that fall into a very narrow range to make life possible. If one of the many factors were slightly off, life would not exist. But God declares He formed it to be inhabited. Now we know a bit more of what that entailed, and the details put us in awe.

There is certainly more to be discovered. There is no other god. God who created all things can tell us with certainty that no other god exists.

¹⁹ I did not speak in secret, in a land of darkness; I did not say to the offspring of Jacob, 'Seek me in vain.' I the LORD speak the truth; I declare what is right. Isaiah 45:19 While God is said to hide Himself, He certainly does not hide the revelation of who He is or make it difficult for us to know what is true. He set Israel at the crossroads of the world so that all nations could hear the truth. He has had the Bible translated into most of the world's languages. There are missionaries in every nation on earth. The Gospel has gone into all the world because God loves the world (John 3:16).

God is very specific about being the only God, speaking the truth, and declaring what is right. We frequently hear the cultures mantra of every path that is sincere leading to God. How can that be when they each claim to be the exclusive way? How can they all be right when they contradict one another? How can they all be truth when they describe attributes of god that don't match with the god of another religion? If they describe a different way to heaven and claim it is the only way, how can they both be true? It is illogical to believe all roads lead to God. If other roads can lead to God, why did God not answer Jesus' prayer, "If there is some other way, let this cup pass from me?" (Matthew 26:39).

²⁰ "Assemble yourselves and come; draw near together, you survivors of the nations! They have no knowledge who carry about their wooden idols, and keep on praying to a god that cannot save. ²¹ Declare and present your case; let them take counsel together! Who told this long ago? Who declared it of old? Was it not I, the LORD? And there is no other god besides me, a righteous God and a Savior; there is none besides me. Isaiah 45:20-21 God is declaring idolaters to be clueless. When their gods do not save them, why do they keep trusting them? Some that have come out of the New Age have shared with me that they turned to Jesus when their philosophies failed them. They were willing to be honest with the failure of their faith. Who predicts the future but the one true God? Those who seek Him will find Him (Matthew 7:7; Proverbs 8:17).

In verse 21 God describes Himself as the righteous God and Savior. He is saying that what He does is just. He does not let evil go unpunished. He will not excuse the guilty, nor will He neglect to reward those who deserve reward (Jeremiah 17:10). He is right in all that He does. Only when we are in Him, when we accept the righteousness of Jesus can we be righteous. The only human to ever live a righteous life offers to take our sin and give us His righteousness. There is no other righteous God and Savior but Him. So when the New Testament declares Jesus is the Savior, we see the oneness of the Father and Son (John 10:30).

²² "Turn to me and be saved, all the ends of the earth! For I am God, and there is no other. Isaiah 45:22 This is the Gospel message. To turn means to repent. We change the direction of our life from selfishness to God centered living. We forsake our idols and put our hope in our righteous Creator and Savior. This is not for the Jews or any particular race. It is a call to the ends of the earth (Acts 10:34-35). Everyone on this planet, regardless of race or nationality or time in which they live, is invited to turn to God and be saved through Jesus. There is no other way (Acts 4:12). God is able to make Himself known to them (Acts 17:26-27).

Has God sent this message out in vain because there are those who haven't heard the details? That kind of thinking underestimates His love and His power. If the invitation is to all, where there is not yet a missionary, the Spirit of God will do the work (Acts 10:34-35). We are hearing of this more and more as world communication has advanced. Dreams, visions, radio, the internet, and the Spirit of God moving on individual hearts, all are God at work drawing those who will turn and be saved.

23 By myself I have sworn; from my mouth has gone out in righteousness a word that shall not return: 'To me every knee shall bow, every tongue shall swear allegiance.' Isaiah 45:23 The power of God's Word creates and transforms. It is the Word delivered in those various means mentioned that saves or condemns every individual that ever lived (John 12:48). There is no such thing as an innocent native who died without being confronted by the Holy Spirit. There are only human beings made in the image of God who accept or reject God's invitation to them. There are idolaters and there are believers. There are none in-between.

While not every soul will be saved, every knee will bow (Romans 14:11-12). Once again we have a passage directly speaking of the Creator YHWH that is applied to Jesus in the New Testament (Philippians 2:8-11).

24 "Only in the LORD, it shall be said of me, are righteousness and strength; to him shall come and be ashamed all who were incensed against him. Isaiah 45:24 All righteousness and strength are in the LORD. There is no other. Our righteousness is like filthy rags (Isaiah 64:6). Every soul that ranted and raved against Jesus and against His demand to repent and turn, and we see many doing so in blatant manner today, will come and be ashamed. Brothers and sisters we are mocked and scorned today because we proclaim that all are sinners in need of God's grace (Romans 3:23). That is ok. I'd rather be scorned here than to be ashamed in eternity. If you take the heat now, you won't face it then.

We see ISIS and secular society incensed against Christians. We just love our neighbors and try to live quiet lives (1Timothy 2:2), but we will not compromise our message. We are hated because Christ is in us. We are hated by those who hate Jesus. They hate Jesus because they hate His Father (John 15:18-23). That is not my thought. It is what Jesus said would happen.

25 In the LORD all the offspring of Israel shall be justified and shall glory." Isaiah 45:25 In YHWH, whom we have already seen is one with the Son, shall the spiritual offspring of Israel be justified. Spiritual Israel are those who prevail with God through Jesus' atoning death. Justified is to be just as if we'd never sinned. We shall glory. We praise God. We glorify God for His saving work for us. We turn from idols to the true and living God. We forsake our life so that we can truly find life (Matthew 10:39). In Him is life and His life is the light of men (John 1:4). Turn to Him and be

232

saved, all the ends of the earth, for He is God and there is no other! We are ambassadors of Christ pleading with the world to experience the joy and peace we have found in Christ. For doing so, we are hated and despised, imprisoned and killed just as Jesus predicted (John 16:2). And our response to persecution should always be love.

Questions
1 What do the converts of verse 14 say?
2 What does "hide Himself" mean?
3 Who is considered "Israel"?
4 Who is the Savior?
5 What happens to idolaters?
6 What is the promise to us?
7 Discuss verse 18.
8 How has God made Himself known?
9 Who is invited in verse 22? How does that happen?
10 What verse is quoted in the New Testament? What is the significance?

Carried - Isaiah 46

In our chapter today we are reminded that idolatry has failed us as well as everyone else who places their faith in created things rather than the Creator. Idols cannot carry you through a difficulty or help you in times of calamity, but God can. He will not only see us through our old age but will provide the righteousness we need to enter eternity.

[1] Bel bows down; Nebo stoops; their idols are on beasts and livestock; these things you carry are borne as burdens on weary beasts. Isaiah 46:1 Bel was the city god of Babylon. When Hammurabi made Babylon the capital of Babylonia, Bel increased in importance until he took the place of other gods in Babylonian mythology and became the main god or lord. That is the meaning of Bel. His name is Marduk, or sometimes Merodach. The Babylonians believed he controlled the destiny of nations.

Nebo, also called Nabu, was another city god, the god of vegetation. In an earlier time, Nebo was considered to be of greater importance that Marduk. Later on, he was thought to be Bel's son.

Every new year these two idols of gold and silver were carried in procession through the streets of Babylon, as if to proclaim the New Year would be good because the god that directs nations and the god of vegetation were with them. But Isaiah sees the obvious, what idolaters cannot see because God has shut their eyes (Isaiah 44:18). He sees the fact that they have to be carried by beasts that are about to collapse under the weight of their load. He sees there is no life in these idols to carry the Babylonians or anyone else. R. Ortlund Jr. commented on this passage, "If a god has to be carried, how can it carry you? If a god can't help itself, how can it help you?

If a god needs your strength, how can it strengthen you?" (R. Ortlund Jr., Preaching the Word, Isaiah, p. 308)

I had to explain who these gods were thought to be because no one remembers them. While they have faded into obscurity only to be learned of in historical works, the cross of Jesus is setting people free in every part of the world (Matthew 24:14). The church may be on decline and under attack in the USA because of the public's increasing love of idols, but in most of the world His truth is marching on.

² They stoop; they bow down together; they cannot save the burden, but themselves go into captivity. Isaiah 46:2 If the animal can't save the idol, how can the idol save anyone? The idol was thought to hold the destiny of nations, but those who carry it are going into captivity. What does that tell you about futility of trusting in it (Jeremiah 48:7)?

Let me remind you of something we looked at last week. Silver and gold are not immoral. It is what man does with them that can be immoral. How appropriate in this day when we are bombarded with "What's in your safe?" If you think it can save you, you've forgotten that God the Father and God the Son are called "the Savior" (Isaiah 44:18).

Why is Isaiah lingering over this issue of idolatry? It was the downfall of Israel and Judah, and now it is about to be the downfall of Babylon. God wants the Jews, and everyone else, to once and for all get the point. The achievements of man aren't meant to be crushed, but idolatry makes it inevitable. When our hopes are placed in what cannot save or endure, when our bondage to any created thing causes us to place our hope in what cannot save, we have destined ourselves to failure and ultimate destruction. We become captive to things we idolize by thinking just a little more will fulfil or satisfy (Ephesians 4:19). Just a little more and we will be secure. It's always a little more, but the end is destruction. If we insist on clinging to a false hope, is it any surprise that we will end up in captivity to that which we hope in (Romans 6:17)?

³ "Listen to me, O house of Jacob, all the remnant of the house of Israel, who have been borne by me from before your birth, carried from the womb; Isaiah 46:3 The idol can't carry you, it has to be carried. By contrast, God has carried you and me from before our birth, even in our mother's womb. Yes, life begins at conception. The idolatry of personal freedom to do whatever we want without the constraint of moral boundaries has resulted in a culture of death. Our nation is hurtling towards its own destruction in the name of tolerance and diversity. But that tolerance and diversity only applies to those who hold to the progressive agenda. They won't tolerate or allow the diversity of those who hold a different view, especially one with moral judgments of right and wrong.

Blessed are you when you are persecuted for righteousness sake, for great is your reward in heaven (Matthew 5:10-12). Jesus said that if the world hates you, remember it hated Him first (John 15:18). Peter and John rejoiced in the privilege of suffering shame for the name of Jesus. If you are willing to speak the truth that life begins at conception, then you don't have

234

to stand in front of an abortion clinic to be persecuted. All you have to do is hold that conviction dear to you and be truthful when asked. The same goes for the sacred nature of marriage.

As our culture is pushed further down the road of liberalism, the now familiar words of Chicago's Cardinal Francis George come to mind. *"I expect to die in bed, my successor will die in prison and his successor will die a martyr in the public square. His successor will pick up the shards of a ruined society and slowly help rebuild civilization, as the church has done so often in human history."* But few know that he went on to say something even more closely relating to our passage today about God sustaining us. *"...only one person has overcome and rescued history: Jesus Christ, Son of God and Son of the Virgin Mary, savior of the world and head of his body, the church. Those who gather at his cross and by his empty tomb, no matter their nationality, are on the right side of history. Those who lie about him and persecute or harass his followers in any age might imagine they are bringing something new to history, but they inevitably end up ringing the changes on the old human story of sin and oppression. There is nothing "progressive" about sin, even when it is promoted as "enlightened."* (Themelios, Vol 39, Issue 3, as edited by D.A.Carson p. 427)

Because the legalists love to nit pic, I have to clarify that I'm not endorsing Catholic theology, I'm simply saying this Cardinal got it right in these remarks. It is a correct historical analysis. You can try to distort history if you want, but you can't change it. Don't be afraid to speak the truth in love. There is such thing as right and wrong. Redefining things does not change the substance. Every human deserves dignity and respect but that does not change the fact that we are all sinners (Romans 3:23).

4 even to your old age I am he, and to gray hairs I will carry you. I have made, and I will bear; I will carry and will save. Isaiah 46:4 What a beautiful verse to assure us as we age! Not only has God carried us from the womb, but He will carry us to our old age. Though we age and change, He is the I am, the eternal unchanging God (Malachi 3:6). His love will never fail (1 Corinthians 13:8a). The *Footsteps* poem tells us he carries us through the difficult times. But God is telling us through Isaiah that He carries us all the way through this life.

My hairs are turning gray and I can say He is still carrying me through each and every day. He made you. If you will put your life in His hands, He will bear you, carry you, and save you. No thing or person can do that. Only God is big enough. Are you being carried? We carry the heavy burden of idols or we are carried by God. We bow down under the crushing load of an idol or we rest in the arms of Jesus.

In our times, many are fearful of old age. We are living longer and many people worry that they will end up in a home and being cared for by people they don't know. I watched my mother go through that and God carried her right to the end. In my role as a pastor I've witnessed God's faithfulness to a number of elderly right up to their passing. He will carry everyone who trusts Him (Psalm 71:18). It may not be easy, but you'll be in His arms, and that changes everything (Isaiah 40:11).

   5 "To whom will you liken me and make me equal, and compare me, that we may be alike? 6 Those who lavish gold from the purse, and weigh out silver in the scales, hire a goldsmith, and he makes it into a god; then they fall down and worship! 7 They lift it to their shoulders, they carry it, they set it in its place, and it stands there; it cannot move from its place. If one cries to it, it does not answer or save him from his trouble. Isaiah 46:5-7 Okay! It's god competition time. My God has all knowledge, all power, and is present everywhere. He made everything. He loves us enough to die for us (Romans 5:8). He is just, but He is also merciful. His lovingkindness endures forever (Psalm 42:8). He carries me through life.

   The idolaters turn. What? Your god can't talk, makes no promises he can fulfill, and can't satisfy your heart's longings (Psalm 65:4)? Does he have any power? Does he know the future? Can he fill your heart with peace no matter what circumstances you face? No? Then I have a much greater God for you to consider!

   8 "Remember this and stand firm, recall it to mind, you transgressors, 9 remember the former things of old; for I am God, and there is no other; I am God, and there is none like me, 10 declaring the end from the beginning and from ancient times things not yet done, saying, 'My counsel shall stand, and I will accomplish all my purpose,' Isaiah 46:8-10 To whom is God speaking? I believe this is to the Jews in captivity. They could recall their transgressions into idolatry and consider the historical results of the failure of idols to help them. Then they could compare how God had done unprecedented things like bringing them out of slavery in Egypt, parting the sea, and on and on. No god of any nation had done anything like the God of Israel. That is because He is the only real God. Even the imaginary ones don't compare.

   Nations can look back on the prosperity and goodness they experienced when their trust was in the Lord. They can compare that with the failure of this world's philosophies to bring anything good. While we experience the decline of our own culture many are unwilling to associate the decline with our rejection of God and embracing idolatry.

   God again reminded them that He is telling them of the future so that when it comes to pass they will have faith to trust Him. Reading these detailed prophecies and knowing of their fulfillment should have the same effect on us. God does as He pleases. What He decides is what happens. To oppose Him is insanity. He is the glorious, eternal God of all.

   And what is His purpose that will stand? It is that you and I be transformed into the image of Christ that we might become His bride (Romans 8:29). It is that He receive glory and praise forever for the great things He has done for us. Do you believe He can do it? If I didn't, I would despair. Knowing He will change everything, it makes the present trials fade in insignificance. It puts a smile on my face when situations would tell me to fear. He's carrying us. What more could we ask?

236

God follows His declaration of knowing all things with another prediction; this time it's of where Cyrus will originate. *[11] calling a bird of prey from the east, the man of my counsel from a far country. I have spoken, and I will bring it to pass; I have purposed, and I will do it.* Isaiah 46:11 God is anointing Cyrus for the task of conquering Babylon and setting the Jews free. He will come from the east. God was going to bring it to pass a hundred years later, which, we'll see in the next verses is a short time to God. To those reading it in captivity, it would come to pass in their lifetime.

God sets up kings and takes them down (Daniel 2:21). Why He lets some despots reign we may never understand in this life, but I'm sure when we get there we will see why. He has His own purposes. Sometimes the storm causes us to seek shelter in the Lord. Persecution draws us together. The church thrives under persecution. We put down our petty divisions and come into unity in Christ and love for one another. Satan has not learned that lesson that persecution purifies and strengthens us. Perhaps he just can't stop himself from his lust for destruction (John 10:10).

[12] "Listen to me, you stubborn of heart, you who are far from righteousness: [13] I bring near my righteousness; it is not far off, and my salvation will not delay; I will put salvation in Zion, for Israel my glory." Isaiah 46:12-13 He told us He'd carry us from the womb to old age, but now He calls us transgressors and stubborn of heart. How can that be? Well, it is because He loves us stubborn-hearted transgressors. He understands our frames are but dust (Psalm 103:14). He knows we must deal with the flesh. Our best help in this battle is to listen to Him.

And when we listen what does He tell us? For those in captivity it was that salvation was on its way. Righteousness was near. God would deliver them from the Babylonians, send them back to Jerusalem, and finance the re-building of the Temple and the walls.

But once again these prophecies have a secondary meaning. God was going to place His righteousness on the restored streets of Jerusalem in the form of Jesus Christ (Isaiah 53:11; 28:16; 1Peter 2:6). He was drawing near to us. Immanuel, God with us. Salvation in the flesh would walk the streets of Zion for Israel, His glory.

We've seen before that Israel is the people of faith (Romans 2:28-29). They are the bride of Christ. They are His glory, for they shine with His attributes of love and mercy, justice and truth. And when the work in us is complete, we will be like Him for we will see Him as He is. That is to be glorious (1John 3:2).

In the middle of this tough message to Israel in captivity, comes this message of hope that is so great and gracious that no one could possibly have comprehended the full greatness it. But now we know. We can stoop under the burden as we carry this world's idols, or we can experience the Lord of all creation carrying us through this life. What a gracious invitation! Are you bent under the load of some idol or resting in His everlasting arms?

Questions

1 What are the Bel and Nebo of today?
2 Why does Isaiah mock the idols being carried?
3 Why does God keep addressing idolatry?
4 When did God begin to carry you?
5 Review Cardinal George quotes.
6 Why is there no need to fear aging?
7 Why is our God incomparable?
8 What is God's purpose?
9 How does persecution help the church?
10 What did God put in Zion?

Prepare! - Isaiah 47

In our chapter today, God is predicting the demise of those who were going to level Jerusalem and abuse the people of Judah. It tells us something of God's ways of dealing with mankind. First, God expects those people who are called by His name to faithfully represent Him (1John 2:6). Secondly, if they don't, He warns them again and again of their idolatry and unwillingness to listen to Him. Thirdly, He sends calamity to get their attention when nothing else will cause them to turn. Finally, He holds accountable those He uses to judge His people, if the people He employs to discipline His children are brutal and use excessive force. He will punish them for their sins as well. God is ever the equal arbitrator of justice, regardless of the nationality of those on the receiving end of that justice. Reaping what we sow is a universal truism (Proverbs 22:8).

¹ Come down and sit in the dust, O virgin daughter of Babylon; sit on the ground without a throne, O daughter of the Chaldeans! For you shall no more be called tender and delicate. Isaiah 47:1 (ESV) Babylon is compared to a young, tender and delicate virgin. The idea conveys the picture of a pampered, self-indulgent life that the Babylonians were enjoying at the expense of the nations they had subjugated. The hanging gardens of Babylon were one of the wonders of the world paid for by oppression. The Lord is saying that instead of a throne to rule the nations and a luxurious lifestyle, the Babylonians would sit in the dust. They were going to be the subjugated. Their time of prosperity was about to end.

Instead of using foreigners for the hard labor that produced their luxury, it would be the Babylonians who had to do the menial tasks. *² Take the millstones and grind flour, put off your veil, strip off your robe, uncover your legs, pass through the rivers.* Isaiah 47:2 The book of Revelation uses Babylon as a foreshadow of the coming judgment on the world. This same sense of luxury is mentioned in John's prophecy. *² And he called out with a mighty voice, "Fallen, fallen is Babylon the great! She has become a dwelling place for demons, a haunt for every unclean spirit, a haunt for every unclean bird, a haunt for every unclean and detestable beast. ³ For all*

nations have drunk the wine of the passion of her sexual immorality, and the kings of the earth have committed immorality with her, and the merchants of the earth have grown rich from the power of her luxurious living."
Revelation 18:2-3

The Babylon of Revelation does not represent Rome or the USA or any one city or country. It is the world in rebellion toward God, persecuting people of faith. The USA is increasingly becoming part of Babylon the Great. You may be aware that the USA is the most prolific exporter of pornography (James 1:21). We also export our entertainment that increasingly portrays Christians as the evil characters and immorality as a pleasure with no negative consequences. Hollywood is indoctrinating the world and getting rich doing it. (Isaiah 33:15).

Jonathan Cahn has written several books, *The Harbinger*, and the *Shemitah* about the soon coming judgment of God upon the United States. I don't know if his date predictions are from God, but I do know his overall conclusions are Biblical. God will eventually judge this nation like the judgment upon Judah. Our nation was also founded upon godly principles. We have also turned to idols, the idols of sexual promiscuity, of luxury, the worship of wealth, the idol of leisure, just to name a few. Many churches openly promote things that God declares to be evil (Isaiah 48:1). Our legal system has been abandoning the rule of law and tyrannically punishing people because of their religious or political convictions, while those of their own persuasion can do the same things and be applauded.

I am apolitical. I am persuaded that while we still have the opportunity, if we still do, we should vote on the basis of godliness, against lawlessness, against condoning immorality. But if the direction of the nation does not turn, God will get our attention (Psalm 9:17). His hand of protection has already lifted to some extent. We are receiving so many warnings from God, warnings in weather, fires, financial, terrorism, judicial decisions; but the nation as a whole is ignoring the warnings. Our response will determine if we will experience what Babylon went through when this prophecy came to pass (Jeremiah 3:12).

A healthcare worker recently told me how difficult it was under Obamacare. They have to refer people to organizations known to profit from abortions. Now we know they also profit from selling the body parts of those unborn babies. This has nothing to do with politics. It's about how low our culture has sunk from God's standards of decency (Proverbs 28:13; Psalm 14:2-3).

[3] Your nakedness shall be uncovered, and your disgrace shall be seen. I will take vengeance, and I will spare no one. Isaiah 47:3 God is just. He repays. It's a warning to turn and be saved. But if we will not turn, we will face His wrath (Isaiah 45:22). All Babylonians suffered the defeat and loss of their wealth. We saw an enormous loss of wealth in '08 when the market tanked due to corruption in politics and business. The naked truth about lying politicians and corrupt investment companies was laid bare. But

what have we done in response? A few laws were passed, but that did not keep us from going right back to our old practices.

The crash of '08 was nothing like what will happen when we face our trillions of dollars of debt and 127 trillion in federal unfunded liabilities (more than twice the nation's total estimated assets). No one will be spared because the economy affects us all (Psalm 37:21; Proverbs 22:7). I'm not saying this to scare you but to prepare you. If Jesus is your highest priority, if you have the calm assurance that He will carry you through, you can lose every physical thing and be at peace.

⁴ Our Redeemer—the LORD of hosts is his name— is the Holy One of Israel. Isaiah 47:4 Isaiah keeps repeating this declaration. God was going to buy back His people out of captivity. He is Lord of the armies of heaven. He is the Holy One described throughout Israel's history. The fate of nations is not in the hands of Bel, or the USA, or the Supreme Court, or for that matter, it's not in any human hands. Our fate is in the hands of Almighty God. If persecution will draw us to Him, then we will be persecuted. But He will also deal with those who persecute us.

⁶ I was angry with my people; I profaned my heritage; I gave them into your hand; you showed them no mercy; on the aged you made your yoke exceedingly heavy. Isaiah 47:6 God gave His reason for the coming judgment on Babylon. While God intended to judge His people through them, they abused their power. They went too far. They were merciless. There have been some real abuses of power against people of faith, but you can expect it to get much worse as the polarization deepens. The gray areas will disappear as we are forced to take sides.

There are those who love darkness and those who are in the light (Isaiah 5:20). The darkness is on the increase in our culture. It is becoming increasingly intolerant under the guise of tolerance. It doesn't matter who is elected, unless the people turn to Christ and we quit executing the unborn and lauding perversion, unless our education system returns to education and abandons indoctrination and being the arbitrator of "correct thinking," we are going to end up with the state religion of secularism (Habakkuk 1:4). Then we will see what merciless looks like. But in time we will also see God's judgment upon it.

⁷ You said, "I shall be mistress forever," so that you did not lay these things to heart or remember their end. Isaiah 47:7 That was Babylon, secure behind their huge impenetrable walls. But nothing can stop the justice of God. Is the attitude of America any different? Go back and listen to the speeches after 9/11. The leaders were unrepentant and arrogant. We did not lay these things to heart or remember their end. Our leaders declared again and again in various ways and through both parties, "We will be a mistress forever!" (Proverbs 21:24)

⁸ Now therefore hear this, you lover of pleasures, who sit securely, who say in your heart, "I am, and there is no one besides me; I shall not sit as a widow or know the loss of children": Isaiah 47:8 This is an arrogant disregard for God and the rest of the world. It's an underserved superiority that will not listen to those with a different persuasion, especially on the subject of what is moral. Anything that would interrupt that in which they find pleasure is labeled and slandered (Psalm 3:1-2).

But there is an eventual price to pay. *⁹ These two things shall come to you in a moment, in one day; the loss of children and widowhood shall come upon you in full measure, in spite of your many sorceries and the great power of your enchantments.* Isaiah 47:9 Fake spirituality that justifies sin will not spare people from God's judgments. False gods will fail them. Eastern mysticism will not calm or protect them (Jeremiah 2:11).

¹⁰ You felt secure in your wickedness, you said, "No one sees me"; your wisdom and your knowledge led you astray, and you said in your heart, "I am, and there is no one besides me." Isaiah 47:10 Compromise the conscience in one area and it becomes easier to do so in another. Recently a web site that promoted adulterous relationships was hacked and the names of the clients who thought "no one sees me" was made public. It was reported that only two zip codes in the entire U.S. were not included in the list of inquiries. The Scriptures warn us that our sin will be exposed eventually (Numbers 32:23). We think no one sees, but God sees. He will make it known because He loves you and doesn't want to see that sin destroy you (Deuteronomy 10:13). How many people have we seen in the news who thought they were so smart they could fool everyone? They really do have the attitude now repeated again in this passage, "It's all about me."

¹¹ But evil shall come upon you, which you will not know how to charm away; disaster shall fall upon you, for which you will not be able to atone; and ruin shall come upon you suddenly, of which you know nothing. ¹² Stand fast in your enchantments and your many sorceries, with which you have labored from your youth; perhaps you may be able to succeed; perhaps you may inspire terror. Isaiah 47:11-12 God is warning them of what will come to pass. They have sown evil and they will reap it (Hosea 8:7). They won't see it coming. If they really believe what they proclaim, then stick with it. If you think the chants will get you through, then chant on. People need to experience the failure of what they put their hope in to realize its ineffectiveness to deliver (Proverbs 6:15).

¹³ You are wearied with your many counsels; let them stand forth and save you, those who divide the heavens, who gaze at the stars, who at the new moons make known what shall come upon you. Isaiah 47:13 We have so many fortune tellers, mystics, and prognosticators (Isaiah 8:19). Some people can't get enough of them. Babylon had the fortune tellers and astrologers too. God mocks them, for they have only worn out their adherents with all their mumbo jumbo. When God brings His judgments, will you turn to them then? They are the luxury of an affluent society because they demand exorbitant fees.

¹⁴ Behold, they are like stubble; the fire consumes them; they cannot deliver themselves from the power of the flame. No coal for warming oneself is this, no fire to sit before! ¹⁵ Such to you are those with whom you have labored, who have done business with you from your youth; they wander about, each in his own direction; there is no one to save you. Isaiah 47:14-15 Here is God's estimation of their substance. They are like stubble. They can't save themselves from the fire. And the fire that consumes them doesn't produce enough heat to help anyone else. They are of no substance (Job 21:18). In the end these people who were looked to for guidance and trusted to tell the secrets of heaven will be just as desperate and lost as everyone else. Why? Because they are just as powerless as what they worship (Psalm 115:8).

In view of this cycle of nations that we have seen through Isaiah and history, the USA stands at a precipice. We went through revivals. We experienced prosperity. We have turned from God and are calling light darkness and darkness light (John 3:19). With the Supreme Court's arrogant decision to redefine marriage, we will face persecution. The dissenting judges warned of that. We've already seen it even before the decision.

In the state of Washington, Barronelle is a florist who had a customer named Rob. She considered him a friend, did many arrangements for him, but when he asked her to be the florist for his wedding with a man, she had to gently and lovingly explain her Christian convictions about the sanctity of marriage. He hugged her and told her he understood. He had no problem finding another florist. His partner however was irate and posted the situation on Facebook. The new attorney general of the state took action. It was the place of the couple or the human rights commission to file a lawsuit, but the attorney general had an axe to grind and in a liberal state it advanced his political stature. Barronelle received lots of hate mail and calls. But then she started receiving support for her stand from believers around the world. The case is still in the legal system.

A Christian photographer in New Mexico, Elaine Huguenin, received an inquiry from a lesbian couple. She politely replied that they only did traditional marriages and gave her referrals to other photographers who would help. Two months later, after the lesbian couple had easily found another photographer, they asked again if she was refusing to shoot a same-gender wedding. She again politely thanked them for asking but said that was correct. Next she got a letter from the human rights commission of New Mexico. She lost in lower and state court and was ordered to pay $7000 in legal fees. The US Supreme Court refused to hear the case. Elaine lost her livelihood for holding to her religious convictions.

I could give you case after case of Christians who politely refused to participate in something that violated their conscience and religious convictions, something that those who tout tolerance are intolerant of (Psalm 120:7). Some have lost their livelihood, while others have had to endure huge legal expenses and time-consuming court cases. Are we losing the very reason for which our nation was founded?

Let me be very clear, because parts of this sermon will be taken out of context and used against us. We love everyone (Luke 6:27). Everyone is made in the image of God. Christians stand for equal rights of all. But we also stand for the freedom of religion that is now overruled by the so called

242

human rights. It is rights for groups with special preferences. I can't ask some people to celebrate my religious convictions, but they will try to force me to celebrate theirs. I believe they are free to live as they please, though I believe there are natural and spiritual consequences, just as there are for abortions and every other sin (Romans 2:6-9).

I am not advocating policing bedrooms as some absurdly claim to be the Christian agenda. I am simply saying that we live in a land where we were once free to hold our religious convictions as long as they did no harm to others. Having to find a different florist or caterer is not harmful. If the business was already booked, you would have to do so anyway. Live how you want to live according to what you think is right. Let Christians do the same.

Does tolerance only work in one direction? Some would say it is to compensate for past discrimination. How are these Christians that are deprived of their livelihood compensated for the persecution of their religious beliefs? Christians are the most persecuted people on the planet, martyred at a rate of over 150,000 a year. There are hateful people who claim to be Christians. There are hateful gays who don't represent their community as well. True Christians are commanded to love their neighbor as themselves (Matthew 22:39), and real love will speak the truth (Ephesians 4:15).

Be prepared to answer when asked of the hope that lies in you (1Peter 3:15). We need to know how to respond when confronted, because we will be confronted. Answer with love, honesty, gentleness, and kindness (2 Timothy 2:25). Then, by the grace of God, be prepared to face the wrath of an intolerant society.

Questions
1 Review the pattern of God's dealing with nations.
2 Describe the before and after of Babylon in verses 1 through 3.
3 What does it have in common with Babylon in Revelation 18?
4 What does America have in common with Babylon of Revelation 18?
5 What could save us from this course?
6 What happens to those who think no one sees?
7 To what does God liken the mystics?
8 Review the cases of persecution.
9 What do Christians believe about our fellow human beings?
10 How should we answer those who confront us about our faith?

Our Refiner - Isaiah 48

How does God get our attention when we refuse to listen? How can He turn our selfish hearts from fixating on His gifts to adoration of Him, the giver of every good gift (James 1:17)? It is His furnace of affliction that refines us. There is an easier way, a way which He would much rather see us take. It is to follow His leading and take heed to His commandments. One way or the other, He will see His name is glorified.

¹ Hear this, O house of Jacob, who are called by the name of Israel, and who came from the waters of Judah, who swear by the name of the LORD and confess the God of Israel, but not in truth or right. ² For they call themselves after the holy city, and stay themselves on the God of Israel; the LORD of hosts is his name. Isaiah 48:1-2 At the first read through, I thought these people who call themselves by the name but not in truth or right could be compared to those who call themselves Christians today but have no idea what it means to follow Jesus. I hear people say they are a Christian and declare that Jesus would be on a certain side of an issue, when in fact the gospels clearly say the opposite. Some people act in a manner that is inconsistent with the Gospel and yet teach it. This is certainly a source of confusion about Christianity in our culture. We can't expect those who are not born-again to catch the Spirit behind the letter of the Word (1 Corinthians 2:14) or discern who is truly born-again.

After reading through this chapter again, I found that it is not the unredeemed being addressed. God is addressing His redeemed children. They confess His name and stay themselves on the God of Israel. But they do not do so in truth or right. They are born-again, but they have not allowed Jesus to be the Lord of their lives.

This passage applies to the Christians who attend church, read their Bibles, and trust the Lord, but are caught up with worldliness. The faith they profess isn't seen in the lives they live. There is a disconnect between what they believe in their hearts and the priorities of their daily lives. Unbelievers point to those lives as a reason to reject the Bible and Christianity (2 Samuel 12:14a).

It happens so easily. It is the pattern of spiritual lives and denominations. Someone described it this way: Man, mission, movement, method, monument. It starts with someone inspired and anointed by God. The mission is clear and focused. Others join in as they see the zeal and fruit that is resulting from it, and it becomes a movement. But then it develops into a method that is taught to others with some success at first. Then it becomes a routine void of the Spirit. Eventually it is merely a monument to what God did in history. In an individual life, it begins with that first encounter with Christ. There is a hunger for the Word and a desire to follow wherever He leads. The person discovers their gifts and calling. There is fruit that results from it. But eventually it becomes a routine done in the power of the flesh (Revelation 2:4). Without renewal it becomes just ritually going through the motions. Testimonies that are shared are only ones from long ago. This passage is going to tell us how to keep from following that pattern.

³ "The former things I declared of old; they went out from my mouth, and I announced them; then suddenly I did them, and they came to pass. Isaiah 48:3 God announced from the founding of the nation that if they

244

worshiped other gods they would go into captivity (Deuteronomy 29:63-64). He did that with the ten northern tribes and was about to do it to Judah. The next verse tells us why.

⁴ Because I know that you are obstinate, and your neck is an iron sinew and your forehead brass, Isaiah 48:4 Prophet after prophet warned them of their impending fate (Jeremiah 7:25-26). Ungodly kings would lead them to a defeated condition, and godly kings would lead them to prosperity. They didn't make the connection but continued to turn away to idols. Our own lives can be just as obtuse to the fruit of sin in our lives.

This pattern reminds me of obstinate way our country views and teaches its own history. The iron sinew neck is a picture of people who will not turn when God is calling them. Their bronze forehead is their refusal to consider the discipline of God. They continue on their way to their own destruction (Ezekiel 18:31). Even believers can be opinionated, self-assured, "know-it-alls." We limit God to our preconceived ideas of how He will work and shun the wild, unpredictable God of the universe.

⁵ I declared them to you from of old, before they came to pass I announced them to you, lest you should say, 'My idol did them, my carved image and my metal image commanded them.' ⁶ "You have heard; now see all this; and will you not declare it? From this time forth I announce to you new things, hidden things that you have not known. ⁷ They are created now, not long ago; before today you have never heard of them, lest you should say, 'Behold, I knew them.' Isaiah 48:5-7 God gives us prophecies so that we won't give the credit to something or someone who has nothing to do with the events that took place. We can be so obstinate that we would give the credit to anything or anyone other than God. Our culture even mocks the idea of God's sovereignty over nature and the course of nations. That is because we don't want to bow our knees and submit our lives. Idols don't demand our all. God deserves our all.

⁸ You have never heard, you have never known, from of old your ear has not been opened. For I knew that you would surely deal treacherously, and that from before birth you were called a rebel. Isaiah 48:8 This is the nature of man, rebellious. It was said of Jesus that His ear was opened (Psalm 40:6). In other words, Jesus' spiritual ear was tuned to the Father and always listening for His instruction and direction. But even the redeemed can refuse to allow their ears to be opened (Matthew 11:15). If we hear, we are then obligated to obey (John 15:22). We deal treacherously by accepting the teachings of the Word but refusing to open our ears to the Spirit's application. The rebellious nature of Adam was never put to death with Jesus on the cross (Romans 6:6).

⁹ "For my name's sake I defer my anger, for the sake of my praise I restrain it for you, that I may not cut you off. Isaiah 48:9 Our refusal to listen does not stop the grace of God. He's angry because He has every right to expect us to listen (Deuteronomy 1:43). After giving us life and so many proofs, after giving His one and only Son for us, it is only right that we open our ears to His instruction. But He defers His anger. His mercy and grace are reasons to praise Him. They are attributes of His name. We deserve death (Romans 6:23), but He restrains Himself from immediate judgment and does what He must do to get us to listen and change our priorities.

10 Behold, I have refined you, but not as silver; I have tried you in the furnace of affliction. Isaiah 48:10 Here is His tool, the furnace of affliction. In other cases, God compares His refinement to that of precious metals (1 Peter 1:7; Ezekiel 22:22). Here, He says it is different. This furnace is not a smelting furnace but the crucible of affliction. It is in the trials that we draw near the Lord and give up that which holds us back from a deeper relationship with God.

11 For my own sake, for my own sake, I do it, for how should my name be profaned? My glory I will not give to another. Isaiah 48:11 It is true that God does things for our good, but ultimately it is for His own sake. That is because He is righteous. His character is holy. What He does is right and good. To bring glory to His own name is to demonstrate mercy and grace. If His promises to Israel did not come to pass, the false gods of other nations would be glorified, and God's name profaned (Numbers 14:13-16). If He did not demonstrate justice and grace as well, His name would be profaned. He acts so that that will not be the case.

12 "Listen to me, O Jacob, and Israel, whom I called! I am he; I am the first, and I am the last. Isaiah 48:12 This is the third declaration of God being the first and the last (Isaiah 41:4; 44:6). Listen up called out children of God! Open your ears. Hear this in the depths of your soul. He is the beginning of all things. He is the end of all things. He will do all that He pleases and His purposes will stand (Isaiah 46:10)

13 My hand laid the foundation of the earth, and my right hand spread out the heavens; when I call to them, they stand forth together. Isaiah 48:13 He is the Creator of the space and all that fills it. He made this planet to be inhabited (Isaiah 45:18). He commands every asteroid, planet, moon, and star the number of which is so great we cannot fathom it (Psalm 8:3-4).

14 "Assemble, all of you, and listen! Who among them has declared these things? The LORD loves him; he shall perform his purpose on Babylon, and his arm shall be against the Chaldeans. 15 I, even I, have spoken and called him; I have brought him, and he will prosper in his way. Isaiah 48:14-15 God especially wanted them to hear His prophecy about Cyrus, the ruler who would set God's people free from Babylon. It would encourage their faith when it came to pass. They would know it was God that did it and not circumstances or idols. They needed this assurance to make a final turn from idolatry and to prepare the way for the Messiah (Isaiah 40:3). *16 Draw near to me, hear this: from the beginning I have not spoken in secret, from the time it came to be I have been there." And now the Lord GOD has sent me, and his Spirit.* Isaiah 48:16 Once again God commands their ears to be open and hear. God inhabits eternity and knows all things. He does not hide His ways or instruction (Isaiah 45:19). It is open to all. It can be tested (John 7:17). It is provable.

The "he" of the previous verse speaks, for He is the Word of God. Jesus does not hide His ways or instruction. It is open to all. He was in the beginning with God (John 1:2). The Son is saying the Father has sent Him and His Spirit. "Has sent" is a singular verb in Hebrew because they are one. There is unity in the diversity of the trinity. "Me" in the verse is the sent One, the Servant of the Lord.

17 Thus says the LORD, your Redeemer, the Holy One of Israel: "I am the LORD your God, who teaches you to profit, who leads you in the way you should go. Isaiah 48:17 Here is the alternative to the furnace of affliction. It was too late to save them from the coming Babylonian captivity, but it was not too late for after the captivity or for us. Our Redeemer teaches us how to be profitable. That is to be useful. It is to ascend in our spiritual life and move beyond that which is vain to that which is eternal (John 6:27). If we will give Him our hearts and our ears, He will lead us in the way we should go.

So often people wonder about what the right choice between the paths before them. They want to do God's will and want the decision to be one that honors Him. If that is truly their heart, He will teach them what is profitable and direct them in the way they should go (Psalm 32:8).

18 Oh that you had paid attention to my commandments! Then your peace would have been like a river, and your righteousness like the waves of the sea; 19 your offspring would have been like the sand, and your descendants like its grains; their name would never be cut off or destroyed from before me." Isaiah 48:18-19 This is God's lament for all who refuse to take heed to His Word. If we would just see the Word as the light to our path and follow it without struggling to convince ourselves our own inclinations are better, what peace we would have! Peace is knowing in your heart that you are being obedient to God in everything He has revealed to you (Psalm 119:165). Knowing Jesus as Lord and Savior and being obedient and surrendered in everything that is revealed to you means your righteousness is like the waves of the sea, wave after wave after wave. That is consistent, dependable, and righteous.

20 Go out from Babylon, flee from Chaldea, declare this with a shout of joy, proclaim it, send it out to the end of the earth; say, "The LORD has redeemed his servant Jacob!" Isaiah 48:20 When God would set them free from captivity, they would know their relationship with God had been restored. They would know He had mercy upon them again and had not forsaken them. They were to go out with shouts of joy, proclaiming to the ends of the earth the wonder of our gracious Redeemer. And that is what we are to do as well when God sets us free from the captivity of sin (John 8:36).

21 They did not thirst when he led them through the deserts; he made water flow for them from the rock; he split the rock and the water gushed out. Isaiah 48:21 Once again God reminds them of the provision of water during the wilderness wandering on the way to the Promised Land. That is because it is a picture of the coming outpouring of the Holy Spirit (John 7:38-39). It promised provision as they journeyed from Babylon to

Jerusalem. It promises our spiritual provision as we journey to New Jerusalem (John 14:26). The overflowing grace of God toward us obstinate, iron sinew necked rebels, keeps inviting us to listen so that we can hear and understand what is real. When we listen and let the Spirit open our eyes as well, we realize Babylon is enslavement. Even if we lose everything by coming out of her, we gain much more in Christ. That is what we shout about. [22] *"There is no peace," says the LORD, "for the wicked."* Isaiah 48:22 Here is the great contrast. We open our ears and obey from hearts of gratitude and have peace like a river. The Hebrew verb "to hear" is used ten times in our passage today to emphasize our great need and the source of our peace.

The wicked will never know the peace we experience. You may have seen the bumper sticker, No Jesus, No Peace – Know Jesus, Know Peace. It succinctly sums up the last part of our passage today. Peace is unattainable to those who refuse to listen to Jesus, because it is only found in a relationship with Him. To hear God, we just need to hear the incarnation of His Word. This contrast between the peace of the righteous and the lack of peace for the wicked emphasizes the need for those who are redeemed to always keep their relationship with Jesus alive by listening to the Spirit, reading the Word, and submitting to Him (John 4:23-24).

Do you know peace in your heart regardless of life's circumstances? Listen in a special place alone with God in prayer and as you go throughout your day. Listen to His Spirit as you read the Word. You can know peace like a river and your righteousness can be as consistent and powerful as the steady waves of the sea. Are you willing to put Him first in everything?

Questions
1 Who is God addressing in verses 1&2?
2 How does the passion and joy die?
3 Why does God give us prophecies?
4 What does "opened ear" mean?
5 Why does God defer His anger?
6 How does God refine us?
7 What does God want us to hear?
8 What does the Redeemer offer us?
9 What/Who can give us peace and righteousness?
10 What should we do when we are freed from sin/captivity?

The Second Servant Song - Isaiah 49:1-13

Our subject today is the second Suffering Servant Song. We call it a song because it is written in prose about God's servant who is rejected by the nation. The first such song we studied in Isaiah 42, and there are several more later in Isaiah (Isaiah 42:1-17; 50:4-10; 52:13-53:11). Together they paint a picture of the Messiah that was to come. This marks a transition in

Isaiah from the previous section focused on promises of raising up Cyrus to send the Jews back to their homeland to this section which focusses on the coming Messiah and His ministry to the world.

¹ Listen to me, O coastlands, and give attention, you peoples from afar. The LORD called me from the womb, from the body of my mother he named my name. Isaiah 49:1 The message God is speaking through Isaiah is for the world of mankind. That is the meaning of "coastlands" and "peoples from afar." Unlike many Bible prophecies to specific nations, God declared that He is addressing the entire world (Isaiah 45:22). This universal call makes this message of the utmost importance for all mankind throughout time.

The message begins in the voice of the Servant of the Lord declaring He is called from the womb. Since this voice is in the first person, this Servant was alive at the time of Isaiah and was at that moment speaking through Isaiah. That is one reason that John the Beloved could say that "In the beginning was the Word, and the Word was with God and the Word was God." John 1:1-2 Jesus was speaking 700 years before His birth in Bethlehem.

While it is true that others were called and named before their birth, like Jeremiah (Jeremiah 1:5) and King Cyrus, it was uniquely applicable to Jesus. The angel Gabriel told Mary this child would be conceived through the Holy Spirit. He declared the child's name would be Jesus and that His kingdom would never end (Luke 1:26-33).

² He made my mouth like a sharp sword; in the shadow of his hand he hid me; he made me a polished arrow; in his quiver he hid me away. Isaiah 49:2 In contrast to Cyrus, whose coming Isaiah had predicted, the Servant would use spiritual weapons of His words and His life. John wrote in the Revelation that out of Jesus' mouth came a sharp two edged sword (Revelation 1:16). The author of Hebrews tells us this sword is the all-powerful Word of God (Hebrews 4:12). Those words can create and they can destroy in judgment.

He was hidden in the shadow of the Almighty's hand. I think of all the attempts on Jesus' life, from Herod the Great to the Pharisees. All were inspired by the destroyer to stop Jesus from fulfilling His mission. Imagine how desperately Satan tried to kill Jesus when He was an infant (Matthew 2:16). But God hid Him in the shadow of His hand. Jesus could say, "My time has not yet come" (John 7:6).

Like a polished arrow Jesus was hidden away. I don't think Satan really knew that arrow was strung and the bow of the cross was bent and aimed straight at him. It gives the word "crossbow" a new meaning. Satan could not perceive that in Jesus giving His life as a sacrifice that arrow would destroy the works of darkness and set innumerable captives of Satan free. One polished arrow could accomplish so much because it was hidden in the hand of Almighty God.

Jesus is still conquering souls today as His Word wins our hearts. But that sharp sword of His mouth will also slay His enemies at Armageddon (Revelation 19:15,21; compare with John 12:48).

³ And he said to me, "You are my servant, Israel, in whom I will be glorified." Isaiah 49:3 The use of the word "servant" alerts us to this as one of the Suffering Servant Songs. Yet, it is also why many Jews claim that this is about the Jewish people. Remember, the name "Israel" means "one who prevails with God." Jacob was simply a foreshadowing of Jesus. What Israel failed to become was fulfilled in Jesus, the ultimate Israel.

Isaiah is writing to the Jews in captivity and telling them of their return, but also telling them of their ultimate freedom through the Messiah (Isaiah 42:7). We read in Nehemiah and Ezra that, even upon the return, they gave their Gentile neighbors reason to reproach their faith because they did not help one another (Nehemiah 5:8-10). They charged interest on food loaned in time of famine, married the pagans around them (something forbidden in the Law), and even bought children of their poor neighbors as slaves.

Verse five tells us that part of the Servant's calling is to gather Israel back to the LORD. That tells us the Servant Israel can't be the people of Israel. That would be like saying Pastor Paul is called to bring Paul Wallace back to God. The individual referred to as Israel is called to bring wayward Israel back to God.

Isaiah is not the only prophet who applies this term "servant" to the covenant people. Jeremiah and Ezekiel do as well (Jeremiah 30:10; Jeremiah 46:27-28; Ezekiel 28:25). Those same prophets apply "servant" to David, the Messiah of promise (Jeremiah 33:21-22, 26; Ezekiel 34:23-24; Ezekiel 37:24-25). It is also used for David's descendant, Zerubbabel, in Haggai 2:23. Of special interest is its connection with the messianic title "Branch" (Zechariah 3:8). (See The Theological Wordbook of the Old Testament)

F. B. Meyer wrote the following in his commentary on Isaiah. "But, it may be asked, how can words, so evidently addressed to Israel, be appropriated, with equal truth, to Jesus Christ? It is sufficient here to say that He was the epitome and personification of all that was noblest and divinest in Judaism. When, in spite of all that they had suffered in their exile, they for a second time failed to realize or fulfil their great mission to the world; when under the reign of Pharisee and Scribe they settled down into a nation of legalists, casuists, and hairsplitting ritualists—He assumed the responsibilities which they had evaded, and fulfilled them by the gospel He spoke and the Church He formed. In the mission of Jesus, the heart of Judaism unfolded itself. What He was and did, the whole nation ought to have been and done. As the white flower on the stalk, He revealed the essential nature of the root." (Christ in Isaiah by Meyer)

It is possible that this very verse (verse 3) was on the mind of Jesus when Judas Iscariot left the table of the Last Supper to betray Him. Jesus said, *³¹ᵇ "Now is the Son of Man glorified, and God is glorified in him."* John 13:31b

The last phrase of verse 3, "in whom I will be glorified" can be translated "in whom I will display my beauty." Has the beauty or glory of the LORD ever been more clearly displayed than in Jesus of Nazareth? He was the friend of sinners, healer of all who looked to Him, allowed Himself to be sacrificed for our sins, and then rose to justify us (Romans 4:25) and assure us of our own resurrection (1 Corinthians 15:20). No individual or nation comes anywhere close to Jesus in revealing the beauty of the Lord.

4 But I said, "I have labored in vain; I have spent my strength for nothing and vanity; yet surely my right is with the LORD, and my recompense with my God." Isaiah 49:4 Jesus must have sensed profound discouragement at the hardness of the human heart. (John 6:66-67; Mark 14:50). Consider what Jesus did in humbling Himself to enter His own creation, speaking the very words of God, and still to have had such a poor initial response! Yet, Jesus knew faithfulness is rewarded. (Hebrews 11:6) He knew God would justly reward His obedient life (Psalm 22:22-31).

Many of the prophets faced the same hardness of hearts and were also murdered. We must follow Jesus with the same attitude and mindset, that God will do what is right and help us through whatever the world throws at us. Our ultimate reward is not in earthly acceptance, but in God's acceptance. Our right is with our LORD and our recompense is with our God (Matthew 5:10-12).

5 And now the LORD says, he who formed me from the womb to be his servant, to bring Jacob back to him; and that Israel might be gathered to him— for I am honored in the eyes of the LORD, and my God has become my strength— Isaiah 49:5 This is an intro to the One speaking in verse 6. It introduces a change of speakers from the Servant to the LORD Himself. The LORD is the One who formed the Servant in the womb. While the expression is said of others, Jesus is the one and only Son of God. He was formed to bring Jacob back and gather Israel to God. That surely includes both physical and spiritual Israel.

The use of Jacob may specifically be referring to the Jewish people as we'll see in the next verse. While only the remnant came back from legalistic religion to a relationship with God through the sacrifice of Jesus, the full fruit of what Jesus did for the Jewish people is starting to become evident in our lifetime (Romans 11:5). We are seeing Messianic congregations on the rise even in the land of Israel.

Jesus is the honored of God, as the Apostle Paul wrote in Philippians 2:9. Because of Jesus' willingness to obey to the point of dying on a cross, God honored Him with a name that is above every name. God was His strength in life, death, and resurrection (John 5:19). In doing so He demonstrated what we must do as well

6 he says: "It is too light a thing that you should be my servant to raise up the tribes of Jacob and to bring back the preserved of Israel; I will make you as a light for the nations, that my salvation may reach to the end of the earth." Isaiah 49:6 This is the message from the LORD. It is from the One who called the Servant to raise up the tribes of Jacob and to bring the world to Himself. The Servant's calling is not only to bring the Jewish people (Jacob) back to God, but He was to become the Light of the world (John 9:5). That is just what Jesus declared Himself to be.

Why did the LORD form Him and make Him the Light of the world? It was to bring God's salvation to the end of the earth. When John wrote that God so loved the world that He sent His only Son (John 3:16), he was following the theme of this verse. God is not willing that any should perish, Jew or Gentile (2 Peter 3:9). All lives matter.

The Apostle Paul would follow this pattern of going to the Jews first and try to raise up the tribes of Jacob through the proclamation of the Servant's message. When the Jews rejected the Word, he would move on to the Gentiles. In Acts 13 Paul was preaching in a synagogue of Pisidia. When those Jews rejected the preaching of the Good News, he quoted verse 6 of Isaiah 49 as the reason he should leave the Jews and go to the Gentiles (Acts 13:47).

This is the wonderful fact about God's message to the world. It is for everyone. We are all sinners in need of the gift of salvation freely offered to us because Jesus paid our sin debt. That is why the Gospel message is reaching the ends of the earth. That is God's will. Jesus predicted that when His message did go to the ends of the earth that the end would come (Matthew 24:14).

7 Thus says the LORD, the Redeemer of Israel and his Holy One, to one deeply despised, abhorred by the nation, the servant of rulers: "Kings shall see and arise; princes, and they shall prostrate themselves; because of the LORD, who is faithful, the Holy One of Israel, who has chosen you." Isaiah 49:7 The path to this global victory goes through being despised and abhorred by His own nation (John 1:11; Philippians 2:8-11). This is another indication of the Servant's suffering and that the Servant is an individual and not the nation.

The LORD tells Him "kings will stand," which is the way of receiving another dignitary. And "princes shall prostrate themselves," which is an act of worship and submission (Isaiah 52:15). Why? It is all because this is God's plan. This is not human idealism or effort, but the Almighty's choice of Jesus to redeem us. He is King of kings and Lord of lords (Isaiah 9:7)! And He has chosen His redeemed sons and daughters to be His own and to bring Him glory.

8 Thus says the LORD: "In a time of favor I have answered you; in a day of salvation I have helped you; I will keep you and give you as a covenant to the people, to establish the land, to apportion the desolate heritages, Isaiah 49:8 The Servant's faith is rewarded. God heard Him and raised Him from the dead. He becomes the New Covenant for the people (Hebrews 9:15). The inheritances restored are the godliness and spiritual abundance of the patriarchs and prophets. In the Second Coming it may well include the land as well, though some of it is already inhabited by Messianic Jews.

252

The first part of this verse was cited in 2 Corinthians 6:2 by the Apostle Paul. Instead of applying it to Jesus, He applied it to our salvation. His point was that God reached out to us with His favor and helped us to be saved. But of course, that is because God answered Jesus with favor first making it possible for us to receive God's favor. Therefore, Paul tells us, now is the favorable time and the day of salvation for God heard Jesus' cry.

9 saying to the prisoners, 'Come out,' to those who are in darkness, 'Appear.' They shall feed along the ways; on all bare heights shall be their pasture; 10 they shall not hunger or thirst, neither scorching wind nor sun shall strike them, for he who has pity on them will lead them, and by springs of water will guide them. Isaiah 49:9-10 Because of the redemption the Servant has obtained for us, we prisoners of sin can hear Him call to us to come out of our prisons and go from darkness to light.

We are fed with the meat of the Word and drink from springs of living water. Our spiritual hunger and thirst is blessed with fullness (Revelation 7:16). We are sheltered from the scorching wind of prince of the power of the air (Ephesians 2:2). The LORD is our guide and leads us as the pillar of cloud led the Children of Israel. Our destination is the Promised Land that is even more glorious than Israel of old.

11 And I will make all my mountains a road, and my highways shall be raised up. Isaiah 49:11 God is the One who prepares the way for His children who trust in Him. As the highway was to be prepared for the coming of the LORD, so He makes a highway for us (Isaiah 40:3-4). He works in our hearts and convicts us of our need for Him. He overcomes our doubts and fears and meets us in our weakness with His strength. Without His help and the work of His Spirit, none of us would ever make it into the kingdom. His sacrifice has made the way before us possible, and His Spirit has given us the strength for the journey.

12 Behold, these shall come from afar, and behold, these from the north and from the west, and these from the land of Syene." Isaiah 49:12 From all over the earth Jews have returned to their homeland. But I believe this is ultimately speaking of the nations of the world spoken of in the first verses that will come to the Messiah. It is a wonderful thing to travel and meet believers in other lands and see their love for Jesus. It is one of the things I enjoy about trips to Israel, meeting the pilgrims from all over the planet who want to see the places they read about in Scripture.

13 Sing for joy, O heavens, and exult, O earth; break forth, O mountains, into singing! For the LORD has comforted his people and will have compassion on his afflicted. Isaiah 49:13 The triumph of Jesus over death (the curse on sin) gives us reason to burst into song. It also gives creation hope that the restoration of creation (the lifting of the curse on the earth) will soon follow (Isaiah 44:23; Romans 8:19-21).

The Jews could relate to this upon their return to the Promised Land, but it is realized in the ends of the earth at the Second Coming of Jesus. That will be such an amazing event that the heavens will sing! The earth will exult. That means to be so excited that you spin around. That is pretty giddy. The fullness of it will be realized when we see our Savior face to face (1 Corinthians 13:12). Ecstatic won't begin to describe it. This is what the Servant has accomplished for all who receive His suffering on their behalf.

Questions
1 Who is to hear this message?
2 Why couldn't Jesus be killed?
3 Who is the Servant?
4 Why shouldn't we think the servant is someone other than the Jewish people?
5 Where do we see the glory or beauty of the LORD?
6 What kept Jesus from discouragement?
7 What was the LORD'S message?
8 Which verses did Paul quote from this chapter? How did He apply them?
9 What does He say to us? (verse 9,10)
10 What does verse 13 attempt to describe?

Promises Fulfilled - Isaiah 49:14-26

Last week we looked at the first portion of this chapter and saw the prophetic look forward to the coming of the Messiah. The Servant was to bring the servant Israel back to the LORD (49:5). Today we see the ultimate fulfillment of the Messiah's work. While it gave the captives in Babylon hope for the future, what they would experience was a far short of the predictions of this chapter. God's ultimate plan is so much greater than our ideas of temporary, immediate satisfaction.

14 But Zion said, "The LORD has forsaken me; my Lord has forgotten me." Isaiah 49:14 Zion was first mentioned in Scripture when David captured this fortress from the Jebusites. The original meaning of Zion is uncertain, but it is equated with the city of David, Jerusalem (2 Samuel 5:7).

Zion is both a place and a people group. We do the same thing today when we call the people in a town's people by the town's name. For example, "I wish Sedona would receive the Gospel." In the psalms, Zion is exhorted to praise the Lord (Psalm 147:12). In Revelation the saints descend as a city called New Jerusalem (Revelation 21:2) New Jerusalem is both the place and the people of Zion in this prophecy.

Zion consists of both fulfilled Jews who have come to know Jesus as the Messiah and Gentiles who have been grafted into the Israel of faith (Romans 11:17-18; Ephesians 2:13-16). It is this Zion that asks if the LORD has forgotten them.

As we go through life in this fallen world, we are experience the frailties of the human condition, persecution from without, pride and selfishness from within, and we wonder if God has forgotten us. Like those captives of Babylon, we wonder if God will ever fulfill His promises to us. We taste the firstfruits of the Spirit and are encouraged to hang on, but how long oh LORD (Ephesians 1:13-14; Revelations 6:10)?

15 "Can a woman forget her nursing child, that she should have no compassion on the son of her womb? Even these may forget, yet I will not forget you. Isaiah 49:15 We will be tempted to think God has forgotten us, but as we saw in a previous chapter, He is carrying us through it all (Isaiah 46:4). God says it is remotely possible that a woman might forget the child she nurses and not be compassionate toward the son she gave birth to, but God can never forget you. It is such a strong expression because what you experience in this fallen world will cause you to doubt. But all we need to do is look at the life of the Messiah to realize that suffering is a part of human existence regardless of how much God loves us. Grace uses every painful experience to prepare us for eternity.

Even when you know in your mind you are not forgotten the hard days of life welcome the comforting blanket of God's love that this verse and the next describes. *16 Behold, I have engraved you on the palms of my hands; your walls are continually before me.* Isaiah 49:16 How the LORD loves us (1John 3:1)! His palms each have a big nail hole that reminds Him of you continually.

The walls are the protection of the city. He is always watching them to see that you are protected. The spiritual walls are faith and self-control (Proverbs 25:28). While they are battered and full of flaming arrows at times, the LORD'S eyes are on them to see that those gifts of the Spirit are withstand the attacks.

While I have made a personal application of the verses above, they are more specifically applicable to the bride of Christ just before the rapture. This world will grow increasingly hedonistic and anti-Christian in the days ahead. The new holocaust is already underway (Gordon-Cornwall Theological Seminary has estimated 1 million Christians have been martyred between 2000-2010), and its main victims are followers of Jesus. That will only increase until the day the LORD returns and lifts us out of this mess. He will deal with Babylon the Great like He dealt with Babylon of old.

17 Your builders make haste; your destroyers and those who laid you waste go out from you. Isaiah 49:17 This was exactly what happened after the return under Nehemiah (Nehemiah 6:15-16). Those who assist in the building of New Jerusalem will make haste. The destroyers who were not annihilated at the Second Coming will run from the saints in glory.

18 Lift up your eyes around and see; they all gather, they come to you. As I live, declares the LORD, you shall put them all on as an ornament; you shall bind them on as a bride does. Isaiah 49:18 This is about the nations of the earth honoring New Jerusalem in the beginning of the Millennial Kingdom. Isaiah describes it more in detail in chapter 60. After a period of gross darkness, the Israel of God becomes a light to the world. The LORD will be the light of the city, and the world will bring their treasures to it (Isaiah 60:2-5).

I'm sure those who returned from Babylon were hoping it would be fulfilled in their time, but the Messiah of the first portion of the chapter had not yet come. I wonder if the Jews of the early church thought about the fulfillment. Perhaps that is one reason why they expected the Lord to return at any moment. The world was dark in those days of Roman persecution, but not as dark as it will become in the days ahead.

19 "Surely your waste and your desolate places and your devastated land— surely now you will be too narrow for your inhabitants, and those who swallowed you up will be far away. Isaiah 49:19 Analysts are already predicting a space crisis for the present Jerusalem by 2030. Israel is slightly larger than New Jersey and by that time will have the same population or greater. The difference is that a large part of Israel has the Negev desert (Zechariah 10:10). Refugees from Sudan are pouring in from the south while Jews are still migrating from the old Soviet bloc. That is why there is such an uproar over settlements. Israel desperately needs them, but Palestinians feel it is an encroachment on their limited space as well.

20 The children of your bereavement will yet say in your ears: 'The place is too narrow for me; make room for me to dwell in.' Isaiah 49:20 This is already the case. Jews from all over the world have returned to Israel and need space to live. In the Millennium everyone will want to be near Zion except those who hate the Lord and His people. The persecutors of the past will want to be as far away as they can get.

21 Then you will say in your heart: 'Who has borne me these? I was bereaved and barren, exiled and put away, but who has brought up these? Behold, I was left alone; from where have these come?'" Isaiah 49:21 When Israel gained sovereignty over the land again in the 1948, Jews began pouring into the land. Many were expelled from surrounding Muslim nations without their possessions, taking only what they could carry. Then the immigration began from all over the entire world. This verse has surely been said many times over the past seventy years. But imagine what the immigration will be like in the Millennium when spiritual Israel from around the world wants to live near the throne of Jesus in the restored kingdom of David.

The verse reminds me of China. When missionaries were forced to leave the country, there were so few active indigenous works. No one really knew for decades if Christianity was surviving. Once China began to open up a bit, we found it not only survived, but thrived. The largest nationality of believers of the world is now Chinese. Who has borne these? From where have these come? They came out of the Cultural Revolution that persecuted believers. The Lord raised them up. God will use us, but He doesn't need us. He can raise up leaders all on His own. He is a mighty God who can do anything (Jeremiah 32:17).

In the Millennial Kingdom, we will witness all those who have become a part of New Jerusalem and ask the same question. Then we will really understand that salvation is the work of God. Sure, He lets us participate in His work, and we should always look for opportunities to join Him in His work, but it is His work.

When we get to heaven we will see just how far and wide the rivers of the Holy Spirit that flowed through our lives became. When you are near the source of a river, you have no idea what it will become. The few souls that the Spirit of the Lord touched through us may have multiplied so that you find you have more spiritual children than an evangelist (Isaiah 54:1). There is a great difference between obedience out of a loving relationship with the Lord and self-initiative. We can do out of duty what we think we are supposed to do, and even do it sacrificially, yet bear little or no fruit. But obeying the Holy Spirit, letting the river flow through you, will produce more than you will see in this life (John 4:14).

[22] Thus says the Lord GOD: "Behold, I will lift up my hand to the nations, and raise my signal to the peoples; and they shall bring your sons in their arms, and your daughters shall be carried on their shoulders. Isaiah 49:22 It happened to a minor extent after the Babylonian captivity. It happened in a much greater way in 1948 and the years that followed. It is still going on with ministries like Ezra International. But the ultimate fulfillment will be in the return at the beginning of the Millennium (Isaiah 11:12).

[23] Kings shall be your foster fathers, and their queens your nursing mothers. With their faces to the ground they shall bow down to you, and lick the dust of your feet. Then you will know that I am the LORD; Isaiah 49:23a The captives in Babylon couldn't imagine this would ever be possible. But Cyrus did what they thought no Gentile King would ever do. He restored them to their land and even helped finance the rebuilding of the Temple. But that was just a shadow of the service the world will render in the Millennium.

In that day, the powers of the world will have been put to shame at Armageddon. Jesus will have shown the world that they are powerless against Him. We will see in future chapters in Isaiah that the world will realize Jesus is Almighty and that those who make up spiritual Israel are His chosen ones (Isaiah 60:16). The world will want the favor of New Jerusalem. Justice will go out from Zion. If nations want blessings, they will know from whence they come (Zechariah 14:16-17). The meek will inherit the earth and the once mighty ones will do their bidding (Matthew 5:5).

[23b] those who wait for me shall not be put to shame. " Isaiah 49:23b This promise is repeated several times in Scripture, because our tendency is to be like King Saul. He saw his army drifting away. He saw the enemy growing in strength, and instead of obeying the prophet Samuel and waiting for him, he made a sacrifice to the Lord on his own (1 Samuel 13:8-9). The minute he did so, Samuel showed up. And that was the start of Saul's downward spiral that ended in his death and David being enthroned. Learn to wait on the Lord.

We look at conditions instead of to the Lord. When we do, we jump into panic mode and act on our own, nearly always making the wrong decisions. How do you think the battle for Jericho would have gone had Joshua not met with the Captain of the hosts (Joshua 6:2)? Why would we fare any better? Our ideas are rarely God's ideas (Isaiah 55:8). Wait and get His direction. Then He promises you will mount up with wings of eagles. You will run and not be weary. You will walk and not faint (Isaiah 40:31) In your own effort you will not have the strength to endure.

We think way too much of our own ability. When we realize how limited we are and how great God is, we find the power in a humble submitted life that waits on the Lord. That was the source of Jesus' strength and success. Though He was God in the flesh, He did nothing without direction from the Father (John 5:30). The fruit of our lives is directly related to whether we wait on the Lord. What appears to be fruit is not always fruit that remains.

²⁴ Can the prey be taken from the mighty, or the captives of a tyrant be rescued? ²⁵ For thus says the LORD: "Even the captives of the mighty shall be taken, and the prey of the tyrant be rescued, for I will contend with those who contend with you, and I will save your children. Isaiah 49:24-25 It was the children of the original readers that would be taken captives. God was promising to set them free and rescue them. He would contend with those who contended with His own. He would save the children of the original readers. God was going to deal with this first world empire by raising up Cyrus.

God is able to rescue us, but as those men facing Babylon's furnace declared, "But if not, we will still not bow to commands that cause us to disobey God" (Daniel 3:18). We will trust God to deliver by life or by death.

²⁶ I will make your oppressors eat their own flesh, and they shall be drunk with their own blood as with wine. Then all flesh shall know that I am the LORD your Savior, and your Redeemer, the Mighty One of Jacob." Isaiah 49:26 God did deal with the Gentile nation of Babylon. He has dealt with all those who harm His children. He said that whoever touches us touches the apple of His eye (Zechariah 2:8). Harm a saint and you poke God in the eye.

I visited a church in a West Africa nation that had a blind man who was always at church first before others, praying for the service. One day a Muslim man took a stick and went into the church and severely beat the blind man. That day the attacker's arm that wielded the stick became like hardened cement. When the blind man heard of it, he went to visit the man and prayed for his healing. The man was healed, and since then, there have not been any more attacks on that church.

As the hearts of people grow harder in the last days, the persecution will be so severe that the Great Tribulation concluding with Armageddon will be the only just answer. After that, Christ will reign on the earth for a thousand years, the glorious kingdom Isaiah has just started to describe will cover the earth. We'll see how we were meant to be governed under Christ; but we will also see the hardness of the hearts of men.

Our passage today once again covers the past, the present, and the future. The Word never fails to speak the truth. How then should we live today?

Questions
1 What is Zion?
2 What are we tempted to think?
3 How does God reassure us?
4 What are our walls?
5 How have 19 and 20 been fulfilled?
6 How might you experience verse 21?
7 How might 22 and 23a come to pass?
8 Why do we need to wait on the Lord?
9 Why don't we wait?
10 What happens to those who harm God's children?

Third Servant Song - Isaiah 50:1-11

Our text today includes the third Suffering Servant Song. It is clearly about our Messiah, Jesus. Two weeks ago we saw the clear difference between the servant Israel, and the suffering servant, the Messiah who was yet to come (49:6-7). The passage today begins with reason for the coming captivity of Judah and then continues with the God's solution to our tendency to be unfaithful. It is the work of the Messiah to create a faithful bride made up of Jews and Gentiles.
¹ Thus says the LORD: "Where is your mother's certificate of divorce, with which I sent her away? Or which of my creditors is it to whom I have sold you? Behold, for your iniquities you were sold, and for your transgressions your mother was sent away. Isaiah 50:1 The eternal God of Israel is asking the people of Judah to consider why they are going into captivity. Why would God send them away like a divorced woman or like a child sold to creditors? He is not saying He has divorced Judah or sold them, but rather why it will seem as if He had.

God answers His own rhetorical question. It was sin that separated them from Him. It was their iniquities that pulled them away. He didn't leave them. They left Him. A few chapters later He will repeat this thought. *² but your iniquities have made a separation between you and your God, and your sins have hidden his face from you so that he does not hear.* Isaiah 59:2 When a nation falls under the judgments of God it is not because God has left them. It is because their sins have separated them from God. He is of purer eyes than to behold evil (Habakkuk 1:13). He will lift His hedge of protection to turn us back to Himself. He is more concerned about our eternal condition than our temporal happiness. It is true for nations and individuals as well.

As our nation turns from God and runs headlong into hedonism what can we expect? We will experience a separation from God because of our transgressions. His hedge of protection will lift (Job 1:10; Isaiah 47:6-11). There will be natural disasters, military failures, attacks on the nation, and a drastic decline in our quality of life. Is it because God divorced our mother? Is it because He sold us to creditors? No. It is because our iniquities have separated us from God. The historical pattern of nations that enjoy success is decadence, decline and defeat.

God did deliver a certificate of divorce to Israel (the northern ten tribes) because of their idolatry. They were conquered and went into captivity, but Judah paid no attention (Jeremiah 3:6-10). Even then God pleaded with Israel to return and acknowledge their sin (Jeremiah 3:12-14). Not only will our nation not acknowledge their sin, but they boast about their tolerance of it and declare all who will not celebrate sin are "bigots."

In the USA we have a wonderful heritage of godly founders. The colonies were divided along denominational lines. If anything, they were too dogmatic about their particular interpretation of the Bible. When they tried to unite around a constitution, they realized they would have to put those differences aside and agree to let individuals be free to come to their own conclusions about faith and the practice of their faith. That is why our first right was the freedom of religion. It prevents the establishment of any one religion over the others and promises that all are free to practice their faith without harassment from others.

Local governments, in their pursuit of political correctness, have decided we will ignore that and establish a new religion. It is the religion of secularism. Its first tenant is the golden rule of Satanism: "Do what thou wilt." That is to say that whatever you think is right is right for you. There are no moral absolutes in this ancient faith with one exception. You absolutely cannot tell anyone something is a sin. You must not just accept but rather celebrate and conform by giving up the right to publicly practice any other faith.

This new religion says that everyone is basically good. That is another reason using the "s" word is forbidden. The word they consider most vulgar is "sin." A religion is being established, and every premise of the First Amendment is being nullified by the very judicial system that was established to defend it.

2a Why, when I came, was there no man; why, when I called, was there no one to answer? Isaiah 50:2a This reminds us of chapter 48 in which the call to hear God went out ten times (48:16). The Holy Spirit was crying out to the people of Judah through the prophets, but no one was listening (Jeremiah 13:10). He is crying out today from Bible believing pulpits and directly to the hearts of men and women. Will anyone answer?

When I asked our city council if they were really aiming to deny the religious rights of those who believe in traditional marriage as a sacred institution, no one answered. Is there anyone to answer when God asks why our nation is so filled with pornography, vile entertainment, drug abuse, and lethargy? Will anyone answer when our nation is facing insurmountable debt? But even more importantly, will each of us face the idols that call us away from keeping God and His Word as the priority of our lives? Will you answer when He calls? Will you be one who will take a stand and dare to be different?

At this verse there is a shift in the focus of this passage from the failure of man to the power of God. What man can never do, God is more than able to do! *²ᵇ Is my hand shortened, that it cannot redeem? Or have I no power to deliver? Behold, by my rebuke I dry up the sea, I make the rivers a desert; their fish stink for lack of water and die of thirst.* Isaiah 50:2b God is able to redeem fallen Judah. He is able to redeem you and me. You and I are unable on our own to resist the temptations of idolatry. We are unable to serve God and be who He has created and called us to be. But God is able! He can reach you right where you are. He can redeem Judah from captivity and you and I from the captivity of sin (John 8:34). He can pay the price that buys us back from the clutches of Satan. He can deliver us from the power of sin.

God gave the example of redeeming and delivering Israel out of Egypt. He made a path through an ocean. He made springs in the desert. He can physically take care of a million people in the wilderness can't He take care of our spiritual need as well (Philippians 4:19). Can't He make a faithful bride out of us adulterous, pleasure loving, iron sinew necked, bronze forehead rebels? What a mighty God we serve!

It is amazing to see a 500 ton A380 lift off the runway carrying up to 980 people and their luggage into the sky. But God has been flying something weighing ten times that from beginning of the earth. The average cloud weighs 5000 tons!

³ I clothe the heavens with blackness and make sackcloth their covering." Isaiah 50:3 At any one moment the Lord has 50 trillion tons suspended above the earth! If He can do that through His design, can't He redeem His people? Now He tells us how He delivers us.

The Deliverer speaks. *⁴ The Lord GOD has given me the tongue of those who are taught, that I may know how to sustain with a word him who is weary. Morning by morning he awakens; he awakens my ear to hear as those who are taught.* Isaiah 50:4 No wonder Jesus invited the weary to come to Him and find rest (Matthew 11:28). No wonder the sinners flocked to hear His message. They were weary of trying to obey the 613 laws of Moses and all the traditions surrounding the Law. Jesus had the solution to the never ending effort of trying to please God. Trust in Him to do what we could never do. Let His life invade our own by the power of the Holy Spirit and walk by faith and not by sight. The beatitudes sustained with a word those who were weary (Matthew 5:3-12). His parables did the same.

And from whence came these words? Every morning His ear was open to heavenly Father. *³⁵ And rising very early in the morning, while it was still dark, he departed and went out to a desolate place, and there he prayed.*

Mark 1:35 His spiritual ears were awake to hear instruction. Every day was lived in obedience to the Father. God opened His ears to hear and He received and obeyed what He heard.

"Why is it that we have such a hard time hearing the voice of the LORD? Jesus told us that His sheep listen to His voice (John 10:3). Could it be that we are not surrendered to obey and therefore our ears are not awakened? If our hearts are determined to do what we want, rather than to obey our LORD, we have rebellious hearts. If we want our ears to be awakened, we must first surrender our hearts to serve in any ways the LORD would direct us. If you are weary, Jesus has a word to sustain you. Surrender your heart to do His will and your ear will be awakened. Follow His example." (Paul Wallace *Through the Bible Again Vol 1*. Sept 18)

5 The Lord GOD has opened my ear, and I was not rebellious; I turned not backward. Isaiah 50:5 This is the example. Jesus' heart was one with that of the Father. While His natural will did not desire to suffer (Mark 14:36), His heart was for the salvation of mankind and yielded fully to the will of the Father. That is key to hearing! What He heard He obeyed no matter the cost. When God called was there a man? Only one! Jesus of Nazareth, the God man!

Not being rebellious and turning not backward had a painful toll. *6 I gave my back to those who strike, and my cheeks to those who pull out the beard; I hid not my face from disgrace and spitting.* Isaiah 50:6 Oh how He gave His back to those who strike. They literally tore the muscles to shreds. Here are a few verses from the Gospels that describe the fulfillment of this verse. *67 Then they spit in his face and struck him with their fists. Others slapped him* Matthew 26:67 NIV)*19 Again and again they struck him on the head with a staff and spit on him. Falling on their knees, they paid homage to him.* Mark 15:19 (NIV) He could have paralyzed every one of them with one word. But He didn't. He demonstrated a greater strength. The power of love for His Father and love for them held Him from action. That's power! Compared to that power the power those soldiers demonstrated was nothing. He would soon utter the words, "Father forgive them, they don't know what they are doing" (Luke 23:34).

Jesus could not do that as a mere man, and neither can you or I. *7 But the Lord GOD helps me; therefore I have not been disgraced; therefore I have set my face like a flint, and I know that I shall not be put to shame.* Isaiah 50:7 It was the help of His heavenly Father that enabled Him to set His face like flint (Luke 9:51). He warned His disciples in advance just what He would endure (Mark 10:34). He knew because it was written of Him. Having quoted from one of the Isaiah passages about Himself (Luke 4:17-19), we see He knew the passage we are looking at today as well as the other Suffering Servant Songs.

Jesus knew the final outcome of obedience to the Father is fruitfulness beyond human comprehension. That is why He knew the final outcome would not end in shame, but joyous victory (Hebrews 12:2; Psalm 22:29-31). The world will call us names and belittle us for standing for the truth of the Word of God, but the end result will not be shame for us, but for those who resist God.

⁸ He who vindicates me is near. Who will contend with me? Let us stand up together. Who is my adversary? Let him come near to me. Isaiah 50:8 Jesus alone can confidently say this. Remember the time He challenged those who were attacking Him to convince Him of some sin He had committed (John 8:46). Who among us would dare to make that claim? Someone might be arrogant enough to do so, unless we told them their wife could testify. The very presence of Jesus was so holy that no one dared to accuse Him to His face during that encounter. Some would be so arrogant as to do so later, but all their false accusations were shown to be slander when God vindicated Jesus by raising Him from the dead.

Some resist Him even today, but when they see Him descend in His glory every knee will bow and every tongue will confess that He is Lord (Matthew 24:30). He was vindicated in the Resurrection and will be vindicated in the Second Coming.

⁹ Behold, the Lord GOD helps me; who will declare me guilty? Behold, all of them will wear out like a garment; the moth will eat them up. Isaiah 50:9 God the Father helped God the Son in human form by empowering Him with the Spirit. Jesus listened and obeyed. That is when we are helped by God. No voice could declare Him guilty of even one sin. Even Pilate declared there was no fault in Him (John 18:38). Every human body that would stand up and resist the Lord will grow old and wear out.

Clothing in Jesus' day was quite costly. People took great care of their clothes because it was so expensive to replace them. Even then, clothes wore out and moths would eat holes in them. That is the human condition. Try to fight aging as we may, we wear out. Will mortal man contend with the eternal Son of God? We do, but how foolish we prove ourselves to be. Jesus could look at His critics and the Roman soldiers and know their bodies would soon be worm food. People think so much of the physical being, but it is so short lived. The next time you are tempted to be angry with someone, remember, that person will soon return to dust just as your body will. Our souls will be forever in one place or another. That should give us a different perspective.

¹⁰ Who among you fears the LORD and obeys the voice of his servant? Let him who walks in darkness and has no light trust in the name of the LORD and rely on his God. Isaiah 50:10 Now God asks us if we fear the LORD and obey the voice of His Servant, Jesus. Have you listened to Jesus' words in the Gospels? He tells us to love God with all our heart, soul, mind, and strength (Mark 12:30). He tells us to seek first the kingdom of God and His righteousness (Matthew 6:33). He tells us that we must be born again (John 3:3).

Are you walking in darkness? Do you know what life is all about, or are you still trying to figure it out? There is light in Jesus who declared Himself to be this Servant, the light of the world (John 9:5), who suffered for you. You can trust in His name, that is, to trust in His nature. He is love.

He will not mislead you. He loves you and will guide you if you will trust in Him. He is the only reliable One.

The chapter ends with a reference back to something Isaiah prophesied earlier. If you have a fear of the righteous judgments of God, then the previous verse invites you come to His light and rely on Him. But if you have no fear of God's righteous judgments, you are relying on yourself or some other spiritual power, like those mentioned in 47:14. Astrologers and mystics were predicted to be consumed like stubble. At the flash of a flame they would be gone.

[11] Behold, all you who kindle a fire, who equip yourselves with burning torches! Walk by the light of your fire, and by the torches that you have kindled! This you have from my hand: you shall lie down in torment. Isaiah 50:11 There is only one provision for sin, the Suffering Servant. He is the Lamb of God who takes away the sins of the world (John 1:29). All other efforts to be spiritual are a delusion. They only lead to hell. Jesus suffered for you so that you could experience His deliverance, have light to see in the darkness of this world, and be sustained through life by His encouraging words. He's calling. Will you answer? Jesus answered the Father's call to save humanity. Will you answer Jesus call to come to Him and walk in His light?

Questions

1 How does man become separated from God?
2 What are the roots of the first amendment to the constitution?
3 Will you answer when God calls?
4 What powerful thing can God do?
5 Who is speaking in verse 4? What does He have for us? Why?
6 How do we follow that example?
7 What were the initial consequences of Jesus' obedience?
8 What were the ultimate consequences?
9 Why was that so?
10 What is the warning in the final verse?

You can watch **God's Comfort Isaiah 51:1-16** by Luke Thorne it at the following link:

http://www.bible-sermons.org/player_video.html?video=141356906

God and Man - Isaiah 51:1-16

[1] "Listen to me, you who pursue righteousness, you who seek the LORD: look to the rock from which you were hewn, and to the quarry from which you were dug. [2] Look to Abraham your father and to Sarah who bore you; for he was but one when I called him, that I might bless him and multiply him. Isaiah 51:1-2 As the nation of Judah dwindled in power and influence, those who were faithful to YHWH wondered where it would all end. For them, they could not imagine the promises of God coming to pass

without a temple and the land God promised to Abraham. What would it mean if another nation took them into captivity as Isaiah had predicted? Did they completely misunderstand God's Word, or had God forsaken them?

To those who still pursued righteousness, the faithful in Judah who sought the LORD, God had a word of comfort. They were to look to the rock from which they were hewn, meaning Abraham. They were to look to the quarry from which they were dug, the womb of Sarah. God did the impossible in keeping with His promise and this elderly couple had the child of promise. God's promises to Abram seemed impossible. How could a solitary man without children, whose wife was long past the stage of menopause, become the father of nations? How could His offspring bless the world and inherit the land? And yet, God was faithful to fulfill His promises.

Part of the theme of Isaiah is the survival of the line of David that would one day give birth to the Messiah. (See the messages on Isaiah 7 and 9 and the Suffering Servant Songs.) Yet, when the godly in Judah looked at the corruption and decline of the nation, it seemed as impossible as ninety-year-old Sara giving birth. But with God, nothing is impossible. God's comfort was to remind them that He is faithful to keep His promises regardless of how impossible they seem.

Perhaps you have thought that your children will never come to the Lord, even after training them in the way they should go (Proverbs 22:6). What does God's Word say? Perhaps you have wondered after falling way short of righteousness that God will give up on you (Hebrews 13:5). What does God's Word say? Whatever thing you think are discouraged about today, remember what God's Word says and be encouraged that nothing is impossible with God. It may not happen on your timetable, and it may appear to be getting worse by the day, but with God… (say it!). What His Word says about the situation is the way it will be.

3 For the LORD comforts Zion; he comforts all her waste places and makes her wilderness like Eden, her desert like the garden of the LORD; joy and gladness will be found in her, thanksgiving and the voice of song. Isaiah 51:3 What a beautiful verse! Zion is the people and the land. God comforts His people with blessings of fruitfulness. While God can cause the land to flourish, the exiles would face famine and a partially occupied land when they returned. It is really only in our day we have seen her wilderness become like Eden and her deserts like the garden of the LORD. 86% of farming water comes from recycled sewage water. Soon 70% of potable water in Israel will come from desalination plants. The Israelis invented the drip system. They produce the majority of Europe's citrus fruits. But this is only a precursor to the Millennial abundance when the early and later rains will be abundant. Then joy and gladness will be found in her, thanksgiving and the voice of song, not just for the fruitfulness of the land, but for the presence and favor of the LORD in her midst.

Is this not true today in the life of the believer? Jesus is the source of our living water (John 4:14). He makes us verdant with the fruits of the Spirit. We rejoice in His presence with thanksgiving and the voice of song.

This beautiful verse is fulfilled in the spiritual sense in the Zion of God. He comforts us when we are discouraged with the wickedness around us and the attacks upon the people of God.

⁴ "Give attention to me, my people, and give ear to me, my nation; for a law will go out from me, and I will set my justice for a light to the peoples. Isaiah 51:4 Again and again we are told to pay attention and hear. Moses said we must listen to the Messiah (Deuteronomy 18:15). Isaiah will repeat this call in Isaiah 55:3, asking us to make a covenant that assures us the faithful love God promised to David. That love promised that one from his lineage would reign forever. That is Jesus.

This call to give attention was for those in Israel who pursued righteousness, and it applies to all those who seek the LORD. "Law" in this verse can also be translated "teaching." Jesus, the Servant of the last chapter has sent out a new law/teaching. This was a Jewish expectation of the work of the coming Messiah. It was true of Jesus revision of the Law. While He nullified much of the rituals by fulfilling it in His life, He strengthened the moral laws by including the heart attitude. "You have heard that it was said… but I say to you…" (Matthew 5:22, 28, 32) The Ten Commandments and sayings of Jesus were the basis for much of Western Law. Only in our generation have we begun to call those laws antiquated, for our culture has decided we know better than Moses and Jesus.

Jesus is referred to as a light to the peoples. He called Himself the light of the world (John 9:5). He was saying that He is the teaching that has gone out from God. He is God's justice that gives light to the world. His justice for our sins was taken upon Himself. That is the light we all need. Only by accepting the truth that He received the justice our sins deserve can we really be in the light of God. If we reject that we remain in the darkness. (John 3:18-21).

⁵ My righteousness draws near, my salvation has gone out, and my arms will judge the peoples; the coastlands hope for me, and for my arm they wait. Isaiah 51:5 If those who pursued righteousness were worried about the promises of the Messiah coming to pass, this verse was telling them it wouldn't be long, at least not from God's perspective.

Jesus is called the "righteous one" in the next suffering servant song (53:11). He was drawing near. It would be another six hundred years, but relative to past and future history it was very near. The salvation of God, Jesus, would go out through the very land predicted (Isaiah 9:1). His words judge the people, for He only judges as the Father declares (John 5:30). The world waited for the proclamation of the Gospel. The next Servant Song also calls Jesus "the arm of the LORD." (Isaiah 53:1) The world was waiting for Him to be proclaimed and still waits for Him to be the true and just ruler in the earth.

⁶ Lift up your eyes to the heavens, and look at the earth beneath; for the heavens vanish like smoke, the earth will wear out like a garment, and they who dwell in it will die in like manner; but my salvation will be forever, and my righteousness will never be dismayed. Isaiah 51:6 Entropy reigns since the fall of man. We age and die. I can name more than a dozen individuals who have gone from this earth to their heavenly home during my ministry here. It reminds us that our life is like a vapor. However, God's salvation, Jesus, is forever, eternal. In Him is eternal life. "Dismayed" can be translated "broken." God's righteousness will never be broken. Satan cannot win. In Jesus, we have the righteousness of God and we will not be broken! There is one solution to entropy, decay, and death... the Victor over death in whom we are made eternally righteous! We may feel broken at times. We are hopefully broken of our stubbornness and pride, but our hope of heaven will never be broken. Jesus said, "It is finished!" (John 19:30)

From a scientific perspective, this verse was millennia ahead of its time. No one until the modern age conceived of the earth wearing out and the heavens vanishing like smoke. Yes, God said He would make a new earth and heavens, but man has always thought of earth as permanent until modern astronomy. Even in the scientific realm, the revelations in Scripture are true.

⁷ "Listen to me, you who know righteousness, the people in whose heart is my law; fear not the reproach of man, nor be dismayed at their revilings. ⁸ For the moth will eat them up like a garment, and the worm will eat them like wool; but my righteousness will be forever, and my salvation to all generations." Isaiah 51:7-8 Once again the godly are told to listen up. While it could be applied to some people in that age (Psalm 37:31), the Law is in the heart of those who have entered the New Covenant (Jeremiah 31:33). This is for us today. No Fear! (Matthew 10:28) We will be reproached and reviled. Don't let it cause you to be dismayed. They did it to Jesus, and they will do it to us.

We should not fear our persecutors because they grow old and die (Romans 8:31). I've had people come against me because I stand on God's Word. I've learned that given time they give up, move, or die. One pastor asked me how to deal with entrenched obstinate members. My advice was, "Outlast them!" Just keep standing firm. When you and I die we go to our reward, because we are in Christ Jesus our righteousness. His salvation is eternal. Why did John keep using the phrase "eternal life?" It's found eighteen times in John's gospel. It's because God said His salvation is to all generations. Jesus is salvation and He is eternal.

⁹ Awake, awake, put on strength, O arm of the LORD; awake, as in days of old, the generations of long ago. Was it not you who cut Rahab in pieces, who pierced the dragon? ¹⁰ Was it not you who dried up the sea, the waters of the great deep, who made the depths of the sea a way for the redeemed to pass over? Isaiah 51:9-10 This is so fascinating when you understand that the visible manifestation of God is Jesus. He is called the arm of the LORD in this verse. It is declaring that Jesus was the one who cut Egypt to pieces in the Red Sea. Rahab and the dragon are referring back to Egypt (Isaiah 30:7; Ezekiel 29:3). Where did they see the manifestation of God? It was the cloud that led them out and shaded them through the desert (Exodus 13:21; 14:9). Isaiah was asking that the arm of the LORD, Jesus, go into action again, delivering them from those who will take them captive. Whenever I come across these passages, it makes me wonder if it was part of what Jesus shared with the disciples after He rose from the dead (Luke 24:44-45).

[11] And the ransomed of the LORD shall return and come to Zion with singing; everlasting joy shall be upon their heads; they shall obtain gladness and joy, and sorrow and sighing shall flee away. Isaiah 51:11 This verse is exactly the same as Isaiah 35:10. If Jesus was to arise like He did when He drowned the Egyptian army, they would be miraculously returned from captivity with singing. Notice that Isaiah calls those who will go into captivity, "the ransomed of the LORD." That can be understood as having your freedom purchased. That is exactly what Jesus did for us. So while Isaiah was praying for Jesus to "awake" and ransom those who would go into captivity, it perfectly applies to what Jesus did for us on the cross. In that case the broken dragon is Satan! Jesus conquered him and returned us to the freedom from sin God intended for us. He awoke from death for our justification (Romans 4:25). The fruit of the Spirit is joy. That is why we sing as we realize the great love God has for us! Everlasting joy is our crown.

The parallels are so rich. When God would move on the heart of Cyrus to issue the decree for the Jews to return to Zion, the captives were filled with joy. They were free and could be in the land God promised Abraham. They could rebuild the temple and worship God according to the directions God gave to Moses. We are freed by the decree of Jesus because our sin debt is paid. Our promised land is life in Jesus. We sing for joy. And though we are traveling through this life that has sorrows, we are on our way to the heavenly Zion where sorrow and sighing will forever flee away.

[12] "I, I am he who comforts you; who are you that you are afraid of man who dies, of the son of man who is made like grass, [13] and have forgotten the LORD, your Maker, who stretched out the heavens and laid the foundations of the earth, and you fear continually all the day because of the wrath of the oppressor, when he sets himself to destroy? Isaiah 51:12-13a The Lord promised to comfort those who pursue righteousness. He asks who we are that we should be afraid of man whose life is so brief. Did the people going into captivity forget the LORD, their Maker, the Maker of heaven and earth? Just because man is on the rampage, should we fear him. Do we not believe that all things are in God's hands? Does He not see what is happening to us? Is He not capable of seeing us through? And if we are to die is this not the time He has ordained for us to enter His presence?

And where is the wrath of the oppressor? [14] He who is bowed down shall speedily be released; he shall not die and go down to the pit, neither shall his bread be lacking. Isaiah 51:13b-14 God promises to care for the captives. In fact, their captivity was not nearly so hard as they imagined it would be. Many of the Jews were so successful that they did not want to return to Jerusalem when they were given their freedom. They not only survived, they thrived, just as God promised in this verse. What we imagine
268

is rarely as bad as it turns out to be. We worry about so many things that never come to pass. Why can't we believe that our Maker can care for us? Haven't we seen Him do so in the past both in Scripture and in our own lives? Where is our trust? Don't we believe He loves us and knows our limitations? If we do, it changes our expectations.

15 I am the LORD your God, who stirs up the sea so that its waves roar— the LORD of hosts is his name. Isaiah 51:15 Scriptures use the analogy of seas to represent people. (Isaiah 57:20; Jude 13). The coming invasion of Babylon was not something God did not foresee. He was the one that stirred them up to take Judah captive. The LORD of the armies of heaven was shaking Judah out of their idolatry and causing them to return to their Scriptures. Our hardships in life are not something that took God by surprise. He ordained them for our good.

16 And I have put my words in your mouth and covered you in the shadow of my hand, establishing the heavens and laying the foundations of the earth, and saying to Zion, 'You are my people.'" Isaiah 51:16 God was still using Israel as His chosen people to communicate His Word. He was still protecting them. The mighty God who spoke all things into existence was saying to the fearful people of Judah, "You are my people." If you are in Christ, that word is for you as well. Hasn't the same all-powerful God put His words in your mouth? Hasn't He covered you in the shadow of His hand? In Christ, we are God's people. Whatever we face, whatever we fear, we are in the hands of Almighty God. He can not only see you through, but He can make you thrive in the process.

Arise! - Isaiah 51:17-52:12

In the first portion of this chapter, the captives of Babylon were to be encouraged that God can do great things that seem impossible to man. He can bring a great nation out of an elderly couple (51:1-2). He can make barren places bloom like Eden (51:3). He can be a light to this dark world (51:4). He can make sinners righteous and give them eternal salvation (51:6-8). The future captives were told to quit fearing man and trust in the Savior who delivered them from Egypt, who stretched out the heavens, and who laid the foundations of the earth (51:12-13). God promised to bring them back to Jerusalem with great joy while providing their needs (51:11, 14). The Servant who is hidden in the hand of God created all things and delivered them from Egypt would raise up a king to deliver the captives and declared those captives would still be His own people (51:15-16). There are many rich parallels in that passage to our life in Christ.

The first "awake" came in verse 9. It was to the "arm of the Lord," who is Jesus (53:1). He does not sleep (Psalm 121:4). It is a call to Jesus arise to display His delivering power and bring the future captives out of Babylon. We could compare it to the ministry of Jesus in our spiritual deliverance from sin. That is predicted in the next passage, the fourth

Suffering Servant Song. In it we are told the arm of the Lord was pierced for our transgressions (53:5).

Our passage today begins with the second call to "awake," or we could also translate it "to arise." *¹⁷ Wake yourself, wake yourself, stand up, O Jerusalem, you who have drunk from the hand of the LORD the cup of his wrath, who have drunk to the dregs the bowl, the cup of staggering.* Isaiah 51:17 This time the ones who are to arise are the people of Judah in captivity. They will have suffered as a consequence of their sins. God will see to it that they reap what they sowed to the full extent of the wrath His justice requires. Though Babylon would be the instrument of wrath, it was God who uses them as a bowl of wrath delivering justice upon Judah (Psalm 75:8). Judah is to arise and prepare to return to their homeland with lessons learned from the consequences of idolatry. After the discipline of the Lord, we are not to wallow in self-pity. We are to arise and take the lesson we learned into a renewed commitment to be faithful.

¹⁸ There is none to guide her among all the sons she has borne; there is none to take her by the hand among all the sons she has brought up. ¹⁹ These two things have happened to you— who will console you?— devastation and destruction, famine and sword; who will comfort you? ²⁰ Your sons have fainted; they lie at the head of every street like an antelope in a net; they are full of the wrath of the LORD, the rebuke of your God. Isaiah 51:18-20 Once again we have the evidence that this portion of Isaiah was written the same time as the first portion and not generations later. God is describing through Isaiah the devastation that would take place before and during the time that the people of Judah would go into captivity and the eventual return.

You might ask how he could describe their return and then jump back to the defeat that made them captives. God sees it all at once. In describing the wrath, they would drink to the full, God predicted the initial wrath which would be the worst part, the devastation that would take place during the conquest of Jerusalem (Lamentations 2:11-12). The city they loved and longed for would lay in ruins. Their sons and daughters would perish by famine during the siege or in the battle. Their idolatry would take a heavy toll. It was their sins that separated them from God causing Him to lift His hand of protection (59:2). When we insist on evil, we must realize that we are insisting on moving away from God. When we do so, we move out from under His protection. We open ourselves up to the consequences of our sins. His wrath upon sin is often the natural consequences from our behavior. We sometimes ask God why He would allow our present condition without realizing it was our behavior that put us in that condition.

God has asked, "Who will comfort you?" He then becomes the comforter by saying He will take the cup of staggering from their hand (40:1; 51:12). *²¹ Therefore hear this, you who are afflicted, who are drunk, but not with wine: ²² Thus says your Lord, the LORD, your God who pleads the cause of his people: "Behold, I have taken from your hand the cup of staggering; the bowl of my wrath you shall drink no more;* Isaiah 51:21-22

One day they would no longer have to drink from the cup of His wrath. Judah's days of discipline would be numbered. Jeremiah the prophet predicted those days would number seventy years (Jeremiah 25:11). It is God alone who can remove His wrath. This is true for every life. The good news is that Jesus removed from us the cup of God's just wrath upon our sins and poured it out upon the cross (John 3:36).

God declares He will take the bowl of wrath out of the hands of Judah and put it in the hands of their tormentors. *23 and I will put it into the hand of your tormentors, who have said to you, 'Bow down, that we may pass over'; and you have made your back like the ground and like the street for them to pass over."* Isaiah 51:23 One way ancient kings used to humiliate their enemies was to have them lay down in the streets and walk over their backs. Judah had suffered great humiliation, but now Babylon was about to experience what they had done to others.

I want us to look beyond the details of what was predicted, even beyond what happened when we came to Christ, and see God's final outpouring of wrath upon Babylon the Great (Revelation 16:19). She represents the world that refuses the grace and mercy of God and insists on rejecting His love. She has humiliated and persecuted the people of God throughout time (Revelation 17:6). At times God has used the wrath of this world's systems to get the people of God to return to Him. Just because God used the world to serve His purposes does not mean He does not hold it accountable.

The wrath in the book of Revelation is described as being poured out of seven bowls, just like the bowl mentioned here (Revelation 16:1). It will be poured out on a world that has rejected God's gracious gift of salvation and gone their own way. Those who have humiliated, and persecuted God's children will one day face the awakened arm of the Lord in the form of the wrath of the Lamb (Revelation 6:16).

Chapter 52 begins with the third call to awake or arise. First Jesus was to arise and deliver the captives from Babylon. Secondly, the people of Judah were arising to return with joy to their homeland. Now the call to arise goes out to all who will come to know Jesus as their Savior, the Jerusalem of God. *1 Awake, awake, put on your strength, O Zion; put on your beautiful garments, O Jerusalem, the holy city; for there shall no more come into you the uncircumcised and the unclean.* Isaiah 52:1 This third call is an introduction to the forth Suffering Servant song. Its superlative language tells us this is not only about previous restorations of Israelites to their land but is the ultimate return of lost souls to the Servant Savior. Let me relate it phrase by phrase. While the previous "Awake" or "arise" have lessons for us, the third one is specifically for us today.

"Arise! Arise!" When we are wallowing in sin we are like the cursed serpent who ended up on his belly in the dirt because of his rebellion (Genesis 3:14). We can only arise out of the dust when we are enabled to end our rebellion by the grace of our Redeemer. "Put on your strength." The Lord is my strength (Exodus 15:2). "Put on your beautiful garments." It is a repetition. The Lord is my beautiful garments and my strength. Put on the Lord Jesus Christ (Romans 13:8). The only ones clothed in righteousness are those who have put on the Lord Jesus! "Jerusalem, holy city," is the city of peace, those who are made holy by what Jesus has done and thus have peace with God (Romans 5:1). Every pain we deal with is from the uncircumcised hearts and unclean minds of man, redeemed or otherwise. The day will come when we will be set free from the persecution of this world and having to deal with fallen man's sin. Hallelujah!

This call to arise, to awake, will go out to the bodies of all who have died in Christ and those who remain on the earth (1Thessalonians 4:16-17). We will put on our heavenly bodies and we will soar into His presence. O come Lord Jesus!

² Shake yourself from the dust and arise; be seated, O Jerusalem; loose the bonds from your neck, O captive daughter of Zion. Isaiah 52:2 In contrast to the Babylonians who were taken off their thrones and made to sit in the dust, and then made to wear the yoke of hard labor (47:1-2), the people of Judah would rise from the dust to sit on thrones and be freed from slave labor. But this passage is speaking of much more than that partial fulfillment. It is of us shedding these frames of dust and rising to be seated with Christ in heavenly realms (Psalm 103:14). The bondage of the flesh, our sinful nature, will be eliminated. Transformed to the image of Christ, we will become His holy bride.

³ For thus says the LORD: "You were sold for nothing, and you shall be redeemed without money." ⁴ For thus says the Lord GOD: "My people went down at the first into Egypt to sojourn there, and the Assyrian oppressed them for nothing. Isaiah 52:3-4 Those who played a role in shaping the nation through affliction were not paid to do so. God moved them to do His will without cost. God would move the Persians to liberate them without being paid. God moves kingdoms for the salvation of His people. He uses the difficulties of life to shape and refine us.

⁵ Now therefore what have I here," declares the LORD, "seeing that my people are taken away for nothing? Their rulers wail," declares the LORD, "and continually all the day my name is despised. ⁶ Therefore my people shall know my name. Therefore in that day they shall know that it is I who speak; here I am." Isaiah 52:5-6 What is the result of the sins of Israel and their captivity? The rulers of Israel wail a lament. The nations despise Israel's God. But the byproduct of this discipline of captivity is that God's people come to know His name. That is that they come to know He is holy and jealous (Exodus 34:14). He will have no other God's before Him. His desires for us to be entirely His are for our good and for righteousness to be revealed in the earth. So, when He returns them from captivity without price, the world should take note that He alone is God. To make known His name is to reveal His nature. "Here I am!" He says. A day was coming when the One who is speaking to the heart of man through the prophet Isaiah would be right in front of them. He would reveal Himself.

Jesus nearly quoted the end of this verse to the woman at the well. She had said that she knew the Messiah was coming. Jesus said to her, "I am he, the One speaking to you." (Interlinear Translation of John 4:26) As the incarnate Word of God, Jesus revealed the nature of God. The people of God know the nature of God because of the life and words of Jesus. When Jesus comes again and finishes the work He started in us, we will know Him even as we are known (1 Cor. 13:12). The world will no longer despise His name because of our failures, but will love or hate Him for who He is.

[7] How beautiful upon the mountains are the feet of him who brings good news, who publishes peace, who brings good news of happiness, who publishes salvation, who says to Zion, "Your God reigns." Isaiah 52:7 For those in captivity this would mean they would return to Jerusalem. Paul the apostle applied this verse to those who proclaim Christ (Romans 10:15). In the ancient world a runner would bring the city the news of a victory in battle (2 Samuel 18:24-27). The evangelist brings the good news of Jesus' victory over death and hell, giving us peace with God. What news of happiness that is, that we will not drink from the bowl of God's wrath! He publishes salvation and says to the people of God that our God reigns. He will not be defeated. His purposes will prevail. In this dark and fallen world, there is a bright light of hope. Those who share the good news of Jesus shine that light.

[8] The voice of your watchmen—they lift up their voice; together they sing for joy; for eye to eye they see the return of the LORD to Zion. [9] Break forth together into singing, you waste places of Jerusalem, for the LORD has comforted his people; he has redeemed Jerusalem. Isaiah 52:8-9 Are you watching for Him? Our King returns victorious from battle. When did the Lord leave Jerusalem? Ezekiel said the Spirit of God departed from Jerusalem when they went into captivity (Ezekiel 10:18-19). This looks forward to a day when His manifest presence returns, only this time He is seen eye to eye. It is the Lord coming suddenly to His Temple (Malachi 3:1). He came through the womb of Mary to redeem His people (Matthew 20:28). But the passage may also be referring to the Second Coming and the joy of His Millennial reign. He will be physically present then as well (Isaiah 24:23). The ultimate comforting of the people of God is not merely the return to the Promised Land, but the wiping of every tear from our eyes (Revelation 7:17). Imagine the joyful messengers that go around the world declaring Jesus reigns over the whole earth.

[10] The LORD has bared his holy arm before the eyes of all the nations, and all the ends of the earth shall see the salvation of our God. Isaiah 52:10 The holy arm of the Lord is Jesus, and the world has seen Him in the gospels and in His people. Everyone's eyes will behold Him at the Second Coming (Revelation 1:7). The word for "salvation" here is "Yeshua," the name of our Savior. I don't know if we will have video news feeds then, but imagine a newscaster saying, "We interrupt this program to bring you a message from the King of kings!"

[11] *Depart, depart, go out from there; touch no unclean thing; go out from the midst of her; purify yourselves, you who bear the vessels of the LORD.* Isaiah 52:11 This was God's call for the priests who carried the vessels of the Temple to be ready to return them to Jerusalem. The Apostle Paul tell us it also applies to us (2 Corinthians 6:17). We are priest as well. We come out of Babylon the Great by walking with the Lord. We are to separate ourselves from the activities of the world that defile our souls. Since Christ has purified us by His blood, we are to live holy lives. We have become God's vessels dedicated to His service in this eternal temple of living stones.

[12] *For you shall not go out in haste, and you shall not go in flight, for the LORD will go before you, and the God of Israel will be your rear guard.* Isaiah 52:12 The captives of Babylon would not be fleeing; they would have the approval of King Cyrus. The Lord went before them and was there rear guard, just as Ezra testified (Ezra 8:22-23). It was like the cloud that went before them in the Exodus and stood between them and the Egyptian army. As we come out of Babylon the Great, this world's evil influence, the Lord goes before us and is our rearguard as well. God directs history to give us spiritual parallels. We don't flee this world and hide in a monastery. We are in the world but not of the world (John 17:6, 14). The Lord surrounds us with His presence and empowers us to be witnesses to a world in darkness (Isaiah 43:13).

The first call to arise is to Jesus to rescue His people from captivity. The second was to the people of Judah in captivity to prepare to be delivered. This third call to arise was to the captives as well, but it is filled with implications of a greater deliverance. The mysterious way in which God would make all this possible is foretold in the fourth and final Suffering Servant Song. Awake people of God, and be prepared to rise!

Questions
1 To whom is the first "arise" given?
2 To whom is the second "arise" given?
3 What comfort did the captives receive?
4 What is does the wrath on Babylon foreshadow?
5 To whom is the third "arise" given?
6 Review the meaning of 52:1.
7 What is the ultimate shaking ourselves of the dust?
8 How is the name of the Lord revealed to us?
9 How did Jesus use 52:6?
10 Who has beautiful feet? Why?

Fourth Servant Song part 1 - Isaiah 52:13-53:5

The preceding text looked forward to the captive Jews in Babylon rising up to return to their homeland. It was a promise that they would be delivered. But there are hints in the passage that there is a greater deliverance that is only foreshadowed by that return (Isaiah 52:6, 8). The Babylonian captivity can be a metaphor of our captivity to sin. The coming Redeemer would present Himself, and they were promised to see Him eye to eye. The joy of the ultimate redemption that was coming would far surpass that of the return to Jerusalem.

As with all the Suffering Servant Songs, most Jews today interpret this passage as referring to Israel. Lenny told me that in the Hebrew school he attended the school even deleted the portion of Scripture we will look at today. Before the eleventh century rabbis interpreted the servant in this song as the Messiah. Later rabbis up to this day teach that the suffering servant is the Jewish people. The change came when Rashi (Rabbi Shlomo Yitsak) interpreted the fourth servant song as referring to the Jews. Maimonides (Rambam), who was generally acknowledged to be the greatest Jewish thinker, Talmudist, and codifier in the Middle Ages, wrote that he was shocked by Rashi's change in the interpretation of the Servant in this passage.

There are practical interpretive reasons that the servant in this song can't be Israel. First and most obvious is the fact that in Hebrew the servant is referred to with plural and singular nouns. The singular ones refer to the Messiah and the plural ones refer to the people of Israel. Another key reason is that the servant is referred to as "the arm of the Lord." When one looks at other "arm of the Lord" passages, it is readily seen that this can't be referring to the nation and must be about the Messiah (Isaiah 51:5, 9; 40:10; 52:10). This passage today speaks of an individual person's experience, one who suffers willingly and silently. Can we say that of Israel? He dies for "my people." He is an innocent and righteous sufferer. His death is vicarious and substitutionary, meaning it is for the sake of others and in their place. He suffers for others' justification. He dies and is resurrected. How can those things be applicable to the people of Israel?

13 Behold, my servant shall act wisely; he shall be high and lifted up, and shall be exalted. Isaiah 52:13 Jesus acted wisely because, Paul wrote, "being found in fashion as a man, he humbled Himself and became obedient to death, even death on a cross." (Philippians 2:8) "High and lifted up" describes the LORD in Isaiah 6:1 (John 12:38-41). By Isaiah using the same description he used for the LORD, he is saying that the Messiah and the LORD are one. This verse must have been on the Apostle Paul's mind when writing Philippians 2:9-11, for Paul writes that because of Jesus' obedience He was given a name above every name that at the name of Jesus every knee should bow, and every tongue confess that He is Lord. Jesus wise obedience resulted in exaltation.

14 As many were astonished at you— his appearance was so marred, beyond human semblance, and his form beyond that of the children of mankind— Isaiah 52:14 I remember some people telling me that the movie *The Passion* went overboard in its depiction of Jesus' suffering. According to this verse, it may have not gone far enough. He was unrecognizable. The Scriptures mention several different times when Jesus was struck on the face with fists and with a reed. The lashes of the lictors' whips could at times go beyond the back and gash the face of the victim. This verse in Isaiah tells us the Servant was marred beyond human likeness.

Look at the contrast with the previous verse. The song begins saying the Messiah will act with wisdom and be highly exalted. The very next verse says He will be so physically abused He will hardly look human. That doesn't sound very wise. However, the song will go on to explain these great contrasting verses. We'll see the reason for both the suffering and the exaltation.

15 so shall he sprinkle many nations; kings shall shut their mouths because of him; for that which has not been told them they see, and that which they have not heard they understand. Isaiah 52:15 To "sprinkle" is a term used in association with the Levitical law's requirements for purification. When the first covenant between God and Israel was made on Sinai, Moses sprinkled the people with the blood of the covenant (Exodus 24:8). The language of this verse implies that God is going to enter a new covenant, but not with the blood of animals, but with the blood of His Servant, not with Israel alone, but with many nations (Hebrews 12:22-24; Isaiah 49:6). Jesus clearly understood this. During the Last Supper He declared the communion cup was the cup of the New Covenant in His blood (1Corinthians 11:25).

Kings will shut their mouths is referring to a sign of respect. They will want to hear from Messiah. The Apostle Paul cited the end of this verse in Romans 15:21 in application to the spread of the Gospel to Gentile nations. Perhaps this is ultimately referring to the Millennial Kingdom when kings will come to New Jerusalem to listen to the King of kings, to learn what had never before been told them.

Again, consider the contrast and message this is declaring. The wisdom of the Servant will result in Him being brutally abused, but end in Him entering into a covenant with nations and being exalted above kings. How can that be?*1 Who has believed what he has heard from us? And to whom has the arm of the LORD been revealed?* Isaiah 53:1 This verse is why we can say the Servant is "the arm of the LORD." The song continues with a revelation of "the arm of the LORD." The song is asking who has believed the prophecies. The Jews did not believe the words of Isaiah. They carried on with their idolatry until they went into captivity. Did they believe God would raise up a Gentile king to deliver them? Did they believe that if they returned God would protect them? It seems only remnant did. Did they believe the Messiah was coming to suffer and die for them? Apparently not.

Then the song asks who has received a revelation of "the arm of the LORD." Jesus tells that we can only come to Him if the Father draws us (John 6:44). While many were curious about Jesus and the miracles He performed, after the resurrection there were only 500 followers (1 Corinthians 15:6). It took the outpouring of the Spirit at Pentecost for multitudes to receive the revelation. This song, however, goes on to explain why many did not recognize Him.

² For he grew up before him like a young plant, and like a root out of dry ground; he had no form or majesty that we should look at him, and no beauty that we should desire him. Isaiah 53:2 Spiritually barren Israel was burdened with stifling oral traditions and a seemingly endless cycle of religious requirements that were impossible to live out. Many just gave up trying and were referred to as "sinners." In that dry ground came this new shoot of life growing in their midst (Isaiah 11:1). As Isaiah prophesied, "Unto us a child is born, unto us a Son is given" (Isaiah 9:6). Jesus wasn't a handsome, attractive person, but His words were a breath of fresh air.

³ He was despised and rejected by men; a man of sorrows, and acquainted with grief; and as one from whom men hide their faces he was despised, and we esteemed him not. Isaiah 53:3 John tells us that Jesus came unto His own and His own did not receive Him (John 1:11). The leaders rejected Him because He did not conform to their traditions and interpretations. They were so intimidated by Him that they decided they had to eliminate Him. After the crucifixion, the Jewish writings about Jesus even changed His name to derogatory words. The only leaders who first esteemed Jesus were Nicodemus and Joseph of Arimathea (John 19:38-40). They surely lost their high positions to align themselves with a man who was accused of blasphemy and crucified.

The people weren't any more receptive. While He miraculously fed and healed them, they were eager to be around Him. But when He refused to be their king or do their bidding, they used His difficult expressions to justify turning away (John 6:66).

It is no different today. I'm always struck with the Bible's accurate depiction of human nature. Billy Graham just published a new book in anticipation of his own death entitled, *Where I Am*. It speaks of heaven and hell and the choice we must make. Liberals are furious about the focus on hell and have made all kinds of claims. They say Franklin wrote it under his father's name, that Billy never emphasized that message, or that it was written like this because his mind is failing, and on and on. Why? They hate the message of impending judgment. They reject the message that we are all sinners in need of a Savior. The real Jesus and His honest messengers will always be despised and rejected by men because they speak of man's fallen condition (2Timothy 3:12).

Jesus is said to be more joyful than His brothers, that is, those who are His followers (Hebrews 1:9). Yet, here He is called a man of sorrows, and acquainted with grief. Jesus faced the rejection of His family, His friends and community, His followers, even His nation. The accusations against Him ranged from accusing Him of being deranged to being demon-possessed (John 10:20). Jesus knew grief and sorrow. He was probably most sorrowful for all who would not hear His invitation and warnings. When those you love ignore your pleas to turn from a disastrous direction, it can be very grievous to your soul. Yet, He found His joy in His fellowship with the

Father and doing the Father's will. Sorrow does not exclude joy, nor does joy exclude grief.

The verse ends declaring "we esteemed Him not." Jesus fellow Jews rejected Him. Yet, remember verses 13 and 15 in the opening of the song declare He will be esteemed. Jesus was esteemed by the Father for His obedience, and He would be esteemed by His followers after the resurrection and ascension. The world will esteem Him when He reigns over the Millennial Kingdom, at least until the final uprising against Him (Revelation 20:7-9). The redeemed will highly esteem Him throughout eternity.

⁴ Surely he has borne our griefs and carried our sorrows; yet we esteemed him stricken, smitten by God, and afflicted. Isaiah 53:4 The word translated "borne" here is used in Leviticus to describe the scapegoat carrying away the sins of the nation into the wilderness (Leviticus 16:22).

Our griefs come from sin in our lives and in the lives of others. Jesus carried all those sins, the source of our grief and sorrow, to the cross.

The enemy of our souls tries to tell us we are missing out on happiness when we say, "no!" to sin. Yes, we are missing out on much of the grief and sorrow sin causes. We may miss some temporal pleasure, but the accompanying grief is never worth it. What an entirely opposite perspective presented to us by the Word and by that of Satan!

Jesus carried our sorrows. The same word "carry" was used in 46:4 to tell us how God carries us through life to our old age. Life is filled with sorrows. We've had our share lately, but God is carrying us through it. He carries our sorrows. Just as we can cast our cares on Him, we can cast our sorrows on Him as well. Let that sink in. You can't carry them alone. He will carry away your grief like the scapegoat carried away the sins of the nation. If He is willing to carry your sorrow, why should you go on carrying it? It may take time to release it into His hands, but know His hands are stretched out to receive all our sorrows. Will you dare to believe that? He gives you His word.

Matthew tells us that what Jesus carried away is the consequences of sin as well, namely illness. When Jesus healed Peter's mother and the sick and demon possessed of Capernaum, Matthew said it was a fulfillment of this verse (Matthew 8:16-17). He quotes the verse as, "He took our illnesses and diseases" in place of "grief and sorrow."

Despite so graciously bearing our sins and carrying our sorrows, we count Him stricken, smitten by God, and afflicted. Stricken is a Hebrew verb usually associated with disease, but in this case, it is the disease of our sins. That isn't what He deserved. It was what we deserved. He deserves our love and gratitude. He deserves our total allegiance, honor, and praise. Why should God smite Him?

⁵ But he was pierced for our transgressions; he was crushed for our iniquities; upon him was the chastisement that brought us peace, and with his wounds we are healed. Isaiah 53:5 He was pierced for our transgressions, not His own (Psalm 22:16). Pierced is a word that survives in Arabic to mean fatally thrust through. Jesus' hands, feet, and side were pierced for your transgressions and mine.

He was crushed for our iniquities. "Crushed" reminds us of the opening verses that say His form was marred beyond human likeness. The just punishment our sins deserve fell upon Jesus, but that brings us peace. We don't have to stand before God and give an account of our rebellion. As the Apostle Paul declared, "We have peace with God through our Lord Jesus Christ" (Romans 5:1b).

"And with His wounds we are healed." This is often cited by people seeking divine healing. Peter cited it in 1 Peter 2:24 (NIV). *24 He himself bore our sins in his body on the tree, so that we might die to sins and live for righteousness; by his wounds you have been healed.* Peter's use of the verse is in context with the Servant Song. The healing referred to here is the healing of our sin sick souls. I believe God sometimes answers our prayers for miraculous healing, but this is not the verse that refers to it. It is one of those verses regularly used out of context because, generally speaking, we don't examine the context and try to apply verses as the Scriptures do. Matthew's use of verse four is more applicable to physical healing.

Ray Ortlund Jr. summed up the message of this song in words that are easier for us to relate to than these that are steeped in Jewish traditions. He wrote, "God wants to glorify himself by flooding our lives with sin-bearing mercy in Christ. The only barrier to being awash in freshness and joy and release is when we cling to our guilt by clinging to our own righteousness. All our guilt must go to Christ, and all our righteousness must come from Christ. This is God's way of release for guilty people, and there is no other." (R. Ortlund Jr. Preaching the Word - Preaching the Word – Isaiah: God Saves Sinners p. 353) That is the truth, the Good News! Lord willing, we will conclude the song next week.

Questions
1 What does the Babylonian captivity picture?
2 When did the Jews change the interpretation of the song?
3 Why should we think the Servant is Jesus?
4 What is the big contrast in 52:13-15?
5 Why is Jesus despised?
6 What were some of Jesus' sorrows?
7 What has and will He do for us?
8 What is behind the words "stricken" and "borne"?
9 Why was He pierced?
10 What wounds does He heal?

Exalted Servant part 2 - Isaiah 53:6-12

Last week we began looking at the amazing predictions of the fourth Servant Song. We saw the remarkable contrast predicting the Servant would be brutalized beyond recognition but be exalted and revered by kings. Another contrast is that though kings would honor Him, people would despise Him. Though He is the mighty arm of the Lord, He bears our grief and carries our sorrows. Though He bears our griefs and carries our sorrows, mankind would consider Him stricken by God. It was for our transgressions that He was pierced, and His wounds bring healing to our souls. The contrasts seem impossible to be fulfilled by an individual, and yet we see them all fulfilled in detail by Jesus of Nazareth.

We pick back up in this prophetic song just after the declaration that it would be for our iniquities that the Servant suffers this abuse. That punishment He received brings us peace and heals us. We ask, what are the wrongs we have done that He should have to suffer like this? How did we lose peace with God? Why do our souls need healing? The next verse gives us the answers. *6 All we like sheep have gone astray; we have turned—every one—to his own way; and the LORD has laid on him the iniquity of us all.* Isaiah 53:6

Every single human being is like a sheep that wanders away from their shepherd (Psalm 23:1). This is a metaphor for our spiritual condition. Sheep stay near their shepherd for protection and provision. He watches out for poisonous plants, for predators, and leads them to where they can find grass and water. Occasionally a stupid, rebellious sheep will wander off ignoring the shepherd. It pays no attention to the shepherds call and refuses to follow where He is leading? If it is fortunate, it will be found by the shepherd before it is devoured by wolves or dies of thirst (Zechariah 10:2).

Shepherds have a way of training this kind of sheep. They will break its leg and carry it until it heals, feeding it by hand. It is a burden, a great sacrifice on the shepherd's part, but that sheep will never again wander. It will stay close to the shepherd's side from then on.

God is telling us that we are all like that stupid sheep that wanders. He will call to us, but our nature is to go our own way. So we wander off into rebellion and are in grave danger. That rebellion should result in our death or at least a broken leg. But the punishment for all our iniquity, all our going astray, God laid on the Servant. This song emphasizes that His suffering is on our behalf. He receives what we deserve. In verse 5 the iniquity was plural as it is each and every sin of every person. In verse 6 it is singular as it is speaking of the sin of mankind, going astray.

Each of us has gone our "own way." I did it my way! We sing it, boast of it, laud it in others because our culture highly values the independent spirit of autonomy. No one can tell me what to do! I decide what is right or wrong for me. The spirit of lawlessness is on the rise. You see it in traffic, the legal system, the media, academia, and daily interactions. We are becoming a "me" centered society. That is to go our own way.

A recent twitter trend was to "shout out your abortion." Women were encouraged not to carry any guilt. Go ahead and tell everyone you aborted a baby and are glad you did. When the conscience is silenced, the results are an increase in lawlessness. Jesus took the punishment we all
280

deserved upon Himself. That is the only place our souls can find peace. That is the only way our sin sick souls can be healed (Acts 4:12).

The path to this sacrifice on our behalf was not an easy one. We saw a hint of it in an earlier Servant Song. *⁶ I gave my back to those who strike, and my cheeks to those who pull out the beard; I hid not my face from disgrace and spitting.* Isaiah 50:6 At the beginning of this song we read that His form would be marred beyond human likeness. This song continues with what He endured on the way to the cross. *⁷ He was oppressed, and he was afflicted, yet he opened not his mouth; like a lamb that is led to the slaughter, and like a sheep that before its shearers is silent, so he opened not his mouth.* Isaiah 53:7 This was depicted so well in Lewis', The Lion, Witch, and the Wardrobe. The lion was a Christ figure named Aslan. With all the demons howling in delight they shaved Aslan's mane, while Aslan lay silent awaiting the blade of the witch.

Jesus said so little during His trials. He had one before Annas, one before Caiaphas, one before Herod, and another by Pilate. At each location Jesus was mocked and physically abused. Before Annas, Jesus only spoke twice. One comment was to encourage the powerbrokers to conduct the trial according to the Law (John 18:20-21). Another was to make everyone aware of the duplicity that was taking place (John 18:23). Before Caiaphas, the Sanhedrin, and the false accusers He only spoke once to warn them of the future (Matthew 26:64). Jesus did not say a word to Herod. He spoke the most before the Gentile ruler, Pilate. The comments He made to Him seemed to be directed to Pilate's lost soul. The Gospel writers declare that Pilate was shocked that Jesus would not say more (John 19:11).

After silently taking the abuse and listening to the false accusations against Him, Jesus was judged guilty of blaspheming, condemned to death by the Sanhedrin, and then when threatened with political extortion, Pilate reluctantly sentenced Jesus to crucifixion. *⁸ By oppression and judgment he was taken away; and as for his generation, who considered that he was cut off out of the land of the living, stricken for the transgression of my people?* Isaiah 53:8 The word "oppressed" was used in the previous verse as well. In Hebrew the word is to tyrannize, or to treat like an animal. It is what a taskmaster does to slaves. This is prophetic of the scourging Jesus received. The verse sounds like Rome's treatment of Jesus: scourged, sentenced, and led to crucifixion (John 19:16).

When that happened, it seemed there was only one onlooker who understood what was happening, a criminal crucified along with Jesus. Who considered that He was stricken for the transgression of my people? The criminal next to Jesus who asked that he be remembered when Jesus came into His kingdom (Luke 23:42). Ron Kess recently shared a great expression with me that I want you to remember. "Heaven is not for good people. It is for forgiven people." The criminal beside Jesus knew He didn't deserve heaven. He was asking for forgiveness.

...who considered that he was cut off out of the land of the living, stricken for the transgression of my people? "Cut off" is an expression in the Law that is the most severe penalty for the breaking of God's law (Exodus 12:19). Our witness to the world is to invite people to consider that Jesus received God's punishment for our transgressions of God's laws.

⁹ And they made his grave with the wicked and with a rich man in his death, although he had done no violence, and there was no deceit in his mouth. Isaiah 53:9 We have come to another of these amazing predictions that sound impossible. If a person dies with the wicked, why would they be with the rich in death? Why would they be die with the wicked if they had done no violence or never spoken deceit? These details were amazingly fulfilled in Jesus being crucified between two criminals and yet buried in the tomb of the wealthy Joseph of Arimathea. Normally a crucified person would be thrown on the Jerusalem trash heap for dogs to consume. At best they might be buried in a hole in the ground as was the case with the recent find of one crucified individual from Jesus' time. But to be put in a wealthy person's hewn out tomb was unheard of. This innocent Servant called "the arm of the LORD" died with criminals but was buried in a rich man's tomb just as this passage predicted.

¹⁰ Yet it was the will of the LORD to crush him; he has put him to grief; when his soul makes an offering for guilt, he shall see his offspring; he shall prolong his days; the will of the LORD shall prosper in his hand. Isaiah 53:10 If the Servant was innocent, how could it be the will of the LORD to crush Him and put Him to grief? There is only one answer. He was bearing our sins, like the scapegoat (Azazel) on the Day of Atonement (Leviticus 16:8).

We need to be aware that many churches that claim to be Christian churches reject the idea of atonement. They reject the belief that Jesus took our sins upon Himself and was punished in our place so that we might have eternal life. However, that is clearly the prophetic word here which was fulfilled and taught in the New Testament. To reject this concept is to reject the Bible. The reason that is done gets back to the same idea I mentioned earlier. If this book accurately predicted future details as no one in history ever has, then it is from God. That means it is truth from God and holds us to an unattainable standard (John 7:19). It means every person that ever lived needs to recognize that without God's mercy and grace each of us will be judged with eternal consequences. It means we are obligated to live lives of gratitude in service to the One who loved us enough to take our punishment. We have to accept Jesus as our guilt offering if we want to be forgiven and be in God's presence forever.

Guilt offerings die (Leviticus 5:16)! The servant died as a guilt offering. But then the text says He prolonged His days. Is that the forty days he walked the earth after His resurrection or His eternal resurrected condition? Perhaps it refers to both. He shall see His offspring. They are all those who come to faith through His offering of Himself (Galatians 5:26). We become children of God, His offspring. God's desire for the salvation of many, the reversing of the curse, is accomplished in Jesus. It was done through His sacrifice, while being hidden in the hand of God (Isaiah 49:2).

This is one of those passages that has second potential translation that can deepen the meaning. *…when his soul makes an offering for guilt,* can also be translated, "when you make His soul an offering for guilt…" When you, (including all who read or hear this), make His soul your guilt offering, you become His offspring, and He sees you as a child of God. He died for you, but you must make Him your offering. God used the Hebrew language in a way so as to give us these rich double meanings.

[11] Out of the anguish of his soul he shall see and be satisfied; by his knowledge shall the righteous one, my servant, make many to be accounted righteous, and he shall bear their iniquities. Isaiah 53:11 This song tells us the anguish of the Servant's soul is when He is marred beyond human likeness, despised and rejected by the people. He carries our sorrows and is innocent, but He is oppressed (scourged) and abused physically. He is crushed by God, our sins are placed on Him, and He is offered up as a sacrifice. That is certainly anguish of soul. But it doesn't end there. He sees the result. He sees the offspring that come from the sacrifice. He knew it before the crucifixion (Hebrews 12:2). That is what He looked forward to your salvation and mine. By bearing our iniquities He has made many to be accounted as righteous.

Jesus said if He was lifted up He would draw all men to Himself (John 12:32). There is another double meaning. It can mean lifted up on a cross, or as in 52:13 it can mean to be exalted. But the two are tied together. It was because He was lifted up on a cross for us that He is exalted over all mankind. Every knee will bow before Him and declare Him Lord. This is so clearly filled with the Gospel message which is repeated again and again. By my count God tells us in seven different ways that the Servant takes our sins upon Himself and pays for them (verses 5, 6, 8, 11, 12). God is driving home the point that Jesus suffered for our sins to bear them away. The Servant takes our transgressions upon Himself so that we can be made righteous in the eyes of God. Hallelujah!

[12] Therefore I will divide him a portion with the many, and he shall divide the spoil with the strong, because he poured out his soul to death and was numbered with the transgressors; yet he bore the sin of many, and makes intercession for the transgressors. Isaiah 53:12 Because the Servant has done this, the Father will divide Him a portion with the many. The glory that Jesus received from the Father is to be shared with those who suffer with Him (Romans 8:17; 2 Thessalonians 2:14). That is one of those truths of Scripture that I have a difficult time grasping because the promise is so great.

I understand the dividing of the spoil with us to be the pouring out of the Holy Spirit. That seems to be the Apostle Paul's thought in Ephesians 4:8. It is the Spirit that gives us power to be a witness (Acts 1:8). It was only Jesus' death that sanctifies us to be vessels of the Holy Spirit (John 16:7).

Though He committed no sin, He was numbered with us, a fellow son of man. But He was also numbered with the two criminals.

Finally, to sum it all up, in spite of pouring out His soul to death and being numbered among the transgressors, *He bore the sin of many and makes intercession for the transgressors.* Notice the word "many." He carries away the sins of those who receive Him. He died for the sins of all (2 Corinthians 5:15). But if our sins are to be carried away as prefigured by the scapegoat, we must receive Him as our guilt offering. We have to realize our indebtedness and dependency on Him (John 1:12).

Also notice the present tense of the last phrase. He makes intercession right now and always for those who transgress. He is at the right hand of the Father, even as I speak, presenting the full payment for our past, present, and future sins (Hebrews 7:25). How thankful we should be. How hopelessly in love we should be with this Servant who loves us so! I close with the chorus on my heart from the hymn *Living for Jesus*.

O Jesus, Lord and Savior, I give myself to Thee, For Thou, in Thy atonement, Didst give Thyself for me; I own no other Master, My heart shall be Thy throne, My life I give, henceforth to live, O Christ, for Thee alone.

Questions
1 Why are we compared to sheep that stray?
2 What happens to our iniquity?
3 What is wrong with autonomy?
4 How was verse 7 fulfilled?
5 How was verse 8 fulfilled?
6 Who is in heaven?
7 How was verse 9 fulfilled?
8 Why did the LORD crush the Servant?
9 Where do we see resurrection in this song?
10 In what is Jesus satisfied?

Something to Sing About - Isaiah 54

The last two weeks we have looked at that amazing fourth Suffering Servant Song in which we saw so many details about Jesus' ministry, His taking our sins upon Himself and suffering in our place, His resurrection, and the outpouring of the Holy Spirit. It was a summary of God's plan to save us, New Testament theology explained in the Old Testament 700 years before it came to pass.

While the song has ended, the prose continues with an expansion of an expression in the song, "He shall see His offspring" (Isaiah 53:10). The phrase comes immediately after God making the Servant's soul an offering for guilt. Guilt offerings die, but through the resurrection Jesus sees His offspring and prolongs His days. The offspring are not His physical descendants, but rather His spiritual children born through faith in what He had done for them. The Apostle John saw this clearly when He wrote that those who are children of God through belief in Jesus' sacrifice are those *[13] children born not of natural descent, nor of human decision or a husband's will, but born of God.* John 1:13 (NIV) This is the connection between the Servant Song and our chapter for today.

[1] "Sing, O barren one, who did not bear; break forth into singing and cry aloud, you who have not been in labor! For the children of the desolate one will be more than the children of her who is married," says the LORD. Isaiah 54:1 Paul explains in his letter to the Galatians that this is telling us that Jew and Gentile believers who had not had spiritual offspring would end up with more than the Jewish nation's children of faith. He wrote, *[22] For it is written that Abraham had two sons, one by the slave woman and the other by the free woman. [23] His son by the slave woman was born in the ordinary way; but his son by the free woman was born as the result of a promise. [24] These things may be taken figuratively, for the women represent two covenants. One covenant is from Mount Sinai and bears children who are to be slaves: This is Hagar. [25] Now Hagar stands for Mount Sinai in Arabia and corresponds to the present city of Jerusalem, because she is in slavery with her children. [26] But the Jerusalem that is above is free, and she is our mother. [27] For it is written: "Be glad, O barren woman, who bears no children; break forth and cry aloud, you who have no labor pains; because more are the children of the desolate woman than of her who has a husband." [28] Now you, brothers, like Isaac, are children of promise.* Galatians 4:22-28 (NIV) Did you hear Paul's use of Isaiah 54:1 in verse 27? The Jews became like Hagar with Abraham, in bondage to the Law, while it is the church that became like Sarah, the mother of the children of promise, the children of faith who experience the freedom that we have in Christ (Romans 4:13).

How could Paul reach this conclusion? He saw in the four suffering servant songs that the Gentiles would be heirs of God by faith in what the Servant did for them (Isaiah 42:6; 49:6). That is one reason Paul considered it an honor to be the apostle to the Gentiles (Romans 11:13). He could foresee the fruit his ministry would bear.

The captives in Babylon probably read this as applying to future fruitfulness after their return to Jerusalem. It would have been a comfort and given them hope for a greater future. But as we read further in the prophecy, we'll see that the details can only be true for Jew and Gentile believers in the Messiah. Some of the predictions never applied to the Jewish people as a nation.

[2] "Enlarge the place of your tent, and let the curtains of your habitations be stretched out; do not hold back; lengthen your cords and strengthen your stakes. [3] For you will spread abroad to the right and to the left, and your offspring will possess the nations and will people the desolate cities. Isaiah 54:2-3 This was the promise to Abraham (Genesis 28:14). Again, Paul sees it happen in a spiritual sense (Galatians 3:16). The descendant of Abraham who would bless the world is Christ Jesus. It is the

spiritual offspring of Abraham, through this Seed that blesses the world, who possess the nations (Psalm 2:8).

Missions are an amazing part of world history that is ignored by the secular world. Think of it, nothing has influenced all of humanity to anything approaching the influence of the message of laborer from the little backwater town of Nazareth. He lived in a nation under the thumb of Rome. He lived in poverty. He never wrote a book. His crowds of followers were large at times, but when He died a criminal's death, He had 500 followers at most. His closest ones deserted Him in fear for their lives. But today, you can travel to any part of the planet and hear praises sung to Him in their own language. Lives from every background have been transformed from hopelessness to meaning and purpose. The disciples of this one man have possessed the nations with His message.

2000 years after Jesus ascended people hate Him or love Him. Radical Muslims so fear His message that they feel they must execute His followers. The Chinese government so fears the power of the Gospel that they try to control the message of the church and punish those who will not conform. In North Korea anyone caught with a Bible can be executed on the spot. The rate of martyrdom has been at around 100,000 a year and growing. Why? Ravi asks, "Are they not courageous enough to allow a healthy, honest, robust civil, discussion on matters of disagreement? Has violence become so absolute that the only answer is to decapitate you literally or otherwise?"

The first Sunday of November is the time we set aside to remember those who are being executed for their faith or held in prisons. You probably saw the men in orange jump suits who were beheaded. Orange was meant to be a protest over Muslim extremists in Guantanamo. One of those men in orange was not a Christian. He was a laborer from Chad. When the executioners got to him they told him he would be spared if he would just accept Mohammed as the prophet and Allah as the only god. Seeing the faith of the Christians he replied, I want their God to be my God. He died in faith because of the witness of those martyrs. Stand up for your faith brothers and sisters. Love never fails. We know who will win in the end (Revelation 11:15).

Here in the USA the intimidation to be quiet about the Gospel is on the increase. A crazed man executed those college students who declared they were Christians. A High School student quarterback in Syracuse, New York, was penalized 15 yards because He lifted a finger to God after a touchdown, intending to give God the glory for his success. A football coach in Washington was ordered by the school to not mention God, pray, or even bow his head. Thank God he is standing his ground and supported by the players and parents though he is on suspension. Public displays of Christianity are being removed while symbols of other religions are accepted. Why? Because Jesus' and His followers are possessing the nations. They should fear us, not because we will do harm to anyone, but because Jesus' message is the most powerful message in the world.

[4] *"Fear not, for you will not be ashamed; be not confounded, for you will not be disgraced; for you will forget the shame of your youth, and the reproach of your widowhood you will remember no more.* Isaiah 54:4 Before we became the bride of Christ, we were like an abandoned widow, left to fend for ourselves. The shame of our youth was that we turned away from the One who cared about us and lived in rebellion toward Him. But because the Servant removed our sins from us, we no longer need to fear. We can forget the rebellion of our past. Like the scapegoat carried off the sins of the nation of Israel (Leviticus 16:10), so our Savior has removed our sins as far as the east is from the west (Psalm 103:12). We no longer need fear the judgment of God or the wrath of man. We won't be ashamed when we stand before God, for we will be clothed in the righteousness of Jesus (Isaiah 61:10).

[5] *For your Maker is your husband, the LORD of hosts is his name; and the Holy One of Israel is your Redeemer, the God of the whole earth he is called.* Isaiah 54:5 We are the abandoned widow no longer. As the bride of Christ, we have the ultimate husband. His provision and protection are incomparable. His names are wonderful (Isaiah 9:6). "LORD of hosts" reminds us that He commands the angel armies. Nothing can happen to us that He has not allowed. "The Holy One of Israel" means that He is the eternal, unchanging God who is holy in all His actions (Malachi 3:6). "Your Redeemer" signifies He is the Suffering Servant who has become our guilt offering, redeeming us from servitude to Satan and our rebellious nature (John 8:36). "God of the whole earth" reminds us that nothing gets past Him. He is present everywhere and sovereign over everything. This is the glorious One to whom we are forever wed.

[6] *For the LORD has called you like a wife deserted and grieved in spirit, like a wife of youth when she is cast off, says your God.* [7] *For a brief moment I deserted you, but with great compassion I will gather you.* Isaiah 54:6-7 I'm sure this spoke to the Jews in captivity and encouraged them to have hope. But it is for us too. Our sins separate us from God, just as the Jews' sins had made them feel as if God divorced them (Isaiah 59:2). God sometimes leaves us to our own devices to wake us up and get us to change our course. The grief in our spirit and feelings of being deserted cause us to examine ourselves and cry out to God for restoration. When we see our wrongs, He is there with open arms of compassion to gather us back to Himself. That time of grief was for our good. It is often in those times of grief that God becomes everything to us and we discover our calling to be His instruments. Out of the ashes comes a life of true value (Isaiah 61:3).

[8] *In overflowing anger for a moment I hid my face from you, but with everlasting love I will have compassion on you," says the LORD, your Redeemer.* Isaiah 54:8 God repeats the promise of hope to be sure we hear it. God's dealings with us are always to bring us into a deeper walk with Him. Because He is our Redeemer, He is always at work in our lives to change us into His perfect bride, to make us holy as He is holy (1 Peter 1:16).

⁹ *"This is like the days of Noah to me: as I swore that the waters of Noah should no more go over the earth, so I have sworn that I will not be angry with you, and will not rebuke you. ¹⁰ For the mountains may depart and the hills be removed, but my steadfast love shall not depart from you, and my covenant of peace shall not be removed," says the LORD, who has compassion on you.* Isaiah 54:9-10 This is clearly not to the Jews but to the people of faith. The Jews saw another rebuke in 70 A.D. and another in 135 A.D. They have experienced numerous rebukes from the hand of God. This can only be the eternal state of those redeemed by the Servant's sacrifice. If He paid for all your sins, past, present, and future, how can the LORD be angry with you? This is describing an everlasting covenant. It is the new covenant in Jesus' blood (Isaiah 52:15). It is the result of the Servant's sacrifice in the previous chapters. The wording of this verse is one clear reason this must be addressing the redeemed people of faith.

God may discipline us, but just as He promised to never flood the earth again, so He has promised that He will never remove His steadfast love from us (Psalm 89:30-34). That new covenant that results in us being at peace with God is not conditional on what we do. It is because of that covenant that God works at transforming us continually until we see Him face to face. You may stumble along the journey, but He will never fail to have compassion on you. The price is paid in full. The covenant is sealed. It cannot be broken.

¹¹ *"O afflicted one, storm-tossed and not comforted, behold, I will set your stones in antimony, and lay your foundations with sapphires. ¹² I will make your pinnacles of agate, your gates of carbuncles, and all your wall of precious stones.* Isaiah 54:11-12 Again we see that it could have given hope to the Jews in captivity, but the real application is to the people of faith. Revelation describes New Jerusalem, the heavenly city of the saints, in a similar way (Revelation 21:18-21). So Paul and John saw this passage referring to the redeemed believers, both Jew and Gentile. Jerusalem was restored and the temple was magnificent, but nothing as glorious as this description.

This description is for every believer who feels they just can't go on. The world can come in like a flood and weigh on us till we want to give up. "O afflicted one, storm-tossed and not comforted," look at what is coming. Look at what the LORD is making out of you through this affliction. The city of God is the people of God, the bride of Christ (Revelation 21:1-2). It is you and me when the Lord has finished His work in us (Philippians 3:21).

¹³ *All your children shall be taught by the LORD, and great shall be the peace of your children.* Isaiah 54:13 I believe we can claim this promise for both our physical and spiritual children (Acts 16:31). Because we are the redeemed, the bride of Christ, our husband, Jesus, will take it upon Himself to teach our children and lead them into great peace. That means He will lead them to righteousness, for Isaiah has declared there is no peace for the wicked (Isaiah 57:21).

288

14 In righteousness you shall be established; you shall be far from oppression, for you shall not fear; and from terror, for it shall not come near you. 15 If anyone stirs up strife, it is not from me; whoever stirs up strife with you shall fall because of you. Isaiah 54:14-15 Not only will our children be established in peace, but we will be as well. God is not saying we will free of strife or oppression. He is saying it will not come from Him. He is reiterating the promise that unlike what has happened and would happen again to the Jews, the strife in our life will not come from God. He also promises that the strife the world brings will not end in us falling, but in their demise (Psalm 17:8-9). When you contend with the bride of Christ, you are asking for a confrontation with her protector. That is why we never need to fear the confrontations that come from this world. Remember that Jesus' name is the LORD of hosts. The angel armies are at His command. He doesn't even need to bother with it Himself. He can just send one angel who is more than enough to deal with any force. (2 Chronicles 32:21).

16 Behold, I have created the smith who blows the fire of coals and produces a weapon for its purpose. I have also created the ravager to destroy; Isaiah 54:16 Whether the army of Cyrus to set the Jews free from Babylon or the angels of God to silence those causing strife in our lives, all things are overseen by God for His purposes.

17 no weapon that is fashioned against you shall succeed, and you shall refute every tongue that rises against you in judgment. This is the heritage of the servants of the LORD and their vindication from me, declares the LORD." Isaiah 54:17 By following the Servant we become the LORD'S servants. We will have many battles in this life, for the enemy of our soul plots to make our life ineffective. The world will want to silence you. But if God is for you, who can be against you (Romans 8:31)? Every weapon, scheme, plot, or effort against us will eventually fail. We are the victorious army of the King of kings. They can kill our body, but they can't harm our soul (Matthew 10:28). They can lie and slander us. They can even catch us in our weakness being hypocritical. But when their words reach the ears of our Redeemer, He knows that He has paid for that sin and their words only condemn themselves for refusal to accept His forgiveness for the very same sins in their lives. Our vindication is from the LORD. Our army is undefeatable because our King goes before us (Deuteronomy 1:30). He has given us a heritage that exceeds our greatest hopes. I have a human heritage, but it is insignificant compared to our spiritual heritage as the servants of the LORD.

Chapter 54 has listed for us some of the gracious benefits received by those of us who have accepted the Servant's offering of Himself as our guilt offering (53:10). Because of what the Servant has done for us we enter into an everlasting covenant of peace with God (54:10). He promises us a multitude of spiritual offspring (54:1), that we will never be ashamed (54:4), to be like a husband to us (54:5), to protect and vindicate us (54:17). Perhaps the greatest of the promises is that His steadfast love will never be taken from us (54:10). That is something to sing about! That is why the LORD started the chapter with the command, "Sing!"

Questions
1 What was the last chapter about?
2 Who is being addressed? How do you know that?
3 How are we possessing the nations?
4 Review the stories of persecution.
5 Why should we have no fear?
6 How do His names reassure us?
7 Why does God hide His face from us?
8 Why does God put up with so much from us?
9 What is the promise in verses 11 and 12?
10 What is the promise of verses 16-17?

Thirst Slaker - Isaiah 55

As we begin looking at Isaiah 55, we should be sure to see it in light of the previous two chapters. Chapter 53 predicted the coming Servant would suffer and die for the sins of many. Chapter 54 describes the gracious benefits received by those who accept the Servant offering Himself as their guilt offering (53:10). Because of what the Servant has done for us we enter into an everlasting covenant of peace with God (54:10). He promises us a multitude of spiritual offspring (54:1), that we will never be ashamed (54:4), to be like a husband to us (54:5), to protect and vindicate us (54:17). Perhaps the greatest of the promises is that His steadfast love will never be taken from us (54:10). That is why that chapter started by telling us to sing.

In chapter 55 the call goes out to the world to be recipients of these blessings. It is a call that is echoed by Jesus during His ministry and also by His bride in the Revelation (Revelation 22:17). That tells me that the early church understood this message given through Isaiah was the message they were to proclaim.

[1] *"Come, everyone who thirsts, come to the waters; and he who has no money, come, buy and eat! Come, buy wine and milk without money and without price.* Isaiah 55:1 Here is the invitation. Come! We are invited four times in this one verse. The Suffering Servant, Jesus, paid the price. We are invited to come and freely partake of Him. Oswald Chambers wrote, "His (Jesus') word 'come' means 'transact.' 'Come unto Me.' The last thing we do is to come; but everyone who does come knows that that second the supernatural rush of the life of God invades him instantly. The dominating power of the world, the flesh and the devil is paralyzed, not by your act, but because your act has linked you on to God and His redemptive power." (Oswald Chambers, *My Utmost for His Highest,* November 4)

There is a theological debate about whether or not you can choose to come to Jesus. One side says that we can't do anything about our salvation. God chooses us. He calls us. He makes us respond. The reasoning behind this opinion is that the Bible tells us God is sovereign and that man can do nothing good (Psalm 14:3). The doctrine is called "the depravity of man." From heaven's perspective, mankind without God is incapable of a selfless, godly action (Isaiah 64:6). It is quite humbling to accept these truths. But does man really have no choice in the matter?

The other side of the debate says that God has given us a gift of freewill. We are invited to choose to come to the waters or we can reject the invitation. Somewhere in the middle is the opinion that God convicts everyone and enables every depraved soul to come, but the majority refuse to come (Matthew 7:13). That is my opinion. I can't see why God would invite us if we have no choice in the matter. Why would the call go out to the world if the world isn't given the opportunity and ability to come? How could God love the world if He just randomly picks a few to be saved? And how could hell be justice unless a soul willfully chooses to reject the loving sacrifice of Jesus (2Peter 3:9)?

What is this "water" that we are invited to partake? Jesus took this up in the beatitudes when He declared, "Blessed are those who hunger and thirst after righteousness, for they shall be filled" (Matthew 5:6). Jesus saw the souls of mankind thirsty to be filled with something. Some will respond to the conviction of the Spirit and hunger and thirst for righteousness. They will come to the water. Jesus is that rock from whence the living water flows (1 Corinthians 10:4). He is our source for righteousness.

The God-sized hole in our heart aches to be filled with something. We try wealth, pleasures, relationships, fame, education, and countless other things. We are all born thirsty. The question is this -what are we thirsting for? When the Spirit of God shows us that the only real way to satisfy that thirst is by accepting what Jesus has done for us, the gift of freewill becomes a blessing or a curse. We choose to drink of the water Jesus has provided or we drink something else that will never fully satisfy the longing He has put in our hearts. Jesus made it clear that He is the water Isaiah is speaking of when He stood up on the last great day of the Feast of Tabernacles and said, "If anyone thirsts, let him come to me and drink" (John 7:37). That is an invitation to all, for we all thirst for something. Jesus was telling the world that He alone satisfies our thirst.

The rest of the first verse tells us we don't need money to obtain the wine and milk that God is offering us. I understand the wine to be the Holy Spirit and the milk to be the Word of God. The Jews saw wine as symbolic of joy (Ecclesiastes 10:19). The second fruit of the Holy Spirit is joy (Galatians 5:22). Peter wrote that young Christians should crave the sincere milk of the Word (1 Peter 2:2). The Spirit and the Word are offered freely to us. True Christianity never asks a price for the things of God. Freely we have received, and freely we give (Matthew 10:8).

2 Why do you spend your money for that which is not bread, and your labor for that which does not satisfy? Listen diligently to me, and eat what is good, and delight yourselves in rich food. Isaiah 55:2 What a penetrating question! Everything the world promises will bring you satisfaction comes with a hefty price tag. It's usually money, but the price can also be your physical health, your marriage, even your sanity. The world cannot give you the bread that satisfies. As I began praying about this passage, it dawned on me that this is what Jesus was speaking of in John 6. He had just fed the multitude and they followed Him trying to get more fish sandwiches (John 6:11). *27 Do not work for food that spoils, but for food that endures to eternal life, which the Son of Man will give you. On him God the Father has placed his seal of approval."* John 6:27 (NIV) *35 Then Jesus declared, "I am the bread of life. He who comes to me will never go hungry, and he who believes in me will never be thirsty.* John 6:35 (NIV) Just as Jesus gives Himself for our spiritual thirst, He also gives Himself for our spiritual hunger. He alone satisfies. The world will always leave you hungry and thirsty for more.

How do we receive this bread that satisfies? Isaiah told us in the last half of verse 2. *Listen diligently to me…* If we will listen to Jesus speak the truth to our hearts, we will find our souls invaded with that supernatural rush of life. It reminds me of Martha and Mary. Martha was busy making the food that perishes while Mary was devouring the rich food by listening to Jesus' speak (Luke 10:41-42).

It is very important for us to ask ourselves this question. Why is the kitchen of busyness so much more attractive to us than this feast that Jesus lays before us? The duty of a servant is to listen, but we would rather be a lord (John 8:47). Maybe we want people to think well of us. Maybe we are afraid that partaking of the feast of Jesus will cause us to be indebted to Him. We are already indebted to Him for our life, every breath, every ability, everything (1 Corinthians 4:7)!

In case we didn't hear the first "listen" (actually the Hebrew is the word "listen" twice), in case our pots and pans were banging too loudly to hear Jesus in the other room, the next verse says it another way. *3 Incline your ear, and come to me; hear, that your soul may live; and I will make with you an everlasting covenant, my steadfast, sure love for David.* Isaiah 55:3 The first verse told us to come to the waters, and we saw Jesus applied it to Himself. Here the Lord says, "Come to me!" That is because the LORD who is speaking through Isaiah is Jesus, the Suffering Servant of chapter 53. Get out of the kitchen, come sit at His feet, and hear Him so that your soul may live! He is the source of everlasting life. When Jesus said, "Come to me all you who labor…" (Matthew 11:28), He was drawing from this passage. Why do we labor for what does not satisfy?

We must come to Jesus to enter that everlasting covenant of love God made with David. This is so richly Messianic! David wanted to build a house for God, a temple to replace the tent of worship. God told David that his son would build the temple. Instead of David building a temple for God, God was going to build David a house. God was saying that He would cause one of David's descendants to reign on David's throne forever. He promised to never remove His love from that One that was coming (Psalm 89:28). It was a promise that the Messiah would come through the line of David (Isaiah 9:7) and build the spiritual temple of living stones (Ephesians 2:21-22). Jesus is the fulfillment of that promise.

How can you enter into that covenant of sure, and everlasting love that God promised David, that house that God was going to build? You enter into Christ (Romans 8:39). You become one with Him as His bride. You become the body of Christ in this world. That happens when we listen and respond to the Holy Spirit (Titus 3:5). When He spoke to you, how did you respond? Are you hearing Him now? How will you respond today?

There are some who tell us God doesn't speak to us today. We just read the Word and do what it says. I understand their concern that we might get away from the plumb line of the Word, but God is looking for those who worship Him in Spirit and truth (John 4:23). We are born again through the Word of God (1 Peter 1:23), but Jesus also said we must be born of the Spirit (John 3:6). Without the Spirit we will forever have the Word in our head and not in our heart. That creates legalistic people who are critical of everything instead of joy filled lovers of God.

4 Behold, I made him a witness to the peoples, a leader and commander for the peoples. 5 Behold, you shall call a nation that you do not know, and a nation that did not know you shall run to you, because of the LORD your God, and of the Holy One of Israel, for he has glorified you. Isaiah 55:4-5 David was a witness of a man with heart after God (1 Samuel 13:14), God's chosen leader of people. How much greater is the Son of David who will reign forever? I see this verse fulfilled in the early Jewish church calling Gentiles into the kingdom. Gentiles in the first centuries ran to the Apostles. Why? Because Gentiles saw a God who loved them enough to die for them. It was also because of the glory of the Lord they saw on those early Jewish believers. When Greeks and Romans with their multitudes of self-serving gods heard of a God who loved them and invited them to quench their thirsty souls and satisfy their spiritual hunger, they responded to the Spirit's invitation. They came to Jesus and drank freely. It continues to this day, as shining, Spirit filled believers offer real satisfaction to the thirsty.

6 "Seek the LORD while he may be found; call upon him while he is near; 7 let the wicked forsake his way, and the unrighteous man his thoughts; let him return to the LORD, that he may have compassion on him, and to our God, for he will abundantly pardon. Isaiah 55:6-7 When can the LORD be found? When is He near? It is when the Holy Spirit speaks to the heart. He convicts the world of sin, of righteousness, and of judgment (John 16:8). It is then that He enables us to seek Him. If we don't, we are refusing His grace and goodness. We are turning our backs on His mercy. You might ask, "Can't He be found any time? Isn't He always near? The problem is our fallen nature I mentioned at the beginning of the sermon. We won't seek except for God intervening in our lives at those perfect times when we are most prepared to hear and respond. Don't let those moments pass you by without responding. Most of you have responded, and that is why you are here today. You want to partake of that milk of the Word and feast on the rich fare He offers us. But if you haven't made that transaction, if you haven't responded to His offer to be your guilt offering to God, don't let the chance pass you by. What God is saying in this verse is a warning not to harden your heart. Once you do, it is easier to do the next time, until eventually you have chosen to never respond. God longs to have compassion and abundantly pardon us.

8 For my thoughts are not your thoughts, neither are your ways my ways, declares the LORD. 9 For as the heavens are higher than the earth, so are my ways higher than your ways and my thoughts than your thoughts. Isaiah 55:8-9 This is our problem. God's thoughts and ways are pure and holy. Ours are not. We often quote this verse when we don't understand what God is doing. In the context of the passage, however, God is telling us the difference from sinful man and a holy God. He is telling us how much we need Him. The ways and thoughts of man in verse 7 were evil and unrighteous. God is announcing through Isaiah why we need the Suffering Servant to take our sins, but also telling us the great promises for those who do seek and call on Him (Romans 10:13).

We can never get to God intellectually. Our most sincere desires to be good aren't enough. We need the Holy Spirit to draw us into that transaction of exchanging our sins for Jesus' righteousness (John 6:44). We must respond to His conviction and deliberately choose Jesus over our own ideas of how we can be good or spiritual. Jesus said, "I am the way" (John 14:6). Argue with it if you like, but it won't change the fact.

10 "For as the rain and the snow come down from heaven and do not return there but water the earth, making it bring forth and sprout, giving seed to the sower and bread to the eater, 11 so shall my word be that goes out from my mouth; it shall not return to me empty, but it shall accomplish that which I purpose, and shall succeed in the thing for which I sent it. Isaiah 55:10-11 Here is the great difference between our words and God's. His accomplishes something. His have lasting value. If we want to join in His thoughts and ways, we have to allow His Word to renew our minds (Romans 12:2). We have to take time to be in His Word and in prayer. We need to learn to wait on the Lord and seek His leading (Proverbs 8:17). Regardless of the hardness of the hearts of people, God's will is going to prevail. You can get on board by seeking Him and calling on His name when He is near. Then as you listen to His voice you can participate in the work of His Word in the world. You can see eternal results from your life.

Christians apply this verse apart from the context as well. We use it to declare the power of the Word of God, meaning the text of Scripture. It can be used that way, but it seems more in line with the passage to refer to that word from the Holy Spirit when the LORD is near to turn the wicked from His ways. If we take it in that sense, God is declaring the power of His Word to transform a life from darkness to light (Ephesians 5:8), from being fruitless to fruitful. God can finish the work He started in us because His Word is powerful (Philippians 1:6).

294

Sometimes when I tell people of the power of God to transform their lives, they tell me I don't know how bad they've been. I tell them they don't know how powerful a Savior God is. They don't know the power of His Word to put our old nature to death and cause the resurrected life of Jesus to be seen in us (Romans 6:4).

¹² *"For you shall go out in joy and be led forth in peace; the mountains and the hills before you shall break forth into singing, and all the trees of the field shall clap their hands.* Isaiah 55:12 This is the transformation that is possible if we will respond when the LORD is near. He'll turn our sorrow into joy. That is what buying wine without cost alluded to. There is joy in a life in Jesus. We will be led in peace, for we now have peace with God through the sacrifice with Jesus (Romans 5:1). How many times have you heard someone say that after they were saved the colors were brighter and everything seemed so full of life? The mountains and hills seem to burst into song. The trees seem to clap their hands, and maybe they literally will in the Millennial Kingdom.

¹³ *Instead of the thorn shall come up the cypress; instead of the brier shall come up the myrtle; and it shall make a name for the LORD, an everlasting sign that shall not be cut off."* Isaiah 55:13 While this has been true in physical Israel, it is true in a spiritual sense for all who come to Christ. The thorns of life seem to be replaced with cypress, and the briars with myrtles. This is pointing to the curse of sin one day being lifted from the earth (Genesis 3:18) The transformation of our lives is an everlasting sign to the world of the power of God. But it all begins by coming to Jesus, the only one who can quench our thirst and satisfy our hunger. Have you responded when He called? Is He calling you this morning? Is He first in every area of your life, or are you still spending your money on what is not food, and your labor on what does not satisfy? Come!

Questions
1 What did chapter 54 promise us?
2 How can sinful man choose Jesus?
3 Why are our souls thirsty?
4 Where does Jesus apply verse 2?
5 What are you laboring for? Does it satisfy?
6 How do we receive spiritual bread?
7 Why is the kitchen more attractive to us?
8 What is the everlasting covenant offered to us?
9 Who is "me" in verse 3? How do you know?
10 How does God want you to respond to this chapter?

God of All - Isaiah 56

The LORD continues the theme from the previous passage, an invitation to all to come and partake of Jesus and find spiritual satisfaction.

We're invited to enter that covenant God promised to David, the Messiah from the line of David who would reign forever, from Whom God's steadfast love will never depart.

¹ Thus says the LORD: "Keep justice, and do righteousness, for soon my salvation will come, and my righteousness be revealed. Isaiah 56:1 This chapter begins with a warning. The readers were not to give up keeping justice and doing righteous acts. While in captivity, the nation of Judah would be tempted to conform to the world around them. Later in captivity they would become prosperous and the lure of unjust gain would entice them. When they returned to Jerusalem they compromised by taking pagan wives and putting their own interests above that of the LORD and the nation.

The warning was that the Messiah was soon to come. "My salvation" and the revelation of the righteousness of God both refer to the Messiah (Isaiah 51:5). In fact, the Hebrew word for salvation here is the name of Jesus, Yeshua. It would be 400 from the return of the Jews to Jerusalem until Jesus was born. Isaiah became a favorite of the Jewish people throughout that time. This is why John the Baptist's message resonated with the people (Matthew 3:3). They expected the Messiah to appear. John's message to repent and prepare for the coming of the Messiah is of the same theme as this verse. We should heed this warning today as the Second Coming approaches. It's time to get our act together and do what is right, keeping justice and acting righteously. The Lord will return. Death does not always give you time to prepare. What will He find you doing?

² Blessed is the man who does this, and the son of man who holds it fast, who keeps the Sabbath, not profaning it, and keeps his hand from doing any evil." Isaiah 56:2 Those who keep justice and do righteousness, who stay in earnest about obeying God, who keep the Sabbath, and refrain from evil are promised a blessing. We are to be just because God is just. If we compromise when justice would cause us loss, why should we expect justice from others? Justice is right because it is the nature of God. We are to be righteous because God is righteous. While the meaning of righteousness includes being just, it is also to be morally ethical. The Hebrew word is derived from a word meaning "straight" (Psalm 145:17). We use the word "crooked" today to mean morally perverse. To be righteous is to conform to God's standards. To keep the Sabbath meant to rest on that last day of the week while worshiping and thanking God for His goodness. Walking in the Spirit makes every day a Sabbath rest (Hebrews 4:9-10).

Why would the LORD warn people to be good if the Messiah was coming? Wasn't He coming because we fail to be good? Absolutely! However, as we'll see at the end of the chapter, those whose hearts are corrupt would find themselves in opposition to the Messiah. Those who were seeking God from the heart, whether they were accepted or rejected by the religious establishment, would flock to Jesus (Mark 12:37).

³ Let not the foreigner who has joined himself to the LORD say, "The LORD will surely separate me from his people"; and let not the eunuch say, "Behold, I am a dry tree." Isaiah 56:3 Not only would those

Jews seeking God from the heart be invited to come to the Messiah, but also the foreigner who was seeking God. We've already seen in Isaiah that the Messiah was coming to be a light to the nations and that His salvation would go out to the ends of the earth (Isaiah 42:6; 49:6). Here it is spelled out so plainly that it is hard to understand why the Jews of the first century did not expect it.

Jews in Jesus' day despised foreigners. Yet here in verse 3 through 8 we see God specifically declare the Gentiles will have a big part in the Kingdom of God. First, God addresses the eunuchs. Many of the leaders who were taken into Babylon were made eunuchs. It was to take away their hope of posterity and get them to serve for the present only. I wonder if Daniel's friends, Shadrach, Meshach, and Abednego had a copy of Isaiah (Daniel 1:6-7). This would have encouraged them to have hope in a spiritual heritage in spite of their lack of physical lineage. We saw in the previous chapter the hope of spiritual lineage (Isaiah 54:1). Those whom they influenced for God's glory would be counted as their spiritual children.

4 For thus says the LORD: "To the eunuchs who keep my Sabbaths, who choose the things that please me and hold fast my covenant, 5 I will give in my house and within my walls a monument and a name better than sons and daughters; I will give them an everlasting name that shall not be cut off. Isaiah 56:4-5 During Jesus' day, eunuchs were not allowed into the temple grounds. That attitude toward them may have been the same during the exile. They were probably seen as those who compromised with the conquering power and as unclean. But as Daniel and his friends are an example, they were more faithful than the rest of the Jewish people. While all people bowed to the king's image, these men refused to compromise (Daniel 3:16-18). It may be because of these promises they read in Isaiah.

They also held fast to the covenant by refusing to eat non-kosher food. They chose to please God in everything they did (2 Corinthians 5:9). God honored them by delivering them from the fiery furnace. He exalted Daniel to one of the highest positions in the land, influencing generations of kings. God did give him a monument and a name better than sons and daughters. That is the Book of Daniel. His name will be forever remembered. This is just one way God honors those who choose to please Him in all they do. I named my son Daniel. He grew up with pictures on his wall of Daniel in the lion's den. The Prophet Daniel's integrity and relationship with God has been a testimony to youth for two and a half millennia. Would the desire to please God in all you do describe your choices?

How does this apply to us who are blessed to understand the grace of God? Verse 3 began by speaking to the foreigners who had joined themselves to the LORD. That is all people who are not of Jewish lineage. We shouldn't say that because we are not Jewish that God will separate us from His people. This is the Apostle Paul's message that being a child of God is not through physical lineage, but through faith (Galatians 3:7). We join ourselves to the LORD by faith when we accept the God of Israel and

His Messiah, Jesus. Our Sabbath rest is Jesus (Hebrews 4:9-11). He is our justice and our righteousness. And because He is righteous we seek to be like Him in all we do and say (1 Peter 1:16). If that is not your aim, be honest about your priorities. What lasts?

Verse 5 needs some cultural explanation to get the full impact of what God is saying about His gift to us of being in His house and within His walls. Jewish homes were small family compounds. When a son in the family was to be married, the son would add on a room to the family buildings that surrounded a courtyard. Only when the new room was added to the others and the father approved it as sufficiently complete, could the groom go to claim his bride. She would move into this new room within the walls of the family compound. The Son is Jesus. He has claimed us for His bride. He has gone to prepare a place for us, and He will come again to receive us unto Himself, that where He is, there we may be also (John 14:1-3). In Jesus, we are accepted into God's family.

6 "And the foreigners who join themselves to the LORD, to minister to him, to love the name of the LORD, and to be his servants, everyone who keeps the Sabbath and does not profane it, and holds fast my covenant— Isaiah 56:6 Who are these Gentiles who are to be the bride of the Son? They are those who have joined themselves to YHWH, the God of Abraham, Isaac, and Jacob. They minister to Him, love His name, and serve Him (John 14:21). He is their Sabbath rest. They will not compromise or ignore their time with the LORD. They cling to the New Covenant in Jesus' blood as their only hope of salvation.

7 these I will bring to my holy mountain, and make them joyful in my house of prayer; their burnt offerings and their sacrifices will be accepted on my altar; for my house shall be called a house of prayer for all peoples." Isaiah 56:7 It is these who God will bring to His holy mountain, which is to say His holy kingdom. It is symbolized by Mount Zion and its temple. The home of God is a house of communion with Him. Our service to God will be acceptable to Him for it is directed by His Holy Spirit. The sacrifices God accepts are a broken and contrite heart (Psalm 51:17).

The Jews had a short wall around the temple on Mt. Zion that forbade Gentiles to enter and warned of execution if they did (Ephesians 2:14). I wonder what they thought of this passage. The only time Gentiles entered that earthly temple, it was considered defiled and had to be re-consecrated. This passage never saw fulfillment in the earthly temple. This promise to the Gentiles is in regards to the heavenly temple.

When Jesus cleaned out the outer court during His last week of ministry, Jesus quoted this verse (Matthew 21:13). While Gentiles were allowed in that outer court, they were never allowed in the house, the temple itself. The area where they were allowed was so noisy with merchants and traffic carrying things from one side of the city to the other that one would have a difficult time praying. This earthly symbol of the heavenly temple so distorted the picture of God's heart that Jesus had to act (Hebrews 8:5). He drove out the merchants and wouldn't allow anyone to carry things through the courtyard (Mark 11:16).

This shows us how passionate God is to commune with us, to include us into His family. Prayer is one of the most neglected disciplines of today's believers. It is one of God's most gracious gifts to us. He actually includes us in bringing His will into the earth. The God of all creation is willing to listen to you. But an even greater privilege is that He wants to speak to your heart (Matthew 6:6; John 16:13).

For years I've tried to cast the vision for volunteers to occupy the prayer room and pray for us as the Word is proclaimed. Most Sundays no one seems to take the challenge. Perhaps I haven't shared the power of prayer and the glory of participating with God. How much more would be accomplished in our hearts if there were those who would put prayer behind the Word of God, praying for us to be impacted by the Holy Spirit through the Word?

Notice that God promises to make us joyful in His house of prayer. The second fruit of the Holy Spirit (joy) is lacking in many believers because we do not take time to enter into prayer. They don't take the time to let God encourage them and declare His love for them. Joy is a by-product of realizing God's love for you and participating with Him in His plans. If you are lacking joy, join the disciples in asking Him, "Lord, teach us to pray." Luke 11:1

8 The Lord GOD, who gathers the outcasts of Israel, declares, "I will gather yet others to him besides those already gathered." Isaiah 56:8 Just in case we didn't get the point God keeps making throughout Isaiah, God makes it very clear here. He is not just gathering the Jews back to Jerusalem; He is gathering the world to Himself. New Jerusalem is made up of Jew and Gentile, all who hold fast to Jesus and the New Covenant He offers us.

9 All you beasts of the field, come to devour— all you beasts in the forest. Isaiah 56:9 Verse 9 is a shift in the text from speaking of Gentiles coming into the kingdom to the failings of Israel's leaders. It was true before, during, and after the captivity. It was especially true in Jesus' day. A call goes out to the predators. When the shepherds don't care about the sheep, the wolves will enter the flock and devour. It is evidence of the failure of the watchmen (John 10:12-13).

10 His watchmen are blind; they are all without knowledge; they are all silent dogs; they cannot bark, dreaming, lying down, loving to slumber. Isaiah 56:10 The Jewish ruling council was supposed to be watching out for the spiritual welfare of the people, but instead they were more concerned about their position, pride, and profit. They couldn't tell the difference between a wolf and the Savior. They were spiritually blind.

Dogs were often used to help protect the flock. But the leaders were like lazy, voiceless dogs that did nothing to protect the flock. There was a false sense of security when they were there. For a Jew to be called a dog was an extremely derogatory expression (Revelation 21:15). But here the description is made worse by the attributes ascribed to these leaders.

¹¹ The dogs have a mighty appetite; they never have enough. But they are shepherds who have no understanding; they have all turned to their own way, each to his own gain, one and all. Isaiah 56:11 Not only are they clueless and lazy, they can never get enough to eat. For all they cost, they do nothing in return. They aren't even there for one another. They are each in it for themselves (Ezekiel 34:2). They don't follow the ways of God. They have their own selfish way.

¹² "Come," they say, "let me get wine; let us fill ourselves with strong drink; and tomorrow will be like this day, great beyond measure." Isaiah 56:12 Eat, drink, and be merry is their plan. But what adds to their shame is that they think they will never have to answer for their selfish disrespect for the position they have been given (Ezekiel 33:6).

There is a contrast here with God's call in the previous chapter to come and drink wine without cost, the joy of the Holy Spirit (Isaiah 55:1). Here the leaders call to come and get drunk on physical wine while proclaiming that there will never be a Day of Judgment. No wonder Jesus' harshest words were reserved for those religious leaders (Matthew 23:27). They were the ones responsible for all the noise in the outer court. They had no regard for Gentiles and didn't care if Gentiles got the wrong impression of the God of Israel. Like many of the passages we have studied in Isaiah, these two parts of this chapter seem so different and yet they came to gather in the Gospels. In this case it was Jesus' cleansing of the temple bringing together the house of prayer and the greedy watchmen.

Sadly, these verses are too often true of the rulers of this world. Power puffs them up in pride. There is no fear of God in their eyes. They live for today while taking the position they have gained for selfish advancement, fame, and pleasure.

We are offered two alternatives to greatness in this chapter. One is God's way of humbly coming into the New Covenant and joyfully living in that House of Prayer as a servant of Almighty God. The other is that of this world's leaders, gaining the respect of man to abuse it for selfish desires. One ends in eternal glory. The other ends in the judgement they deserve. Grace goes out to all. There are exceptions to evil watchmen. The Gospels tell us of the salvation of two noted leaders of Israel, Nicodemus and Joseph of Arimathea. Grace is extended to us all. The call to come rings in our ears from both the Lord and from the world. One is offering true life, the other is a call to death while we live (1 Timothy 5:6). Both are costly. One ends in eternal glory, the other judgment. Choose this day whom you will serve.

Questions
1 Who is God's salvation and the revelation of His righteousness?
2 How do we get the blessing of verse 2?
3 What two types of people are encouraged in verse 3?
4 Who specifically may this have encouraged? How?

5 How does God honor those who choose to honor Him in all they do?

6 Describe the bride in verse 6.

7 What is she promised in verse 7?

8 How valued is prayer to you?

9 Which verse tell us Gentiles are part of God's kingdom?

10 What was wrong with the leaders back then? Today?

Two Paths - Isaiah 57

¹ The righteous man perishes, and no one lays it to heart; devout men are taken away, while no one understands. For the righteous man is taken away from calamity; ² he enters into peace; they rest in their beds who walk in their uprightness. Isaiah 57:1-2   I often think of these first verses at the memorial service of a godly person. God knows when to take us home to spare us from some future calamity. He also knows how to keep us alive until we are prepared for that day. Some pastors prefer to officiate funerals rather than weddings because the hearts of those attending are more likely to hear the message and consider how short this life is (Ecclesiastes 7:2).

When the righteous, those who walk in their uprightness, graduate from this life, they are taken away from calamity. They enter peace that is so complete we cannot comprehend it now (Philippians 4:7). That is the reward for a life united with Christ. This chapter is presenting to us two very different paths. In these first two verses we have the path of the godly who have the righteousness of God through faith in the grace and mercy provided for us in Christ Jesus. The other is seeking satisfaction in something else, anything else. We could say it another way, - God or idolatry.

The chapter has started by telling us of the good end of the righteous person, but warning us that no one lays it to heart. What will be your epitaph? What will people say at your funeral? How did your life affect others? And more importantly, how does God view your life? Where will you spend eternity? Have you prepared for it? The Egyptians laid up treasures in the tombs of their kings, all of which now sit in museums. I've seen so many lives focused on wealth only to see it tear apart the family as it fights over the inheritance. If you had a revelation of the results of your life one month after your death… what difference would it make in your priorities today?

³ But you, draw near, sons of the sorceress, offspring of the adulterer and the loose woman. Isaiah 57:3 God invites those who do not take the death of the righteous to heart to draw near and hear Him. He calls them sons of the sorceress, offspring of the adulterer and the loose woman. Over and over again, the Bible refers to idolatry as unfaithfulness, adultery, or fornication. The reason is two-fold. God calls Himself the husband of His people (Isaiah 54:5). To seek for satisfaction elsewhere is to be unfaithful to Him. But the second reason is that most of the idolatry in Biblical times and today involves physical lust. Sensuality was a part of most pagan religions. We don't call it a religion today, but it is still seen as a source of satisfaction. Americans lay about four billion dollars on the altar of pornography each year. Sons of the adulterer is a spiritual reference to those who follow the path that leads to destruction (John 8:41-42). Their spiritual parent is lust of one kind or another.

God invites all who would abuse creation out of God's intended boundaries to draw near and hear His warning. The world sees this as harsh but remember the opening verses. God is concerned about your eternal condition. If He is to be true to His nature He must judge what is evil, destructive, and harmful. If He did not, He would not be holy or just. God's harsh rebuke is to wake people from the stupor of lust to see where true satisfaction and eternal peace is really found. We are lied to day in and day out by advertising, educators, politicians, and our old nature. That is why God must use these drastic terms (Isaiah 55:2).

⁴ Whom are you mocking? Against whom do you open your mouth wide and stick out your tongue? Are you not children of transgression, the offspring of deceit, Isaiah 57:4 On a rare occasion I will look at comments to a news article. There was one article about the extremely low percentage of Christians among the Syrian refugees that were already given asylum in the U.S. In the article, an official for an NGO that worked for religious freedom stated that the refugees come from UN camps, but most UN camps are infiltrated by Jihadists. Comments on the article suggested we should accept Christian refugees in a greater number because they are non-violent. But one commenter went on and on about how stupid Christians are. He cited the number of stars discovered as proof that God didn't exist. He mocked Christians and all who believe in God. I would guess that he was suggesting that no religious asylum seekers be allowed into the U.S., and that we'd be better off as a nation of atheists.

Against whom was he opening his mouth wide and sticking out his tongue? What motivated him to be so anti-god? Was he not the offspring of deceit? I have one simple question for those who take his perspective. Where do they think that multitude of stars came from (Psalm 19:1)? Nothing? And if the answer would be that it always was, then simple physics says all mass would have long since slowed to a steady state. Instead we see the universe expanding with increasing speed.

I'm sure you could share many illustrations of your own of those who mock people of faith. The evidence for a Creator has never been more abundant and clear than in our day, but the anti-god rhetoric never so extreme. The major premises of evolution have been debunked. There is no such thing as a simple cell. There are no missing links. Yet, we go on indoctrinating each new generation.

⁵ you who burn with lust among the oaks, under every green tree, who slaughter your children in the valleys, under the clefts of the rocks? Isaiah 57:5 The motivation for much of the railing against God and those who believe in Him or any moral standard comes for the most part from

302

those who seek satisfaction in what God has forbidden. And why has He forbidden it? Because He knows it is harmful, an abuse of His perfect design. His prohibitions are words of concern and love (Deuteronomy 10:13).

This verse describes the common ways to practice idolatry at the time Isaiah was writing. Even today in eastern nations, people attach spiritual significance to old trees. The slaughter of children is worldwide (Jeremiah 19:4). Who are the most innocent among us, if not the unborn? Babies were offered to red, hot heated arms of an image called Molech. He was supposed to give them fertile crops in return. Besides, it was one less mouth to feed. Abortions today promise a similar financial benefit and convenience.

⁶ Among the smooth stones of the valley is your portion; they, they, are your lot; to them you have poured out a drink offering, you have brought a grain offering. Shall I relent for these things? Isaiah 57:6 While living in Japan, I would sometimes walk mountain trails and come across smooth granite stones. There would be offerings in front of them as if a spirit of some kind inhabited them and could do something for the one who offered the gift. I never saw the stone consume the cups of sake or eat the bowls of rice which are the equivalent of grain and drink offerings. The Jews knew better, but did it anyway. We know better. But do we look to things we know can't see, feel, hear, or think? Do we make offerings of wealth to what cannot satisfy?

⁷ On a high and lofty mountain you have set your bed, and there you went up to offer sacrifice. Isaiah 57:7 The high places were where people thought the gods would hear them. "Set your bed" is another reference to God seeing idolatry as spiritual adultery. James tells us that adultery is friendship with the world. *⁴ You adulterous people, don't you know that friendship with the world is hatred toward God? Anyone who chooses to be a friend of the world becomes an enemy of God. ⁵ Or do you think Scripture says without reason that the spirit he caused to live in us envies intensely?* James 4:4-5 (NIV) The "world" that James is referring to is the fallen nature of man in a fallen planet who crave everything other than a relationship with God our Creator (1John 2:15-17).

God yearns for our spirits to wake up from the stupor of self-indulgence and see that the greatness of His love is the only thing that will satisfy our hearts (Ephesians 3:18-19). If you are not in a love relationship with Jesus that affects your entire life, you are seeking satisfaction in this world. God is jealous for you. He doesn't want you to settle for something far less, that in the end will be harmful for you. He wants you to know the greatness of His love and the wonder of what He has planned for those who love Him in return (1Corinthians 2:9).

⁸ Behind the door and the doorpost you have set up your memorial; for, deserting me, you have uncovered your bed, you have gone up to it, you have made it wide; and you have made a covenant for yourself with them, you have loved their bed, you have looked on nakedness. Isaiah 57:8

Spiritual adultery used to take place in secret in America. Now people are proud of it. They don't hide it behind closed doors (Jeremiah 6:15). They boast of it. Some of the most perverted forms are still done in secret. Jared of Subway advertising fame just received a fifteen-year sentence for child pornography. But how long will our culture find that abhorrent when we refuse to define right or wrong by any objective standard? We also have the temptation to act as if we are Christ followers while we worship materialism behind the door, trying to live in both worlds, hoping for the blessings of God and the pleasures of sin for a season. It's not possible. We fool ourselves to think God is pleased with anything less than our whole heart.

⁹ You journeyed to the king with oil and multiplied your perfumes; you sent your envoys far off, and sent down even to Sheol. Isaiah 57:9 If we can't find what satisfies in this culture we go to another. How many journey to Thailand for some pleasure they would be looked down on here? They sent down even to hell! Some people realize that there is a spiritual realm, and if they can't get the thrill they want from their perception of god, they will literally turn to hell to find it. They'll try anything and everything but God.

¹⁰ You were wearied with the length of your way, but you did not say, "It is hopeless"; you found new life for your strength, and so you were not faint. Isaiah 57:10 Sin will make you weary. But the hard heart of man will encourage itself that just a little more, somewhere else, in some other person, object, some other drug, some other experience their soul will find satisfaction it craves. They find new life for their strength and go on searching experience after experience only to find increasing destruction to their body and mind (Ephesians 4:19). The last line says the result of renewed strength is that they were not faint. It could be translated "were not sick." We ought to be sick of some of the depravity man turns to, but man can overcome that natural disgust.

¹¹ Whom did you dread and fear, so that you lied, and did not remember me, did not lay it to heart? Have I not held my peace, even for a long time, and you do not fear me? Isaiah 57:11 The captors of the Jews would demand they worship their gods, but they did so before they were taken into captivity. God asks if someone threatened them to turn from God? Why would they lie or forget God? Why wouldn't we remember the warnings of God? Is it because His justice hasn't swiftly dealt with us? Do we think we won't be held accountable? Is that why we have no fear of God? Sinful indulgence often borders on the edge of insanity. Why would politicians throw away their positions for an affair? Have we forgotten the promise that our sins will find us out (Numbers 32:23)?

¹² I will declare your righteousness and your deeds, but they will not profit you. Isaiah 57:12 Jesus said there will be those on the Day of Judgment who declare all they did for the Lord, but He will tell them to depart from Him (Mathew 7:21-23). He never was their source of satisfaction. They never responded to His call to them (Isaiah 1:18). They never turned from their pursuit of the world. Their good deeds won't save them. It's not about good deeds. It's about our relationship with our Creator.

13 When you cry out, let your collection of idols deliver you! The wind will carry them all off, a breath will take them away. But he who takes refuge in me shall possess the land and shall inherit my holy mountain. Isaiah 57:13 In this verse the two paths come to their destination. If we have chosen something other than God to save us, we can cry out to it as we watch it vanish away. Our hope will be gone. Its temporal satisfaction will be exposed as meaningless (1 John 2:17). On the other hand, those who took refuge in the suffering Servant, the Messiah, Christ Jesus, who bore our sins, will inherit the kingdom of God. That is God's holy mountain. They will have their share in the heavenly land, like the Jews each had a plot of land in Israel (John 14:2).

14 And it shall be said, "Build up, build up, prepare the way, remove every obstruction from my people's way." Isaiah 57:14 I explained that the harsh rhetoric comes from a heart of love that would wake us and turn us from a path to destruction. Here again we see God's passionate desire for any who will choose Him over the world. Isaiah tells us that God will prepare the way for us to come to Him. That is the grace that convicts us of sin and opens our eyes to the meaninglessness of trying to find satisfaction in this world. But He also asks us to prepare the way for Him to come to us. That was the message of John the Baptist, to repent and get ready to meet Him (Luke 3:4). So as He prepares the way for us to come to Him, and by His grace we prepare our hearts to receive Him. Our hearts are broken for our past rejection of Him and seeking pleasure in the abuse of His created things that were meant for our good (Isaiah 40:3; 62:10).

15 For thus says the One who is high and lifted up, who inhabits eternity, whose name is Holy: "I dwell in the high and holy place, and also with him who is of a contrite and lowly spirit, to revive the spirit of the lowly, and to revive the heart of the contrite. Isaiah 57:15 God's self-description tells why reality is what He has described in this chapter. He is holy. That means He will not tolerate sinfulness. His just nature demands that He deal with it. He is so pure that He is said to dwell in a high and holy place. It is much higher than the mountains on which the idolaters worship. It is higher than this created universe. But the great wonder is that He is also with the contrite and lowly in spirit (Psalm 34:18). How can that be? Their repentance has prepared the way for Him and they have chosen the path He leveled for them (Isaiah 66:2). We meet in the loving embrace of forgiveness made possible by Jesus' sacrificial death in our place on the cross (Hebrews 10:14). When we find there is no condemnation to those who are in Christ Jesus, our lowly spirits are revived (Romans 8:1). The heart of the contrite is revived. We have peace with God. We are His and He is ours (Song of Songs 2:16). The work He has begun He will complete (Philippians 1:6).

16 For I will not contend forever, nor will I always be angry; for the spirit would grow faint before me, and the breath of life that I made. Isaiah 57:16 This passage told the captives that God was going to end their captivity and restore them to the land. But it speaks of something much more universal. If God did not provide salvation for us in Jesus, no human would survive. We would all be delivered to judgment. But God made a way. Jesus declared, "I am the way!" (John 14:6).

17 Because of the iniquity of his unjust gain I was angry, I struck him; I hid my face and was angry, but he went on backsliding in the way of his own heart. 18 I have seen his ways, but I will heal him; I will lead him and restore comfort to him and his mourners, Isaiah 57:17-18 Even when God dealt with Israel and Judah, they insisted on continuing in injustice and idolatry. Even into captivity, the people had hard hearts. But God would still have mercy and restore them to the Land of Promise. He would comfort them. And He will comfort all who come to Him for mercy.

19 creating the fruit of the lips. Peace, peace, to the far and to the near," says the LORD, "and I will heal him. Isaiah 57:19 This mercy and comfort results in the fruit of the lips that the author of Hebrews says is praise (Hebrews 13:15). God longs to be at peace with us. You see, sin is actually to set yourself in battle against the Lord. It is to join those in rebellion against Him. He longs to be at peace even with the worst of rebels. That is why He prepares the way for us to return as He did with Paul.

Those far and near is quoted in Ephesians 2:17. It is there interpreted by the Apostle Paul to mean Gentile and Jew. God will heal every sin sick soul that will meet Him on that path He has prepared for us. The end of the road for those who choose Him is peace.

20 But the wicked are like the tossing sea; for it cannot be quiet, and its waters toss up mire and dirt. 21 There is no peace," says my God, "for the wicked." Isaiah 57:20-21 Those who refuse the path prepared for them and insist on going their own way will find their life in constant turmoil, muddied by the confusion and chaos resulting from sin. They can't be still, for they deplore their own emptiness. They cannot know peace.

God's descriptions are very clear. Which of these paths are you on? It should be obvious. You know peace or you don't. If you don't, you can know it by turning from the path you are on and choosing the one God has prepared for you. Let go of trying to find something of creation that will satisfy. Acknowledge that in trying to do so you have been at war with God who loves you (Isaiah 50:8). Prepare the way for Him to take over your heart by repenting of those choices you have made in the past that only hurt you and others. Welcome Jesus as your Savior and experience the forgiveness He is ready to pour over you. Know Jesus, know peace. No Jesus, no peace.

Questions
1 What should we consider when a righteous person dies?
2 Why does God use such harsh language?
3 Why do people hate the idea of God?
4 What are some of today's idolatrous practices?
5 What is spiritual adultery?
6 Contrast two forms of renewing your strength?

7 Why would we ignore God's warnings?

8 Where does each path end?

9 Who prepares a way for whom?

10 Where does God dwell?

11 Who has peace?

Two Fasts - Isaiah 58

In the last chapter we saw two very different paths that we could take in life. One led to peace and the other a complete lack of peace (Isaiah 57:21). If the reader might have mistakenly thought he or she was in that category of the righteous, but had deceived their self, this chapter helps us see hypocrisy. There is a difference between religion and relationship. Religion is done out of duty to supposedly earn favor with God or man. Relationship comes from the heart and results in genuinely caring about the things that God cares about. This chapter asks us to examine our ways and see if we are religious or if we are in a relationship with our Creator (Jeremiah 9:24).

1 "Cry aloud; do not hold back; lift up your voice like a trumpet; declare to my people their transgression, to the house of Jacob their sins. Isaiah 58:1 Judah had not yet gone into captivity. While still practicing temple rituals, they also worshiped other gods that promised them wealth and strength. The people being addressed in this chapter were not necessarily those engrossed in idolatry as much as they were in outright worship of mammon (Matthew 6:33). They had the American dream long before the pilgrims struggled with it. They thought that if they just kept up the religious routine that God didn't mind what they did to get ahead (Isaiah 29:13). That is why God tells Isaiah to cry aloud and not hold back. It's not about attacking individuals for their hypocrisy but is addressing a nation for this mindset that allows them to be comfortable with sin (Micah 3:8). A few voices today are being lifted up like a trumpet. Is anyone paying attention? When we declare the transgression of the nation, we are looked down on as ignorant, self-righteous nuts. And that may be the case if we simply have religion and not a relationship with the living God.

The other extreme of not saying anything about sin can be just as evil. If we so long to fit in and be accepted that we refuse to declare the transgressions of the nation, we are guilty as well (Ezekiel 3:18). This chapter is going to give us a litmus test to see if we have discovered true faith, a life lived in relationship to God.

2 Yet they seek me daily and delight to know my ways, as if they were a nation that did righteousness and did not forsake the judgment of their God; they ask of me righteous judgments; they delight to draw near to God. Isaiah 58:2 This is a description of a sense of righteousness that is abhorrent to God. They had prayer, religious language, a call for righteous judgment, and delighted to go to the temple (Isaiah 1:11). Notice that it is "as if they were a nation that did righteousness." In other words, all this religious behavior was hypocritical. It is spiritual routine without surrendering to the will of God. It is declaring God to be the one true Lord while living as they pleased.

Paul had to defend against the idea that grace meant you could live as you want. He wrote, *¹ What shall we say then? Are we to continue in sin that grace may abound? ² By no means! How can we who died to sin still live in it?* Romans 6:1-2 To be in relationship with God results in a hatred of sin. Our renewed minds see things as they truly are. The destructive deception of sin is clear and we avoid it like a plague. We may fall back at times, but we are convicted rather than seduced to go further with it. It is often difficult to tell the religious from the redeemed because the religious can appear so delighted with the things of God. By their fruits you shall know them (Matthew 7:20). Many churches fall under the influence of the religious who gain influence over the church as an organization. They encourage others to do be religious, but the way they treat others reveals that their hearts have not been redeemed. They will point you to duty rather than a relationship with God (Matthew 15:9).

³ᵃ 'Why have we fasted, and you see it not? Why have we humbled ourselves, and you take no knowledge of it?' Isaiah 58:3a This is the religious person's attitude toward God. "Why doesn't He see all I've done? Why doesn't He answer my prayers like He has promised to do? Surely God should answer me after all I do!" (Malachi 3:14)

God gives the answer that they usually refuse to hear. This is what Isaiah was to cry aloud. This is the tune that his voice like a trumpet declares. *³ᵇ Behold, in the day of your fast you seek your own pleasure, and oppress all your workers.* Isaiah 58:3b Even while they go through their religious routines such as fasting with sackcloth and ashes, bringing a sacrifice to the temple, singing the psalms of worship, they were seeking their own pleasure and oppressing all their workers. They were withholding good from him to whom it was due when it was in the power of their hand to do it (Proverbs 3:27). Their fasting was not for God. It was to manipulate God to get what they want. "If I do this for God, then surely He will answer my prayer!" That idea is a form of paganism. God will not be manipulated (Isaiah 45:11). He needs nothing from us. God doesn't need us to fast. We need to fast for our own sake. We need to sever our bondage to our desires and driving influences so that we can give ear to the one influence we need the most.

⁴ Behold, you fast only to quarrel and to fight and to hit with a wicked fist. Fasting like yours this day will not make your voice to be heard on high. Isaiah 58:4 In the midst of the fast they are acting out of anger, quarreling and fighting. That kind of a fast doesn't invite God to hear you. It invites His judgment on you. Men often struggle with anger. There should be a correlation between humility and a reduction in anger. The greater our awareness of our own imperfections, the less likely we should be to lash out at someone for theirs (Matthew 6:14). The greater our awareness of God's abundant grace upon our lives, the readier we should be to extend that grace to those who offend or wound us. A true fast is a time of humbling ourselves before the Lord. To quarrel and fight with others while fasting are contradictory actions. It shows our fast is not really before our holy God. It is just going through the motions for the respect of others or to attempt to manipulate God. That is false humility.

⁵ Is such the fast that I choose, a day for a person to humble himself? Is it to bow down his head like a reed, and to spread sackcloth and ashes under him? Will you call this a fast, and a day acceptable to the LORD? Isaiah 58:5 There is genuine humility of the heart under conviction before God, and there are outward expressions of humility for the respect of men. Perhaps Jesus had this passage in mind when He told people to not appear outwardly to fast. Instead, He said to wash your face and anoint your head with oil so that only God knows you are fasting (Matthew 6:17-18). We have such a tendency to seek respect from others that we should be careful that our worship is for God alone. The outward show is rewarded by man's respect, not by God's favor (Matthew 5:16). It's not even acceptable to God.

⁶ "Is not this the fast that I choose: to loose the bonds of wickedness, to undo the straps of the yoke, to let the oppressed go free, and to break every yoke? Isaiah 58:6 This is the kind of fast that God has chosen. It's that fast that Jesus chose (Isaiah 61:1). He chose to go to the cross so that the bonds of wickedness would be loosed from our hearts. He undid the straps of the yoke this world places on us and invited us to take up His easy yoke (Matthew 11:28-30). He lets those oppressed by sin go free through the power of His Spirit. That is the fast He wants us to choose. It doesn't mean that we don't fast from time to time to draw near to the Lord. It means that our relationship with Jesus should result in a life that aims to be like His. We don't die on a cross, but we do take up our cross to show the love of Christ (Matthew 16:24).

We do this as a congregation through our mission giving, but that doesn't mean God won't give us the opportunity to do this personally. I know a number of you have taken up this fast. The real needs we see around us are broken hearts and confused lives. Discipling others is a way to loose the bonds of wickedness and undo the strap of the yoke. Sharing Christ with the lost breaks every yoke (John 8:32).

⁷ Is it not to share your bread with the hungry and bring the homeless poor into your house; when you see the naked, to cover him, and not to hide yourself from your own flesh? Isaiah 58:7 There is a difference between professional beggars and the genuinely hungry. Don't give cash that can be misused. Take the person somewhere for a meal. Then you can sit with them and make sure they know the Lord and His love for them. We can meet that clothing need by helping with the Hope Cottage Christmas gifts. Our support for homeless shelters does that as well. The generosity of this congregation shows you have a relationship with Jesus and have chosen His fast.

Hiding yourself from your own flesh means to divorce yourself from the needs of your relatives. God is warning us that we should care for our own (1Timothy 5:8). What does it say about our relationship with God if we won't even help our own family members with necessities? This is all about seeing our fellow man as created in the image of God and as those for whom Christ died (1John 3:17).

Now God moves to the reward of the fast of caring for others. If the religious people thought they would get something from God for their ritual service, He tells them the reward is for those who serve their fellow man from the heart. *⁸ Then shall your light break forth like the dawn, and your healing shall spring up speedily; your righteousness shall go before you; the glory of the LORD shall be your rear guard.* Isaiah 58:8 This is the way to truly be righteous. If they were praying for healing, here is the way to have the ear of the Lord for that request. They would have a truly godly reputation, and the LORD will cover their back. Already in Isaiah God has said He would go before us and be our rear guard (Isaiah 52:12). When the Israelites left Egypt, the Lord went before them in a pillar of cloud. The Amalakites would pick off the stragglers in the rear who couldn't keep up (Deuteronomy 25:17-18). Here and in chapter 52 God promises to be our rear guard as well. That means that if we should fall behind, He will keep us safe. If our walk with the Lord is delayed, we know that when we share God's love with others we have a Protector who will be with us and help us catch up.

⁹ Then you shall call, and the LORD will answer; you shall cry, and he will say, 'Here I am.' If you take away the yoke from your midst, the pointing of the finger, and speaking wickedness, Isaiah 58:9 If you choose the fast that God has chosen instead of a self-righteous display, then the LORD will hear your prayers. If you remove the yoke from others when given the opportunity, and if you don't gossip about others (Proverbs 26:20), and if you refuse to speak wickedness, then the LORD will hear your prayers. He'll be there when you call out to Him. You'll know His presence. These are conditional promises. A few more conditions with promises are given in the next verses.

¹⁰ if you pour yourself out for the hungry and satisfy the desire of the afflicted, then shall your light rise in the darkness and your gloom be as the noonday. Isaiah 58:10 This "if" includes giving to the physically and spiritually hungry, as well as helping the afflicted. Then your gloomy situations will become as bright as anything you've experienced (Isaiah 61:3). Then your righteousness will be seen, not because you want others to see it, but because you are acting at the leading of the Holy Spirit instead of your selfish desires. You are sharing God's heart for the needy.

I'm reading the biography of Adonirum Judson. He gave himself completely to the Lord in the hardest field on earth, Burma. His beloved wife and child died, and he suffered immensely. He was rejected by those who supported him because it took so long to make progress in that difficult field. The Lord was with him. When he returned to New York for his only

310

return visit from the mission field, the orphans in the streets called him Ol' Glory Face, because of the way his face shone (Ecclesiastes 8:1).

But that is not all the LORD will do for those who give themselves to the needs of others. *11 And the LORD will guide you continually and satisfy your desire in scorched places and make your bones strong; and you shall be like a watered garden, like a spring of water, whose waters do not fail. 12 And your ancient ruins shall be rebuilt; you shall raise up the foundations of many generations; you shall be called the repairer of the breach, the restorer of streets to dwell in.* Isaiah 58:11-12 God so loved the world! Why does He promise such blessings to those who care for the needy? It's because He loves each and every one of us (Romans 5:8). He hurts with each one. He wants to minister to the needy through you. I don't know how many we've helped physically or spiritually, and the number doesn't matter. Their response doesn't matter. What matters is that we show the heart of God. When we do, He promises to guide continually and satisfy our desire. When His desires become our own, we do these things from the heart. We can never be more satisfied than when we are satisfied with Him. He is the source of those waters that never fail (John 7:37-38). For the Jews, verse 12 meant if their relationship with God was right they would return and rebuild Jerusalem. For us it means churches and families will be restored to what they should be.

13 "If you turn back your foot from the Sabbath, from doing your pleasure on my holy day, and call the Sabbath a delight and the holy day of the LORD honorable; if you honor it, not going your own ways, or seeking your own pleasure, or talking idly;
14 then you shall take delight in the LORD, and I will make you ride on the heights of the earth; I will feed you with the heritage of Jacob your father, for the mouth of the LORD has spoken." Isaiah 58:13-14 We've seen that the Lord is our Sabbath rest. His holy day is now every day (Romans 14:5). We can walk with the LORD every day, or we can walk in our own ways seeking our own pleasure. The LORD truly becomes our delight, not the false kind of delight we saw in verse 2. These promises are for those who are truly in relationship with Him and seeking His pleasure. You will ride on the heights of the earth and have the heritage of Jacob (Genesis 27:39-40). Remember, Jacob got the blessing, the birthright, *and* the promises given to Abraham.

While the religious were trying to get God to hear their prayers through ritual forms of worship, those in relationship with God who serve Him from the heart are promised more than they could ever ask. There is a fast of religion that is somber and selfish. There is a fast from selfishness to serve the God with whom you are in relationship that is joyful and full of glory. How strange that in giving up our selfishness to serve the Lord out of love, we'd find a pleasure that surpasses all others. Have you found it?

Questions
1 What was to be loudly proclaimed?

311

2 What's wrong with the religion of verse 2?
3 Why are the religious upset?
4 What was wrong with their fast?
5 What are the two ways to fast?
6 How can we best do verse 7?
7 What are the rewards in verse 8?
8 What is the condition of verse 9?
9 What are the rest of the conditions and promises?
10 Which fast have you chosen? How can you be sure?

The Cycle Ends - Isaiah 59

Judah's transgressions and those of the world are no different. They just knew better. This chapter is a transitional chapter that begins by answering Judah's complaint against God. It moves on to describe their wickedness, and then moves into the rebellion of mankind as a whole. It ends with God's salvation of the Jews and the judgment of the world, which lead into the Millennial Kingdom described in the following chapters.

¹ Behold, the LORD's hand is not shortened, that it cannot save, or his ear dull, that it cannot hear; Isaiah 59:1 In our previous chapter we saw the people of Judah complaining about God not answering their requests when they would fast (Isaiah 58:3). God answered with a description of their hypocrisy. He answers that question again in this chapter with more specifics. But first He tells them that He is not impaired in any way. He hears just fine. His hand is more than able to save. He tells them just how He will save at the end of the chapter.

If God is not answering our prayers when and how we desire, we need to know that it isn't because He can't. It is either our sin that is in the way, or our request is something that wouldn't be good for us in the long run (James 4:3). His timing is perfect. His answers are best. He loves us enough to not give us everything we demand, just as we don't give our children everything they desire.

² but your iniquities have made a separation between you and your God, and your sins have hidden his face from you so that he does not hear. Isaiah 59:2 In the case of Judah before captivity, it was their sins that kept God from answering their prayers. His refusal to answer was a wakeup call to get them to open their eyes to the destructiveness of their sin. He hid His face from them for their good.

I should add that there are times in a believer's life when God will seem to hide His face from us to increase our faith (2 Corinthians 12:8-9). It isn't always because of sin. When sin is the cause, God uses difficulties and the natural consequences of sin to turn us back to Him. In some cases, He even uses the lack of consequences to show that He is merciful and wants us to turn before severe consequences result. God's response to our situation depends on the condition of our hearts. But He will not condone or tolerate continued rebellion. He loves us too much to leave us as we are.

³ For your hands are defiled with blood and your fingers with iniquity; your lips have spoken lies; your tongue mutters wickedness. Isaiah 59:3 Verses 3 through 8 are a description of the iniquity of Judah which is the same as that of the world. Hands, fingers, lips, and tongue remind us of a few of the Psalms (Psalm 51:14-15). Psalm 8 tells us the work of God's fingers include the moon and stars, yet He gave to man dominion over the works of His hands and put all things under our feet. He gave us this glorious creation, and yet, we abuse it. The innocent are slain. We lie to one another. We speak wickedly. Language seems to have degenerated into one vulgar expression after another. Live recordings of people on the street have so many bleeps when broadcast that you can hardly understand what the person is trying to say. A lying tongue and foul mouth is evil because God is true and holy (Proverbs 8:7). To be unlike Him is to be in rebellion toward Him, which is un-godly.

⁴ No one enters suit justly; no one goes to law honestly; they rely on empty pleas, they speak lies, they conceive mischief and give birth to iniquity. Isaiah 59:4 Insurance rates are as high as they are because of all the fraud and abuse of the system. Someone tried to sue our church because they fell in a drainage ditch in our parking lot a year prior to notifying us. Their attorney said there was no sign warning of the ditch. You have ridiculous labels on things for this very reason. Caution: This hot coffee is hot. The sad thing is that it is less costly for insurance companies to settle out of court than to go through a long drawn out court case. That is why people can make a living from frivolous law suits, which means those who pay for insurance also pay these people who conceive mischief (Proverbs 1:19).

⁵ They hatch adders' eggs; they weave the spider's web; he who eats their eggs dies, and from one that is crushed a viper is hatched. ⁶ᵃ Their webs will not serve as clothing; men will not cover themselves with what they make. Isaiah 59:5-6a In poetical form, the people of Judah are compared to spiders whose fruit produces death, and whose offspring are called vipers. In other words, they produce evil and the children are much worse than the parents. Each successive generation is worse than the one before.

⁶ᵇ Their works are works of iniquity, and deeds of violence are in their hands. ⁷ Their feet run to evil, and they are swift to shed innocent blood; their thoughts are thoughts of iniquity; desolation and destruction are in their highways. Isaiah 59:6b-7 God refers to their hands and feet again. It is our physical actions that express what goes on in the mind. If the mind dwells on evil, it will eventually be expressed in our actions. Our mind is where our spiritual battles are fought (2 Corinthians 10:5). Our heart decides the outcome (Proverbs 21:2).

On the very day I started working on this sermon, December 4th, as God would have it, Oswald Chambers devotional was explaining that life is a battle physically, mentally, morally, and spiritually. (Oswald Chambers,

My Utmost for His Highest, December 4) To be physically healthy internally we must have sufficient vitality inside to resist the destructive forces from the outside, viruses, germs, and the like. The same is true of our mental life. Temptations from the world, the devil, and our old nature compete for time in the contemplation of the minds. The world, the flesh, and the devil never tell you the whole story, otherwise it wouldn't be a temptation. And when given enough contemplation, we can talk ourselves into compromising and figure out a way to justify it.

"Swift to shed innocent blood" seems to be the mantra of ISIS. "Desolation and destruction are in their highways" also fits pretty well. But we should never fool ourselves that without Christ we wouldn't be as vulnerable to deception and lust as they are. It is only the grace of God, and His grace is even reaching some of them (Jeremiah 17:9). Our lust for violence and bloodshed is seen in our entertainment industry.

⁸ The way of peace they do not know, and there is no justice in their paths; they have made their roads crooked; no one who treads on them knows peace. Isaiah 59:8 Whether ISIS or the ungodly that look so refined within our own culture, a wicked heart does not know the way of peace. As a previous chapter stated, "There is no peace, says my God, for the wicked." Isaiah 57:21 Sin is a hard taskmaster. It drives us to seek more and is never satisfied. And when sin reigns there is no justice in their paths. Everything is skewed by passion for sin (Romans 8:5).

"Crooked roads" in Scripture means an immoral lifestyle. No one on that path knows peace. That is because sin wont fill the emptiness within, and the subconscious acknowledgement that we will reap what we sow (Galatians 6:7).

⁹ Therefore justice is far from us, and righteousness does not overtake us; we hope for light, and behold, darkness, and for brightness, but we walk in gloom. ¹⁰ We grope for the wall like the blind; we grope like those who have no eyes; we stumble at noon as in the twilight, among those in full vigor we are like dead men. Isaiah 59:9-10 Verses, 9-13, tell of the fruit of their choices. They are choices to contemplate wickedness, to act on it, to justify it, and even make it a goal. First, the wicked never seem to get justice from others. That is because they have sown injustice. Righteousness never overtakes them because the refuse to seek it. They hope for some light and clarity to life and their situations, but light is in the Lord whom they have rejected (1 John 1:5).

They grope around to find something that really satisfies, something that can make sense of life, a reason to go on, but they are spiritually blind. Compared to people who are alive in Christ, they seem like dead men. Have you noticed how some people exude life and joy while others seem to be so lifeless? In Christ we have a reason to live, a reason to go on, regardless of the circumstances we face.

¹¹ We all growl like bears; we moan and moan like doves; we hope for justice, but there is none; for salvation, but it is far from us. Isaiah 59:11 This is a description of despair and frustration. As believers, we can fall back into the old nature and be right there with these unbelievers in complaining as if everything were hopeless. If we have life in Christ, we should be the ones lifting the conversation to another level. We should be speaking of what is praiseworthy and the goodness of God in the midst of this fallen world (Philippians 4:8). I can moan and growl with the best of them, but I don't believe that pleases the Lord. It certainly doesn't draw others to Him.

¹² For our transgressions are multiplied before you, and our sins testify against us; for our transgressions are with us, and we know our iniquities: ¹³ transgressing, and denying the LORD, and turning back from following our God, speaking oppression and revolt, conceiving and uttering from the heart lying words. Isaiah 59:12-13 Acknowledgment of sin comes before there can be genuine repentance (Psalm 32:5). But when we see our sins and yet refuse to forsake them, we are laying up judgment against ourselves (Romans 2:5). To deny the LORD is to deny the conviction of the Holy Spirit and turning away from His love (Matthew 10:33).

That last line of verse 13 is something I've witnessed too many times. Even among Christians we see some who conceive a lie for their own advancement or gain, and then utter from the heart lying words. I've looked into the eyes of individuals and asked them about a sin they were involved in and had them answer without blinking that they weren't. Every time the sin eventually becomes known, but in the meantime, damage is done to the reputation of the church and an excuse given to those who want to deny the validity of the Gospel (Luke 6:46).

¹⁴ Justice is turned back, and righteousness stands far away; for truth has stumbled in the public squares, and uprightness cannot enter. ¹⁵ᵃ Truth is lacking, and he who departs from evil makes himself a prey. Isaiah 59:14-15a The rest of the chapter tells us God's description of the general condition of man and what He intends to do about it. He first addresses the injustice and denial of truth. Ideology can be idiotology. It can blind people to the truth, and it often results in a purposeful denial of truth. The whistle blowers are persecuted. The Christians are called bigots for pointing out the facts. Those ISIS members who have a revelation of Jesus are likely to be beheaded. He who departs from evil makes himself a prey (2 Timothy 3:12). Been there!

¹⁵ᵇ The LORD saw it, and it displeased him that there was no justice. ¹⁶ He saw that there was no man, and wondered that there was no one to intercede; then his own arm brought him salvation, and his righteousness upheld him. Isaiah 59:15b-16 God hates injustice! He hates it when the truth is denied and the godly are persecuted (Proverbs 12:22). He wondered that there was no one to intercede. Who can straighten out the mess in our world? I don't think this is addressing intercessory prayer as important as that is. It is expressing amazement that with the multitude of people on the earth and the abundance of truth God presents to us, no one has stood up and been the answer to the injustice of this world.

The only answer is the God/man, the arm of the LORD (Isaiah 53:1), Christ Jesus. He is the source of eternal justice for our sins and final justice for the sins of the unrepentant world as well. He is the Captain of the Hosts (Joshua 5:14). He is the One who fought and won on Calvary for all who will come to Him. And He will fight and win the Battle of Armageddon (Revelation 19:11-16). All will stand before His judgment seat.

17 He put on righteousness as a breastplate, and a helmet of salvation on his head; he put on garments of vengeance for clothing, and wrapped himself in zeal as a cloak. Isaiah 59:17 The beginning of this verse reminds us of the armor we are to put on, which is listed in Ephesians 6:10-17. The last half of the verse is what He alone wears so well, garments of vengeance. Remember vengeance belongs to the Lord alone (Deuteronomy 32:35), as He is the only One who can administer it in justice. He wraps Himself in zeal as a cloak. He is zealous for justice to reign, for all wrongs to be righted, and to have truth and righteousness prevail in the earth. As much as we desire it, we can know He desires it even more. The disciples saw just a glimpse of it when Jesus cleansed the temple. They remembered the verse, "Zeal for your house has consumed you" (John 2:17) and *we* are His house.

18 According to their deeds, so will he repay, wrath to his adversaries, repayment to his enemies; to the coastlands he will render repayment. Isaiah 59:18 This is justice for the world! Repayment is inevitable because God is just. If our sins are not covered by His atonement, they will meet repayment at His hand. To all those who fight goodness and resist righteousness, repayment for every deed will be rendered.

19 So they shall fear the name of the LORD from the west, and his glory from the rising of the sun; for he will come like a rushing stream, which the wind of the LORD drives. Isaiah 59:19 In Isaiah 57:11 God asked if they had no fear of God because He held off His judgment. When He delivers justice to the world, there will be a worldwide fear of the LORD (Romans 2:6). His judgment will come like a flash flood driven by a tornado!

20 "And a Redeemer will come to Zion, to those in Jacob who turn from transgression," declares the LORD. Isaiah 59:20 Jesus will come to reign in Zion. The Redeemer will come to the Jews who turn to Him in that time called Jacob's Trouble. Only one-third will have survived, but all those will turn to Him and be saved (Zechariah 13:8-9).

21 "And as for me, this is my covenant with them," says the LORD: "My Spirit that is upon you, and my words that I have put in your mouth, shall not depart out of your mouth, or out of the mouth of your offspring, or out of the mouth of your children's offspring," says the LORD, "from this time forth and forevermore." Isaiah 59:21 Isaiah's prophecy has gone from the reason the prayers of the hypocritical Jews were not answered to laying out all their sins and the consequences. They were not unlike the so called "godly" who go through religious routines but do not know the Lord. Then Isaiah predicted the return of the LORD to judge the earth and establish the kingdom of God. The Redeemer of chapter 53, who is our guilt offering and died for our sins, will make a new covenant with Israel (Isaiah 53:10; Hebrews 10:10). His Spirit will be upon them, His words will be in their mouths, and the mouths of the generations that follow. Isn't that one of the greatest desires of those who know the Lord, that their children will know Him as well? Israel's history of backsliding will be over. The cycle of sin, rebellion, repentance will finally end. The following chapters are glimpse into that time to come. This chapter has covered Isaiah's time to the near future. Only those who are living in Christ are ready for that day. Are you ready?

Questions
1 Give some reasons God doesn't answer prayer?
2 What is the connection with verse 3 and Psalm 8?
3 Are you surprised false lawsuits go back to 700BC?
4 Why is it so important to guard our thoughts?
5 What are "crooked roads" in Scripture?
6 Why do things seem dark to the wicked?
7 Why would we moan and complain?
8 Why does truth stumble in the public squares?
9 Why do those who depart from evil become a prey?
10 Summarize the chapter and its part in Isaiah.

Coming Kingdom - Isaiah 60

Our previous studies in Isaiah have shown us that there are multiple applications of many of the prophecies. That is not to say each prophecy was specifically for numerous times. In every case there is one specific fulfillment. However, there are intermediate applications that generally fit some of the prophetic predictions. That is the case with most of the prophecy we will look at today. Some of the wording would have been great encouragement to the people of Judah who were about to return from captivity in Babylon. Some of it sounds quite a bit like the coming of Jesus and the spread of the Gospel message. The very next verse after this chapter was quoted by Jesus as a prediction pertaining to Himself (Isaiah 61:1). But the specific wording of this chapter shows us that it is about the establishment of the Kingdom of God on the earth.

¹ Arise, shine, for your light has come, and the glory of the LORD has risen upon you. Isaiah 60:1 "Your Light" and "the glory of the LORD" is the same thing stated differently. The verse is expressing the same thing in two different ways. Isaiah chapter 9 verse 2 speaks of the Light being Jesus' ministry in the darkness of northern Galilee. For Jews light in general meant the blessing of God. For those reading these words in the time of the captivity, it would be read as the favor of the Lord returning to the Jewish people. Isaiah has already indicated that that time was coming (Isaiah 40:1-2).

For Christians since the time of Christ, it could be seen as God's favor on us because of the forgiveness we have received through Jesus. We shine because of His indwelling presence. When we express the fruits of the Spirit, people catch a glimpse of the glory of God (2 Corinthians 2:14). Like the rising sun gives light and warmth after a cold dark night, so the risen Son gives truth and grace to those who turn to Him (Malachi 4:2). This verse could be said to anyone who is ready to turn from self-reliance to faith in Jesus. It can be said to each of us as believers after we turn away, wallowing in self-pity but are ready to turn back to the Lord and have faith in Him. "Arise, shine for your Light has come, and the glory of the LORD is risen upon you!"

Can the Holy Spirit apply a verse out of its context and use the wording to speak to other situations? We have a good example of that in Matthew 2:15. Matthew tells us that baby Jesus return to Nazareth from Egypt was a fulfillment of a prophecy in Hosea (Hosea 11:1) when that verse specifically says it is about Israel. We should be very cautious to do so and be certain it is the Holy Spirit's leading, lest we abuse Scripture. Matthew was obviously led to do so and shows us in the process that Jesus is the true Israel (the One who prevails with God). Therefore, we can say to the person who has accepted Jesus as Lord of their life, "Arise, shine, for your Light (Jesus) has come, and the glory of the LORD is risen upon you!"

The context of this verse, however, is of the final conversion of the Jewish people and the establishment of the Kingdom of God on the earth. The captivity they experienced was not as severe as the future Great Tribulation. The Light will be the Messiah reigning in the heavenly city which will be established in Jerusalem.

2 For behold, darkness shall cover the earth, and thick darkness the peoples; but the LORD will arise upon you, and his glory will be seen upon you. 3 And nations shall come to your light, and kings to the brightness of your rising. Isaiah 60:2-3 "The darkest hour is just before the dawn" is not speaking of a physical condition. It's a spiritual one. Those in captivity would find that hope was waning just before their return. Those in Jesus' day thought the corruption of the priests and oppression of Rome was an unbearable combination. But the end of the Great Tribulation will seem as if all hope for mankind is gone. That is when the light dawns. That is when the Lord shows up and delivers the world from darkness. In the return of the Jews it was a physical deliverance and freedom. In the time of Christ to this day it is spiritual freedom. In the Second Coming it will mean both physical and spiritual deliverance (Zechariah 12:7-10).

Even verse 3 can be seen in the three different ways. Nations assisted in supplying material for rebuilding the temple. Kings and Queens have made pilgrimages to see the places Jesus ministered. But in the Millennial Kingdom, they will come to honor the King of kings and bring Him gifts and offerings (Zechariah 14:16).

4 Lift up your eyes all around, and see; they all gather together, they come to you; your sons shall come from afar, and your daughters shall be carried on the hip. Isaiah 60:4 Once again we see the return from the Babylonian captivity. It could also be seen as those coming into the family of God through the Gospel. Wherever you go in the world, you can find brothers and sisters in Christ. It could also be seen as the return to Israel in 1948. But the ultimate fulfilment will be when the gates of the heavenly city on earth are opened.

⁵ Then you shall see and be radiant; your heart shall thrill and exult, because the abundance of the sea shall be turned to you, the wealth of the nations shall come to you. ⁶ A multitude of camels shall cover you, the young camels of Midian and Ephah; all those from Sheba shall come. They shall bring gold and frankincense, and shall bring good news, the praises of the LORD. Isaiah 60:5-6 This could hardly be said of the return from Babylon, though there were taxes and physical goods offered up for the rebuilding of the temple (Ezra 6:3-10). You could say it was partially true when the wise men brought the gifts to baby Jesus (Matthew 2:11). The prosperity gospel would claim this for today, but the testimony of many saints show us that is not the case. This is the point where we begin to see the main application solely for that day to come.

There is quite a contrast here between the first readers in captivity and this prophecy. Though the Jews had done fairly well in captivity, they were still second-class citizens who lived under laws they often didn't agree with. This day that is predicted is a complete reversal of the suffering and ridicule the people of God have endured in this world. In that day the whole world will have to recognize that our message was the one true message. The gifts and good news the nations bring into New Jerusalem will be for the praises of the LORD. We will be honored as the beloved of the LORD. We will see all this and be radiant. Our hearts will thrill and exult! "Exult" means to be widened. It's the heart made large with joy! We will be so glad to know the whole world is under the reign of Christ, and that injustice has ceased, and that truth will no longer be ridiculed that we will shine with joy as hearts swell in our chests. I interpret the treasures to also mean those who turn to Christ as Lord and Savior in that age.

⁷ All the flocks of Kedar shall be gathered to you; the rams of Nebaioth shall minister to you; they shall come up with acceptance on my altar, and I will beautify my beautiful house. Isaiah 60:7 How could there be an altar in that day when Jesus has already been our sacrifice? Just as the Jews looked forward to the coming of the Lamb of God through the sacrifices, so in that day they will look back by means of the sacrifices to the greatest of all sacrifices, the cross. Zechariah predicted that in that day the world will celebrate the Feast of Booths (Zechariah 14:16). That feast has prescribed sacrifices (Leviticus 23:33-36). While it did represent the Jews' wilderness journey to the Promised Land, perhaps in that day it will represent our journey through life in the tents of our mortal bodies to the heavenly promised land.

⁸ Who are these that fly like a cloud, and like doves to their windows? Isaiah 60:8 We could see in this verse the three interpretations we've seen in some of the other verses. It could be the blessed return from Babylon to Jerusalem. It could also be seen as those who come to hear the Gospel. But ultimately it will be the rapture of church as she is transformed into the bride of Christ (1 Thessalonians 4:17), New Jerusalem.

⁹ For the coastlands shall hope for me, the ships of Tarshish first, to bring your children from afar, their silver and gold with them, for the name of the LORD your God, and for the Holy One of Israel, because he has made you beautiful. ¹⁰ Foreigners shall build up your walls, and their kings shall minister to you; for in my wrath I struck you, but in my favor I have had mercy on you. Isaiah 60:9-10 The coastlands are the rest of the world. Many around the world have placed their hope in Jesus. He makes us beautiful for He is our covering. He transforms us from the inside out. He had favor on the Jews at the return to Jerusalem, in the coming of Jesus, but especially when all Israel will be saved (Romans 11:26).

¹¹ Your gates shall be open continually; day and night they shall not be shut, that people may bring to you the wealth of the nations, with their kings led in procession. Isaiah 60:11 Now the prophecy is moving clearly and solely into the Millennial Kingdom. This verse along with some of the others are quoted or alluded to in the description of New Jerusalem. Here is the book of Revelation's parallel to this verse and some of the previous thoughts. *²⁵ On no day will its gates ever be shut, for there will be no night there. ²⁶ The glory and honor of the nations will be brought into it.* Revelation 21:25-26 (NIV) Open gates mean there is no threat of conquest. After Armageddon none will dare attempt it until the end of a thousand years when it will be too distant to remember.

¹² For the nation and kingdom that will not serve you shall perish; those nations shall be utterly laid waste. Isaiah 60:12 The Jewish nation ceased for 1900 years. The Roman Empire ended. The Soviet Union fell apart. ISIS is next. You don't mess with God's people and get away with it (Zechariah 2:8).

¹³ The glory of Lebanon shall come to you, the cypress, the plane, and the pine, to beautify the place of my sanctuary, and I will make the place of my feet glorious. Isaiah 60:13 (See 1 Kings 5; Ezekiel 40-42) The place of God's feet is a reference to the temple. It could be interpreted on all three levels. The temple the Jews restored which was renovated by Herod the Great was said to be one of the wonders of the world. The temple built in the Tribulation period will no doubt be incredible. Jesus is the temple of the New Jerusalem (Revelation 21:22).

¹⁴ The sons of those who afflicted you shall come bending low to you, and all who despised you shall bow down at your feet; they shall call you the City of the LORD, the Zion of the Holy One of Israel. Isaiah 60:14 Again we see the great reversal. Israel's captors were defeated, and those who resist the Gospel and persecute believers now and in the Great Tribulation will bow down at our feet. We will be called the city of the LORD, as seen in Revelation 21 (Revelation 21:9-11). We have now seen the title "The Holy One of Israel" in all three sections of Isaiah, which attests to its continuity.

15 Whereas you have been forsaken and hated, with no one passing through, I will make you majestic forever, a joy from age to age. Isaiah 60:15 This can only be fulfilled in the Millennial Kingdom. It is for the bride of Christ and speaks of our eternal reign with Him (Revelation 22:5). What a contrast from where the readers were, and even those in the time of Christ. (See last half of vs 17.) "Passing through" may refer to conquering armies or it could refer to the way the temple was abused. The location of the temple in Jerusalem and the topography of the city resulted in a short cut route right through the temple from one side of the city to the other. This was one of Jesus' contentions with the way the outer court was misused. Not passing through would mean you only came before the throne to worship and nothing else (Revelation 21:27). I imagine so, with Jesus physically present in His glory! Who would dare?

16 You shall suck the milk of nations; you shall nurse at the breast of kings; and you shall know that I, the LORD, am your Savior and your Redeemer, the Mighty One of Jacob. Isaiah 60:16 We can clearly see here that the language is figurative, for kings don't lactate. ☺ The whole world will honor the LORD and His bride. In that day there will be no doubt that YHWH, the eternal God of Israel, is Jesus, the Savior, the One who redeemed us on the cross. He is also call the Mighty One of Jacob. That may be alluding to the fact that it is all by grace. Jacob was the conniving rascal who tried to cut deals with God (Genesis 28:20-22). But God's grace prevailed and made Jacob one of the patriarchs, just like His grace prevails in our lives to make us sons and daughters of God (1 Corinthians 15:10).

17 Instead of bronze I will bring gold, and instead of iron I will bring silver; instead of wood, bronze, instead of stones, iron. I will make your overseers peace and your taskmasters righteousness. Isaiah 60:17 We won't have second best in that day. Everything for the bride of Christ will be a step above. We may go without in this life, but we will never have anything but the best when Jesus reigns. Once again the contrast is drawn between their condition in captivity in Babylon and Egypt, with that coming day. Their overseers and taskmasters abused and drove them. In the coming age the overseers are peace and the taskmasters are righteousness.

18 Violence shall no more be heard in your land, devastation or destruction within your borders; you shall call your walls Salvation, and your gates Praise. Isaiah 60:18 No more violence or destruction for us! Gun laws won't do it, politicians won't, and religion can't; Jesus must reign. That is because our walls are called Yeshua, the name of Jesus! Our gates are called Praise, and we enter His courts with praise (Psalm 100:4).

19 The sun shall be no more your light by day, nor for brightness shall the moon give you light; but the LORD will be your everlasting light, and your God will be your glory. Isaiah 60:19 This verse is also quoted as pertaining to New Jerusalem. *23 And the city has no need of sun or moon to shine on it, for the glory of God gives it light, and its lamp is the Lamb.*

Revelation 21:23 The Shekinah that lit the Holy of Holies will illuminate the entire city! Our glory will be God Himself! (Also see Revelation 22:5.)

²⁰ Your sun shall no more go down, nor your moon withdraw itself; for the LORD will be your everlasting light, and your days of mourning shall be ended. Isaiah 60:20 The LORD will be our *everlasting* light! Every scar on our hearts will be gone (Revelation 21:4). Everything for which we grieve will be forgotten. We will be overwhelmed by His presence and the ever-increasing knowledge of His love for us.

²¹ Your people shall all be righteous; they shall possess the land forever, the branch of my planting, the work of my hands, that I might be glorified. Isaiah 60:21 Israel as a branch is finally rooted and productive in spite of their past, for the grace of God has prevailed. The branch also refers to Jesus in several instances. This may then refer to the body of Christ, Gentile grafted into Jewish roots (Romans 11:23). All this is for the purpose of glorifying God. The wonder of what He has done with us displays His glory.

²² The least one shall become a clan, and the smallest one a mighty nation; I am the LORD; in its time I will hasten it. Isaiah 60:22 The captivity wasn't the end of Israel. The persecution of believers wasn't the end of Christianity. The Great Tribulation will not end in Satan being victorious (Revelation 20:10). God has destined us to be fruitful. When the time has come, it will proceed with haste, Jesus said it will be like that of woman in labor (Matthew 24:8). I can't help but feeling that time is near.

> Questions
> 1 What are the three applications of much of this chapter?
> 2 How may verse one apply to any believer?
> 3 What kind of deliverance is meant in verses 2-3?
> 4 How could there be an altar in that day?
> 5 What are three interpretations of verse 8?
> 6 How can we be sure of verse 11 interpretation?
> 7 What is the great reversal of 14 and 15?
> 8 Why may God use the name "Mighty One of Jacob"?
> 9 What are the walls, gates, and light of that city?
> 10 What is the purpose of all this?

Coming Kingdom part 2 - Isaiah 61

Almost two thousand years ago there was a small village of about four hundred residents. They named their town the Branch because they were all descendants of King David. Branch was used in the manner we use it in a family tree. There were prophecies dating back a thousand years earlier that it was this family line from which would come an individual man who would change the course of history and reign forever (Isaiah 11:1-2; 9:7). The anticipation of His coming had reached a fevered pitch. Even the non-Jewish world expected a great king to arise in Israel.

Thirty years earlier there were rumors of angelic visitations and messages (Luke 1:32-33). A young woman in the town claimed to have miraculously conceived a child. Some thought it might be true, but most thought that it was just to cover up relations she had had with the man who later married her. Certainly her Son was a decent and honest man, but he showed no desire for warfare. He never even complained about the oppression and taxation of Rome. He was more of a studious type of person. When his father died, he faithfully went to work each day as a builder for the Greeks in the nearby city of Sephoris to support the family.

Sometime later, John the Baptist began preaching in the wilderness of Judea. Expectations of the coming Messiah rose even higher. After all, if this one to come would overthrew the Romans and set up His kingdom, the entire city of the Branch would be favored as the royal family. Surely, they would be freed from all taxation. Some thought it might be John the Baptist, but John denied it (John 1:20).

One day, the quiet man, the one whose mother claimed he was miraculously conceived, left his work and traveled south. He had gone to Judea to be baptized by John the Baptist (John 1:29-30). When He returned a few months later, He had followers with Him. On the Sabbath, He was going to address the congregation in his hometown (Luke 4:16). What would He say about John? What would He say about the coming Savior? It was an excited village that gathered that Sabbath. He opened the scroll to the reading for that day. The portion He was to read was from the prophet Isaiah (the passage we refer to as chapter 61). He read, *[1] The Spirit of the Lord GOD is upon me, because the LORD has anointed me to bring good news to the poor; he has sent me to bind up the brokenhearted, to proclaim liberty to the captives, and the opening of the prison to those who are bound; [2a] to proclaim the year of the LORD's favor...* Isaiah 61:1-2a *[20] Then he rolled up the scroll, gave it back to the attendant and sat down. The eyes of everyone in the synagogue were fastened on him, [21] and he began by saying to them, "Today this scripture is fulfilled in your hearing."* Luke 4:20-21 (NIV) Whispering broke out everywhere. Maybe Mary was telling the truth. Maybe Yeshua was named salvation because He really was the One! Excitement began to build. The whispers turned to a rumble of conversation. What an amazing passage to apply to Himself! Maybe the muscles He developed working with stone could be used to swing a sword in victory, like the time Jonathan and his armor bearer routed the Philistines. Was this the year of the Lord's favor on the town called "Branch." *[23] Jesus said to them, "Surely you will quote this proverb to me: 'Physician, heal yourself! Do here in your hometown what we have heard that you did in Capernaum.'" [24] "I tell you the truth," he continued, "no prophet is accepted in his hometown. [25] I assure you that there were many widows in Israel in Elijah's time, when the sky was shut for three and a half years and there was a severe famine throughout the land. [26] Yet Elijah was not sent to any of them, but to a widow in Zarephath in the region of Sidon. [27] And there were many in Israel with leprosy in the time of Elisha the prophet, yet not one of them was cleansed--*

only Naaman the Syrian." [28] All the people in the synagogue were furious when they heard this. [29] They got up, drove him out of the town, and took him to the brow of the hill on which the town was built, in order to throw him down the cliff. [30] But he walked right through the crowd and went on his way. Luke 4:23-30 (NIV) This was the rejection of Jesus in his hometown of Nazareth which brought about His move to Capernaum, a more central location for His ministry.

The first verses of our chapter today are like many of the prophetic passages about the Messiah. It has predictions of both the first and second coming. It speaks on different levels with multiple applications. The emphasis is on the preaching of good news (Matthew 11:5). Those words are behind our word "gospel." As Jesus quoted verse one and a portion of verse 2, we know it was specifically meant for His first coming. The liberation he was proclaiming was not physical as the people had hoped, but rather was a spiritual one. When Jesus clarified that point by references to the Old Testament explaining that the Gentiles would be more willing to accept Him, they became angry. Their excitement turned to rage and an attempted execution. They thought, "How dare He say they would reject the Messiah, but Gentiles would seek Him?"

The physical deliverance they were hoping for will come at the Second Coming which is evidenced by the very point where Jesus stopped reading. The part He did not read was, *[2b] and the day of vengeance of our God;* Isaiah 61:2b The Second Coming is the day of vengeance. Jesus understood the two separate events. He predicted that on that day at the Second Coming all the tribes of the earth would mourn when they see His sign in the sky (Matthew 24:30). Jesus is rejected now for the same reason He was rejected then. He doesn't offer what the world is looking for. He didn't come to give us what we desire. He came to deliver us from sin and bring us into a relationship with God. The Day of the LORD is a day of vengeance upon evil (Zephaniah 1:14-18).

to comfort all who mourn; [3] to grant to those who mourn in Zion— to give them a beautiful headdress instead of ashes, the oil of gladness instead of mourning, the garment of praise instead of a faint spirit; that they may be called oaks of righteousness, the planting of the LORD, that he may be glorified. Isaiah 61:2c-3 Who are these mourning in Zion. Zechariah, who prophesied over a century after Isaiah gives us the answer. *[10] "And I will pour out on the house of David and the inhabitants of Jerusalem a spirit of grace and supplication. They will look on me, the one they have pierced, and they will mourn for him as one mourns for an only child, and grieve bitterly for him as one grieves for a firstborn son.* Zechariah 12:10 (NIV) A few verses later we are told of the comfort they receive. *[1] "On that day a fountain will be opened to the house of David and the inhabitants of Jerusalem, to cleanse them from sin and impurity.* Zechariah 13:1 (NIV) In the Last Days, in an act of final desperation, the Jewish people will turn to Jesus at His return and be delivered from the enemies that were about to annihilate them.

What is this beautiful headdress they wear instead of ashes? Isaiah has already told us. *⁵ In that day the LORD Almighty will be a glorious crown, a beautiful wreath for the remnant of his people.* Isaiah 28:5 (NIV) The glory of the LORD will be our crown! I don't separate this Jewish remnant from the rest of the body of Christ. In Him we are one (Ephesians 2:13-18). Though some of these prophecies are specifically about events in their future, salvation gives us a unity that is inseparable. Gladness and praise is the result of our salvation. Joy in the Lord is for every believer regardless of what we endure. It is the deep abiding realization that we are forgiven and loved. Nothing can change that. Oaks of righteousness, a planting of the Lord speaks of our being firmly rooted and strong "for the glory of the LORD," or it can be translated, "that He might display His beauty."

⁴ They shall build up the ancient ruins; they shall raise up the former devastations; they shall repair the ruined cities, the devastations of many generations. Isaiah 61:4 The captives in Babylon probably took this as applying to their return, but the rest of the chapter gives us a definite wording that applies to an ultimate fulfillment when the Kingdom of God is established on earth. Throughout Israel today there are mounds of ancient cities that were abandoned. One day Israel will be so full that these will all be rebuilt. The words "many generations" tell us this was for a distant time yet to come.

⁵ Strangers shall stand and tend your flocks; foreigners shall be your plowmen and vinedressers; Isaiah 61:5 The USA and a few other affluent nations import much of their manual laborers. This is speaking of the future prosperity of the people of God in the Millennial Kingdom. The next verse explains why we will be served.

⁶ but you shall be called the priests of the LORD; they shall speak of you as the ministers of our God; you shall eat the wealth of the nations, and in their glory you shall boast. Isaiah 61:6 Just as the Levitical priests were to be supported by the people, so they could devote themselves to ministering to the LORD (Numbers 18:24), so in the Millennial Kingdom we will be supported as we minister to the LORD and to the nations. God always intended His people to be priests in both the old and new covenant eras (Exodus 19:6; 1Peter 2:9) This is that great reversal in the last chapter (Isaiah 60:5).

⁷ Instead of your shame there shall be a double portion; instead of dishonor they shall rejoice in their lot; therefore in their land they shall possess a double portion; they shall have everlasting joy. Isaiah 61:7 Once again, the idea of the great reversal is emphasized. Perhaps God was driving it home so that the captives in Babylon would have hope for the future. Surely it has given hope to the persecuted people of God since it was first written. I can imagine the believers in the Middle East today clinging to this passage. Dishonor and shame are often the lot of the believer in this life (2 Timothy 3:12). We see things differently from the world. Our hope is not here. We will not compromise. We speak the truth in love (Ephesians 4:15).

We should not be living for the praise of man, and that means we will inevitably make enemies. In Pakistan the Christians can only find jobs as laborers. I have had friends who lost their business or job when it became known that they were Christians. Even this Christmas season a friend told me that at an Amazon shipment center there were Muslim and Jewish Holiday signs but no Christian signs, though many of the workers were Christians. Why do they think it was their busiest season? In that day there won't be any other gods mentioned. Everyone will know there is but one true God (Zechariah 14:9).

The double portion is mentioned two other places in the Bible. One is for the firstborn son's inheritance so that he can carry on the responsibilities of the family. The other was Elisha asking for twice the anointing of Elijah (2 Kings 2:9). We can see the spiritual and physical overlap. This Kingdom double portion will surely be both. We will be anointed to minister to a greater extent than we have ever witnessed, and every good thing we can use will be ours.

8 For I the LORD love justice; I hate robbery and wrong; I will faithfully give them their recompense, and I will make an everlasting covenant with them. Isaiah 61:8 God will deal out justice as each person deserves, whether blessing or punishment (Isaiah 4010). God's sense of justice is something impartial, for which we should be very grateful (1 Kings 8:39). Injustice today is one of the most discouraging aspects of this fallen world. It is one of the things atheists point to when trying to prove there is no God. But God says the day is coming when He will indeed settle the books (Matthew 16:27). We saw in previous verses that the return of the LORD will result in salvation for the remnant of the Jews (Romans 11:23). They will enter the same everlasting covenant that we have entered through faith in Jesus.

9 Their offspring shall be known among the nations, and their descendants in the midst of the peoples; all who see them shall acknowledge them, that they are an offspring the LORD has blessed. Isaiah 61:9 I don't believe the resurrected saints of New Jerusalem will be having children in the Millennium, so what is this referring to? Could it be those Jews who are converted at the return of the Lord, who enter the Millennial Kingdom without dying? Or it may be that all the children of the blessed of the Lord in their resurrected state are honored? I tend to think it is referring to the former. These who survive the Great Tribulation and enter the Millennium will have children, grow old and die, and receive their heavenly bodies in the second resurrection (Revelation 20:5; Isaiah 65:20).

10 I will greatly rejoice in the LORD; my soul shall exult in my God, for he has clothed me with the garments of salvation; he has covered me with the robe of righteousness, as a bridegroom decks himself like a priest with a beautiful headdress, and as a bride adorns herself with her jewels. Isaiah 61:10 Isaiah sees what is to come and is overwhelmed with gratitude. He doesn't just rejoice; he *greatly* rejoices! His soul spins around in joy. I had a Labrador that would whirl around in circles when I would return home after a long time away. That is what Isaiah says his soul will do. The reason for this joy is that he has been clothed in the garments of salvation.

Jesus tells the story of a wedding feast in which a man entered without the robe given to all the guests. He must have come in the back door. He was promptly thrown out (Matthew 22:11-12). Paul tells us to put on the Lord Jesus Christ and make no provision for our flesh to fulfill its lusts (Romans 13:14). With such a future before us, are you sure you are clothed with the garments of salvation? Does your soul whirl for joy for what God has done for us?

¹¹ For as the earth brings forth its sprouts, and as a garden causes what is sown in it to sprout up, so the Lord GOD will cause righteousness and praise to sprout up before all the nations. Isaiah 61:11 What Israel and the church failed to do, God will accomplish in His time. Even then, the nations will have a choice. We must respond to the opportunity that is set before us. When we witness truth and are given grace we must respond. Righteousness and praise sprout up before us. Is the world witnessing it sprout up on our lives today? Will you be among those with a double portion in that day?

Questions
1 What did Nazareth expect?
2 Where had Jesus been before returning to Nazareth?
3 Why did the mood in the synagogue change?
4 Why did Jesus stop reading where He did?
5 Why was Jesus rejected then and now?
6 Who will mourn in Zion? Why?
7 What comfort do they receive?
8 Describe the great reversal?
9 Why are we a part of this?
10 What is our crown? Our clothing? Our response?

The Lord's Delight - Isaiah 62

I could have entitled this Coming Kingdom Part 3, but I chose to emphasize one particular aspect of what is to come by entitling it The Lord's Delight. In the last two chapters we've seen the promises of that kingdom that is to come and our amazing role in it. Isaiah continues in this chapter to expand on that theme.

¹ For Zion's sake I will not keep silent, and for Jerusalem's sake I will not be quiet, until her righteousness goes forth as brightness, and her salvation as a burning torch. Isaiah 62:1 The people, the city, and the land are all spoken of as one. Zion was originally the fortified hill in Jerusalem between the Kidron and Tyropean valleys. In Scripture "Zion" is used to refer to that hill, or to all of Jerusalem, or to the entire covenant people (Isaiah 1:27; Psalm 97:8). We can see that usage in the description of New

Jerusalem in Revelation 21:1-3. The city of peace is the people of God who have peace with Him through Jesus (Romans 5:1). In the Psalms and Lamentations Zion is almost always referring to the city of God in the new age. It is the dwelling place of God. In that, we again see it as the hearts of those who are His. What makes Zion so special is that God resides there (Isaiah 8:18).

God is declaring that He is not going to be silent or quiet for Zion or Jerusalem's sake. The first two lines are Hebrew parallelism, saying the same thing in two different ways. God will keep speaking. His words create. His words are creating is His ultimate creation, the bride of Christ. She must not only be redeemed; she must be transformed. While her positional righteousness comes from Jesus' sacrifice, her experiential righteousness comes by the transforming power of the Spirit speaking to us, changing the way we think (Romans 12:2), convicting us of certain actions and words, which causes our righteousness to shine brighter and brighter (Proverbs 4:18; Philippians 1:6). In God's eyes we are clothed in the righteousness of Jesus. In our day to day experience, we find we fall far short of Christ likeness. But God is at work in us. And He is going to keep speaking to our spirits and growing us *if* we are willing to listen. This is the application for us today. It results in preparation for our future, a time when the saints will reign over the earth in the Millennial Kingdom.

Isaiah has spoken of this future shining of the people of God a number of times (Isaiah 58:8, 60:1) Scripture speaks of the shining of God's face which is brilliance of His glory (Numbers 6:25). When we reign with Christ over the earth, we will be His perfect representatives (2 Timothy 2:12). Glory is the outshining of perfect attributes, the fruit of the Spirit. While in our day we hear people's excuses for rejecting Christ to include the hypocrisy of people who say they are Christians, in that day there will be no excuse. Our salvation will stand out as a burning torch. It should today! The more we let the transforming voice of the Spirit convict and guide us, the more we will shine even now.

[2] *The nations shall see your righteousness, and all the kings your glory, and you shall be called by a new name that the mouth of the LORD will give.* Isaiah 62:2 There have been those through history who so shined with the light of Jesus that nations saw their righteousness and kings sought them out. Even today there are believers who are invited to speak to the UN and to national leaders. We should pray for these people, like Franklin Graham, Ravi Zacharias, and Joel Rosenberg. Wouldn't it be wonderful if it were said of you? It will be! When God's work in us is complete, when we reign with Christ, the nations will see your righteousness and all the kings your glory. Do you grasp the fact that this is truly our destiny?

In Jesus' letter to the church of Pergamum and Philadelphia, the conquerors (overcomers) are promised a new name, given to them from the LORD (Revelation 2:17; 3:12). In the latter case, the name of God, the name of the city of God, and Jesus' new name is written on them. Roman slaves in the first century were branded with the name of their owner. The

328

more important the owner, the more respect and deference given them in the marketplace. Though we are the bride of Christ, we serve Him as His helpmeet (Genesis 2:18). We wear His name. We come with His authority. Imagine the respect that we will be given as the servants of the Creator of all!

Even now we wear His name. When people know you are a Christian, they think of you as representing Him. We represent Him in how we drive, how we speak, in our priorities, in our compassion or lack thereof. How are you wearing His name? Are you attracting others to Him? No doubt some will be repelled by what you represent, even when you represent Him faithfully. But we certainly don't want to repel those who are seeking or open to the truth.

To the conquerors of Pergamum, a white stone was promised with their new name. It is, I believe, a name unique to each individual, and I suspect is a name that has to do with our personal relationship with Jesus, as He and you alone know it. I think both new names are referred to here in verse 2, the name by which the world refers to us and Jesus' personal name for you. As a new creation, you will receive a new name (2 Corinthians 5:17).

³ You shall be a crown of beauty in the hand of the LORD, and a royal diadem in the hand of your God. Isaiah 62:3 When Jesus has finished His work in us, when we see Him in glory, we will be the crowning beauty of God's creation. All the scars of sin will be gone. Aren't there times when you get frustrated with your failure to keep your thoughts and words pure and unselfish? Don't you sometimes feel like you just aren't growing in Christ as you should and wonder if you'll ever be what He is calling you to be? This verse tells us we will be a crown of beauty in His hand (Zechariah 9:16). He who began a good work in you will be faithful to complete it (Philippians 1:6). There will be no flaw in us (Romans 7:24-25).

What is more, we will be a royal diadem in God's hand. That is the rod of ruling authority. Because the work in us is completed, we can faithfully represent God in caring out justice with His authority in that day. Whereas we were once at the mercy of courts of those who accept bribes and judge by personal preference, we will judge with the righteous justice of all-knowing God. That is the implication of being a diadem in God's hand.

⁴ You shall no more be termed Forsaken, and your land shall no more be termed Desolate, but you shall be called My Delight Is in Her, and your land Married; for the LORD delights in you, and your land shall be married. Isaiah 62:4 The Jews in captivity felt they were the forsaken of God. The land of Israel was desolate. Christians today and throughout history have felt the same at times. I'm sure the Syrian and Iraqi Christians would say it is true of them today. We can be looked down on in our own culture because we do not conform to the contemporary acceptable attitudes of our culture. But as we saw in previous chapters, the great reversal is coming (Isaiah 61:7).

In that day, people will call us Hephzibah (God delights in us). It will be obvious to the entire world that we are the ones in whom God delights. That thought of being God's delight should be a great motivating encouragement to us all to persevere through the times of being called "Forsaken."

Our land being called Beulah, which is to say Married, means that God is in covenant with us to make us fruitful. Heaven would be boring if we had nothing to do. Yes, we will be quite occupied with worship of our Redeemer, but He is going to have assignments for us. The book of Revelation tells us that His servants will serve Him (Revelation 22:3). We won't be sitting around on clouds with harps. We will have productive and enjoyable work to accomplish for God's glory.

5 For as a young man marries a young woman, so shall your sons marry you, and as the bridegroom rejoices over the bride, so shall your God rejoice over you. Isaiah 62:5 This is poetical imagery of the inhabitants of Zion cherishing their city. Children will often plan to leave the place they grew up and desire some other city that looks like it has greener grass. That won't be so in New Jerusalem. Since it is made up of the people of God and the very presence of Christ, our love for one another and Jesus will forever be a part of our eternal home. How could we not love it as it is a place of joy, delight, righteousness, peace, and beauty?

Jesus, our groom, will delight in us! It's almost as if God knew this would be hard for us to fathom, so He repeats it again. He delights in us now, for He sees us clothed in the righteousness of God (2 Corinthians 5:21). He delights in the finished work He sees even now, what we are becoming by faith (1 John 3:2). Our love for Him will only grow as we realize how great His love is for us.

ESV Study Bible notes comment, "Isaiah explains that in God's great plan of salvation, he not only forgives his people, protects them, heals them, provides for them, restores them to their home, reconciles them to each other, transforms them so they are righteous, honors them, exalts them above all nations, and makes them a blessing to all nations, as he called them to be—but more than all these things, he actually *delights* in his people."

6 On your walls, O Jerusalem, I have set watchmen; all the day and all the night they shall never be silent. You who put the LORD in remembrance, take no rest, Isaiah 62:6 The chapter began with God saying He would not be silent until our righteousness shines forth and our salvation like a blazing torch. One way He does that is through His watchmen. Watchmen stand on the walls of the city and keep lookout for the enemies that would sneak up to conquer and take us captive.

The walls are the boundary lines between the city and the world. In a previous chapter the walls were salvation, that is Yeshua (Isaiah 60:18). These watchmen are preachers and evangelists who standing on the rock of Christ Jesus proclaiming the Gospel message. They warn people by reminding them that there is a holy and righteous God who will hold us all to account for what we have done with Jesus (Romans 14:12). What did we do

330

with the grace and faith given to us? The watchmen warn of the enemy of idolatry that would take our souls captive. Isaiah was one of those watchmen. As watchmen, we are to continually and faithfully declare the message without compromising with the ever-changing currents of this world (1 John 2:17).

⁷ and give him no rest until he establishes Jerusalem and makes it a praise in the earth. Isaiah 62:7 We are not only to proclaim to the world without rest, but we are to give God no rest by continually praying for our work to be fruitful that souls might come into the kingdom. When that last soul enters in (2 Peter 3:9), God will establish Jerusalem, the city of God, the people of God, making them a praise in the earth.

⁸ The LORD has sworn by his right hand and by his mighty arm: "I will not again give your grain to be food for your enemies, and foreigners shall not drink your wine for which you have labored; ⁹ But those who garner it shall eat it and praise the LORD, and those who gather it shall drink it in the courts of my sanctuary." Isaiah 62:8,9 YHWH swears by Jesus, who is His right hand and mighty arm, the robbery of the past, physical and spiritual, the stealing away by evil birds of the seed we planted in the hearts of men will be a thing of the past. The saved souls in the Millennial Kingdom will immediately enter New Jerusalem and be secure (Matthew 13:4). All our labor will bear fruit and be a blessing to us. There will be no more frustrated endeavors. We will no longer be misled into programs that don't bear fruit. Every work will be fruitful and glorify our Savior.

¹⁰ Go through, go through the gates; prepare the way for the people; build up, build up the highway; clear it of stones; lift up a signal over the peoples. Isaiah 62:10 These are the saints of New Jerusalem heading out of the city to prepare the way of salvation for the multitude that will come into the kingdom. We first saw this in chapter 57 verse 14. *¹⁴ And it shall be said, "Build up, build up, prepare the way, remove every obstruction from my people's way."* Every stone of false teaching will be removed. Every excuse of hypocrisy will be cleared away. The choice will be as plain as it could possibly be. That is why at the end of the Millennium, Satan will so easily convince the world to come against New Jerusalem (Revelation 20:7-8). The people will have already have made their choice and entered in or chosen to remain outside.

The signal we raise is the exaltation of the Lord Jesus. He was declared to be that signal in Isaiah 11:10 *¹⁰ In that day the root of Jesse, who shall stand as a signal for the peoples—of him shall the nations inquire, and his resting place shall be glorious.* Jesus is the root of Jesse, who was the father of David. The nations can come to inquire of the glorified Christ before they decide to accept or reject His grace.

¹¹ Behold, the LORD has proclaimed to the end of the earth: Say to the daughter of Zion, "Behold, your salvation comes; behold, his reward is with him, and his recompense before him." Isaiah 62:11 The daughter of Zion was a term sometimes used in addressing the people in captivity (Isaiah

52:2). They had been forced out of Zion. God proclaims to the end of the earth and to the captives, "Your Savior is coming. His reward is with Him and His recompense before Him." This is the Second Coming. While we could see it applied to the return or to the first coming, for He brought the reward of salvation to those who would accept Him, the language is of the final White Throne Judgment (Revelation 20:11-12). The righteous will be rewarded for their labors. Those who reject Christ will receive the recompense their deeds deserve. All books will be settled. Justice will be complete and final.

12 And they shall be called The Holy People, The Redeemed of the LORD; and you shall be called Sought Out, A City Not Forsaken. Isaiah 62:12 "They" refers back to the daughter of Zion. While they were despised at the time, a day will come when the world will refer to God's children as the Holy People, the Redeemed of the Lord. We will be called Sought Out. Instead of trying to get people to listen to the Gospel, and waiting for opportunities, people will be coming to us to hear the Good News. Instead of being the forsaken ones, we will be called A City Not Forsaken. This is the glorious future of those called "My Delight is in Her," those who have placed their faith in Jesus. Will you be among them?

Questions
1 What is Zion?
2 Who won't keep quiet? Why?
3 How is the bride made ready?
4 What is the "new name"?
5 What were we called? What will we be called?
6 What does "sons marry you" mean?
7 Why repeat that God will delight in us?
8 What is a watchman?
9 What is the promise to us?
10 Why do we prepare a road? How do we?

Day of Vengeance - Isaiah 63

Chapter 59 of Isaiah told us of Israel's unfaithfulness, but ended with God's faithfulness to save them and His promise to judge their enemies who are His enemies as well. Chapters 60 through 62 told us of the coming Kingdom of God. The first six verses of 63 tell us what will take place between the salvation of the Jewish people and the setting up of the kingdom, in other words, the details of the promise given through Isaiah in 59:19b. *19b For he will come like a pent-up flood that the breath of the LORD drives along.* Isaiah 59:19b (NIV) What imagery of Jesus' zeal for justice!

1 Who is this who comes from Edom, in crimsoned garments from Bozrah, he who is splendid in his apparel, marching in the greatness of his strength? "It is I, speaking in righteousness, mighty to save." Isaiah 63:1 Edom was in what is today Jordan. Edom was settled by the older twin brother of Jacob whose name was Esau but was also called Edom. The name comes from Adam, which means "red." Bozrah means sheep pen. It is a small village today near Petra. Much of what I will share in this sermon is speculation, trying to understand the Bible's prophetic details of the end-times.

The Edomites were often enemies of Israel. This passage may be using Edom to refer to all of the enemies of the Lord, in which case Armageddon and Edom would be the same. However, I'm going to present a different scenario. Since Bozrah was the capitol of Edom, I believe it is speaking of that literal location in today's Jordan.

When we look at the passages about Armageddon, that final battle of the world gathered against Jesus, Joel chapter 3, and Revelation 19, there are a number of terms that show up in this chapter of Isaiah. Common terms include, treading the winepress, wrath of God, all the nations, and great quantities of blood. The problem I encountered is that Edom is southeast of Israel and Armageddon is in northern Israel.

Isaiah chapter 34 gives us this same language of this Day of Vengeance but says the slaughter takes place in Edom (Isaiah 34:6). *6b For the LORD has a sacrifice in Bozrah, a great slaughter in the land of Edom.* Isaiah 34:6b Whenever I find what appears to be contradictions, I search for the way to bring it all together into a more complete picture (2 Timothy 2:15). Those who don't believe the Bible just say it is proof that the Bible isn't inspired by God. Those of us who do believe it is inspired by God seek to understand what points we are missing. One side says they know it all. The other says they need to know more (Proverbs 22:4).

For example, the gospels list a different group of women going to Jesus' tomb (Matthew 28:1; Mark 16:1). The skeptic says, "Aha! See the error." The believer says, "Oh, that woman was there also." To the believer it is proof that the writers didn't collaborate to make up a story. To the skeptic, it is evidence they fabricated the story. We see the same thing but come to different conclusions. Both conclusions are faith based as neither of us were there. It helps to know that Jewish writers often only included the individuals they thought were essential to their account.

In our first verse, we are confronted with a question from the watchman on the wall in the last chapter (Isaiah 62:6). We are quickly given an answer. Who is this, coming from Edom in splendid clothing stained red, marching in great strength? He is the One giving the revelation to Isaiah. He is the One who is speaking in righteousness. He is mighty to save. The angel told Joseph to name the child Jesus, for He will save His people from their sins (Matthew 1:21). We know He will eventually save this world from the forces of evil. He is the ultimate superhero who rescues us.

Right now, Jordan/Edom is mostly Muslim, but it is a fairly safe haven for Christians as far as Middle Eastern countries go. We are welcomed to visit Petra. Refugee camps there are sometimes infiltrated by radicals, but Jordan keeps a close eye on it. So why would there need to be a slaughter in Edom? As we watch Russia in league with Iran invading Syria, we are seeing end-time predictions fall into place (Ezekiel 38:14-16). Russia now has a base from which to invade Israel. But this situation in Jordan doesn't quite seem to fit prophecy, at least not yet. Things can change suddenly as we have recently seen.

² Why is your apparel red, and your garments like his who treads in the winepress? Isaiah 63:2 The watchman asks Jesus why His splendid apparel is red like someone who has trod the winepress? Now we have a clear link to the battle of Armageddon. *¹¹ Then I saw heaven opened, and behold, a white horse! The one sitting on it is called Faithful and True, and in righteousness he judges and makes war. ¹² His eyes are like a flame of fire, and on his head are many diadems, and he has a name written that no one knows but himself. ¹³ He is clothed in a robe dipped in blood, and the name by which he is called is The Word of God.* Revelation 19:11-13 (ESV) *¹⁵ From his mouth comes a sharp sword with which to strike down the nations, and he will rule them with a rod of iron. He will tread the winepress of the fury of the wrath of God the Almighty.* Revelation 19:15 (ESV)

If we weren't sure He is Jesus from the description in verse one, we now know He is Jesus from this cross-reference. Jesus is the Word made flesh (John 1:14). His apparel is red because it is dipped in blood. He has fought the nations of the world at Armageddon. But if I understand these passages correctly, the battle is not over.

³ "I have trodden the winepress alone, and from the peoples no one was with me; I trod them in my anger and trampled them in my wrath; their lifeblood spattered on my garments, and stained all my apparel. Isaiah 63:3 The winepress was Armageddon, a great valley where numerous wars in history have been fought. Today it is a rich farmland. Though Jesus brings us with Him (Revelation 19:14), He alone does the fighting, just as He did when the armies came against King Jehoshaphat (2 Chronicles 20:15-17). But there may be additional winepresses in the Kidron Valley and Bozrah.

⁴ For the day of vengeance was in my heart, and my year of redemption had come. ⁵ I looked, but there was no one to help; I was appalled, but there was no one to uphold; so my own arm brought me salvation, and my wrath upheld me. Isaiah 63:4-5 Some people will be troubled by the vengeance of God and the bloody scene described in Isaiah, Joel, and Revelation. We would like to think the best of others and be merciful. That is a good thing. Mercy and grace are wonderful attributes. But we should understand that these armies that have gathered to fight against God will be the epitome of evil. They will see the Lord from heaven and be determined to try and kill Him. They want nothing to do with goodness and righteousness. There is no struggle in their hearts. They have chosen to take a stand against their Creator and reject the salvation offered to them. To offer grace to those who have given themselves over to evil can become enabling of that evil (Proverbs 3:7). Discernment is so important.

We struggle with the wrath of God because we don't recognize the horror of sin. What is the consequence of one sin? Let's look at the first one (Genesis 3:6). Eve disobeyed God. What was the result? All the pain and suffering throughout the ages of mankind! If we could erase all that and put you or me in her place, would it be any different? If we erased all the consequences of sin to this day and could start again, sinless, it wouldn't take long to equal the suffering and pain of our times. Think of it, every person violated, every heart broken, every loved one lost to death, every sickness and injury, every malnourished child, all of it and more, including the crucifixion of our Maker, all are the compounding repercussions of one sin.

People refuse the Holy Spirit's conviction and harden their hearts against seeing sin's damage in their own lives, or, once they have seen it, become hardened and refuse to repent. Would heaven be heaven with them present? If they refuse to be changed by the Holy Spirit, they would infect heaven with the same suffering we have on earth. That is why those who reject the work of the Holy Spirit in their hearts must be separated from God and the heavenly realm (Matthew 7:23). And from where will their torment come? It comes from being with one another. I wish it wasn't so. God wishes it wasn't so. But He will not force His will upon them. He can only offer grace and give them faith to repent, but they must choose to apply it. I realize some may not agree with this, but I would ask you to consider that it is God's will that none perish (2 Peter 3:9)? How could God be love if He merely determined they were doomed without giving them the opportunity to repent and enabling them to do so (1 John 4:8)?

This understanding helps me as I read these horrific passages. God is just. He's also loving and merciful. That is why He calls that day of vengeance the year of redemption, or we could translate it "the year of the redeemed." The world will be redeemed from evil that has ruled it for so long. It is for the sake of the redeemed and for His glory that He rids the world of evil. Satan's authority in the earth will be suspended. And this is where Bozrah comes in. Why does Jesus have to go from Armageddon to Bozrah?

Remember Bozrah means "sheep pen." It is a town just outside of Petra. Many believe that the saints of the tribulation will be miraculously cared for in Petra for the last three and a half years of the tribulation, during God's wrath on the earth (Revelation 12:6). Edom, Ammon, and Moab somehow escape the anti-Christ's hand (Daniel 11:41). It may be that the anti-Christ, hearing of the defeat at Armageddon, sends forces to wipe out God's sheep pen. That would account for the slaughter of the forces gathered against those kept by God at Petra.

Then Jesus, followed by the saints, marches up the Kidron Valley to take Jerusalem (Micah 2:12-14). This is what the watchman, Isaiah, was prophetically seeing in the beginning of the chapter. That would also be when the Jews see Jesus coming and the remnant of surviving Jews converts and joins the battle against the remaining force of the anti-Christ in

Jerusalem (Zechariah 12:5-10). The anti-Christ and false prophet are captured and thrown into the lake of fire (Revelation 19:20).

⁶ I trampled down the peoples in my anger; I made them drunk in my wrath, and I poured out their lifeblood on the earth." Isaiah 63:6
The closing description of God's wrath seems to coincide with the victory over those final forces of the anti-Christ outside the gates of Jerusalem (Revelation 14:20). The Kidron Valley may be what the prophet Joel calls the Valley of Jehoshaphat (Joel 3:2). It is the valley in which the blood of the sacrifices from the altar of God flowed. Then it will flow with the blood of the final forces of the anti-Christ. With those who outright resist God now annihilated, Jesus will set up His throne in Jerusalem. From there He will reign as the King of kings as we have seen in the previous three chapters.

My understanding of the order of these events may be incorrect. Search the Scriptures. Read other opinions written about that time and these passages. God warned Daniel that the prophecies he received would be sealed until the end-times (Daniel 12:4). Of some things we can be certain, Jesus will return for His own. He will judge those who reject His love and grace. He will reign on the earth to give the survivors of the Great Tribulation every reason to receive Him as Lord. When the final judgment examines each and every soul, there will not be one who had a legitimate excuse to reject the salvation Jesus so graciously offers us.

It's not a fantasy. It's the fulfillment of the prophetic passages, many of which have already come to pass. Isaiah predicted that the Messiah would be born of a virgin, minister in northern Galilee, be rejected, be put to death for our sins, buried in a rich man's tomb, rise from death, Gentile nations would put their hope in Him, and that He'd be called Mighty God. Isaiah correctly predicted every one of these unique details of the first coming. These final few chapters we've been studying will just as surely come to pass in as much detail. We'd be foolish to think otherwise.

What difference should this make in our lives today? When I'm wronged, this climax of man's rule of the earth gives me a different perspective. If I have the heart of God, I will long to see those who wronged me come to Jesus and know the same forgiveness that I know. It makes me realize that I don't need to react or try to take things into my own hands. God declares that vengeance is His. He will repay (Romans 12:19). That is because only He knows the heart of any individual. He knows if there is hope or if they will never receive His grace.

It should give us an eternal perspective. This life is a drop in the ocean of eternity. In the end, it won't matter what titles we have or our net worth. Everything is going to change. We don't have to be anxious about ISIS, or the decline of morality in our nation, or world conflicts. We know where it is all headed. Those with humble hearts who are willing to receive the grace and forgiveness offered to us through Jesus' sacrifice will reign with Him over the earth.

Those who resist all goodness and who love violence and power will face the wrath of the Lamb and be defeated. That's what we love about every good story. The bad guy gets what he deserves and the good people live happily ever after. Only our happily ever after is filled with meaning and purpose, new adventures, but most of all with a love which we will forever find to satisfy our deepest longings.

Every one of us is on one side or the other. It depends on what we have done with Jesus, with the conviction of the Holy Spirit. We accept His conviction and realize how evil we have been, or we resist and declare we are just fine without God. We accept the fact that Jesus died for our sins and receive His forgiveness, or we say we don't need it. We let the Spirit of God change us, or we insist we don't need to change. Which will it be for you?

Questions
1 What are the terms common in the final war?
2 Who does the watchman see coming? How do you know?
3 Where has this One been?
4 What did He do at Armageddon? Why?
5 Is God too vengeful? Why or why not?
6 Where does He go next? Why?
7 Where does He lead His sheep?
8 Where might the final winepress be?
9 What happens after justice is served?
10 What does it mean to us today?

Held - Isaiah 63:7-19

Biology, eschatology, soteriology, are all wonderful studies, but the greatest study of all is theology, the study of God. It is out of God that we have all things which we study. And if we were to begin a study of God, it would have to start with His nature. The most common description in the Bible of the character of God is the Hebrew word "*hesed*." It is translated into English as lovingkindness, or steadfast love, and also as mercy (Lamentations 3:22 KJV).

Isaiah begins this next section of chapter 63 by contrasting the wrath of God upon the wicked with the steadfast love of the Lord. One commentator has said that the Greek word for grace (*charis*) is the most beautiful word ever penned. I would say it is this Hebrew word, *hesed*. I say that because it is out of God's steadfast, merciful love that we are offered grace. It is also because of this unfailing love that God's wrath will be poured out on the wicked. For if those who hate the goodness of God were allowed to be with those who love God, then injustice would continue. Suffering would never cease. Wrong would continue to prevail.

It is due to this supreme attribute of God that in verse 7 Isaiah moves from the wrath of God to a prayer of praise for His steadfast love toward God's own. To him there is no contradiction. *⁷ I will recount the steadfast love of the LORD, the praises of the LORD, according to all that the LORD has granted us, and the great goodness to the house of Israel that he has granted them according to his compassion, according to the abundance of his steadfast love.* Isaiah 63:7 The Israel of God eventually responds to the love and mercy of God, but the rest of the world will not. Remember the Israel of God are those who come to God by faith, just like Abraham did (Romans 4:16; Galatians 6:15-16). Isaiah has predicted several times that the Messiah is coming for the ends of the earth, to set captives free, and bring the prisoners out of darkness, to shine His light throughout the earth (Isaiah 49:6; 61:1).

Even the coming captivity was an expression of God's steadfast love to Israel. It would be apathetic for God to let them go on in their sin of idolatry. It is love that disciplines to turn a nation or an individual back to God. Isaiah praises the Lord for His great goodness and for all He has granted them. Stop for a moment and consider all He has granted us as a nation... as individuals... How has His abundance of loving kindness blessed your life? When was the last time you counted your blessings? To not praise God for His loving kindness is ingratitude. To praise anything or anyone else for your blessings is to spit on the loving nail pierced hand that is stretched out to us.

Isaiah goes on to describe the expressions of God's abundant loving kindness. He graciously calls us His own and hopes for the best from us. He saves us physically *and* spiritually. He rescues us again and again, even when we are the ones who gone astray. *⁸ For he said, "Surely they are my people, children who will not deal falsely." And he became their Savior.* Isaiah 63:8

⁹ In all their affliction he was afflicted, and the angel of his presence saved them; in his love and in his pity he redeemed them; he lifted them up and carried them all the days of old. Isaiah 63:9 He even suffers with us. Please hear this, for it is one of the most wonderful expressions of His steadfast love. When you suffer, it is so helpful to have someone at your side who feels with you. It is one of the greatest expressions of love. I watch spouses often suffer even more than their loved one who has some kind of physical affliction or heartache. They so love their spouse that the pain their spouse endures hurts them even more.

Now, understand that God loves you like that. I know that is hard to accept. The reason it is so hard is that we know we don't reciprocate that kind of a love. We try to when we celebrate communion. Some of His saints have asked to share His broken heart for the lost. And surely we can bear but a tiny fraction of what His heart is burdened with, but are we even willing to ask for that? Yet, He continually feels our deepest pain (Hebrews 4:15). *We may be sure that He who permits the suffering is with us in it. It may be that we shall see Him only when the trial is passing; but we must dare to believe that He never leaves the crucible.* (From Streams in the Desert.)

The "angel of His presence" is Jesus (Colossians 1:15). He is the One who saved them again and again. He was the cloud that stood between them and the Egyptians (Exodus 14:24). He was the Captain of the Hosts that met with Joshua (Joshua 5:14). He went before them in Canaan and drove out the Canaanites (Exodus 33:2). He raised up judges to deliver them from oppressors (Judges 2:16). He is God with us. One Immanuel would become the Lamb of God on the altar of the cross to save the souls of everyone who places their faith in God. How many times has the "angel of His presence" saved you from an early death?

I can tell you of a few times in my own life. One experience that was clearly one of those times was when three of us teenage boys were going to ditch school to enjoy a heavy snowfall. We borrowed an older brother's 4-wheel vehicle to go to the Snowbowl. When we hit the old Slide Rock Bridge the vehicle spun sideways and was headed off that cliff into the creek. The vehicle did an amazing, instantaneous 180 degree turn and slammed into a rock wall totaling the vehicle. We had put on our seat belts thirty seconds before. When it was all over, I reached forward and grabbed the Bible I had put on the dashboard. We just sat there in silence wondering at what had just happened. The angel of His presence saved us! That's what happened. He was giving us a little wake up call. Never tried to skip school again! ☺

The verse goes on to say it was in his love and pity that He redeemed them. He knew at the time the very next verse would be true. He knew they would rebel and grieve His Holy Spirit. But He loves us! He knows we will fail again, but His steadfast love endures forever. Like babies learning to walk, we fall down and cry, and He lifts us up and carries us like those days when He carried them out of Egypt (Deuteronomy 32:10-12). And He has done the same for us! Isaiah already spoke of that in Isaiah 40:11. I hope you have not forgotten this wonderful promise of what our Savior does for us. *He will tend his flock like a shepherd; he will gather the lambs in his arms; he will carry them in his bosom, and gently lead those that are with young.*

We think we get through things on our own. Ha! Haven't you seen two different people face the same struggle or tragedy and come out with a completely different response (Proverbs 11:24)? One trusts in Jesus and is carried in His everlasting arms (Luke 15:5). The other tries their best and finds that isn't enough. There is a contemporary Christian song that expresses this, Just Be Held by Casting Crowns. Here is the first verse. *Hold it all together, everybody needs you strong. But life hits you out of nowhere and barely leaves you holdin' on. And when you're tired of fighting, chained by your control, There's freedom in surrender, lay it down and let it go.* And the chorus, *So when you're on your knees and answers seem so far away, You're not alone, stop holding on and just be held. Your worlds not falling apart, its falling into place. I'm on the throne, stop holding on and just be held.* That's sound advice. Just let Him carry you through it. He is more than willing if you will let Him.

[10] *But they rebelled and grieved his Holy Spirit; therefore he turned to be their enemy, and himself fought against them.* Isaiah 63:10 In spite of all that love and grace, we rebel just like they did. We turn to our own ways. We seek our own pleasures instead of looking to Him to be our delight. He

speaks to our hearts, and we turn away, grieving the Holy Spirit. Our rebellion forces Him to turn against us. He fights against us by lifting the protection He had placed around us. Our actions demand His justice and the consequences come. They come to turn us back from our path of self-destruction. Sadly, we sometimes respond by questioning His love, accusing Him of not caring, and all the while He is suffering with us, feeling our pain, and our grief.

¹¹ Then he remembered the days of old, of Moses and his people. Where is he who brought them up out of the sea with the shepherds of his flock? Where is he who put in the midst of them his Holy Spirit, ¹² who caused his glorious arm to go at the right hand of Moses, who divided the waters before them to make for himself an everlasting name, ¹³ who led them through the depths? Like a horse in the desert, they did not stumble. Isaiah 63:11-13 As soon as we repent, He is ready to pour out His blessings again. God remembers the way He went with Israel through the wilderness. In the midst of our deserved calamities we wonder where the God is who helped us in past times. Where is the God who saved me from that car accident? Where is the God who sent His servant to put me back on the right road, the God who filled me with His Spirit (Luke 11:13)?

He took Israel through a wall of water on each side and drowned their enemies on that same path. He fed the multitude in the wilderness. He led every one of us through some kind of water He divided for us. He has fed us the words of life, manna from heaven in the wilderness of this fallen world (John 6:51).

¹⁴ Like livestock that go down into the valley, the Spirit of the LORD gave them rest. So you led your people, to make for yourself a glorious name. Isaiah 63:14 Our good Shepherd has led us to green pastures and by still waters (Psalm 23:1-2). He watches over us so we can feed peacefully without fearing the enemy. We are at peace with Him watching over us. When we come to Him, He gives us rest (Matthew 11:28-30). In all these actions He is displaying His steadfast love, which is the same as making for Himself a glorious name. A name to the Hebrews meant the attributes of that person. It's the way we describe a person. The glorious name God is making for Himself is a way to describe all of His perfect attributes. He makes them known through the ways He deals with us (Psalm 76:1).

¹⁵ Look down from heaven and see, from your holy and beautiful habitation. Where are your zeal and your might? The stirring of your inner parts and your compassion are held back from me. Isaiah 63:15 After declaring God's steadfast love in spite of the repeated rebellion of the people, Isaiah offered up a prayer for mercy. He had just had a vision of Jesus in His glory after treading the winepress of the wrath of God. It disturbed Him as it should have. God's heart is broken for all those who would never repent. He is not willing that any should perish (2 Peter 3:9). Our hearts should be broken as well.

In seeing the coming exile of Israel and the future wrath of God on the world, Isaiah feels as if the steadfast love of God had somehow failed.

He just declared that in all their afflictions God was afflicted, but now he feels that God is withholding that compassion toward him. A verse from the song I mentioned fits here. *If your eyes are on the storm, you'll wonder if I love you still. But if your eyes are on the cross, you'll know I always have and I always will. And not a tear is wasted, in time you'll understand. I'm painting beauty with the ashes; your life is in My hands.*

There will be times when we feel like Isaiah did. We don't understand what has happened or why. Circumstances will stretch our faith. They cause us to be more earnest in prayer. And when we come out on the other side, we learn that God can carry us through whatever He allows to come our way (1 Corinthians 10:13).

16 For you are our Father, though Abraham does not know us, and Israel does not acknowledge us; you, O LORD, are our Father, our Redeemer from of old is your name. Isaiah 63:16 This is wonderfully true for all people. You don't have to be Jewish. You don't have to come from a godly family. You just need to be redeemed and God will be a Father to you, a perfect father (John 1:12). The perfect father loves, guides, protects, provides, and disciplines his children (Hebrews 12:7). He hurts when you hurt. He rejoices with your growth and victories. He wants the best for you. And He wants you to be like Him (Romans 8:29).

17 O LORD, why do you make us wander from your ways and harden our heart, so that we fear you not? Return for the sake of your servants, the tribes of your heritage. Isaiah 63:17 Isaiah was asking why God made them to wander from Him and harden their hearts. But actually, God allows us to harden our own hearts (1 Samuel 6:6); Psalm 95:10). Pharaoh hardened his own heart before God hardened it further (See Exodus 7 – 14). The problem with a hard heart is that we have no fear of God's justice and the consequences of sin (Proverbs 16:6). That means we won't hesitate to rebel and harden if further to our own destruction.

I think many of us are praying the last half of this verse for our country. How has this nation so hardened its hearts that there is no fear of God? We pray with Isaiah, "Return for the sake of your servants, the tribes of your heritage."

18 Your holy people held possession for a little while; our adversaries have trampled down your sanctuary. Isaiah 63:18 Isaiah could see the future battle in which the temple would be destroyed. For the Jews it was the very place of God dwelling among them. It would be as if all hope was lost. The favor of God seemed forever removed. That is why His prayer is that God return to them. God returns to us when we return to Him (Jeremiah 15:19). While we watch the favor of God seem to lift from our own nation, we pray with Isaiah that God would return and cause our hearts to fear Him. We pray He would soften the hearts of those who hate Christianity and want it removed from the public square. We pray for boldness to stand against this spirit that would intimidate us into silence and misrepresent that for which we truly stand.

19 We have become like those over whom you have never ruled, like those who are not called by your name. Isaiah 63:19 Think of the nations that have no Christian heritage. Look at the nations of Africa and the turmoil before the Gospel was proclaimed. Look at the Hindu, Buddhist, and Islamic nations and see where we would have been had it not been for the light of Christ. There's a reason they all want to come here. And now our nation seems to be running headlong away from our Christian heritage. Instead of gratitude for our past, we seem to be running from all that brought God's blessings on us. Prayer: O Lord God of all creation, God of steadfast love, look down from heaven and see. Return O Lord for the sake of your servants. Hold us LORD. Our eyes are on You. Teach us to pray for our homes, our city, our nation, and the upcoming elections. Give us eyes to see You at work, ears to hear Your Spirit, and hearts longing to obey.

Questions
1 What is the most commonly mentioned attribute of God?
2 How has God blessed America? You?
3 How does God feel about your pain? Why?
4 Has "the angel of His presence" saved you? When?
5 Why does He carry us?
6 Why does He turn against us?
7 Why does God allow hardship in our lives?
8 How can God become our Father?
9 What is the problem with a hard heart?
10 What is the difference between a nation with a Christian heritage and a pagan one?

Isaiah's Prayer - Isaiah 64

1 Oh that you would rend the heavens and come down, that the mountains might quake at your presence— Isaiah 64:1 Isaiah continues his prayer from the last chapter. He's asking God to manifest Himself in power, as He did in their history, to turn the people back to God and save them from annihilation (Habakkuk 3:2). In Exodus 19:16-18, God came down upon Mount Sinai in a cloud. The mountain was scorched and the smoke went up like a furnace. In the video, The Search for the Real Mount Sinai, a couple of researchers snuck into Saudi Arabia to see a mountain the Arabs call Jabel al Mousa, Moses' mountain. All the tell-tale signs from the book of Exodus are there. The mountain is scorched. The remains of the pillars (Exodus 24:4) that were erected, the split rock (Isaiah 48:21), and the altar are all still there. The whole area is enclosed with barbwire fencing and guarded. Muslims would rather we did not discover the roots of Judaism and evidence of the truth of the Bible.

The language of Isaiah's prayer reminds us of what happened on that mountain. The whole mountain trembled at the presence of God. There were trumpet blasts along with lightning and thunder. God came down and made a covenant with the people. They were so fearful that they asked Moses to speak with God for them. *²⁰ Moses said to the people, "Do not fear, for God has come to test you, that the fear of him may be before you, that you may not sin."* Exodus 20:20

Isaiah continues in prayer describing God's intervention on Sinai. *² as when fire kindles brushwood and the fire causes water to boil— to make your name known to your adversaries, and that the nations might tremble at your presence!* Isaiah 64:2 Isaiah wants the manifest presence of God for several reasons. He wants the name of the Lord (His authority and character) to be known to God's adversaries. He wants the nations to tremble at God's presence. But the allusion is to Sinai where it was Israel that feared. That fear did not stop them from building a golden calf to worship just forty days after that encounter with God (Exodus 32:8). Later in the prayer we see that nation of Israel was just as guilty at the time of Isaiah's prayer as they were at Sinai.

We often pray what we hope for but find that God has a better plan. Isaiah was hoping to divert the coming assault by Babylon through intercessory prayer. But in reality, the adversaries of God that needed to know the name of God were the Israelites. It was through the captivity that they would come to know His name again. It was the Israelites that needed to tremble at God's presence (Proverbs 3:7).

We are watching our country sink into the abyss of immorality while mocking God and using His name as a curse, or worse yet to gain the votes of the religious. We could pray with Isaiah against ISIS, Putin, and Al Qaeda, that God would rend the heavens and come down, that they might know God's true name and tremble at His presence. I do pray that. But perhaps we are in the same condition as the nation of Israel in that it is our own people who need the fear of God.

My heart breaks for the increasing number of children of single parents. The statistics tell us those children will have a very difficult time succeeding. Worse yet, how will they understand the love of God, the father heart of God, when they have never experienced a loving father? Many of them will follow the same path as their parent. Only the grace of God can break that cycle. What will wake us up? What can turn us from these destructive sins that grip our nation? Rend the heavens and come down that the fear of God might be before us that we might not sin (Proverbs 16:6). The answer isn't political; it is spiritual.

³ When you did awesome things that we did not look for, you came down, the mountains quaked at your presence. Isaiah 64:3 The Bible is full of the amazing deeds of God. Isaiah is praying, "Do it again!" The armies of the Canaanites gathered to stop the Israelites from taking the Promised Land, but God fought for Joshua (Joshua 10:10-11). King Jabin came against Barak and Deborah with an overwhelming force and superior technology, but God fought for Israel and his army was defeated (Judges 4:15). God had Gideon take just three hundred men against a group of armies with so many men they could not be counted. God came down! King Jehoshaphat faced a huge army. God told him to put the singers in front of his army to praise God. The LORD ambushed the enemy and they turned on themselves. The Israelites picked up the spoils for days (2Chronicles 20:22)! Isaiah is pleading for God to do it again.

In our own lives God has done awesome things we did not look for. We never dreamed of the entry to Sedona going by our front door. Two of our sisters had some serious surgery and were up walking around without pain the next day. We project a deficit and God gives us a surplus. But greatest of all the wondrous deeds of God in His sending His only Son to take *our* sins upon the cross. Then, He gave us the grace to turn to Him and be saved. Our God is an awesome God - sing it!

⁴ From of old no one has heard or perceived by the ear, no eye has seen a God besides you, who acts for those who wait for him. Isaiah 64:4 O Lord, help us to wait on You, not to run ahead, or lag behind, but to act when You lead. There is no God like our God. The so called God of Islam is capricious. No matter how you live or how you seek him, he can arbitrarily send you to heaven or hell. Buddhism and Hinduism have no eternal God. The stories of the gods of Hinduism are often viler than men (Isaiah 37:19). Our God is the Creator of all. He gave you the freedom to choose or reject Him. He loves you so much that while you were rebelling against Him, He died for you (Romans 5:8). He paid your just penalty to reconcile His justice with His love and mercy. He uses the weak and loves the powerless. His most mentioned attribute we saw last week, steadfast love (Isaiah 63:7). You can dream a lifetime and not come up with a better God. He is a God who answers prayers, that is, if they are for our good, and His will is always for our good. He longs to be with us forever. He invites us to participate with Him in the earth, so He can justly reward us in heaven.

What does it mean to wait on Him? It means to trust that He will answer your prayer in His time. It means to be still and let Him speak to your heart. It is to read His Word and let Him speak to you through it. It means to love and serve Him with all your heart. He acts for those who wait for Him!

⁵ You meet him who joyfully works righteousness, those who remember you in your ways. Behold, you were angry, and we sinned; in our sins we have been a long time, and shall we be saved? Isaiah 64:5 Who are these joyful workers of righteousness? They are those who are led by the Spirit of God to participate in God's work in the world (Ephesians 2:10). It may be sharing the gospel with a hungry heart caught in the bondage of sin. It may be feeding a homeless man and telling him of the love of Jesus. It might be serving in your local church. It is joining God in what He is doing in the earth, being His instrument to serve others like Jesus served us (Mark 10:45). The joy we experience is a fruit of the Spirit often most realized in the blessing of service.

Some people have the idea that living for Jesus means sad sacrifices and doing things you don't want to do. There is nothing more joyful than surrendering yourself to the will of God and the leading of the Holy Spirit.

That is because you come to realize God loves you and wants to bless you in the process. Sometimes it costs more than you want to pay, but then you find God blesses you in ways that more than make up for any loss. Those who remember God in His ways are those who strive by the power of the Spirit to act in accord with the nature of God. Moses once prayed that God would show Him His ways so that he could know God and be in His favor (Exodus 33:13). If God is patient, loving, and compassionate, then we should be as well. That is, if you want to know Him and be in favor with Him. If He is just and honest, then that is what we should be as well. Those are the people He meets and whose prayers He hears.

The last half of verse 5 turned to confession. Isaiah is acknowledging that this does not describe the Israel of his day. Instead of righteousness, they sinned. They had been caught up in sin for a long time. He asks if there is any hope for their salvation. *6 We have all become like one who is unclean, and all our righteous deeds are like a polluted garment. We all fade like a leaf, and our iniquities, like the wind, take us away.* Isaiah 64:6 This verse is often used to declare the sinfulness of mankind. While man is without question sinful, the subject is not man in general but Israel at that particular time just before the captivity. The people were ritually unclean, meaning they were not presentable to God. They had no business coming into the temple. Their so called righteousness was like a menstrual rag to God. That was considered something that made a person unclean and therefore unable to be with others for seven days (Leviticus 15:19). They still brought offerings, but God did not accept them, for the worshiper was also worshiping idols. The offerings in the temple were efforts to manipulate the God of Israel. "Here, I give you what you want, so now give me my request!" Isaiah is confessing the people's actions were abhorrent to God.

Sin has repercussions. Isaiah says they were fading like a leaf. They watched the glory of Israel fade day by day, as the natural consequences of their sins. Drying out like a leaf, they were about to be blown away (Psalm 90:5-6).

7 There is no one who calls upon your name, who rouses himself to take hold of you; for you have hidden your face from us, and have made us melt in the hand of our iniquities. Isaiah 64:7 Whoever calls on the name of the Lord shall be saved (Joel 2:32), but no one called. No one rouses themselves to take hold of the LORD (Isaiah 43:22; 56:4). How do we take hold of the LORD? We do so in earnest, fervent prayer. No one was stirring themselves to get serious with God in prayer. Are we? Are we taking the time with God to cry out to Him for our nation with all our heart? Are we asking God to show us our own sins and not letting go until He speaks to us?

Isaiah knew the people weren't taking hold of God because he was watching the decline of the nation. He saw that as God hiding His face from them. And what a description he gives for the consequences of sin, "melt in the hand of our iniquities." I was sitting in the surgery waiting room and couldn't help but overhear the discussions around me. Lust, greed, and selfishness seemed to be the dominant themes from the young adults. They couldn't even see they were melting in the hand of their iniquities. God help us rouse ourselves to lay hold of God in prayer for the younger generations of our nation.

   ⁸ But now, O LORD, you are our Father; we are the clay, and you are our potter; we are all the work of your hand. Isaiah 64:8 Isaiah's prayer now turns to a plea for mercy. He is reminding himself and God of the covenant. God had promised to be a Father to the nation (Isaiah 63:16). But remember, fathers exercise discipline (Hebrews 12:7). We are the clay and God is our potter. God molds us. We are the work of His hands. But when the clay on the wheel becomes out of round, unstable, the potter has to remove it from the wheel, pound it into one lump, beat all the air bubbles out of it, slap it on the wheel and start spinning it again. The other options are to discard that clay. The readers of the prayer would have known that.

   ⁹ Be not so terribly angry, O LORD, and remember not iniquity forever. Behold, please look, we are all your people. Isaiah 64:9 Isaiah is beginning the portion of this prayer in the prophetic perfect tense. While Babylon has not yet come, Isaiah can see what will happen as if it had already taken place. Remember, he has lived under a good king and some very bad ones. He watched his nation decline. He longs for the days when the nation was under the favor of God. But now the clay has rebelled against the Potter. No one seeks God. Idolatry is rampant. He knows what God is about to do in His anger and tries to intercede. "Remember not iniquity forever! Look, look! We are all your people."

   Isaiah is asking for God to remember the covenants and reshape them. He knows when God looks, He sees with eyes of mercy. However, the only solution was captivity. Isaiah had already predicted it as a sure thing (Isaiah 5:13). We should note however that the traditional view is that captivity did not take place for another one hundred years. His intercession may have held off the judgment of God, but it wouldn't hold it off forever.

   ¹⁰ Your holy cities have become a wilderness; Zion has become a wilderness, Jerusalem a desolation. Isaiah 64:10 Here is what Isaiah prophetically sees. The cities are desolate. Everyone is taken captive to live as slaves, or at best as subjects of a foreign power. The hill where God's house was, is turned into a wilderness (Isaiah 1:7). Jerusalem, where throngs once came for the holy feasts, is desolate. How heart breaking it must have been. But then I wonder about the great cathedrals of Europe. They were once full of worshipers of Jesus. Did they see the same kind of decline Isaiah saw? Did they foresee these days when those great cathedrals are merely wonders of architecture? Some have even been turned into mosques.

   ¹¹ Our holy and beautiful house, where our fathers praised you, has been burned by fire, and all our pleasant places have become ruins. Isaiah 64:11 Isaiah had witnessed wonderful worship in the temple, the lights at the Feast of Tabernacles, the throngs that sacrificed the paschal lambs at Passover and songs of the Levite choir. Now in a vision he sees the glorious temple stripped of its glory, burned, vacant! It would become simply a heap of ruins.

How could that be? How could the God who had done such wonderful deeds for His people, who had come down and intervened for them, putting fear in their enemies and making His name known in the earth, how could He let it become a pile of ruins?

No people, denomination, or movement will last without a living relationship with our Creator. Every one of these will devolve into methods and routines if each generation does not seek God with their whole heart. Jesus warned us in the parable of the sower that the weeds that choke the plant and keep it from becoming fruitful are the cares of the world and the deceitfulness of riches (Matthew 13:22). If we do not disciple the next generation, the same will happen here. Are you sharing with your children and grandchildren the importance of a living relationship with Jesus? Does your life demonstrate that joyful life of righteousness, walking in His ways, a person God meets?

12 Will you restrain yourself at these things, O LORD? Will you keep silent, and afflict us so terribly? Isaiah 64:12 "God, is this really unavoidable," the prophet asks? Will You sit back and watch this happen and not act. Will you allow such a devastation to occur? Isaiah has roused himself to lay hold of God, but the people will not turn from their iniquity. That day of desolation would come, but desolation was not the end. The Potter was remolding His clay through captivity. He was preparing a people for the coming of Messiah, the final solution to sin. He was preparing the way for the Holy Spirit to descend at Pentecost so that we might be changed (Luke 24:49; Titus 3:5).

Have you allowed Him to change you? We have this treasure in earthen vessels of clay. What Israel lacked to persevere in the faith, we have available to us. The Holy Spirit has been poured out (Acts 2:38). If you lay hold of Him and let Him lay hold of you, your fruit will remain (John 15:16). There will be no need for those cycles in your life. There is victory in Christ. God will turn His face toward you, for you will live in the victory we have through the blood of Jesus.

Questions
1 What was Isaiah asking God to do? Why?
2 What amazing things has God done?
3 What's so special about our God?
4 What is "waiting on God"?
5 Who does God meet?
6 Why do we need to know the ways of God?
7 Does verse 7 speak to you? How?
8 What is the picture in the potter and clay?
9 Why does Isaiah ask God to look on them?
10 What does Isaiah see coming? What does He ask?

Here I Am! - Isaiah 65:1-16

Isaiah ended the last chapter with a prayer question. He was wondering if God would ever be gracious again to Israel (Isaiah 64:12). God's response is that He is going to be gracious, but it is to a people who never sought Him and weren't called by His name. Fortunately, we have the Apostle Paul's use of this verse in Romans 10:20 to clarify that this is about the Gentiles.

¹ I was ready to be sought by those who did not ask for me; I was ready to be found by those who did not seek me. I said, "Here I am, here I am," to a nation that was not called by my name. Isaiah 65:1 This is a wonderful truth I've shared on several occasions, that God's love and grace go out to everyone in the world, even if they don't ask for it. Then each one must decide what he or she will do with it. We could translate the Hebrew of the first line to read, "I permitted myself to be consulted" (Edward Young), which is a consultation that results in the desired knowledge. The people who never sought God found Him anyway. In other words, God's free grace reached out to those who could care less about God. These discovered God. Undeserving people who had no concern for God found the freely given grace of God and acted on it.

In the previous chapter, Isaiah's prayer was pleading with God to have mercy on the Jews by asking God, "Behold us; look on us." But that was the problem; when He looked He saw sin. They needed to look at God again like they once did. God's repetition of "Here I am," or we could read it, "Behold me!" emphasizes God's revelation of Himself to those who are not called by His name. It is Israel that is called by His name (Genesis 48:16). That means God is telling the rest of world He is there for them. Israel saw Him and went their own way. Now He is reaching out to the Gentile world. See Him in the wonder of nature and the sciences. See Him in the revelation of Scripture. See Him in those who are filled with His love. God is continually reaching out to everyone saying, "Look at me! Here I am!" He is not willing that any should perish (2 Peter 3:9). But will we allow ourselves to see Him?

I was reading about DNA the other day. A microscopic speck of DNA smaller than a grain of dust could hold the information of the DVDs of every movie ever made and have enough storage capacity left to hold the movies created in the next 100 years! That screams out, "Here I am!" With all our advances in science we know the exact composition of DNA but we can't reproduce it. Only living things can do that. But somehow we are supposed to believe it was an accident of time and chance? All I hear is God saying, "Here I am! Behold me!" A thunderstorm rolls through the canyon and the sound of the thunder echoing on the canyon walls says to me, "Here I am!" I see the birth of a baby, the miracle of what the human body does before, during, and after that child is born... I'm awestruck with wonder. But other people can see the same things and have no response to God's thundering voice (Job 37:4-5).

 ² *I spread out my hands all the day to a rebellious people, who walk in a way that is not good, following their own devices;* Isaiah 65:2 Paul applies this verse to the Jewish people. He is continually reaching out to them as well. The difference is that they knew God's will and rebelled against it. Though they were taught by God the way that is good, they still followed their own devices (Isaiah 55:8-9). The Hebrew for devices is often translated "thoughts." They just follow their own plans instead of God's. James 4:17 tells us, *whoever knows the right thing to do and fails to do it, for him it is sin.* They had found God. They were called by His name. But they did whatever they wanted and misrepresented Him to the world. But it gets worse than that.

 ³ *a people who provoke me to my face continually, sacrificing in gardens and making offerings on bricks;* Isaiah 65:3 God now describes their way that was not good. They provoked God to His face by continually worshiping idols as if all their blessings came from a carved rock or molten image. Instead of sacrifices in the temple to the God who revealed His laws and an acceptable form of worship, they offered sacrifices to idols in gardens and put their offerings on bricks. It's as if they turned a defiant face toward the temple while they carried out their sacrifices in the gardens, just daring God to act (Exodus 23:21).

 ⁴ *who sit in tombs, and spend the night in secret places; who eat pig's flesh, and broth of tainted meat is in their vessels;* Isaiah 65:4 It sounds as if they were consulting the dead and eating pork, both of which were forbidden by God (Deuteronomy 18:11; Leviticus 11:7-8) The rotten meat in their vessels was some sort of disgusting pagan ritual. God has His welcoming arms stretched out to them, ready to forgive, even while they practice this perverseness. Most idolatry is a form of trying to get what we want without too much commitment. What would cause someone to think that these things would ever result in something good?

 ⁵ *who say, "Keep to yourself, do not come near me, for I am too holy for you." These are a smoke in my nostrils, a fire that burns all the day.* Isaiah 65:5 While practicing this vile idolatry, they see themselves as super-spiritual. Christianity humbles us (Luke 18:9). We see the great need for a Savior and recognize we can do nothing without Him. Paganism exalts self with the idea that we can manipulate God. This verse is where we get the phrase, "holier than thou." It can be Christianity or any religion without recognizing our sinful nature and the mercy and grace of God. New Age folks have shared with me a number of times that they used to be where I am but evolved to higher level. In other words, they used to attend a Christian church, but then they realized they are gods (Ezekiel 28:9).

We have to watch out it in the Christian world for statements like these: "I have the right interpretation and everyone else is wrong." Woe (Philippians 2:3)! "We are the only church that has the whole truth." Yikes! "Our church is the instrument through which God is going to do this mighty work!" Well, I hope so, but not to the exclusion of your other brothers and sisters in Christ in your community. Exclusivism is the sure sign of a cult. If feeds our pride. It says, "We are doing it right and no one else really is."

⁶ Behold, it is written before me: "I will not keep silent, but I will repay; I will indeed repay into their lap Isaiah 65:6 Ignoring Him is the sin of the people (Jeremiah 17:1). God keeps records. Every idle word is recorded (Matthew 12:36). God's response to this defiance and stubborn rebellion is the promise to give retribution. God will always balance the books in His time. Always! He repays blessing to those who serve God, and judgment upon those who refuse to repent and continue to rebel. The retribution will be poured onto their lap (Ruth 3:15). There is no escaping it. The wheels of God's justice often grind exceedingly slow, but they grind exceedingly fine (Jeremiah 16:18).

⁷ both your iniquities and your fathers' iniquities together, says the LORD; because they made offerings on the mountains and insulted me on the hills, I will measure into their lap payment for their former deeds." Isaiah 65:7 The above-mentioned sins of the people who were going into exile, and the sins of their fathers, who are those who were first to read Isaiah's work are the reason for this pouring out of judgment. God repeats it to be certain that they hear the reason and the consequence. They insulted God through their idolatry on the hilltops, so God will measure out the justice they deserve and lay it on their laps.

⁸ Thus says the LORD: "As the new wine is found in the cluster, and they say, 'Do not destroy it, for there is a blessing in it,' so I will do for my servants' sake, and not destroy them all. Isaiah 65:8 Now the tone changes to the survivors, often referred to as the remnant (Ezra 9:8; Isaiah 11:11; Romans 9:27). They are the Jews God has kept from going astray. I want to warn you of that term, "remnant," because it is often used today by groups that claim they are God's special work, the only ones that God has spared from the world's corruption. In another sense, everyone who has come to Jesus for salvation and trust in Him alone is part of the remnant out of this world. Yet, there are those who will claim that if you do this activity or learn these secrets, you can become part of this elite end-time group. It is often based on some kind of works. That appeals to our pride. Our boast should be in the Lord (1 Corinthians 1:31). Every child of God is special. Be led by and convicted by the Holy Spirit, not man. Don't follow me or any other man. Follow Jesus. What any worthwhile pastor shares is not a special revelation or something new, but the teaching of the church through the ages.

The vineyard is Israel (Isaiah 5:7), and the fruit is bad. It's time to pluck up the vines. But there is one cluster that is good. There is a blessing in that cluster. I believe the blessing is the line of the Savior that God is going to preserve. God's servants are those who would survive captivity and return to the Land. But in a more general sense they include all those redeemed, forgiven, and set apart.

350

⁹ I will bring forth offspring from Jacob, and from Judah possessors of my mountains; my chosen shall possess it, and my servants shall dwell there. Isaiah 65:9 While this was surely read by those in captivity as a promise their offspring would return to the Promised Land, it is ultimately about the people of faith consisting of both Jew and Gentile as we read in verse one. Paul explains in Romans 4 that the offspring of Abraham are the people of faith. We inherit the heavenly Canaan. The geographical features are symbols of that heavenly land.

¹⁰ Sharon shall become a pasture for flocks, and the Valley of Achor a place for herds to lie down, for my people who have sought me. Isaiah 65:10 Sharon is on the far west of Israel and Achor on the far eastern side. The entire land will return to God's people who seek Him. It will have everything they need for their support. So while these verses would give hope for return of the captives to the Promised Land and all they need when they return, it speaks to the children of God of spiritual provision and heaven's abundance.

¹¹ But you who forsake the LORD, who forget my holy mountain, who set a table for Fortune and fill cups of mixed wine for Destiny, Isaiah 65:11 Isaiah now returns to a description of those who turn against God. They turn their back on the God who brought their ancestors out of Egypt and gave them His words. They forgot the temple where God dwelt among them. Instead they serve the gods of fortune and fate with food and drink offerings.

How easily we can do the same. We turn away from the cross and devote ourselves to amassing a fortune and controlling our destiny. When we make wealth and security the priority of our lives, and put them above God, we are forgetting that holy mountain of the cross where the Word made flesh died for us. We pour out our time and effort to obtain what will inevitably fail us one day (Isaiah 2:20).

¹² I will destine you to the sword, and all of you shall bow down to the slaughter, because, when I called, you did not answer; when I spoke, you did not listen, but you did what was evil in my eyes and chose what I did not delight in." Isaiah 65:12 There was a word play in the first word translated "destine." The Hebrew word "to number," as in God numbering our days, sounds like the name of the god of Destiny. So the ESV translators went ahead and used the word "destine." They worshiped destiny, but God is the One who determined their destiny was to be cut down when Babylon invaded. The worshipers of idols would die in the siege.

The reason for this is clearly stated here and throughout Jeremiah (Jeremiah 7:13). God called, but they would not answer. He spoke, but they did not listen. This is the unpardonable sin (Mark 3:29). God reaches out to us all, Jew and Gentile. He yells, "Here I am!" But if we refuse His voice, the conviction of the Holy Spirit, the grace to turn and repent, then we will face justice. I can't emphasize enough the need to be still and let the Word of God and the voice of the Holy Spirit speak to our hearts and respond to Him (John 10:3).

I recall a true story, perhaps from the Daily Bread devotional. A man was impressed by the rich truths his friend was sharing with him. One day he asked, "I learned what I know of the Bible from seminary, but where did you learn these rich truths you are sharing with me?" The man replied, "On my knees in prayer each morning before my open Bible." Education can be very helpful, but rich spiritual truths are learned in times of quiet meditation on the Word of God. Spiritual growth requires that we listen to God. He delights in you hearing His voice and taking it to heart (John 10:3-4).

[13] *Therefore thus says the Lord GOD: "Behold, my servants shall eat, but you shall be hungry; behold, my servants shall drink, but you shall be thirsty; behold, my servants shall rejoice, but you shall be put to shame;* Isaiah 65:13 Here is the spiritual and eternal contrast. Those who serve God will eat, drink, and rejoice. But those who reject His voice and do evil, who chose what God hates, will be hungry, thirsty, and put to shame. The world will not satisfy. It just leaves you hungry and thirsty for more. It may bring the honor of man, but in the end, it only brings the shame of investing their lives in vanity (Ecclesiastes 1:2).

[14] *behold, my servants shall sing for gladness of heart, but you shall cry out for pain of heart and shall wail for breaking of spirit.* Isaiah 65:14 God's servants will sing in this world and in our heavenly home for gladness of heart. But those who rebel against God and refuse His call to them will cry out in pain of heart. When we try to stuff the world into the emptiness of our heart, it just leaves us emptier than before. There is the wailing of a breaking spirit that is chilling. It is a cry of hopelessness. When one rejects God and then finds the world will never satisfy, they are left with nothing but lonely pain.

[15] *You shall leave your name to my chosen for a curse, and the Lord GOD will put you to death, but his servants he will call by another name.* Isaiah 65:15 The very name of the rebels against God is a curse. Think of the name Judas. But we will receive a new name. We went over that when we studied Isaiah 62:2. The name is both a personal name known only to us and God, and collectively the name is the very name of our God and the city of God that will be on our foreheads (Revelation 2:17; 3:12).

[16] *So that he who blesses himself in the land shall bless himself by the God of truth, and he who takes an oath in the land shall swear by the God of truth; because the former troubles are forgotten and are hidden from my eyes.* Isaiah 65:16 Those who survive the captivity, and perhaps this applies to those believers who survive the tribulation, who want to declare a blessing, will do so by the God of truth, or literally "the God of Amen." The same is true for taking an oath. The difficulties of the past will be forgotten. The faithfulness of God to His Word and His promises will be clear for all to see. All will realize there is but one God and that all others are a lie.

Do you know the God of truth? Is it His blessing you seek? Will you listen and respond to the God who stretches out His nail pierced hands to you? Are you willing to hear His voice today and every day (Mark 1:35)?

352

flood, which may be because the Lord restores the pre-flood conditions. To die at one-hundred years of age will be like dying in one's youth.

Since there are still sinners present, this can't be the eternal kingdom. The sinner will be accursed at one hundred years of age. I think this is because of man's insatiable appetite for satisfaction. That longing is meant to be filled by the Lord. But when we look for that satisfaction in the creation, we end up increasingly abusing creation and being excessive in our enjoyment of what was meant for good. This lack of moderation harms us. The longer we continue in it the more we indulge in excess and the greater the curse we experience. I like bacon, but if I eat bacon for every meal because I find my satisfaction in food, my arteries are going to clog up and my weight will double. The natural consequence of sin is a curse. So while the curse may be lifted from the earth, those living on it will still be able to choose sin and experience for themselves why God's commands are always for our good (Deuteronomy 10:13).

21 They shall build houses and inhabit them; they shall plant vineyards and eat their fruit. 22 They shall not build and another inhabit; they shall not plant and another eat; for like the days of a tree shall the days of my people be, and my chosen shall long enjoy the work of their hands. Isaiah 65:21-22 We live in an age when it is hard to relate to this passage. For most of human history one's labor was often taken from them by force, either by conquerors or by land owners. But in that age to come, the saints will ensure justice and peace throughout the earth. Not only will we enjoy the fruit of our labor, but we will enjoy it for a long time (Ezekiel 28:26). Too often, the joy that comes from the fruit of our labor is taken away by theft, taxation, or decay. That will end. The political solution is Christ the King. He is the only ruler who can't be corrupted by power, for He has always had all power. Maybe we could write Him in on our next presidential ballot?

23 They shall not labor in vain or bear children for calamity, for they shall be the offspring of the blessed of the LORD, and their descendants with them. Isaiah 65:23 Repetition is driving home the point that what you earn or labor for will not be taken away. The Babylonians would come and take away everything the readers had worked hard to possess. Inflation and devaluation of our currency will take away what we labored for to provide for ourselves in old age. But not in that age! Never again will children be stricken with illness, taken as slaves, or killed by an oppressor (Deuteronomy 28:41). Those who have received forgiveness in Christ will have children who will be blessed, as well as grandchildren and great-grandchildren (Isaiah 61:9).

24 Before they call I will answer; while they are yet speaking I will hear. Isaiah 65:24 We often claim this verse for our time, and it is applicable to some extent. In that age prayers will *always* be in line with the will of God and have quick and wonderful answers. That is the blessing of those believers in that age. Isaiah has already said it is true for those who take up the fast of the Lord, which is a fast of looking out for the poor and needy and not being judgmental. *⁹ Then you shall call, and the LORD will answer; you shall cry, and he will say, 'Here I am.' If you take away the yoke from your midst, the pointing of the finger, and speaking wickedness*, Isaiah 58:9 Because those in that age who belong to the Lord will be sharing God's heart and doing His will, His answer to their prayers will come quickly. James tells us that the prayer of the righteous person is powerful and effective (James 5:16). That is because they pray the heart of God. Their prayers are not self-centered, but God centered.

²⁵ The wolf and the lamb shall graze together; the lion shall eat straw like the ox, and dust shall be the serpent's food. They shall not hurt or destroy in all my holy mountain," says the LORD. Isaiah 65:25 This famous verse has been interpreted as the peace that will prevail in the earth between aggressive and passive personalities, the powerful and the weak. We should remember that the Hebrews don't separate the physical and spiritual. While it is pictorial language, I believe it will literally be the case in the animal world too (Isaiah 11:6-7). The re-creation will make it possible. One thousand years of peace will be an amazing thing. Has the world ever seen a decade of peace from war? It certainly has not had a second of peace from strife between individuals.

The serpent eating dust implies that Satan will not have influence (Genesis 3:14). The sin the world experiences will come from within the heart of man choosing to disobey God (James 1:14-15). Satan is bound for all but the very end of those thousand years (Revelation 20:7-8). Then when he is released, he immediately gathers the world to try to wrestle the throne from Jesus.

The holy mountain is Zion, but it also represents God's kingdom. Remember that in the vision in Daniel the stone from the mountain struck the earth and became a mountain that filled the earth (Daniel 2:35). Jesus will reign over the whole earth, so the animals will not hurt or destroy, nor will Satan have influence. All of mankind will see the world as God intended it to be. Everything man needs will be available to us if he is willing to do a little enjoyable work. Justice will prevail in every situation because God's servants will see that it is so. Man will have no excuse at all for turning against Jesus on the throne in Jerusalem.

I've been discussing the justice of eternal punishment with a brother. I think it is something we should all wrestle with, not because we question God's fairness, but because we would not wish hell upon our worst enemy. We should understand that God does not want to send a single soul to hell. Souls are eternal and must dwell with or without God, and there is only one way to dwell with God, which is by accepting the forgiveness He freely gives us through what Jesus did for us on the cross. By refusing that, we condemn ourselves to separation from Him and His goodness.

What the Millennium will illustrate is that even if man lived in the perfect environment with complete understanding of right and wrong and who their Creator is, even after a thousand years they would still choose not to accept His forgiveness and rather live without Him. They would be miserable in heaven. I don't believe they would ever change their minds. A hardened heart filled with hatred can grow so hardened it will not be changed. We must guard ourselves from this condition by being quick to forgive and refusing to mull over past injustices and evil done to us. We must never blame the evils of this world on God, but always on this fallen world, our flesh, and the devil. In the age to come they will only have their evil hearts to blame.

I wonder if the torment of hell is mostly from the fact that everyone there is as selfish and demanding as those who surround them. There will be no caring people in hell. There will be no one who would change their mind had they only known. What one sows, throughout eternity they will reap. They will sow and reap from one another again and again and again. It grieves the heart of God that they would choose that course. It should grieve our hearts as well, but also cause us to be grateful for what God has saved us from.

There is a glorious future for those in Christ, even greater than that thousand-year reign. We will be filled with overwhelming joy and gladness for all that God has done for us and for our greater understanding of the depths of His love (Ephesians 3:17-20). What a contrast is set before mankind! How eager we should be for every opportunity we are given to share our hope with those who will listen.

C.S. Lewis wrote, *If I find in myself a desire which no experience in this world can satisfy, the most probable explanation is that I was made for another world. If none of my earthly pleasures satisfy it, that does not prove that the universe is a fraud. Probably earthly pleasures were never meant to satisfy it, but only to arouse it, to suggest the real thing.... I must make it the main object of life to press on to that other country and to help others do the same.* (C.S. Lewis, *Mere Christianity*, p. 106)

Jesus endured for the joy that was set before Him (Hebrews 12:2). Part of that joy was our redemption, the end of suffering and sorrow, and the joy and gladness of His bride when He makes all things new (Revelation 21:5). Let us follow the example He set and endure for the joy that is set before us.

Questions
1 Why do we need a new heaven and earth?
2 Why won't we remember the past?
3 What will we be joyful about?
4 What will be the Lord's joy? Why?
5 What are some of the things that will be no more?
6 How can verse 24 be for us today?
7 What is the picture in verse 25?
8 Why should we take it as physical and spiritual?
9 Why is hell eternal?
10 What does the contrast encourage us to do?

God's House - Isaiah 66:1-14

In Isaiah 64, Isaiah offered up a prayer for mercy. The last verses of that chapter pleaded with God not to let the temple be destroyed in the manner Isaiah had prophetically seen (Isaiah 64:11-12). The final chapter of Isaiah begins with God declaring why the temple will be destroyed and goes on to explain the changes that will take place.

¹ Thus says the LORD: "Heaven is my throne, and the earth is my footstool; what is the house that you would build for me, and what is the place of my rest? ²ᵃ All these things my hand has made, and so all these things came to be, declares the LORD. Isaiah 66:1-2a Even though God gave the design for the tabernacle, after which the temple was modeled, we need to understand that God cannot be confined to a building, nor is any human structure sufficiently glorious enough for the God of creation. Solomon acknowledged that when He built the temple (1Kings 8:27). After all, God's real throne is heaven itself, though even the universe cannot contain Him. Now that we know the universe is larger than we can comprehend, that should give us an even greater sense of awe regarding the wonder of God's magnificence (Psalm 19:1).

If the earth itself is only sufficient to be God's footstool, how can we build a house for Him? Everything we have to work with is merely a tiny piece of His creation. The great cathedrals of Europe were made to declare God's glory, and they are inspiring. But in this verse God is saying the works of man falls infinitely short of being glorious enough for Him. We call our church a sanctuary or house of worship, and it is those things, but we must never call the church building God's house. That demeans God. This tiny structure, as nice as we have tried to make it and as blessed as we are to have it, is merely a shelter from the weather so we can focus on corporate worship. One day it will probably become a shop with tourist trinkets.

As a young boy, I worshiped at the corner of Apple and Jordan. That building is now a tourist shop. The members of that church built Crestview Community Church. But one day all these church buildings will be gone (2 Peter 3:10). The Antichrist will see that they become something else or a place to worship him. But that should not alarm us. It won't affect God or our worship of Him.

²ᵇ But this is the one to whom I will look: he who is humble and contrite in spirit and trembles at my word. Isaiah 66:2b Here is the material that God is using to build His church, the humble who are contrite in spirit and tremble at His Word. They are the living stones that Peter wrote about. 1 Peter 2:5 *⁵ you yourselves like living stones are being built up as a spiritual house, to be a holy priesthood, to offer spiritual sacrifices acceptable to God through Jesus Christ.* Paul described the same thing in Ephesians 2:19-22 (NIV) *¹⁹ Consequently, you are no longer foreigners and aliens, but fellow citizens with God's people and members of God's household, ²⁰ built on the foundation of the apostles and prophets, with*

Christ Jesus himself as the chief cornerstone. [21] In him the whole building is joined together and rises to become a holy temple in the Lord. [22] And in him you too are being built together to become a dwelling in which God lives by his Spirit.

I believe Peter and Paul saw that truth from this passage in Isaiah, and of course, through Jesus' teaching. Jesus said that if we love Him, we will obey His teaching and He will make His home in us (John 14:23). The ones who love Jesus and obey His teaching are the humble and contrite ones. It is pride that keeps us from Jesus. Pride tells us we have no need to repent. Pride says we owe our Creator nothing and don't need to obey anyone (Psalm 10:4). Everyone will end up one side or the other eventually, humble and contrite or proud and hardened toward God and His Word.

Are you a living stone that God is using to build His eternal temple? Would those who really know you describe you as humble and contrite? Do you tremble at God's Word? Recently I read a scripture that clarified to me that my mindset on an issue was ungodly. I grabbed hold of that verse and memorized it. When my mind would go back to that former way of thinking I would quote the verse to myself, renewing my mind with the Word (Romans 12:2). I tremble at the Word. We must realize how desperately we need its correction to keep from going astray in thought and action.

[3] *"He who slaughters an ox is like one who kills a man; he who sacrifices a lamb, like one who breaks a dog's neck; he who presents a grain offering, like one who offers pig's blood; he who makes a memorial offering of frankincense, like one who blesses an idol. These have chosen their own ways, and their soul delights in their abominations;* Isaiah 66:3 The Lord continues with the reason the captivity had to come. Worship in the temple was anything but humble, contrite in spirit, and trembling at God's Word. While the people went through the motions of worship, God saw their hearts. Going through the right motions for the wrong reason is abominable to God (Isaiah 1:11-13). That is because it distorts and misrepresents true worship. Unbelievers see it and say, "If that is what being a Christian is like, I don't want to have anything to do with it." The result is inoculation against the teaching of the Gospel.

Obedience must come out of a heart of love for God to be acceptable to God. It is an abomination to God if it comes out of duty, or trying to earn favor with God, or to manipulate God. In the New Testament this is expressed as the battle between grace and works. Paul and Barnabas went out as missionaries to the Gentiles and planted some thriving Gentile churches. When they came back to Antioch they were soon faced with former Pharisees who had become Christians in Jerusalem. These men had come to tell the Gentiles that they had to be circumcised to be saved (Acts 15:1).

Nothing has changed in two-thousand years. There will always be someone telling us we aren't saved unless we do something their way, or have a particular gift, or practice a certain ritual, or something else they believe is necessary. Salvation is faith in the grace of God offered to us through Calvary plus NOTHING! The love that fills our hearts for God's grace freely given to us will cause us to want live for Him and express the gifts He gives us, but in no way should we consider our actions as something that satisfies His justice. Only Jesus' death on the cross can do that. That is the conviction of the humble and contrite in spirit who tremble at His Word.

The last part of verse three reminds us of the song, "I did it my way!" Pride puts our own ways above God's ways. Man's way delights in sin to our own destruction and damnation. Our way leads to hell. His way leads to eternal delight in heaven with Him.

4 I also will choose harsh treatment for them and bring their fears upon them, because when I called, no one answered, when I spoke, they did not listen; but they did what was evil in my eyes and chose that in which I did not delight." Isaiah 66:4 God deals with us harshly to get us to see our sin and turn from our wicked ways. He will bring that which we fear upon us if we do not answer when He calls. This is because He loves us and will act for our eternal good.

The indictment of verse 3 is the same message we saw in chapter one. Isaiah is rounding out the book by saying that even after all his prophecies, nothing has changed. People still refuse to listen. They won't answer God's call to turn from their ways. We see this message to our human weakness again and again. God called them through the prophets (Hebrews 1:1-3). He calls us through preaching of the Word and the voice of the Holy Spirit. Will you answer? That is the most important message God has given, "Hear me!" That is what God said on the Mount of Transfiguration. *"This is my Son, whom I love; with Him I am well pleased. Listen to Him!"* (Matthew 17:5)

Judah as a nation refused to answer or listen. They made deliberate choice to go against God and His ways. They chose that in which God abhorred. We always have this choice before us. Will we be a delight to God, choosing what is good, listening to Him, or will we refuse to listen and go our own way?

5 Hear the word of the LORD, you who tremble at his word: "Your brothers who hate you and cast you out for my name's sake have said, 'Let the LORD be glorified, that we may see your joy'; but it is they who shall be put to shame. Isaiah 66:5 Now to those who do hear, who do tremble at His Word, the Lord has a warning. The sincere, faithful ones are always persecuted by those with a religious spirit. Jesus must have had this verse in mind when He uttered John 16:2-3 (NIV) *2 They will put you out of the synagogue; in fact, a time is coming when anyone who kills you will think he is offering a service to God.*
3 They will do such things because they have not known the Father or me. Those who are caught up in thinking their works please God will always persecute those who worship in Spirit and in truth, who know it is all by God's grace. The reason for some persecution is that our example convicts, and for others it is because we refuse to conform. The later actually think they are serving God when they slander you. Some Jews believed it was

their duty to God to follow Paul from town to town and stir up opposition toward him to the point of even having him stoned (Acts 14:19).

⁶ "The sound of an uproar from the city! A sound from the temple! The sound of the LORD, rendering recompense to his enemies! Isaiah 66:6 Isaiah prophetically hears what is coming, God judging those in the temple for their hypocrisy and pride. It happened when the Babylonians came, and again in AD 70. The last stronghold was the temple. Those who fled to it for safety had rejected Christ and believed that God would save them if they just came to His house for refuge. But as God declared at the beginning of the chapter, His house wasn't in their hearts or in that building.

⁷ "Before she was in labor she gave birth; before her pain came upon her she delivered a son. Isaiah 66:7 Now the subject changes to the birth of the church. The 120 were in the upper room crying out for the Promise of the Father. Boom! The mighty rushing wind comes, tongues of fire dance over their heads. They go out to the crowd gathered, and after a short sermon the church is 3120 souls (Acts 2:41)!

⁸ Who has heard such a thing? Who has seen such things? Shall a land be born in one day? Shall a nation be brought forth in one moment? For as soon as Zion was in labor she brought forth her children. Isaiah 66:8 This new nation is the family of God, all those who by faith have trusted in God for their salvation. The 120 were on Zion. You could say they were Zion for they had received the Words of Jesus. He called, and they answered. He spoke and they listened and believed and the church was born.

Some people interpret this as Israel coming out of captivity in Egypt or the return from captivity in Babylon. Today some apply it to the formation of Israel in 1948. I believe the message is really about the day of Pentecost. That was the solution to Israel's hypocrisy and to the hypocrisy of those with a religious spirit today. They need the Holy Spirit, who convicts us of our pride, causing us to be contrite in spirit, and to tremble at His Word (Isaiah 6:5).

⁹ Shall I bring to the point of birth and not cause to bring forth?" says the LORD; "shall I, who cause to bring forth, shut the womb?" says your God. Isaiah 66:9 Did Jesus come and nothing change? Was God going to give mankind the greatest revelation of Himself to no avail? Or was Pentecost the Kingdom of God coming to earth in the hearts of those who received Jesus? We've been reborn to be the habitation of God by His Spirit! Hallelujah?!

¹⁰ "Rejoice with Jerusalem, and be glad for her, all you who love her; rejoice with her in joy, all you who mourn over her; Isaiah 66:10 Jerusalem is the city of peace, the people of God. The city will be inhabited by the children of God (John 1:12). Jesus will reign in our midst. All who mourn for what the city has become, and all who rejoice in her rich history and what God has done there will rejoice with her in joy. Finally, it will be the city God intends. We will be the people God created us to be.

¹¹ that you may nurse and be satisfied from her consoling breast; that you may drink deeply with delight from her glorious abundance." Isaiah

66:11 During Jesus' millennial reign, the whole earth will be nourished from the spiritual milk that flows from Jerusalem. The Word will go forth from Jerusalem to an extent we have never seen. Every question we have in Scripture will be answered. Every misinterpretation clarified. There are some very good teachers of God's Word, but we haven't seen anything yet! The rich, deep treasures in God's Word will sparkle with clarity we have yet to see.

12 For thus says the LORD: "Behold, I will extend peace to her like a river, and the glory of the nations like an overflowing stream; and you shall nurse, you shall be carried upon her hip, and bounced upon her knees. Isaiah 66:12 We see this description of Jerusalem during the millennium in Zechariah and Revelation as well. The nations of the world will want to honor Jesus. They will want to come like children come to their parent for love and to be spiritually fed.

13 As one whom his mother comforts, so I will comfort you; you shall be comforted in Jerusalem. Isaiah 66:13 The world will come for comfort like the comfort of a mother toward her child. All who seek the comfort of the Lord will find it in Jerusalem. We go to the Lord by faith right now and receive very real comfort (2 Thessalonians 2:16-17). But then it won't have to be by faith. It will be a present physical comfort from the Lord Himself.

14 You shall see, and your heart shall rejoice; your bones shall flourish like the grass; and the hand of the LORD shall be known to his servants, and he shall show his indignation against his enemies. Isaiah 66:14 Our faith will be visible. Our hearts will overflow with joy. Bones flourishing refers to being healthy and tranquil (Proverbs 14:6). God's hand is His provision and aid. The servants of the Lord will experience that provision and assistance, while His enemies will know His indignation. Even during the millennium there will be those who refuse to listen and do not tremble at His Word. How accountable they will be in that day when truth is abundantly clear. I trust that you are among the humble and contrite who tremble at His Word. If you are not, turn to Him today. Know the comfort and tranquility that only He can give.

Questions
1 Why can't we build a house good enough for God?
2 With what material is God building His house?
3 To whom does God look?
4 Why does God hate ritual without heart?
5 What do we need to add to Calvary?
6 What's wrong with "my way"?
7 What is the indictment against Judah?
8 What is the choice God gives us?
9 How did Jesus use verse 5?
10 What was born in a day?
11 What is the theme of verses 7-12?

God's Justice - Isaiah 66:15-24

The previous passage introduced this final section of Isaiah by declaring that the LORD would show his indignation against His enemies (Isaiah 66:14). *15 "For behold, the LORD will come in fire, and his chariots like the whirlwind, to render his anger in fury, and his rebuke with flames of fire.* Isaiah 66:15 Fire is the tool of purification (Numbers 31:23). When Hebrew stone vessels were defiled, they could be cleansed by putting them through the fire. We recognize today that this is actually a way of destroying germs and bacteria. When we leave this earth the testing of our works is compared to a fire consuming the temporal things we did while at the same time revealing the lasting work of God in and through us (1 Corinthians 3:15). God is compared to a consuming fire in Isaiah 33:14 and to a refiner's fire in Malachi 3:1-2. In the literal or figurative sense, the idea is one of purging what is temporary and worthless so that that which is of God, of true value, will remain.

While God desires that all come to repentance, He is angry with the wickedness of man. That is because it is evil, destructive, misleading, and harmful to mankind. It is contrary to the perfect nature of God. He has held back His justice upon evil, waiting for every last soul who will repent and come into the light (John 3:19-21). But as man's sin adds every day to the horrible mountain of evil that causes pain and suffering to mankind, God's passion for justice to be executed grows until that day His chariots will burst forth like a whirlwind to render his anger in fury and his rebuke with flames of fire (2 Kings 6:17). God is eager to rid the world of all that corrupts His creation.

16 For by fire will the LORD enter into judgment, and by his sword, with all flesh; and those slain by the LORD shall be many. Isaiah 66:16 This sounds like the final purging of the earth at the end of the millennium. The Babylonian attacks on Jerusalem were a foreshadowing, as is Armageddon at the end of the tribulation. Revelation 19:15 tells us that at the end of the Tribulation, Jesus will destroy those who have gathered against Him with the sword that comes from His mouth. But at the end of the millennium, when the world again comes against Jesus and the city of God to try to defeat Him, fire comes down out heaven devours them (Revelation 20:9). This is also the point at which the new heaven and earth appear (Revelation 21:1). This final portion of Isaiah seems to refer to both, almost as if Isaiah sees them together, but then that is how the prophets saw the first and second coming of Jesus.

This verse mentions both the sword and the fire God uses for judgment. While it may ultimately speak of the final judgement, we can see in it the intermediate foreshadowing events that are precursors to the final one. The next verse shows us this was meant to wake up the people of that day to the coming judgment by Babylon, but of course these same people will be at the final judgment as well. The theme of the very first chapter of Isaiah was God's coming judgment upon Judah that was compared to a fire (Isaiah 1:31). The book closes on the same theme as Judah did not receive the warning of God that came through Isaiah's many years as a prophet.

Before we leave this theme of final judgment, we should pause to consider the application to ourselves. God was trying to wake up Judah to the immediate *and* eternal consequences of rebellion against Him. All through Isaiah we have seen that our nation stands at the very same threshold. While it took a hundred years to come to pass in Judah, we can't say for certain for certain how close it is to us today. We can say the nation has turned its back on God.

We look to man instead of to God. We look to our military might. Imagine how far a candidate for President would get if his every answer to every policy question was to repent and turn to the LORD. He'd be labeled as a nut job. But that is the only solution to our many problems. It has been the answer throughout our history. Read Peter Marshall's books, The Light and the Glory or From Sea to Shining Sea. But we refuse to learn from our history. Turning to God is the solution to single parent homes, to the decline of morality, to race relations, to the radical Muslim threat, to our economic insolvency, and every other problem we face. God has never failed us, but we have written Him out of our history.

As individuals we need to see God is the solution to our own problems as well. What is the priority of your life? Will your life's labor be consumed by the fire when you pass from this earth? Will Jesus say, "Well done, good and faithful servant (Mathew 25:21)," or will He ask us why we wasted our life on vanity?

[17] *"Those who sanctify and purify themselves to go into the gardens, following one in the midst, eating pig's flesh and the abomination and mice, shall come to an end together, declares the LORD.* Isaiah 66:17 This verse is God's verdict on the idolaters of Judah. They would go to God's temple and go through the rituals prescribed by Moses and then go to gardens on hilltops and worship foreign gods in ways that were an abomination to God (Leviticus 11:7). God is declaring that He will not put up with it forever. Hypocrisy will only be allowed to continue for so long. When you see people who call themselves Christians and yet play with fortune tellers and New Age concepts, who live solely for worldly pleasure, you can be certain that there is an end (Matthew 15:7-8). God declared they would come to an end together. That would happen when Babylon invaded, and will happen again at the last judgment.

The following verses appear to me to be speaking of the end of the tribulation and beginning of the millennial reign. [18] *"For I know their works and their thoughts, and the time is coming to gather all nations and tongues. And they shall come and shall see my glory,* Isaiah 66:18 The believers who survive the tribulation will be gathered before the Lord and they will see His glory. Because there are some who have survived, this must speak of early in

364

the Millennium. We see this in Revelation 7:9-10 (NIV) *⁹ After this I looked and there before me was a great multitude that no one could count, from every nation, tribe, people and language, standing before the throne and in front of the Lamb. They were wearing white robes and were holding palm branches in their hands. ¹⁰ And they cried out in a loud voice: "Salvation belongs to our God, who sits on the throne, and to the Lamb."*

The passage also has elements of the final judgment as described in detail in Revelation 20:11-15 (NIV) *¹¹ Then I saw a great white throne and him who was seated on it. Earth and sky fled from his presence, and there was no place for them. ¹² And I saw the dead, great and small, standing before the throne, and books were opened. Another book was opened, which is the book of life. The dead were judged according to what they had done as recorded in the books. ¹³ The sea gave up the dead that were in it, and death and Hades gave up the dead that were in them, and each person was judged according to what he had done. ¹⁴ Then death and Hades were thrown into the lake of fire. The lake of fire is the second death. ¹⁵ If anyone's name was not found written in the book of life, he was thrown into the lake of fire.*

Jesus described it in Matthew 25:31-32 (NIV) *³¹ "When the Son of Man comes in his glory, and all the angels with him, he will sit on his throne in heavenly glory. ³² All the nations will be gathered before him, and he will separate the people one from another as a shepherd separates the sheep from the goats.* You can see the combination of seeing the glory of God and God knowing each person's deeds and thoughts in that final judgment.

¹⁹ and I will set a sign among them. And from them I will send survivors to the nations, to Tarshish, Pul, and Lud, who draw the bow, to Tubal and Javan, to the coastlands far away, that have not heard my fame or seen my glory. And they shall declare my glory among the nations. Isaiah 66:19 God will set a sign among them. Several places in Isaiah speak of a sign. The virgin birth was a sign (Isaiah 7:14). Jesus' life was a sign (Isaiah 11:10). The recovery of Israel to a verdant land was a sign (Isaiah 55:13). Miraculous gifts are called signs in Mark 16:17. Perhaps the last one is the sign of these the Lord will choose to send as missionaries to the ends of the earth. This happened in an intermediate sense with the people who saw Jesus and His resurrection. God chose some to see His glory and resurrection and to be witnesses, sending them to the nations (Acts 1:8). The nations mentioned were the farthest ones the Jews knew of at the time Isaiah wrote. The term "coastlands" we have seen before means the ends of the earth. These missionaries will declare the glory of Jesus to the world during the millennium.

At the beginning of the millennium, all surviving believers are gathered to see Jesus and will come to worship Him. There will still need to be those who explain to the world what the Lord has done for us. They will have some kind of sign, perhaps the same as that of the Apostles. The sign shows they are truly representatives of the Lord.

²⁰ And they shall bring all your brothers from all the nations as an offering to the LORD, on horses and in chariots and in litters and on mules and on dromedaries, to my holy mountain Jerusalem, says the LORD, just as the Israelites bring their grain offering in a clean vessel to the house of the LORD. Isaiah 66:20 Jew and Gentile become brothers through faith in Jesus (Ephesians 2:14). Everyone who comes to faith in Jesus is and offering to the Lord, a living sacrifice (Romans 12:1). In the Millennium, each new convert will be brought to Jerusalem. The grain offerings were a shadow of this reality, just as the firstfruits of distant fields were brought to the Lord. In Christ our bodies are sanctified vessels. The offering they contain is our hearts.

²¹ And some of them also I will take for priests and for Levites, says the LORD. Isaiah 66:21 While every believer is priest in the sense (1 Peter 2:5) that they can come into the Lord's presence in prayer at any time (Hebrews 4:16), it sounds to me like the Lord is going to choose some of these Gentile converts to stay in Jerusalem to minister to the Lord in the third Jewish temple.

²² "For as the new heavens and the new earth that I make shall remain before me, says the LORD, so shall your offspring and your name remain. Isaiah 66:22 The children of these converts apparently will not take place in the rebellion at the end of the millennium but will also be born again. They will become a part of the household of God, the New Jerusalem, the heavenly temple. The new heaven and new earth seen in Revelation 21:1 are created after the final rebellion at the end of the millennium. It is only then that the New Jerusalem descends out of heaven from God.

²³ From new moon to new moon, and from Sabbath to Sabbath, all flesh shall come to worship before me, declares the LORD. Isaiah 66:23 The new moons and Sabbaths were special days of worship to the Jewish people, and they will be again in the millennium. Zechariah even speaks of celebrating the Feast of Tabernacles (Zechariah 14:16). Then the meaning behind these days of worship will be seen as fulfilled in Jesus.

²⁴ "And they shall go out and look on the dead bodies of the men who have rebelled against me. For their worm shall not die, their fire shall not be quenched, and they shall be an abhorrence to all flesh." Isaiah 66:24 Those in that day can go out and look on the valley of Armageddon and see the carnage of those who rebelled against Jesus. It will be a reminder of their eternal state in hell (Revelation 21:8). Jesus quoted a portion of this passage when He described hell (Mark 9:48). Yet, at the end of the thousand-year reign, those who have not turned to Jesus will rebel again.

The heart of man is incredibly corrupt. That any of us should be saved is the miracle of God's grace. That grace is available to all who will come to Him by faith. He pleads for us to come. He has done all the work. He paid our debt. All we need to do is receive the free gift He offers us. It will transform our life, but not because He demands we give up pleasure, but rather, He offers us a greater and richer joy than we could ever find in this passing world.

In Isaiah's prophecies to Judah, we have seen the problem with our own hearts and our nation. The refusal to listen to God's warnings was the main indictment. Though they knew what God required of them and the blessings of God when they obeyed, they kept going after foreign gods, thinking there was something to be gained by experimenting with them.

We saw the real solution to the problem of the heart of man and our sinfulness is the Son that would be born of a virgin (Isaiah 7:14). We saw that the Son God would give us is our Prince of Peace, the Mighty God (Isaiah 9:6). He is also our suffering servant. In four songs written of this One to come we saw that He would be rejected by His own people and yet become a light to the world (Isaiah 49:6). He would bear our iniquities and become our sin offering (Isaiah 53:6).

In our final chapters we saw how God will conclude it all with a final chance for the world to recognize His love and mercy. The millennial reign will rid everyone of any doubt, so that those who oppose Him in the end will be without excuse.

We also saw the glorious future for those who are His throughout eternity. Joy and gladness will be ours forever (Isaiah 65:18-19). Past sorrows and pain will be forgotten. We will enjoy eternal fellowship with our Lord and Savior Jesus Christ.   God has laid the choice before us. History illustrates the two paths over and over again, but the choice is ours to make. Choose this day whom you will serve.

Questions
1 Why does God come with pent up fury?
2 What is significant about fire?
3 How could this address multiple events?
4 Apply the warning of verse 1 and 2.
5 Where should we turn in times of trouble?
6 What two times are all men brought before Jesus?
7 Who is sent to the nations?
8 Why do some Old Testament rituals remain?
9 What warning remains through the millennium?
10 Review the main themes of Isaiah.

Other books by Pastor Paul Wallace:

Through the Bible Daily Devotional
Through the Bible Again volumes 1&2
Jesus Concealed in the Old Testament
John's Rabbi
Divine Messiah?
Preaching Through Genesis
Preaching Through Exodus
Preaching Through Isaiah
Preaching Through Zechariah
Preaching Through Matthew vol 1&2
Preaching Through John
Preaching Through Acts
Preaching Through Romans
Preaching Through Ephesians
Preaching Through Philippians and Colossians
Preaching Spiritual Disciplines
Preaching the Attributes of God

Coming soon:
Preaching Through Luke

www.ingramcontent.com/pod-product-compliance
Lightning Source LLC
Chambersburg PA
CBHW021133090426
42740CB00008B/770